COLD WAR FILM GENRES

Traditions in American Cinema
Series Editors Linda Badley and R. Barton Palmer

Titles in the series include:

The 'War on Terror' and American Film: 9/11 Frames Per Second
Terence McSweeney

American Postfeminist Cinema: Women, Romance and Contemporary Culture
Michele Schreiber

Film Noir
Homer B. Pettey and R. Barton Palmer (eds)

In Secrecy's Shadow: The OSS and CIA in Hollywood Cinema 1941–1979
Simon Willmetts

Indie Reframed: Women's Filmmaking and Contemporary American Independent Cinema
Linda Badley, Claire Perkins, and Michele Schreiber (eds)

Vampires, Race, and Transnational Hollywoods
Dale Hudson

Who's in the Money? The Great Depression Musicals and Hollywood's New Deal
Harvey G. Cohen

Engaging Dialogue: Cinematic Verbalism in American Independent Cinema
Jennifer O'Meara

Cold War Film Genres
Homer B. Pettey (ed.)

edinburghuniversitypress.com/series/tiac

COLD WAR FILM GENRES

Edited by Homer B. Pettey

EDINBURGH
University Press

To Jo Anne Jenkins, a fine woman and a great mother, *in memoriam*

Edinburgh University Press is one of the leading university presses in the UK. We publish academic books and journals in our selected subject areas across the humanities and social sciences, combining cutting-edge scholarship with high editorial and production values to produce academic works of lasting importance. For more information visit our website: edinburghuniversitypress.com

© editorial matter and organization Homer B. Pettey, 2018
© the chapters their several authors, 2018

Edinburgh University Press Ltd
The Tun – Holyrood Road
12 (2f) Jackson's Entry
Edinburgh EH8 8PJ

Typeset in 10/12.5pt Sabon by
Servis Filmsetting Ltd, Stockport, Cheshire

A CIP record for this book is available from the British Library

ISBN 978 1 4744 1294 0 (hardback)
ISBN 978 1 4744 1295 7 (webready PDF)
ISBN 978 1 4744 1296 4 (epub)

The right of the contributors to be identified as authors of this work has been asserted in accordance with the Copyright, Designs and Patents Act 1988 and the Copyright and Related Rights Regulations 2003 (SI No. 2498).

CONTENTS

List of Illustrations	vii
Acknowledgments	ix
Notes on the Contributors	x

1. Introduction: Cold War Genres and the Rock-and-Roll Film   1
   Homer B. Pettey

2. Social Factors in Brainwashing Films of the 1950s and 1960s   21
   David Seed

3. The Berlin Crisis? Piffl!: Billy Wilder's Cold War Comedy, *One, Two, Three*   42
   Ed Sikov

4. The Small Adult Film: A Prestige Form of Cold War Cinema   62
   R. Barton Palmer

5. "I'm Lucky – I Had Rich Parents": Disability and Class in the Postwar Biopic Genre   79
   Martin F. Norden

6. Rogue Nation, 1954: History, Class Consciousness, and the "Rogue Cop" Film   99
   Robert Miklitsch

CONTENTS

7. Internal Enmity: Hollywood's Fragile Home Stories in the 1950s and 1960s   123
   Elisabeth Bronfen

8. Suburban Sublime   144
   Homer B. Pettey

9. Domestic Containment for Whom? Gendered and Racial Variations on Cold War Modernity in the Apartment Plot   163
   Pamela Robertson Wojcik

10. Success and the Single Girl: Urban Romances of Working Women   181
    Jennifer Lei Jenkins

11. Paris Loves Lovers and Americans Loved Paris: Gender, Class, and Modernity in the Postwar Hollywood Musical   204
    Steven Cohan

12. Straight to Baby: Scoring Female Jazz Agency and New Masculinity in Henry Mancini's *Peter Gunn*   228
    Kristin McGee

Index   259

FIGURES

1.1	Bill Haley and the Comets playing "Rock-a-Beatin' Boogie" for appreciative dancers in *Rock Around the Clock*	8
1.2	Elvis Presley singing and dancing "Jailhouse Rock" in *Jailhouse Rock*	9
1.3	Bob Dylan the "anarchist" with a cigarette in *Dont Look Back*	17
2.1	Alien point-of-view in *It Came From Outer Space*	23
2.2	Pod creature of Dr. Miles Bennel in *Invasion of the Body Snatchers*	32
3.1	Otto Ludwig Piffl riding his motorcycle toward Berlin's Brandenburg Gate in *One, Two, Three*	50
3.2	Piffl entering East Germany with a "Russki GO HOME" balloon on his motorcycle in *One, Two, Three*	50
4.1	Teacher Richard Dadier squares off against swtichblade-toting punk in *Blackboard Jungle*	67
4.2	Philip Green and Kathy Lacey share uncomfortable silence after Philip reveals his plan to become a Jew in *Gentlemen's Agreement*	71
5.1	Franklin Roosevelt charms his daughter Anna with a story in *Sunrise at Campobello*	83
5.2	Marjorie Lawrence sings "Over the Rainbow" for disabled World War II veterans in *Interrupted Melody*	85
5.3	Cole Porter is surprised to see his wife in the audience during a Yale concert performance in *Night and Day*	89
5.4	"You haven't got what it takes – guts!": Jane Froman receives a reprimand from her nurse in *With a Song in My Heart*	91

FIGURES

6.1	Chris Carmody about to pay off newsstand stoolie Selma in fotobusta for *Rogue Cop*	106
6.2	Barney Nolan with the loot in *Shield for Murder*	116
7.1	Attack on the Hilliard home in *The Desperate Hours*	133
7.2	Mary Ann's bridge to tomorrow in *Something Wild*	135
7.3	Ned arrested in the frame of his home ruin in *The Swimmer*	141
8.1	Dr. Boyer unwittingly drives his convertible into the new swimming pool that his wife Beverly forgot to mention in *The Thrill of It All*	149
8.2	The Blandings watch their classic home being brought down in order to build their dream home in *Mr. Blandings Builds His Dream House*	152
8.3	Parents barbecuing some fresh meat for dinner in *Parents*	160
9.1	Jan Morrow on the party line with Allen in his *Playboy*-style apartment in *Pillow Talk*	168
9.2	Chantal Stacy enters photographer Eugene Wright's apartment in *If a Man Answers* and begins the taming process	170
10.1	Gladys Glover sign in Columbus Circle in *It Should Happen To You*	185
10.2	Peg Costello, Sylvia Blair, Ruthie Saylor, and Bunny Watson in front of EMERAC in *Desk Set*	190
10.3	Violet Newstead, Doralee Rhodes, and Judy Bernly at the office in *9 to 5*	194
10.4	Michael Dorsey's first appearance as Dorothy Michaels in *Tootsie*	197
11.1	Jerry Mulligan dances with Lise Bouvier to "Love is here to stay" along the banks of the Seine in *An American in Paris*	208
11.2	Fashion editor Maggie Prescott, fashion photographer Dick Avery, and bookshop girl Jo Stockton sing "Bonjour, Paris!" in *Funny Face*	214
12.1	Peter Gunn and Edie Hart share a private moment on Mothers backstage balcony in Episode 1, *The Kill*	238
12.2	Lola Albright and Henry Mancini's *Peter Gunn* tie-in album *Dreamsville* from 1959	246
12.3	Lynn Martel sings her "Meaning of the Blues" in Peter Gunn's "Lynn's Blues"	251

ACKNOWLEDGMENTS

Because of their splendid scholarship and analysis, my first appreciative thank you extends to the contributors of this volume. Their vision for these unrepresented films from the Cold War far exceeded my initial desires for this project. I also wish to thank them for their patience, because this project had to be delayed owing to illnesses and a death in my family.

As usual, I should like to thank my old pals, Chip Johannessen and Carter Burwell, from whom I still keep learning so much about the industry and with whom I can still get into the right kind of trouble. I would also like to thank Allan Arffa and Kay Matschullat for their faithful friendship over the years. Likewise, my admiration for the *Harvard Lampoon*, its Castle, and its staff and alumni still remains.

As always, my life only stays sane because of Jennifer, Melissa, Olympia, Josephine, and Thomas.

NOTES ON THE CONTRIBUTORS

Elisabeth Bronfen is Professor of English and American Studies at the University of Zürich. She has published on a wide range of literary and visual cultural topics. Her most recent books are *Specters of War: Hollywood's Engagement with Military Conflicts* (2012) and *Night Passages: Philosophy, Literature and Film* (2013).

Steven Cohan is Dean's Distinguished Professor Emeritus at Syracuse University and President-Elect of the Society for Cinema and Media Studies. His books include *Telling Stories: A Theoretical Analysis of Narrative* (1988, coauthored with Linda M. Shires), *Screening the Male* (1993, coedited with Ina Rae Hark), *The Road Movie Book* (1997, coedited with Ina Rae Hark), *Masked Men: Masculinity and the Movies in the Fifties* (1997), *Hollywood Musicals, The Film Reader* (2001), *Incongruous Entertainment: Camp, Cultural Value, and the MGM Musical* (2005), *CSI: Crime Scene Investigation* (2008), and *The Sound of Musicals* (2010). At present, he is writing a book on the backstudio picture and the branding of Hollywood from the 1920s to the present day.

Jennifer Lei Jenkins teaches film history and theory, archival practice, and American literature at the University of Arizona. She is the author of *Celluloid Pueblo: Western Ways Film Service and the Invention of the Postwar Southwest*, forthcoming from University of Arizona Press. She has published on film adaptations of *Lolita*, *Invasion of the Body Snatchers*, and *Sweeney Todd*, as well as on the history of Mexican cinema. She is Curator of the American Indian Film Gallery.

Kristin McGee is an Associate Professor of Popular Music in the Arts, Culture and Media Department at the University of Groningen in the Netherlands. She has written on the subject of jazz, gender and popular music and audiovisual media in a variety of articles and books, including her book *Some Liked it Hot: Jazz Women in Film and Television, 1928–1959* (2009). She is currently completing a typescript on the crossover jazz scenes of the Netherlands. She is also a saxophonist and sometimes theater music composer.

Robert Miklitsch is Professor in the Department of English Language and Literature at Ohio University. His work on film and television has appeared in *Film Quarterly*, *Journal of Film and Video*, *Journal of Popular Film and Television*, *New Review of Film and Television Studies*, and *Screen*. He is the editor of *Psycho-Marxism* (1998) and the author of *From Hegel to Madonna* (1998), *Roll Over Adorno* (2006), and *Siren City: Sound and Source Music in Classic American Noir* (2011) which was named a Choice Outstanding Academic Title of 2011. His edited collection, *Kiss the Blood Off My Hands: On Classic Noir*, recently appeared from the University of Illinois Press (2014) and has been nominated for an Edgar Allan Poe Award by the Mystery Writers of America. The author is currently completing a book on classic noir in the "atomic age."

Martin F. Norden teaches film history/theory/criticism and screenwriting as Professor of Communication at the University of Massachusetts Amherst. He is the author of *The Cinema of Isolation: A History of Physical Disability in the Movies* and numerous other publications. He has lectured across North America and Europe on the movie representation of people with disabilities.

R. Barton Palmer is Calhoun Lemon Professor of Literature at Clemson University where he also directs the Film Studies program. Palmer is the author, editor, or general editor of nearly fifty volumes on various literary and cinematic subjects including, most recently, *Larger Than Life: Movie Stars of the 1950s* (2010) and (with Robert Bray) *Hollywood's Tennessee: the Williams Films and Postwar America* (2009). He has also recently edited (with Steven Sanders) *The Philosophy of Steven Soderbergh* (2010), (with David Boyd) *Hitchcock at the Source: the Auteur as Adapter* (2011), (with Murray Pomerance) *'A Little Solitaire':John Frankenheimer and American Film* (Rutgers, 2011), (with Steven Sanders and Aeon Skoble), *The Philosophy of Michael Mann* (2013), and (with Homer B. Pettey), *Film Noir and International Noir* (Edinburgh University Press, 2014).

NOTES ON THE CONTRIBUTORS

Homer B. Pettey is Professor of Film and Comparative Literature at the University of Arizona. He serves as Founding and General Editor for three book series: *Global Film Studios* and *International Film Stars* for Edinburgh University Press, and *Global Film Directors* for Rutgers University Press. With R. Barton Palmer, he coedited two volumes on film noir for Edinburgh University Press (2014): *Film Noir* and *International Noir*. Also with Palmer, he is coeditor of *Hitchcock's Moral Gaze* (2017) and another contracted volume on *Biopics and British National Identity*. He has several forthcoming chapters: Wyatt Earp biopics for *Invented Lives, Imagined Communities: Biopics and American National Identity*, coedited by William Epstein and R. Barton Palmer (2015); on violence, the Production Code, and noir for David Schmidt's edited collection on violence in popular culture (Praeger, 2015); and on Hitchcock's American noirs for Jonathan Freedman's *Cambridge Companion to Alfred Hitchcock* (2015). His current project concerns *Transnational Silent Film* (Edinburgh University Press).

David Seed is an Emeritus Professor of American Literature at the University of Liverpool. His publications include *American Science Fiction and the Cold War* and *Brainwashing: The Fictions of Mind Control*.

Ed Sikov is the author of seven books about films and filmmakers, including *On Sunset Boulevard: The Life and Times of Billy Wilder*; *Mr. Strangelove: A Biography of Peter Sellers*, and *Laughing Hysterically: American Screen Comedies of the 1950s*. His textbook, *Film Studies: An Introduction*, is in wide use around the country. He has taught at Columbia University, from which he earned a Ph.D., Haverford, and Colorado College.

Pamela Robertson Wojcik is Professor in the Department of Film, TV, and Theatre at the University of Notre Dame. She is author of *The Apartment Plot: Urban Living in American Film and Popular Culture, 1945 to 1975* (2010) and *Guilty Pleasures: Feminist Camp from Mae West to Madonna* (1996); and editor of books on film stardom, film acting, and film music.

1. INTRODUCTION: COLD WAR FILM GENRES AND THE ROCK-AND-ROLL FILM

Homer B. Pettey

From the end of World War II in 1945 to the fall of the Berlin Wall in 1989, the Cold War period ushered in new film genres that reflected and deflected political and social anxieties of the period. In general, cinema scholars view Cold War-era cinema as tending toward two essential aims: to be reliable expressions of American freedom in the face of Communist oppression; to reinforce individualism against collectivism as a distinctly American trait. Traditionally in cinema studies, Cold War films fall into two main categories, American "propaganda" to comply with the House Un-American Committee's (HUAC) anti-Communist agenda or as "allegories that offer disguised comment on American politics."[1] Film critics have interpreted 1950s sci-fi films and Westerns as fulfilling these cultural mandates, if not serving as warnings of complacency and complicity in the face of an ominous Communist, atomic threat. Communist-themed films hardly constitute the majority of films that Hollywood produced during this very inventive, genre-expansive period. Many of these popular film genres have received little notice by film scholars, as though transformative and emerging generic film innovations did not represent the Cold War period. Such a viewpoint relegates several decades to somewhat doctrinaire views of a major period in American filmmaking. This collection of essays not only wishes to expand historical and critical viewpoints but also wishes to display numerous recognizable and diverse approaches to emerging film genres during this period.

For American cinema, the Cold War supplied ample conflict and anxieties about the new postwar period, particularly with the intrusion of the federal government. Several fine studies have made detailed cases from recently accessible archival materials. Tony Shaw's *Hollywood's Cold War* (2007) examines the "state–private networks" of two image-makers, Hollywood and Washington, D. C., that imposed upon filmmakers a propaganda machine to promote doctrinaire capitalism:

> This led to a range of pressures being imposed on filmmakers which affected both the content and distribution of movies. It also entailed a whole range of official organisations – including the FBI, State Department, Pentagon, CIA, and USIA – constructively engaging with filmmakers in myriad ways. This proactive approach included openly lending logistical and financial assistance to trustworthy filmmakers, and secretly setting up consortia of famous directors, producers, and actors to sell American democracy.[2]

John Sbardellati's *J. Edgar Hoover Goes To The Movies* (2012) focuses upon the FBI director's obsession with rooting out Communist subversives in Hollywood, especially with the assistance of the Motion Picture Alliance (MPA):

> The MPA's guiding lights included Sam Wood, the famed Hollywood director of several Marx brothers classics: Walt Disney, whose rabid anti-Communism had been fueled by labor struggles at this studio in 1941; Lela Rogers, mother of Ginger Rogers; and Ayn Rand, the screenwriter, novelist, and pseudo-philosopher who penned the *Screen Guide for Americans*, which the FBI adopted as its manual for detecting subversion in the movies.[3]

Films deemed subversive led the House Un-American Activities Committee to investigate directors, producers, and actors. This history's effects on Cold War cinema has been documented in several admirable accounts, among them: Jeff Smith's *Film Criticism, the Cold War, and the Black List: Reading the Hollywood Reds* (2014); Peter Stanfield, et al., *'Un-American' Hollywood: Politics and Film in the Blacklist Era* (2007); and Patrick McGilligan and Paul Buhle's *Tender Comrades: A Backstory of the Hollywood Blacklist* (1997).

The Cold War certainly produced its brand of propaganda that clearly reconfigured the world geopolitically. The West against the East, democracy against Communism, United States against Soviet Union – all relied on real-world tensions between the aims of liberal capitalism and those of Marxism–Leninism. Symbols of this cultural, social, and ideological divide became Churchill's metaphorical Iron Curtain of 1946 and then, the physical Berlin Wall of 1961. Undeniably, the news media, politicians, government surveillance and intelligence agencies, and private organizations relied upon symbolic rhetoric that divided the world as much ideologically as physically. Of course, Hollywood did make overtly political films and politically laced thrillers during this period, such as *I Was A Communist for the FBI* (1951), *Big Jim McLain* (1952), *North by Northwest* (1959), *The Manchurian Candidate* (1962), *Seven Days in May* (1964), and *Fail Safe* (1964). Standard and established Hollywood genres directly or indirectly alluded to the new world order. War films about the Korean conflict often had anti-communist themes combined with the need for: American unity in Samuel Fuller's *The Steel Helmet* (1951); the American moral necessity in Tay Garnett's *One Minute to Zero* (1952); the effects of torture and loyalty in Andrew Marton's *Prisoner of War* (1954) and Arnold Laven's *The Rack* (1956); and the hidden menace in Anthony Mann's *Men in War* (1957). For Vietnam, the depravity of the Viet Cong dominates seemingly unrelated Vietnam films, such as John Wayne's *The Green Berets* (1968) and Michael Cimino's *The Deer Hunter* (1968); or, the home front emerges as a vague, new battleground without much rhyme or reason but always leading to a kind of American victory, even if physically and emotionally pyrrhic, as in Hal Ashby's *Coming Home* (1978), Karel Reisz's *"Who'll Stop The Rain"* (1978), and Ted Kotcheff's *First Blood* (1982). Westerns, that mainstay of Americanism in cinema, revealed a divided social structure of suspicion, most famously in *High Noon* (1952), although Nicholas Ray's *Johnny Guitar* (1953) can be either anti-HUAC or anti-totalitarianism.

Still, the history of Cold War filmmaking also includes the development of new genres, sub-genres, and cycles which demand analysis. This collection works out new interpretations of emerging genres of the Cold War period. Geopolitics took on an inward topography in American filmmaking, so that the divisive world vision now reflected rifts, schisms, and ruptures in the American scene. Geopolitical space, in particular, became reoriented from the macro to the micro level in American cinema of the Cold War period. That shift in spatial orientation both produced new private spaces, such as the development of suburbia and new model family home, and renewed public spaces, in particular, life in the American metropolis, especially in apartments and the workplace. To populate these new spaces required American cinema to focus upon new social figures that had not received a place in the Hollywood narratives before World War II: the displaced person, to use Flannery O'Connor's apt expression, the outsider, the unknown, the alien, the social other, and the simply not-seen-before figure on screen. Geopolitics and geopsychological displacement in Cold War Hollywood shifted in directions that HUAC, the FBI, and the studios could not have suspected at the end of World War II.

American cinema of the Cold War period introduced new sub-genres, genres, and cycles mainly structured around a concept of class in America. Sub-genres emerged for film noir, family melodramas, and musicals that dealt specifically with corruption from within, rather than from without, thereby problematizing the usual Cold War political paradigm. New genres emerged that told stories of a different America from the conventional middle-class, nuclear family. Some of these genres responded to the absurdity of Cold War politics with parodic, inane comedies, creating what can best be categorized as the political comedy. New European art-house films found competition in small adult films that eschewed the staid values of Hollywood's morality and its penchant for spectacle and melodrama, as it did the overly sexualized art-cinema products from Italy. Instead, small adult films retained their theatrical and literary origins from Broadway dramas that conveyed a different America, one not suffering from political paranoia or capitalist optimism. New genres also emerged in order to convey the changing socioeconomic life of America during the postwar period. In particular, the comedies of the workplace and apartment-living whose contemporary foibles, comic romances, and harmless sins revealed to viewers a new urban American Adam and Eve. The working, single girl, the bohemian couple, the playboy bachelor now offered to spectators a new American social class and consciousness and, along with it, a cycle of similarly gendered plots that continued from the 1950s well into the 1980s. Along with the new urban scene, America expanded beyond the metropolis into the suburbs and with that came a new landscape for cinema. So popular were suburban-themed films, especially comedies, that studios relied upon them as continual moneymakers, even if profits were modest. Like science-fiction films of invasion, suburban invasion by city dwellers became an expected narrative for moviegoers during the Cold War, so much so that a cycle of familiar comic plots of modernity turning against consumers flourished for several decades.

These cinema experiments, which opened up new content for postwar Hollywood filmmaking, did not rely upon socialist counterarguments to McCarthyism but took new perspectives on the American and international scene. New moral and social issues pervade these films, so much so that American cinema history needs to reconcile audience interests with sociopolitical realities. Class did not solely rely upon Marxist or even capitalist economic hierarchy; instead, class issues during the Cold War expanded to include the struggles for single working women, new urban living conditions, trials for people with disabilities, non-Marxist proletariat viewpoints, reversals and inversions of the "Us *v.* Them" HUAC model to become "Us *v.* Us" narratives, as well as critiques of the American dream and the new postwar freedoms against conformity and containment. Additionally, new film genres emerged for adult-themed cinema, sociopolitical comedies, police noirs, and comedies of the suburbs.

Certainly, traditional readings of Cold War existential angst, political upheaval, and social crises retrospectively provide for fruitful discussion of this significant period in American cinema. Such readings of the film industry have tended to echo many concerns of postmodernism, late capitalism, and mass-induced acceptance, if unconsciously, of hegemonic control. And yet, such interpretations of American political schisms or schizoid consciousness deflects from real-world, day-to-day moods and expectations of American film audiences. Instead, this collection favors investigating and questioning assumptions of the Cold War-period cinema studies to expand that discipline to include sci-fi treatments of brainwashing, political satires, completely new genres devoted to international musicals, working-women films, apartment plots, rogue-cop films as enemies from within, the alienated home as the site of political upheaval, new types of biopics concentrating on the disabled other, and moneymaking suburban comedies. Moreover, efforts to homogenize modern art and jazz during the Cold War period find these art forms accepted in musical scores, particularly film noirs such as *Odds Against Tomorrow* (1959) and in modernist mise-en-scène such as *In A Lonely Place* (1950).[4] For that unsung movement, this collection concludes with a look at jazz in the television series *Peter Gunn* as a way to expand, if briefly, the notion of screen genres for this period. Like much of television during the Cold War period, *Peter Gunn* represents emerging screen genres of this period, ones that included gender, race, and class issues as major themes in their narratives. In some respects, this collection wants to offer analyses of neglected, emerging film genres that were popular with movie-goers, financially successful, and challenged the financial funding model for studios.

One obvious, though neglected, outgrowth of the Cold War era was the rock-and-roll film genre. As with many other emerging genres of this period, the Cold War does not have much of an effect on the thematic content of these films. Not that they suffer from the revisionist and long-accepted view of the 1930s, whereby the whole escapist cinematic world wore gowns and tuxedos as they danced and drank the night away at the Ritz. Instead, these genres presented the other America, not the Other American experience, but those forgotten aspects of the American scene. Certainly, the class issues of rock-and-roll films correspond to these developments. While not too detailed in terms of plot structure, usually following the innovator overcoming odds to become a success format, these rock-and-roll films opened up cinema, like television of the era, to those newest of viewers – teenagers. Here, for the first time, Hollywood and independents saw a market share in a burgeoning, growing, America-wide segment who would accept these films. Beginning with *Rock Around the Clock* (1956) and concluding with *This Is Spinal Tap* (1984), this period covers both fictionalized and supposedly faithful biopics, rockumentaries, rock-star-vehicle films, and rock parodies. In short, the Cold War period turned out to be a time to expand the viewing audience and to experiment with very new plots and genre conventions. Most appealing about the Cold War geopolitics remains how cinema magic could convert apocalyptic, atomic doom into an ignored presence whose threats meant far less than the next hit 45, the next Elvis film, or the next concert footage. Certainly, Soviet aggression, the Cuban Missile Crisis, the Vietnam war – all had resonance in emerging Cold War film genres but those international crises hardly deterred innovative filmic techniques and content. Like rock-and-roll films generally, the Cold War period really never curtailed cinematic expression and new art forms.

Among the film genres to emerge during the Cold War Period (1945 to 1989), the rock-and-roll film, with it several subgenres, captivated the burgeoning postwar youth market as much as it did studio executives seeing a ready stream of profits. Commercial interests of record corporations and film studios will propel rock and roll into the mainstream, because the age-old economics of necessity prevail – profits produce popular culture. The rock-and-roll film may well be the most flexible new cinematic genre of this period, because it includes subcategories of rock biopics, rock-and-roll business films, beach party films, rockumentaries, underground avant-garde rock cinema, filmed rock concert performances, mockumentaries, teenage angst, high school adolescent, and radical counterculture films with added narrative elements from rock-and-roll soundtracks. Of course, the various types of rock music spanning this period could well constitute their own subgenre, from British Invasion films, such as *Help!* (1965), through the Jamaican *The Harder They Come* (1972) to punk rock films and musical comedies, such as *Rock and Roll High School* (1979). Rock economics certainly justifies scholarly study of these films as not just pop cultural schlock, which most are not, but as representative expressions of both filmgoer attraction and corporate sponsoring of popular culture. More than these economic and historical indicators, the rock-and-roll film served as a *sui generis* cinematic genre that emerged during a period that it occasionally acknowledged but that it most often ignored – the Cold War. Studios sought profits as any business does or else they would fail. To glom onto current popular cultural movements reveals Hollywood studios' contained, yet astute cultural and economic acumen. As rock-and-roll music retrospectively shifted the music business, the film industry would follow suit, if only to make money on the newest fad in popular culture, especially one that had not just legs but wheels.

Rock Around the Clock (1956) concocts a cinematic myth about the birth of rock and roll, not coming out of a long tradition of both Mississippi Delta and urban blues, country swing à la Bob Wills and the Texas Playboys, American jazz traditions, and big band era rhythms, but springing somehow on its own from a new generation with its own new sound. Past musical success of the big bands now fading in popularity, manager Steve Hollis (Johnny Johnston) travels to find a new sound, only to find himself in small-town, rural America on a Saturday. The hubbub about the "dance" among everyone in the town entices the cynical Steve to the teenagers' hop, where the local band headlines: Bill Haley and the Comets. The band needs a savvy manager because they are paid usually in produce, mostly turnips. Like early rock-and-roll films, *Rock Around the Clock* employs a thin plotline to showcase current popular groups and especially the latest dance routines. The spectacular dancing sequences exhibit the athletic and artistic abilities needed to perform these astounding new moves. The eroticism of rock dancing takes the form of a romance between Steve and the prima rockarina, Lisa Johns (Lisa Gayle), the actress also appearing the same year in the low-budget Fats Domino vehicle *Shake, Rattle, & Rock!*. Even at a distance of over sixty years, these extraordinary dance numbers captivate in the same way that the grand ballroom moments of Fred Astaire and Ginger Rogers did or as the lavish Busby Berkeley extravaganzas did in the 1930s. Commercially, *Rock Around the Clock* keyed into the essential interplay between musical stage performances and their youth culture translation on the dance floor. The film's plot, like that of so many of this new genre, relies upon the up-and-coming latest musical sound that needs to find a wider audience and more money. In essence, *Rock Around the Clock* mimics both the music and film industries' financial scheme for broad exhibition and distribution to this new teenage audience. In early rock-and-roll films, usually some authoritarian obstacle initially blocks that road to newest postwar American dream. In the case of *Rock Around the Clock*, the corporate booking chieftess, Corinne Talbot (Alix Talton), tries to play out her emotional jealousy for Steven's infatuation with Lisa as a way to sabotage this feisty group of working-class musicians. In the end, her business acumen overrides her feminine wiles and unstable emotions and she backs Bill Haley and the Comets, even acknowledging the marriage of Steve and Lisa. Upward class mobility, future financial security, and corporate gains can always be found at the heart of rock-and-roll films.

Because its successful box office of $1.1 million placed it ninety-ninth among the top-grossing films for 1957, *Rock Around the Clock* spawned numerous films, mostly regenerating familiar plots for this new, seemingly insatiable youth market.[5] In *Don't Knock the Rock* (1956), Haley and the Comets reprise that year's roles by returning to their small town where they face an adult ban on rock-and-roll music. Predictably, dancing will save the day but this time by showcasing the Charleston, the adults' own youthful indiscretion, at an art and culture pageant. Realizing their hypocrisy, the adults, allegorical representative of high-culture America, rescind their taboo and the film ends with a rock-and-roll sequence. The film's review in *Variety* had the subheading, "Top rock 'n roll artists in tune-loaded juve story, probably destined for substantial boxoffice response," since *Rock Around the Clock* more than doubled its under $500,000 budget and *Don't Knock the Rock* beat out the original by 100,000 dollars.[6] Curiously, *Go, Johnny Go!* (1959) has no face

Figure 1.1 Bill Haley and the Comets playing "Rock A-Beatin' Boogie" for appreciative dancers in *Rock Around the Clock* (1956).

but only the hands on the guitar strings ripping through Chuck Berry's song for the opening credits. That oddity only becomes clear as Berry plays himself in a secondary role to Johnny Melody (Jimmy Clanton), a semi-delinquent rising star who finds success and marriage with the help of Alan Freed. Star line-up remained the film's appeal for, along with Berry playing "Memphis, Tennessee" for a television variety show, appeared The Flamingos, Eddie Cochran, The Cadillacs, Jackie Wilson, and Ritchie Valens. In 1961, Columbia Pictures relied upon cultural amnesia when it brought out the Chubby Checker vehicle *Twist Around the Clock* which had the exact same plotline and even some of the same shot sequences and dialogue as *Rock Around the Clock*. Here, the discouraged manager confronts the supposed decline of Jerry Lee Lewis-style rock and roll, whose replacement he discovers in a small town. The Twist will beat out old, stale rock and roll in the hearts and hips of America's youth. With twist steps so new, they require a new technique – sandpapering one's shoes to achieve that slick, slip-and-slide ankle turn that gyrates upward to bent knees and shaking bottoms. Of course, it was followed by *Don't Knock the Twist* (1962). Both films rehashing and even denuding already trite plotlines served one purpose – to showcase dancing sequences and to draw in the teenage audience. Columbia's model for rock-and-roll films consisted of a double-the-output with the profit scheme, with short shooting schedules, small budgets, and quick distribution and exhibition, such as the ten-day shoot and $200, 000 for *Twist Around the Clock*.[7]

The most successful rock-to-riches film of this early genre's era has to be

Elvis Presley's *Jailhouse Rock* (1957). Moving beyond the usual rock-and-roll cinematic formula, *Jailhouse Rock* has Elvis convicted of manslaughter during a bar fight, sentenced to Central Prison in North Carolina, involved in a prison riot, and flogged in punishment. The naive Elvis is befriended and coached by an older con who turns out to be a has-been country singer. Almost following a weepy biopic formula, the film's trajectory follows Vince (Elvis) from his release through his hardships to becoming a singing star and his eventual public success, but private failure, and finally to his repentance. Excesses of ego are the bane of rock-and-roll stars. The frame device of a physical altercation climaxes with the film when Vince's mentor–con, Hunk (Mickey Shaughnessy), strikes smug Vince a blow directly at his vocal cords, threatening his career; however, all ends with Vince in the hospital, humble, remorseful, and restored to his humanity. Of course, this rock melodrama ends with Vince singing to his girl, Peggy (Judy Tyler), to reassure her of his two most powerful gifts, his voice and his love. Much of the film's success had little to do with the melodramatic moments but rather with the now iconic "Jailhouse Rock" full-stage dance routine, with Elvis gyrating freely without any mild to extreme censorship. For his 1956 appearance on *The Steve Allen Show*, Allen dressed Elvis in white tie and tails to contrast his lowbrow image in the public. Allen, then, brought out a basset hound on stage, to whom Elvis sang a very atypical version of that old number. In his first appearance on *The Ed Sullivan Show*, even though in a full body shot, Elvis moved in subdued rhythm to "Hound Dog." His final spot on *Ed Sullivan* in January, 1957 included "Don't Be Cruel," which was shot from the waist up although his movements certainly inspired loud female screams from the audience. The "Jailhouse Rock" number remains one of the great choreographic moments in rock-and-roll film

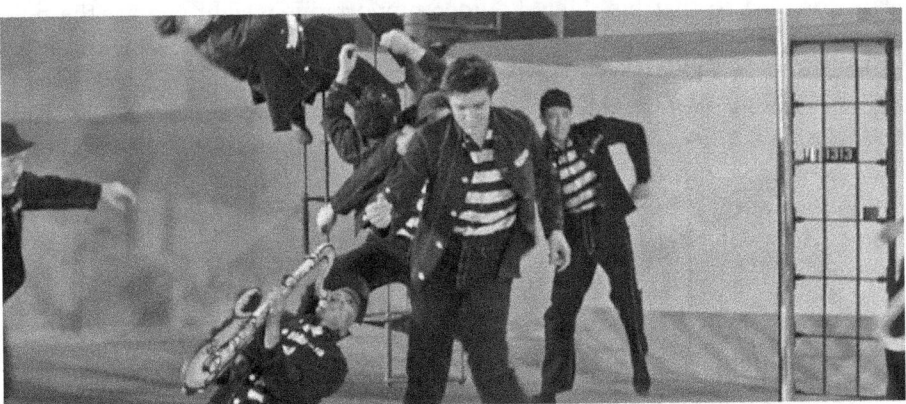

Figure 1.2   Elvis Presley singing and dancing "Jailhouse Rock" in *Jailhouse Rock* (1957).

history, and Elvis's virtuoso performance. Renowned Alex Romero worked out this synchronized yet expressive and anarchistic choreography for the film. Elvis's character dresses, like all the prisoners in the sequence, in black jeans jacket with numbers over heart-pocket, black broad-horizontal stripes on a white T-shirt, and black jeans. He introduces the number before a visible television camera. Here, the irony and visual conceit remain no matter how often censors obstructed or removed Elvis's hip shaking in order to protect the television-viewing audience. Clearly, the initial draw of this film had to be for teen audiences to see Elvis really dance for the first time.

This remarkable three-minute sequence consists of twelve alternating cuts between long shots of all the prisoners dancing with Elvis in the center of the frame and medium shots from Elvis's torso upward singing the main chorus. The camerawork functions in tune with the chorus and refrain of "Jailhouse Rock," with the lyrics shifting into chorus much like Elvis's expressive dance-work. In the establishing long shot, two television cameras with booms angled toward the center background flank left and right foreground sides of the frame, while the center of the frame reveals two tiers of ten prison cells with barred doors. This opening shot creates a televisual illusion of the 1950s' three-camera studio setup. Television crewmen pull the two cameras and booms out of the frame. Sixteen convicts, two per cell, occupy the first four cells on each tier. In syncopated steps, the cons leave their cells, singing "One, two, one, two": cons on the top tier move to the left of the frame toward a spiral staircase, which they descend, while the convicts below dance in an elliptical pattern before their cells. Cut to a medium long (cowboy) shot of Elvis as the last con still on the top tier, with a pole to the left of him and a cell with the number 1313 behind him. With his thumbs hooked into the top of his jeans, his hands then move down along his hips as he sings. Cut to a long shot as Elvis leans forward so that his right shoulder supports his weight against the pole while his knees alternate to each side of him in time to the song before Elvis slides down the pole on "Let's rock." After sliding down the pole, Elvis holds onto it with his right hand and leans forward, in opposite stance from the shot with the pole above, as he does his famous tiptoe hip shake. He then moves forward away from the pole, as prisoners dance to "Spider Monkey" on the saxophone and "Little Joe" blowing on the trombone in coordinated movements with the lyrics. Then, cut to another long shot as Elvis shimmies side to side on his toes in the center of the frame, and on "Let's rock," he jumps back and straddles the pole with this legs, before a prisoner spins him so that he comes off it. On "Everybody in the whole block/Was dancin' to the Jailhouse Rock," Elvis goes into a side-dance walk to the right of frame.

Cut to a medium shot of Elvis singing about "Number forty-seven said to Number three/You're the cutest jailbird I ever did see," before cutting to a long shot of Elvis dancing provocatively to the suggestion of those words.

Cut to long-shot Elvis jumping frame right and onto a long table arranged seesaw fashion. Cut to a medium shot of Elvis singing about "The sad sack ... weepin' all alone" until the warden suggests that he "If you can't find a partner use a wooden chair." On "Let's rock," Elvis falls to the extreme right end which the cons flip up so that Elvis slides off to the table to the left. On "Everybody in the whole cell block," cut to a long shot as Elvis reverses his previous side-dance walk movements to the left of the frame. Cut to a medium shot on the "Shifty" and the prison-break portion of the song, then the refrain, before cutting to a long shot on "Everybody in the whole cell block" as Elvis shimmies to the left of the frame as a prison guard with a club conks a con on the head whom another con drags away. Cut to a medium shot of Elvis in front of the pole again and the camera follows him as he approaches the stairs and continues as he ascends, along with his fellow prisoners. Cut to a long shot of Elvis on the second tier as the camera pulls back to the establishing shot with the two television cameras and booms coming into view. All the while the cons dance back toward their cells, singing the refrain "Dancin' to the Jailhouse Rock," before settling down, some hanging their legs over the top tier. Then, machine-gun fire sends them back to their cells, where they slam shut the doors. Few moments in this rock-and-roll film genre convey the essential and experimental relationship that developed among lyric, music, and dance. These short three minutes forged a film language of these intersections that has not varied significantly to this day.

During the first days after the release of *Jailhouse Rock*, an advertisement with a guitar-wielding-like-an-axe Presley exclaimed new MGM boxoffice highs with "At press time, 1,000 saturation bookings" that have "ELVIS GOING LIKE HELVIS!"[8] By mid-November, 1957, *Jailhouse Rock* was fourth nationwide behind a conventional Hollywood epic and musicals, *Around the World In Eighty Days, Pal Joey,* and *Les Girls*.[9] By late November 1957, *Variety* reported the astonishing success of the first run of *Jailhouse Rock* in Los Angeles, because the film "shapes sturdy $24,000 in three first-runs plus an additional $96,000 from four nabes and 10 drive-ins, making a mighty $120,000 total for 17 playdates."[10] These financial gains represent Elvis's prowess at the box office and his sex appeal. In its early January, 1958 review of the top-grossing films for 1957, *Variety* reported that *Jailhouse Rock* had achieved fifteenth place with its four million dollars in revenue.[11] For MGM, this first major Elvis film beat out Twentieth Century-Fox's Tracy–Hepburn *Desk Set* by $2.3 million dollars and by $1.5 million over MGM's own *Silk Stockings*.[12] Of course, not everyone reacted so favorably to Elvis's performance. Warden W. F. Bailey of North Carolina's Central Prison near Raleigh complained about the inaccuracies in the film, particularly the scene in which Presley receives a severe lashing for his participation in a riot: "We sure don't allow lashings here. We absolutely do not."[13] Cold War imprisonment and torture might be read into this film but that would certainly be a typical overreading of films of this era. In Baytown, Texas, during a screening of the film, a young man was arrested for "malicious destruction of property" for throwing a cowbell at the image of Elvis on screen.[14] Such a response had little to do with pervasive Communism but rather with homegrown envy and perhaps a heap of Christian guilt. *Jailhouse Rock* remains an Horatio Alger story far more than it does a Cold War ideological commentary.

While Elvis Presley and Jerry Lee Lewis ("Great Balls of Fire") represented earthy male sexuality, much of Little Richard's appeal relied on negating male sexuality, so that the erotics of rock and roll could be tamed. Tame hardly describes Little Richard with his impersonation in full feminine makeup, his carnivalesque showmanship, and his outrageous shouting, stomping, and screaming. Still, as Bruce Tucker points out, that very outrageousness worked to change unacceptable erotics into "a bit of exotica so other as to be meaningless."[15] Having cross-dressing, female impersonating, homosexual Little Richard scream out "The Girl Can't Help It" about Jane Mansfield sums up the peculiar sexual incongruity of 1950s popular culture. For studios, as for record producers, soaring rock-and-roll profits revealed that commercial necessity depended upon the invention and acceptance of the outrageous. In fact, the outré soon became the norm for rock and roll, as though a business model followed the success of the offbeat and the marginal, thereby making the socially unacceptable acceptable.

Little Richard, with the not-so-disguised early hit "Tutti Frutti," oddly covered later by Pat Boone, appeared in three rock-and-roll films: *The Girl Can't Help It* in 1956 and two in 1957, with music promoter Alan Freed, *Don't Know the Rock* and *Mr. Rock and Roll*. *The Girl Can't Help It* begins with a black-and-white 4:3 aspect-ratio shot of Tom Ewell in a white tie and tails surrounded by hanging rock-and-roll musical instruments, while an orchestral tuning sequence segues into a rendition of Jean-Paul-Égide Martini's "Plaisir d'amour." Four years later Elvis Presley would make it a number-one hit, "Can't Help Falling in Love," from *Blue Hawaii*. Ewell explains that this film was "photographed in the grandeur of CinemaScope" before clicking the sides of the frame to expand to the actual aspect ratio. He reiterates the initial point and adds that it was also filmed "in gorgeous, life-like color by Deluxe." only to shout the words again until the screen transforms from black and white to color. Ewell continues: "Our story is about music. Not the music of long ago, but the music that expresses the culture," as the camera pans right to expose a jukebox, "the refinement and politeness of the present day," and upon the word "day," a loud rock-and-roll version of "The Girl Can't Help It," with Little Richard screeching away, drowns out Ewell entirely. The camera zooms to the new emcee, the jukebox, as the starring credits of Tom Ewell, Jane Mansfield, and Edmond O'Brien appear, before cutting to the title superimposed in a large stage with teenagers dancing boogie-woogie as poodle skirts twirl. *The Girl Can't Help It* also showcases Little Richard's "Ready, ready to rock-and-roll," Fats Domino's "Blue Monday," The Platters' "You'll Never, Never Know," Gene Vincent and the Blue Caps' "Be-Bop-a-Lula," Eddie Cochran's "Twenty Flight Rock," among other 1950s rockers. This opening satire from Twentieth Century-Fox obviously points to the teenage market, as well as to studio executives' commercial understanding that the new culture now dominates the market. This opening can be seen only as the studio's admission that Beethoven has truly rolled over for the new music and new profits, with a production budget of $1.31 million and an overall box office profit of nearly $5 million.[16]

In 1961, the film industry in the United States crested one and one-half billion dollars, much of that due to a substantial teenage audience and large commercial profits from teenage, mostly rock-music-oriented films:

> The lucrative teen-age box-office, like its counterpart in publishing and in the rock-and-roll recording business, is a phenomenon that has reached its height, or its depth, in the U.S. These cults have their own heroes and standards. A gigantic job of spoiling is taking place, with producers turning out films tailored for kids, and the kids yelling for more, until it is impossible to determine who is forcing whom.[17]

In the Cold War era, rock-and-roll films that began as narratives of some rebellious musicians and their struggle for industry acceptance transformed into a full array of teenage-oriented genres – the beach and surfing film, the star-based rock-and-roll cum actor, such as Elvis films, the concert films, the retrospective rock biopic, the rock opera, such as The Who's *Tommy* (1975), and the mockumentary, such as *This Is Spinal Tap* (1984). These films share little in common except for the focus upon rock and roll.

After the Elvis films phenomenon, surfing and beach films had highly profitable box offices, beginning with Sandra Dee in *Gidget* (1959) and extending through the Annette Funicello and Frankie Avalon in *Beach Party* (1963), *Muscle Beach Party* (1964) and *Beach Blanket Bingo* (1965). *Gidget* made one and one-half million dollars while *Beach Party* had just over two million dollar box office, with both films made for under one-half million dollars.[18] In his own article in *Variety*, director of the Funicello–Avalon franchise for *American International Pictures*, William Asher remarked on the benefits of these films:

> The series of young people's pictures that I've written and directed for American International have had stories that follow the concept of simply visiting ordinary young people of today and allowing the audience to vicariously enjoy whatever their current activities might be.

> Judging from the boxoffice success of these films, it would appear that the adult audience, as well as younger viewers, find this technique to their liking.[19]

On the same page in *Variety, American International Pictures* Advertising and Publicity Director, Milton Moritz, claimed that preproduction publicity, exploitation during production, and extensive promotion through the theater exhibitions "insure American International's pictures for boxoffice," especially by making "montages of production stills and offstage hi-jinks while the picture is shooting" as a lure for exhibitors and by using "the propaganda media available," such as large newspaper ads, repeated radio spots, and significant use of television spots for promotion. Touring the actors, à la P. T. Barnum, for Moritz also fills theater seats:

> We believe that the moviegoing public like to see the stars – close-up; so we have sent out our contract players – Frankie Avalon, Annette Funicello . . . to the four corners of the country on repeated public appearances.
>
> Others appearing in our pictures . . . the Bikini Beach girls – have chalked up thousands of air miles and contributed mightily to bulging books of tearsheets which prove that the public loves to see Hollywood folk on tour.[20]

Moritz and Asher use teenager media and the teenage cult of fandom in particular as the means to sell their films. In a rare reference to the Cold War global conditions, *American International Pictures* sales Vice President, Leon P. Blender, explained that success of beach films could be attributed to escapism from "today's turbulent world."[21] Even though film critics often wrote off beach films, they were more subversive, particularly with the themes of their songs, than usually thought with "sexuality, parodic irreverence, and non-conformity" as essential "elements from teenage culture, Rock-and-Roll, bohemian philosophy, and beat culture and mixed with a heavy dose of parody."[22]

Pop music critic of the late 1960s and 1970s, Ellen Willis places *Easy Rider* (1969) within the fantasy pastoral tradition of America, with its desire for freedom, the open road, and individual liberty. The film's radical soundtrack integrated non-diegetic rock music to amplify the narrative, such as the inclusion of songs by The Band, Jimi Hendrix Experience, and The Byrds. The memorable opening credit sequence employs two songs by Steppenwolf to establish the film's plot. "The Pusher" reinforces the drug-selling scheme of Wyatt (Peter Fonda) and Billy (Dennis Hopper) with its prophetic, lyrics "You know, I've seen a lot of people walkin' round/With tombstones in their eyes." As the credits roll, Wyatt and Billy head eastward on their choppers to fulfill their version of American freedom, while "Born To Be Wild" provides prophetic lyrics that announce their deaths at the film's conclusion, "Fire all of your guns at once/And explode into space." Much like outlaw anti-Westerns of the period, such as Sam Peckinpah's *The Wild Bunch* of the same year, *Easy Rider* really narrates the pursuit of the American dream as an utter failure. Its cowboy–hippie heroes come to understand that this kind of failure strikes at the very heart of countercultural delusions against capitalism:

> *Easy Rider* is about the failure of America on all levels, hip and straight. Billy and Wyatt on their bikes, riding free down the open road, are living another version of the rugged individualist frontier fantasy, and the big dope deal that made them financially independent is just hip capitalism. It won't work, and by the end of the movie Wyatt knows it.
>
> The key line of the film is his admission, "We blew it!" I have no idea if the allusion is intentional, but *The Electric Kool-Aid Acid Test* ends with the same line. There it refers to the failure of Ken Kesey's particular frontier fantasy.[23]

This sense of doom pervades *Easy Rider*, as attentive audiences came to understand. As with most of the social rock-and-roll films, the upshot is not utopian but the reality of aggressive self-interest couched in hippie revolutionary platitudes that remain little more than ego trips. The same may be said for the failed student-protest administration building takeover of *The Strawberry Statement* (1970) in which radicals of all stripes clash more with one another than with the Man. This film employs non-diegetic revolutionary anthems as much for emotional effect as for thematic content, such as Thunderclap Newman's "Something In The Air" and the soundtrack narrative accompaniments by Buffy Saint-Marie and Crosby, Stills, Nash, and Young. *The Strawberry Statement* was released one month after the Kent State shootings in May 1970. Any nostalgia for the hippie era and protest movements misconstrues the dispiriting and discouraging endings of these films.

In general, the rockumentary follows patterns of fictive realism of documentaries: that attempt to capture a fleeting essence of the ephemeral experience of concert performances, backstage exploits, and personal moments as rock stars divulge influences, creative expressions, and personality traits. Fictive remains the operative term here, because rockumentaries almost exclusively disclose not the reality of rock and roll but acting, its staging, its acknowledgment of a constructed world for the camera. *Dont Look Back* (1967) reorients the reality of documentary-style realism by expanding musical performance in its prologue into Bob Dylan's street theater for "Subterranean Homesick Blues." In an alley in London between the Savoy Hotel and Queen's Chapel, Dylan stands in the right foreground holding a cache of handwritten cards with phrases from, or related to, the song, which he flips through in time to the recording of the song from his album *Bringing It All Back Home* that forms the diegetic soundscape. Dylan's sardonic gaze into the camera and responses to the words on the cards reveal, as William Rothman pointed out, a clear "collaboration," if not "co-conspiracy" between director D. A. Pennebaker and performer Dylan.[24] This prologue would be the primogenitor for not only rock videos, particularly the much later MTV format, but also the language play, tempo, and rhyming patterns for hip-hop. As Keith Beattie's insightful study points out, the film emphasizes the collusion between director and star to eschew a probing for the real Bob Dylan and instead such attempts are "deferred or rejected within and through the persona projected before the acknowledged presence of the camera."[25] The same adoption of a guise characterizes Dylan's enigmatic, occasionally hostile relationship to members of the press who wish to extract from Dylan the meaning of his songs, his message. One interviewer faced the brunt of Dylan's hostility when he tried to probe into Dylan:

> DYLAN: I know more about what you do and you don't even know to ask me how or why or anything just by looking, you know, than you'll ever know about me ever. I mean, I could tell you, I could tell you I'm not a folk singer and explain to you why, but you wouldn't really understand. All you could do, you could nod your head, you would not nod your head.[26]

Along with press interviews, *Dont Look Back* includes previous performances by Dylan in Mississippi in 1963 singing "Only a Pawn in Their Game," hotel-room antics, stage performances, backstage preparation routines and dialogue, and limousine conversations, all of which would become staples of rockumentaries. Still, *Dont Look Back* seeks out and critiques a new film genre, the rockumentary, before the genre ever established itself by defying viewers' expectations and flying in the face of pure, direct *cinéma-vérité*. As politically charged as Dylan's early albums had been, *Dont Look Back* concludes with a recognition of the Cold War period at the same time that Dylan mocks politics:

> DYLAN: Anarchist? You're kidding. What papers did you see that in?
> GROSSMAN: Well, two or three. Today, yeah. Just 'cause you don't offer any solution.
> DYLAN: You're kidding!
> GROSSMAN: Of course.
> DYLAN: Anarchist.
> GROSSMAN: Yeah.
> DYLAN: Hmmm. Gimme a cigarette. Give the anarchist a cigarette . . .
> GIRL: At least they didn't say communist.

INTRODUCTION

Figure 1.3   Bob Dylan the "anarchist" with a cigarette in *Dont Look Back* (1967).

> DYLAN: But it probably took them a while to think of that name ... anarchist. They couldn't say communist. (151–2)

As with so much of *Dont Look Back*, Dylan gives a wink and a nod to the absurdity of political terms imposed by the press and stares out the window of the limousine as the world passes by.

Woodstock (1970) would try for the improvisational *vérité* approach to concert filming with new cinematic editing by Thelma Schoonmaker and Martin Scorsese of multiple split screens to capture the rhythms of onstage performances and crowd reactions. Dylan's "Subterranean Homesick Blues" film would re-emerge as the bouncing ball for Country Joe and the Fish's antiwar sing-along, "Feel Like I'm Fixin' To Die Rag." *Woodstock* became well known for iconic performances: Jimi Hendrix's acid version of "The Star Spangled Banner," Santana's rousing instrumentals and memorable drum solo on "Soul Sacrifice," Alvin Lee's guitar-blaring "I'm Going Home," The Who's instrument-destroying conclusion to "Summertime Blues," as well as its glimpses into innocuous, very middle-class youth counterculture in America. By the time we got to *Woodstock* the film, most of the artists and performers had been mainstreamed by television, among them: Jefferson Airplane lip-syncing on *The Smothers Brothers Comedy Hour* in May, in June 1967, and November 1968, as well as on Johnny Carson's *The Tonight Show* in April 1968; Crosby, Stills, Nash, and Young on Los Angeles's *Music Scene* in September 1969, with Stills and Young having already been on the *The Smothers Brothers* as Buffalo Springfield in February 1967; Graham Nash with The Hollies on *The Smothers Brothers* in November 1967; The Who on *The Smothers Brothers* in September 1967; and *Dick Cavett* hosting Janis Joplin in 1969 and 1970, then Jimi Hendrix in 1970. Clearly, the counterculture of rock-and-roll music had embraced conventional media and that commercial recognition diminished whatever political radicalism might have been voiced earlier. For example, when Yippie Abbie Hoffman asked Jefferson Airplane to play at demonstrations against the Democratic National Convention in the summer of 1968, the group refused flat out, as Paul Kantner explained: "I couldn't see any reason for us to go and get beaten up."[27]

Unlike the love-in of *Woodstock*, *Gimme Shelter* (1970) offered a much darker view of America's counterculture – extreme, unpredictable violence. This rockumentary followed the Rolling Stones from a concert in Madison Square Garden to studio work in Muscle Shoals, Alabama, finally to the infamous Altamont Speedway outdoor concert where pool-cue-carrying Hell's Angels served as their private security force. During their set, an Angel coldcocked Jefferson Airplane's Marty Balin and, by the time the Rolling Stones took the stage, the atmosphere shifted to homicidal passions. As Mick Jagger began "Under My Thumb," the crowd surged toward the stage only to be repelled by a host of Angels. Caught on film is the fatal stabbing by Hell's Angel Alan Passaro of a gun-wielding, African American young man, identified later as Meredith Curly Hunter, Jr. The gruesome killing turned the concert film into a version of the nightly news broadcasts of the Vietnam War, with the camera dispassionately recording violence that darkly fulfilled Jagger's press conference claim that this free concert would create a "microcosmic society." Ironically, that society *Gimme Shelter* certainly did reveal, making the film what Amy Taubin referred to as "Rock and Roll Zapruder."[28]

This Is Spinal Tap (1984), with its umlaut cleverly or stupidly placed over the "n," created the mockumentary, parodying all of the essential components of numerous rockumentaries. This marvelously funny film parodies and critiques the entire history of rock and roll from folk rock to protest rock to hippie rock to rock fusion to heavy metal rock, all the while pointing a well-placed finger at the Cold War culture that not only accepted this new popular genre but also saw it, so unthinkingly, as a medium for social change. Few moments in this film sum up both the serious enterprise of new genres in early Cold War period and their dismissal by its end with complete detente with the new Russia as

Spinal Tap having to play at a staid, conservative Air Force base dance. In so many ways, *This Is Spinal Tap* sums up not the new emerging films of the early Cold War period but, rather, their parodic, yet insightful versions. This collection, then, presents new cinematic genres that emerged during these four decades, established themselves as popular formats, and transformed popular culture. That *This Is Spinal Tap* parodies the conventions of the rock-and-roll genre so deftly only indicates the immediate recognition of this genre and its variety. So, too, will be evident for these new, emerging, and transformative film genres during the Cold War era in this volume.

Notes

1. Jeff Smith, *Film Criticism, The Cold War, and the Blacklist* (Berkeley: University of California Press, 2014): 2. Though Smith focuses on the 1950s, these categories extend to film criticism in the 1960s.
2. Tony Shaw, *Hollywood's Cold War* (Edinburgh: Edinburgh University Press, 2007): 4–5.
3. John Sbardellati, *J. Edgar Hoover Goes To The Movies – The FBI and the Origins of Hollywood's Cold War* (Ithaca, NY: Cornell University Press, 2012): 6.
4. Greg Barnhisel, *Cold War Modernists: Art, Literature, and American Cultural Diplomacy* (New York: Columbia University Press, 2015): 4. Barhinsel's "Introduction" makes the claim that the dissemination of modern art in the 1950s transformed "public understanding of modernism, deactivating or nullifying its associations with radicalism and antinomianism and making it safe for consumption by American middle-class audiences" (4).
5. "Estimated Grosses Past Year" *Variety* (Wednesday, January 2, 1957): 4. "Top Grossers of 1957" *Variety* (January 8, 1958); 30.
6. "Don't Knock the Rock" *Variety* (Wednesday, December 26, 1956): 6.
7. "Fred Karger on 'Clock'" *Variety* (Wednesday, November 15, 1961): 4.
8. "ELVIS GOING LIKE HELVIS!" *Variety* (Wednesday, November 6, 1957): 15. The ad also proclaimed that in a "Late Flash," "Go spots beat famed 'Black-board Jungle!'"
9. "National Boxoffice Survey," in "Pictures," *Variety* (Wednesday, November 13, 1957): 3.
10. "Picture Grosses: 'Jailhouse' Terrif 120G . . ." *Variety* (Wednesday, November 20, 1957): 8.
11. "Top Grossers of 1957," *Variety* (January 8, 1958): 30.
12. "That Was 1957 – At the Cash Box," *Variety* (January 8, 1958): 6.
13. "Prison Chief Grimaces; 'Jailhouse Rock' Link To Carolina Unfavorable," *Variety* (Wednesday, November 13, 1957): 20.
14. "Threw Cow Bell at Presley, Out on Bail," *Variety* (Wednesday, November 13, 1957): 24.
15. Bruce Tucker, "'Tell Tchaikovsky the News': Postmodernism, Popular Culture, and the Emergence of Rock 'N' Roll," *Black Music Research Journal* 22 (2002): 37. [23–47]
16. For figures on this film and other Twentieth-Century costs and profits, see Aubrey Solomon, *Twentieth Century-Fox: A Corporate and Financial History* (Lanham, MD: Scarecrow Press, 1988).
17. Gretchen Weinberg, "The Teen-Age Box-Office," *Vision: A Journal of Film Comment* 1.1 (sSpring, 1962): 10. [9–10]

18. Tom Lisanti, *Hollywood Surf and Beach Movies: The First Wave, 1959–1969* (Jefferson, NC: McFarland, 2005): 29.
19. William Asher, "AIP Director's Key to Vitamin Youth: Participate In Their Fun," *Variety* (Wednesday, July 22, 1964): 8.
20. Milton Moritz, "AIP's Barnuming No Soft Sell," *Variety* (Wednesday, July 22, 1964): 8.
21. Leon P. Blender, "Key to Fullest Merchandising Potential: Diversity of Product," *Variety* (Wednesday, July 22, 1964): 8.
22. R. I. Rutsky, "Surfing the Other: Ideology on the Beach," *Film Quarterly* 52.4 (summer, 1999): 13. [12–23]
23. Ellen Willis, "See America First: *Easy Rider* and *Alice's Restaurant*," *Beginning To See the Light: Sex, Hope, and Rock-and-Roll* (Minneapolis: University of Minnesota Press, 2012): 55. While Willis views both *Easy Rider* and *Alice's Restaurant* (1967) as fundamentally apolitical, she aptly points out how disillusioning both are for their sense of failure and, in Guthrie's case, "the decay from within" that characterize the counterculture (56).
24. William Rothman, *Documentary Film Classics* (Cambridge: Cambridge University Press, 1997): 149.
25. Keith Beattie, *Dont Look Back* [BFI Film Classics] (London: Palgrave, 2016): 22.
26. D. A. Pennebaker, *Bob Dylan–Dont Look Back* (1968; New York: Ballantine Books, 2006): 125–6.
27. As quoted in Patrick Burke, "Tear down the Walls: Jefferson Airplane, Race, and Revolutionary Rhetoric in 1960s Rock," *Popular Music* 29.1 (January 2010): 67.
28. Amy Taubin, "Rock and Roll Zapruder," Criterion Collection, DVD booklet, 6. In this same booklet, Sonny Barger, head of the Hell's Angels, blamed the Stones' "ego trips" for wanting the crowd to be in a frenzied state, the crowd's bottle throwing and "messing with our bikes," and the long hours of waiting in the sun (32). When a topless, fat hippie chick came on stage, Keith Richards taunted Barger by asking why it took three Angels to subdue her, so Barger "just walked over to the edge of the stage and kicked her in the head. 'How's that?'" (33). Additionally, Barger explained that Hunter had shot a Hell's Angel: "Since the guy he shot was a fugitive at the time, we couldn't take him to a doctor or an emergency ward. It was just a flesh wound anyway" (33).

2. SOCIAL FACTORS IN BRAINWASHING FILMS OF THE 1950s AND 1960s

David Seed

Ron Robin opens his study of how universities dealt with the Cold War by declaring: "throughout most of the Cold War rumors of an enemy plagued the United States [. . .] The mutant enemy appeared everywhere – in foreign lands and at home. Exorcising his presence became a national obsession" (Robin 2001: 3). In a similar spirit, Peter Biskind has argued that in films of the 1950s "the idea of the alien was profoundly influenced by the Manichean Us/Them habit of thought that was an occupational hazard of the cold-war battle of ideas" (Biskind 2000: 111). But suppose that this polarity can exist within a single body? And suppose home became alien?[1] Soon after the Korean War broke out in 1950, the term "brainwashing" entered the language and, in the same period, a series of films began to appear depicting the takeover of human subjects by alien forces. Though the nature of these forces was to vary, there was a broad congruence of subject in that, especially within the polarities of the Cold War, brainwashing was interpreted as a seizure of the mind by malign agencies. Whether these were identified as Communist or extraterrestrial, the outcome of the two processes was identical in that the subject to all outward appearances stayed the same and yet details of expression, posture and gait all suggested that an inner transformation had taken place. In short, the subject had become alien.

These films repeatedly focus on the brain as the center of vital selfhood and a number speculate on the possibility that the brain somehow survives beyond death. Thus, in *Donovan's Brain* (1953), the brain of a wealthy businessman is kept alive after a plane crash in the desert. This is narrated as a triumph of the will of the deceased who comes to possess the body of the scientist. The 1962 British film *The Brain* repeats the same subject, except that the scientist is now used as a medium for a dead person seeking his murderer. In cinematic terms, of course, the brain is not normally visible. Hence our attention in takeover films contrasts before and after, and induces what Vivian Sobchack has described as an "attentive paranoia," because it is only through the small discrepancies and absences of behavior that the transformation can be perceived (Sobchack 2001: 124). Sobchack anticipates later interpretations when she stresses that the small-town settings favored in 1950s U.S. movies initially evoked a "community which is [. . .] familiar, predictable, snug and unprivate;" and therefore all the more dramatic when under attack (Sobchack 2001: 121). She helpfully identifies a social dimension to the action, which risks being lost if critical attention focuses on special effects or the identity of the aliens, a dimension right in the foreground of the action in one of the formative alien invasion films of the decade.

Alien Takeovers

On release, *It Came from Outer Space* was heavily promoted for its use of 3-D technology through a sensational trailer, which opened with the warning "It's coming right at you!" Despite the promise of threat and danger, the film presents an unusually intelligent dialogue between the human and alien, the known and the unknown. A small town – Sand Rock, Arizona – is used as a portal to the nation. We are told in the opening voice-over that Sand Rock is a "nice town, knowing its past and sure of its future." The protagonist, a local astronomer, named John Putnam, has a house on the border between the town and the desert planning to get "all the benefits of home" with the help of his fiancée Ellen, a schoolteacher who has "responsibilities to the community." The polarity of setting between town and desert is crucial to the action and one reviewer, after ironically commenting on its stereotyped subject, admitted that the new visual effects did give "impressions of depth and true vastness" (A. W. 1953).

When a massive "meteor" crashes near Putnam's house, he takes Ellen in a helicopter to the site. Shot from underneath, this helicopter resembles a giant insect when viewed from the perspective off the ground. Once Putnam starts exploring the crater, perspective reversals increase, alternating between his glimpses of a strange spacecraft and shots of him through a bubble lens, as if from an alien being. Ray Bradbury's original treatment significantly extended this effect to a panning shot: "The CAMERA GLIDES across the vast, burnt and steaming floor of the crater and GLIDES SLOWLY up the crater side, as if it were a visitor, a creature, a man gliding with great ease and slow assurance to look out upon the world."[2] Bradbury's aim was clearly to set up the

Figure 2.1 Alien point-of-view in *It Came From Outer Space* (1953).

alien perspective as a mirror to the astronomer's but this effect was cut to a minimum in the film in the interests of pace and suspense. In this episode the film also establishes Putnam's role as the mediator, investigator, and commentator, guiding the viewer through different possibilities hinted at in the indeterminate title.[3]

The arrival of alien beings is repeatedly linked with the threatening life of the desert. As Putnam and Ellen drive away from the crash site, she screams when she sees a mysterious object only to realize that it is a Joshua tree which becomes a sign of the desert's bizarre life forms. Later Putnam even stands under a Joshua tree calling on the mysterious creature to emerge. Shortly afterwards, he explains about the desert that "it's alive and waiting for you" over shots of cacti and a lizard scurrying across a rock. This brief lesson is countered by a "bubble-lens" shot of their car driving away, a clear hint of alien mobility. To complicate the play of perspectives further, they next meet two telephone engineers, one of whom is hearing strange sounds over the wire. He shrugs off their oddity by attributing them to the desert's impact on habits of perception. At this point he appears to be simply reinforcing Putnam's own commentary but then a more sinister development takes place. When Putnam and Ellen later discover the telephone truck abandoned, a replicant technician steps forward, reassuring them not to be afraid, though the real shock comes through his changed manner: a wooden expression, toneless speech and mechanical gait. The movie's two settings, desert and town, become ominously connected when the two replicant telephone engineers are spotted in the main street. Putnam follows them down an alley and into a building where nothing but shadows can be distinguished. One warns Putnam: "Give us time or terrible things will happen." By this point, the action has taken on a clear social dimension, not least when Putnam and the sheriff sum up recent developments such as a theft from a local hardware store.

It Came From Outer Space is unusual in the attention it devotes to the media coverage of the crash. No sooner has the crash happened than a television truck goes straight to the site. The local newspaper ridicules Putnam's report with the headline "Star Gazer Sees Martians," and he becomes progressively alienated from the community whose spokesman, the sheriff, declares: "this town doesn't understand you." Indeed, Putnam's report is treated with skepticism by scientists and the army alike. The media reports give a serial commentary on events though the film reveals the disparity between events and these misinterpretations. For example, three prospectors working in an old mine are taken over and immediately afterwards a radio announcer ridicules stories of "bug-eyed monsters." The film further develops its ironic awareness of generic clichés when Ellen answers the doorbell, screaming when she sees a spaceman, or rather a boy in costume, standing outside. At such points, the film bounces its action off the science-fiction clichés circulating in the media without ever negating its action.

As the strange occurrences multiply, it becomes clear that a plan is being put into operation but not necessarily a malign one. Putnam learns that the aliens simply want to repair their spaceship and then continue their voyage. They declare as much by saying "let us stay apart." Despite his skepticism towards Putnam's original account of the landing, the sheriff articulates a paranoid perspective more reminiscent of 1950s pulp science fiction when he complains: "how do we know they're not taking over?" The duplication of humans, dramatized in late scenes where we can see both originals and replicants, comes to embody the polarities of response between Putnam's rational consideration of giving help and the increasingly hysterical determination of the sheriff to raise a posse to destroy the aliens. This division is figured through a fissure in the mine separating Putnam from the Ellen replicant. It is only when Putnam asks to see the aliens that there is a brief image of a torso with an eye and limbs, scarcely glimpsed before it is naturalized through a comparison with a spider.[4] In one of Bradbury's treatments, he avoids such lurid effects through suggestion. In a scene where Ellen is alone with the transformed linesmen, a close-up of one of their faces briefly reflects the stars. When Ellen looks "into the shadows of his face. We get the merest glimmer, a suggestion only, of something from a nightmare, something which suggests a spider, a lizard, a tiger, something dark and terrible [. . .]"[5] The problem in this description is the disparity between the momentary visual impression and the duration of the syntax which attempts to draw out that effect. Ellen, predictably, screams.

Brief though it is, the image of the arachnoid creature makes an awkward concession to the bug-eyed monster cliché whereas the film engages primarily with the idea of the alien. By setting up Putnam as a judicious perspective character, the focus gradually shifts to the mounting hysteria and knee-jerk reactions of the townsfolk. Bradbury originally attempted to include substantial dialogue sequences where events and particularly the identity of the "invaders" are discussed but, in the final film, Putnam engages in an extended debate with the town sheriff who points out the destabilizing logic of body takeovers when he complains: "Nothing would ever add up. I couldn't even be sure that you were John Putnam standing beside me." The sheriff wavers uneasily between downright skepticism towards Putnam's story and reluctant acceptance which then results in a collection of town vigilantes who shoot down the replicant linesman in a roadblock and set off to attack the spaceship. By holding off this mob, Putnam ultimately saves the victims who were duplicated, as the originals are held in the spaceship. His pleas for a delay are made through a dialogue between himself and his replicated double, who now speaks for the space travelers, an effect that makes explicit the film's broader interpretive dialogue between hypothesis and counter-hypothesis. Once the captives are released, the vessel leaves the mine in a kind of eruption, flying back into the sky, but it falls to Putnam to deny final closure to the movie when he declares: "they'll be back."

Also from 1953, *Invaders from Mars* manages to avoid many of the clichés of the emerging genre by focusing its action on a small boy and by dramatizing his progressive estrangement from family and friends. David is already an amateur astronomer and is astonished to see a spaceship landing in a back lot during a thunderstorm. When he wakes his parents to tell them, they assure him that it was all a dream in a reassuring tableau of domestic unity. The film, however, exploits a surreal setting behind the house where a path and fence run up a hill reminiscent of *The Cabinet of Dr. Caligari* and where the unusual perspective gives an impression of shrinkage as characters walk away from the camera (Erickson 2002). When David's father goes to investigate, he appears to fall into a sandpit and disappear. The scene toward this pit seems foreshortened throughout the film, not least because, instead of stretching into a background, the fence curves down into the sand. This pit thus seems to be at once near and also strange, the place where the spaceship disappears. Instead of representing a place of play for the child, it becomes the site of concealment and threat.

After two policemen appear to search the area, both disappearing into the sand, David's father reappears suddenly in a close-up which frames his stern expression. As mother embraces him, he stares impassively over her shoulder and closes off their conversation by repeating "period." Similarly, when David questions him about an object embedded in his neck, he strikes him across the face. Parental care has shifted dramatically into demands for obedience, delivered mostly with averted gaze. By this point, David's astronomical interest has shifted into a concentrated visual attention to those around him, specifically to telltale signs of change. In a panic, he runs to his neighbor to tell them that their little girl is missing, at which point, in a reprise of his father's return, Cathy suddenly appears in close-up, frozen in the door frame. Once he suspects that Cathy set fire to her house, David realizes that the changes taking place are more dangerous than he thought and he rushes to the local police station. Here the film weaves further variations on perspective, exaggerating the length of the corridor as David runs towards the duty officer and then the height of the desk as he approaches. The camera's position above the officer's head reduces David's size and magnifies the daunting authority of the location. At this point the police chief enters their dialogue with an apparently benign question, "What's the trouble, Mac?" immediately negated by his stern full-face image in close-up. As the camera follows David's line of vision away from the desk, the internal lamps give a diminishing perspective on the chief who appears somewhat dwarfed in the second doorway. The effect is of yet more estrangement as a potentially reassuring authority figure turns into a threatening guard after he glimpses the device in the chief's neck.

Up to this point, the film has traced out a psychological action consistent with a child's overheated imagination, where the frame of David's bedroom window has been replaced by the bars of the police cell where he is held. Then, thanks to the proxy maternal sympathy shown by a health officer, to whom he tells his story, and later to a paternalistic scientist, David's story achieves credibility through the family roles vacated by his parents. At this point, the subject shifts toward a national drama of attack and defense, a link embodied in the fact that David's father works in a nearby atomic plant. It emerges that the implants in victims' necks transform them into servomechanisms with the specific direction to sabotage any defense installations. One attack is partially successful, by which time the U.S. military has swung into action, shown through the incorporation of library footage of tank transports. In his analysis of this film, Rob Latham has argued that the relation between the Martians and their human victims is problematic because the latter are already involved in the military–industrial system, concluding that "the paranoia about alien invasion and takeover may merely serve to deflect anxieties about how seamlessly militarist power has inscribed itself into the suburban American landscape" (Latham 1995: 201).[6]

In the film's denouement, the Martians are forced to carry on their journey through space. In the American version, a montage of previous scenes is shown over David running (in panic?) and the explosion of the spacecraft jolts him awake as if from a nightmare. The print prepared for European audiences avoids the closure of the dream frame and shows refugees, including David, in flight from the site of the spaceship, which then explodes. A tableau scene with the doctor and scientist reconstitutes the family unit where the doctor reassures David that his parents are "going to be alright."

Like *It Came from Outer Space*, the action of *The Brain from Planet Arous* (1957) is played out in a border area on the edge of the desert where a family group is getting ready for a barbecue. The disruption to an otherwise routine domestic situation comes when the protagonist, a scientist named Steve, picks up radiation which seems to be emanating from the nearby Mysterious Mountain, described by him as the "most godforsaken spot in the desert." An immediate tension is set up between the arid desert and the home, between the scientific impulse to investigate and the more prosaic attractions of the barbecue. This is imaged in the conversation between Steve, his fiancée, and his assistant through a kitchen window, the latter two inside, Steve in the yard. The two men drive to the mountain and explore a cave where the perspective alternates between close and distant shots as if they are already under observation. A brief climax comes with them confronting a giant brain with eyes that contract onto Steve's body. The optical feature carries a symbolism highlighted in the publicity posters for the movie which showed a man gazing upward with rays emanating from his eyes. Despite a time gap of almost a week, the film cuts to Sally inside her kitchen talking on the phone to her father while under observation from Steve outside. His estrangement is signaled through his expression and through his framing in the window. Shortly afterward, Steve's face undergoes lateral distortion when he has a seizure behind a watercooler. Partly these details suggest that Steve is undergoing a psychodrama of possession where he seems to oscillate between two identities. His estrangement is further dramatized when his dog attacks him and when Sally registers a change toward passion ('a regular caveman') but away from her, declaring: "it was as if he was a stranger."

The theme of possession duplicates when a second, more benign, brain manifests itself to Sally and her father, explaining that it is there to block the activities of Gor, the malign consciousness that has "invaded" Steve. As proof of its good intentions, the second brain lodges itself in the family dog. At this point the film opens up into a drama of national survival. During one of his "unpossessed" phases Steve and Sally drive to the top of a hill and gaze down on to the nearby town. Steve declares: "that's our world out there" but Gor has other plans, later willing a passenger plane to explode. As usual in 1950s movies, the fate of the family is shadowed by that of the nation. Indeed,

Pentagon officials discover that the corpses from the air disaster have died from intense radiation. At many points, the film dramatizes events as a parable of the known and unknown. It is radiation that first attracts Steve to the mountain and the disaster reflects its potential as a weapon through the conversion of Steve into an instrumentality triggering a series of deaths starting with his assistant's, extending to the sheriff's – the town's embodiment of order – and culminating with Sally's father.[7] At the moment when he is killing the sheriff, and later an army officer, Steve's eyes transform into metal, the key sign of his alienation. The dynamics of family cohesion are displaced onto a melodrama of invasion as Gor reveals his intention to take over the nation and then the world. The same imagistic motifs persist, however. When Steve demonstrates to international leaders his power to destroy another plane, this is figured by him gazing through a window in a reprise of earlier domestic scenes. The film traces out the evocation of what Steve describes (and adopts) as a "power from outside of this world," the action can only conclude with the purging of this force and the tableau kiss between Steve and Sally in the final scene.

By the end of the decade, the features of the genre had become fixed and *The Brain Eaters* (1958) is useful for demonstrating the pattern which had become established in alien takeover movies. Set in Riverdale, Illinois, "just another quiet small town" until its "living nightmare" begins one night when two men, one carrying a glowing orb, bump into each other. The orb falls and breaks, and its carrier attacks the second man. The orb's origin lies in a mysterious cone which has crashed outside the town, discovered by the scientist protagonist and his fiancée. After a mysterious absence from his office, the mayor is confronted and behaves in a strangely defiant way, culminating in his fatal attempt to shoot his way out. The resulting autopsy shows the traces of a parasitic growth which, like the implants in *Invaders from Mars*, injects acid into the base of the neck, ultimately destroying the victim's nervous system. The breaking of contact with the outside world is by now a familiar strategy. When the senator in charge of the investigation attempts to send a telegram to the state governor, the wire operator reverses his message to read: "Everything peaceful here. Space ship pure bunk." The scene then cuts to a human shadow in profile facing the American flag. Despite such symbolism of national crisis, the film fails to generate suspense, not least when the protagonist enters the cone and confronts a human form who speaks for the parasites, declaring "we shall force upon man a life free from strife and turmoil." This restates the purpose evoked in *Invasion of the Body Snatchers* and the radiant globes function like the pods in that movie. What is missing, however, is the drama of estrangement from familiar figures, and the derivative nature of the film became evident when Robert Heinlein sued the production company for plagiarism from his 1951 novel *The Puppet Masters* which, in 1958, was under consideration for a Hollywood adaptation (Patterson 2004: 173–4).[8] In the latter, Earth is under attack from flying saucers carrying slug-like parasites that attach themselves to the backs of their victims, taking over their will completely, even inducing a temporary dissociation of consciousness of the protagonist.

All brainwashing movies, in varying degrees, dramatize their subjects through gender relations. A repeated pattern is that of a male protagonist undergoing mysterious changes which are particularly registered by his fiancée. *I Married a Monster from Outer Space* (1958) pursues gender estrangement in close detail by opening with a scene where a group of young men in a bar joke about marriage as "mass suicide." On his way to his wedding, Bill stops when he imagines he sees a body in the road; then the scene dissolves in smoke. The extraterrestrial takeover literalizes this male hostility. As Cyndy Hendershot explains, "the film creates two pseudo-communities of threatening men: on the one hand, Bill's cynical friends, who regard marriage as a prison; on the other hand, the aliens, which take over male human bodies exclusively in order to use female humans to repopulate their race" (Hendershot 1999: 58). The director Gene Fowler found himself with a "ridiculous title" but trying to make a "very realistic and very honest film" despite it (Warren 2010: 385). He managed this by placing the alien invasion theme in the background to a drama of marital dysfunction.

The marriage night at the beginning of the film takes place against a melodramatic backdrop of thunder and lightning, the latter momentarily revealing Bill's monstrously distorted face. Otherwise, he comes across as so abstracted that his wife, Marge, records in her diary: "Bill isn't the man I fell in love with." The film's power lies in the disparity it dramatizes between the material comforts of Marge's married life and her growing estrangement from Bill, reflected in contrasting long shots of Bill looking at Marge in the kitchen and vice versa. As substitute for the baby she had hoped for, on their first anniversary she gives Bill a dog named Junior which takes an instant aversion to him. Far from cementing the family group, Junior is strangled by Bill in the basement. The sheer silence between the newly-weds gives an understated tension to the first half of the film while further seizures of local men suggest that the problem is by no means an individual one.

In a crucial discovery scene, Marge follows Bill one night when he goes out for a walk without explanation. She follows him out of town, the road symbolically giving way to track and wild woodland where she sees an astronaut emerge from Bill's immobile form. Marge now faces the problem of conveying her message to others. In the bar, she is dismissed as another "lush" and seems to get a better reception in the police station although the police chief is revealed as taken over through his distorted features. The paranoid dynamics of the film include the alienation of authority figures and, more dramatically, the disruption of telephone and telegraph services, even a roadblock.

At the point where Marge has become trapped, she confronts her "husband" declaring: "You're not Bill. you're some thing that crept into Bill's body," whereupon he finally explains that the women have all died out on his planet. Ironically, the most substantial dialogue since their marriage is the one articulating their total estrangement. The denouement, however, maximizes the role of the town doctor who gathers a posse and the national guard to confront the aliens. As men and dogs approach the spaceship, Bill breaks open Marge's bedroom door, demanding to know who helped her. It seems as if both actions are converging on an outburst of violence. Taller and stronger in physique, Bill in half profile poses an obvious threat to Marge who is, however, imaged full face in a mirror as she voices her defiance. The defeat of the aliens restores the status quo but leaves the gender prejudices untouched.

INVASION OF THE BODY SNATCHERS

The takeover of a small town by extraterrestrial pods in *Invasion of the Body Snatchers* (1956) has been taken as an "overt metaphor for Communist brainwashing" but others have claimed that the film is about the threat of fascism (Biskind 2000: 140). Addressing the latter, director Don Siegel has claimed that his intention was to attack a "much more general state of mind that is found in everyday life" (LaValley 1989: 159). The focus of criticism on this film has also fallen on its depiction of gender, with Nancy Steffen-Fluhr declaring that "the inner game of *Invasion* is a very traditional version of the War Between the Sexes in which the overt antagonism has been suppressed and reprojected as a War of the Worlds" (LaValley 1989: 209). Focusing tightly on the shifting relation between Miles and Becky, she reads the pods as encoded human qualities which Miles and the film as a whole reject, concluding that a covert misogyny informs the plot. The debate continues on the exact significance of the pods and how far the film is exploiting allegory whether as a parable against conformity or not.[9]

Invasion avoids the schematic topography of most alien invasion films by locating the source of the aliens within the heart of the community. When Miles Bennell returns to Santa Mira from a medical convention, he expects to find his home town as he left it but already a disturbance is taking place within its families, estranging one member from another. The first scene to dramatize this occurs when little Jimmy Grimaldi runs in front of Miles's car shouting that his mother isn't his mother. Then Miles stops at a friend's who insists that her uncle has become a stranger, admitting that "there is no difference that you can actually see" (LaValley 1989: 43). In the cruder versions of this theme, characters have become so zombified that they are immediately identifiable. When Miles goes to speak to Wilma's uncle, however, he is the very personification of normality, waving at him while he mows the lawn and puffs on his pipe. The perspective of the doctor, uniquely placed to know the townsfolk personally, introduces the film's main analogy with disease and also induces a visual unease in the viewer because, as Vivian Sobchack has argued, "we cannot automatically believe what we see" (Sobchack 2001: 128). A supplement to Miles is offered by a local psychiatrist who declares that there is a kind of "epidemic mass hysteria" but there is no reason to suppose that he is exempt from the very disease he is claiming to identify (LaValley 1989: 48). Peter Biskind has taken the latter's role as an indicator of a general ideology, arguing that "the vehemence of the film's villainization [sic] of Dr. Kaufman is an indication of the degree to which radical films insisted on the primacy of the individual over community vision" (Biskind 2000: 139). Positing a polarity between individual and community, however, does not do justice to the social dynamics of the film which opens with a knowable community where individuals fit in comfortably. Kaufman becomes sinister because he denies change and because he serves as spokesman for the supposed peace that that change will bring.

It is crucial to our processing of the film that the action is framed with a scene at a hospital's emergency admissions where Miles rushes in on the verge of hysteria with a warning. The film then presents an extended flashback where Miles's voice-over constantly guides our reactions to increasingly strange events. When the scene shifts to a gathering at Jack's, where a human form is stretched out on a pool table, the details in the decor strengthen its symbolic force. A molding hanging on the wall suggests the process of shaping; a sounding cuckoo clock hints at the usurpation of a "nest." And, when the form opens his eyes, his close resemblance to Jack introduces the issue of replication. Strange occurrences gradually converge on Miles who, in a burst of panic, discovers a replicant of his beloved Becky being formed in her basement. These instances converge on what is arguably the film's climactic scene which starts as a barbecue between four friends, disrupted by the sights and sounds of pods opening in the glasshouse. Some scenes are canted at an angle; others use the window frame to give a dark barring effect across the images. In a rapid sequence of shot–reverse-shots, we see the pods bursting open and the shocked horror on the faces of the observers. The scene establishes the imperative to destroy the pods and coincides with the "closure" of telephone lines from the town.

By this stage the action has developed into one of social emergency, realizing the symbolism of the opening frame. What remains impressive throughout is the film's evocation of the alien without using any special effects other than the pods. Scenes such as the dialogue between Sally and Becky's father about putting the baby to bed with a pod become a travesty of family intimacy where care is displaced by figurative deaths. The famous scene where Becky and Miles gaze down on the town square represents another travesty, this time of town

Figure 2.2 Pod creature of Dr. Miles Bennel (Kevin McCarthy) in *Invasion of the Body Snatchers* (1956).

life represented through a process of distribution, just as the pod installation toward the end of the film is the site of mass production. In this section, Miles's estrangement from his community peaks with the townsfolk as enemies, pursuing him and Becky up the hill outside town. When the two hide in a disused mine tunnel, Michael Hardin glosses this as a birth scene, presumably counteracting Becky's romantic death to Miles (Hardin 1997).

Throughout the film the process of transformation is a plot mechanism, far less important than its consequence, which is progressively to alienate characters from one another. Homes become sources of danger, and one of the last refuges is sought in the surgery where Miles and Becky hide in a closet. The barred light falling across their faces makes a visual reprise of the glasshouse episode and renders their flight as a kind of imprisonment, prematurely relieved by the arrival of their friend Jack – who has changed. Another character recommends this change in quasitherapeutic terms, declaring: "They're taking you over cell for cell, atom for atom. There's no pain [. . .] and you're reborn into an untroubled world" (LaValley 1989: 88). These lines play to contemporary anxieties about Communism and radiation but only by suggestion. Within the social reversals of the film, birth is promised as tranquillized release and it is a pointed irony that Miles escapes this threat of "treatment" by jabbing hypodermics into the spines of his former friends in travesty mimicry of epidurals. Far from being the place of collective therapy, the surgery has reversed into a site of violence, marking the sheer estrangement of Miles from his home town.

In the coda to the film, Miles rushes up to the nearby packed freeway which briefly glimpses the fast-paced tempo of urban America excluded from Santa Mira. The return to the frame does not give narrative closure, only confirmation of Miles's story with the report of an accident involving a truck carrying pods. Miles's repeated cry "You're next!" explicitly denies closure.

As Barry K. Grant has pointed out, "once everyone is transformed by the pods, they become distant, vacant, passing each other on the street without regard" (Grant 2010: 71). The open frame suggests that the process is continuing, as did the coda to Jack Finney's novel which evokes an urbanization of its small town, where "the people [...] may seem to you strange, listless and uncommunicative, and may impress you as a little weird" (Condon 1989: 215).[10] The codas of both novel and film share a common evocation of loss.

Such pathos is lost in the 1978 *Invasion of the Body Snatchers* basically because the action has been moved to San Francisco. Even before the pods start their process, early shots of the city streets show crowds bustling by who are already, by implication, strangers to one another. As the screenwriter W. D. Richter states, "it was more interesting to locate the paranoia in a large city [...] if we had fears today it had more to do with how we were losing the centre of our civilization, because our cities were starting to seem strange" (McCarthy and Gorman 1999: 107–8). Of the two Health Department protagonists, the estrangement of Elizabeth's boyfriend is mysterious rather than a source of pathos because we have never seen their earlier intimacy and, when she sees him passing strange packages to others, the evocation of a secret urban network suggests possible analogies with narcotics or criminal organizations. Much more than in the 1956 movie, it now becomes an issue what can and cannot be seen. Many scenes take place at night, and the city is evoked as a labyrinth that could be concealing any number of mysteries, an effect heightened by the hills of the city. And extensive use is made of part images, where a section of the screen is hidden from the viewer, as if to suggest again and again that far more is going on than is revealed.

The Manchurian Candidate

In the takeover films discussed above, the action typically expands from small town to nation. *The Manchurian Candidate* (1962), however, foregrounds the nation right from the start and draws on a number of elements beginning to show themselves in the films of the preceding decade, not least that "the role of mother is becoming a threatening one" (Hardin 1997). Now she steps into center stage as the main conspirator. In addition, the 1958 film *The Fearmakers* describes how an American GI returns to Washington from Korea, where he has undergone brainwashing, to find that his old PR company has become infiltrated by Communists who may be trying to shape public opinion. *The Manchurian Candidate* picked up on these themes and also on the problem of returning to normality from the war which, in his original novel, Richard Condon had depicted in cinematic terms. Thus we are told after the first episode: "The Korean War was over. That camera which caught every movement of everyone's life was adjusted to run backward so that they were all returned to the point from which they had all started out to war. Not all" (Condon 1975: 101). Films of the Korean War reflected an extended crisis in national self-confidence which *The Manchurian Candidate* pushes to a satirical extreme (Young 1998).

Apart from its Cold War melodrama and the Freudian conflict between Raymond Shaw and his mother, the media are repeatedly shown to transform American politics into theater. This process starts as soon as Raymond returns to Washington where the solemnity of a quasidocumentary gives way to farce and near chaos as his mother elbows her way through the reporters to claim photo shoots with Senator Iselin, Raymond and a general. Raymond complains about her "disgusting three-ring circus" but the scene establishes the political malleability of the media by political interests. In other words, the theme of manipulation is dramatized as a domestic feature before any reference to external brainwashing.

One of the film's most famous set pieces is framed as Captain Marco's nightmare sequence but then, as Greil Marcus has pointed out, the sequence possesses none of the usual characteristics of dream sequences (Marcus 2002: 25). Shot with hard-edged clarity, the sequence opens with a women's gardening meeting in a New Jersey hotel, perfectly plausible in itself, except for a group of drowsy-looking American GIs in the audience. As the camera performs a slow, 360-degree pan, the female speaker's words segue into a lecture on brainwashing, then she transforms into a Chinese specialist, Yen Lo, addressing uniformed dignitaries in a tiered lecture theater who yet again transform into American women while discussing the relative merits of programming. The abrupt cut which opens this sequence gives the reader no hint of what is coming, and the serial transposition of dialogue and appearances totally destabilizes our sense of reality. The director, John Frankenheimer, has stated in interview that he planned the film as an attack on the idea of fanaticism, which usually posits an enemy, but this lecture sequence has the bizarre effect of domesticating brainwashing and thus runs counter to its depictions in the 1950s (Tobias 2000).

Although Marco remembers Yen Lo "grinning like Fu Manchu," Lo is a complex figure, malign and yet insisting on humor in his proceedings, alien and yet well aware of American culture. During his lecture, he notes that "brainwashing" is the "new American word" and comments on their cigarettes, made from yak dung, which "tastes good like a cigarette should."[11] Quoting a famous advertising slogan from the period relates his actions to the mainstream of American culture, and later in New York, when he visits a clinic, Yen

Lo jokes further about the term "brainwashing" which, he comments, could just as easily be called "dry-cleaned." What offsets his humor is the graphic image of Raymond lying in the middle of a complex system of medical pulleys. Greil Marcus argues that the whole film straddles both absurdism and naturalism which are encapsulated in the figure of Yen Lo, the arch conspirator and comic commentator. This point can apply to the mixed tone of specific scenes as well as to the movie's constant shift in tone from episode to episode. Rather than establishing a tension between two modes, we could argue that the film is multigeneric, combining aspects of melodrama, romance, and political drama.

If the central subject of *The Manchurian Candidate* is manipulation, collective and individual, the action is shown to be heavily mediated and the film's main satirical thrust is directed against the news media, particularly its role in promoting anti-Communism. In his novel, Condon devised a narrative where Raymond's mother was at once his "American operator" in a Communist conspiracy and also the wife of Senator Iselin who was modeled closely on McCarthy. This apparent paradox is heavily ironic because, as Senator Jordan states in the film, "if John Iselin were a paid Soviet agent, he could not do more to harm the country than he's doing now."[12]

The mother's role is crucial in domesticating brainwashing as a collective effect of the news media. Shortly after the assassination of President Kennedy, the novelist Richard Condon published an article entitled "Manchurian Candidate in Dallas" where he explained the double subject of his original novel. "On its melodramatic surface," he stated, "the book is a study of the consequences of a mind warped by alien violence, but I had also hoped to suggest that for some time all of us in the United States had been brainwashed to violence [...] I meant to show that [the nation's attention] is focused upon violence when it appears on the front page of all newspapers, throughout television programming [...] in most motion pictures" (Condon 1963: 449). Director John Frankenheimer has explained how at the time of release he had to take great care over its ridiculing of extremism: "Certainly in 1962 or '63, the picture was something that attacked McCarthyism and was very effective then, because we lived with it. I think the only difference is that in 1988, the audience knew it was okay to laugh. But in 1962, everyone took McCarthy so goddamned seriously because they were right there to witness it" (Tobias 2000).

Early in the film the press conference for the defense secretary dramatizes the manipulative process at work. As the secretary is answering a question about cuts (with help from his aide Marco), the camera moves away from him to show the lights and massed news cameras facing him, and halts with Raymond's mother profiled in close foreground. She nods a cue to Iselin in the background who launches into his performance with the declaration that he has a "question so serious that the safety of our nation may well depend on your answer." His charge, a reprise of McCarthy's notorious claim in 1950, is that he holds a list of 207 Communists in the State Department. At that point, the event breaks down into near chaos as cameras swing to Iselin. Charles Ramirez Berg (who categorizes the film as a thriller) has rightly described this as a "scene about media narration" and one which shows how a news story takes shape (Berg 2011: 39). The foregrounding of Raymond's mother implies that she is the director of the scene, and the monitor she faces shows in close-up how Iselin's television image can take on a force once detached from the chaotic context. The episode breaks down into farce in the cloakroom as Marco tries to verify Iselin's number, at which point he fluffs his lines. The inconsistencies in McCarthy's original claims become explicit business in the film where Iselin pleads with his wife to give him a fixed number. The press conference shows a successful performance. Thereafter, we see Iselin behind the scenes, rehearsing with prompt cards, being made up and getting stern directions from his wife: "I keep telling you not to think. Just keep shouting 'point of order!' at the cameras."

In his first scene after the press conference we see Iselin's image reflected in the glass frontage of a portrait of Abraham Lincoln, and the film repeatedly positions characters close to the icons of American culture.[13] Senator Jordan is positioned at one point in front of the bald eagle with outstretched wings on the great seal of America. Once again the effect is ironic. The recurrence of images of Lincoln suggest the loss of freedom, not the opposite, and this imagery reaches its climax with the costume ball organized by Raymond's mother. The first shot is of caviar molded into the Stars and Stripes. Iselin is dressed in a Lincoln costume, his wife as Bo-Peep, and Raymond as a gaucho. The whole episode is one of masquerade and leads imagistically into the final political convention where the Lincoln costumes persist. Above all, Raymond's mother plans the episode as theater yet again. Disguised as a priest, Raymond will shoot down the presidential nominee, Iselin will pick up his body "gallantly," "Then Johnny will really hit those microphones and those cameras [. . .] rallying a nation of television viewers into hysteria." It is to be his star performance but. in the final climax, Raymond seizes back the control of his "camera-eye" sights, shooting first Iselin then his mother.

Brainwashing in Britain: *The Ipcress File*

The British context for these movies was quite different from that in America. The Korean War made far less impact and, as we have seen, Hollywood was promoting a fashion for alien-invasion movies. The primary British text for brainwashing was *Nineteen eighty-four*, which went through two television adaptations – CBS in 1953 and BBC in 1954 – before the release of Michael Anderson's film in 1956 starring Edmond O'Brien. Although the film introduces its narrative as set in the immediate future (in this case 1965), it opens with a scene which would still have been familiar to many viewers: during an air raid characters running across actual bomb sites toward the city shelters. The London shown in the film is a hybrid of ruins and futuristic buildings, the latter exemplified in the circular ministry building where Winston Smith works, which resembles a huge panopticon, ideal for official surveillance. The interrogation makes extensive use of lights, sometimes eye shaped as if peering into Winston's mind, and, late in the process, he is placed in an electric chair suggestive of the death of his older self.[14]

While there is no doubt about the purpose of Winston's brainwashing here, *The Mind Benders* (1963) speculates on the relationship between scientific experimentation and its political applications. The film opens with one professor Sharpey somberly fingering an envelope full of money before he throws himself to his death from a train to Oxford. It transpires that he has been participating in secret experiments in sensory deprivation. Indeed, the film concludes its titles by acknowledging its debt to "Reduction of Sensation," experiments then current in the United States which use an isolation tank where subjects float in water at blood temperature.[15] When an officer from military intelligence is shown a film of this project, he exclaims: "this is an experiment on the fringes of brainwashing," becoming convinced that Sharpey had sold results to foreign agents. The film then shows the experimental immersion of the leading scientist to see if it can induce distrust of his wife – with apparent success. Scenes of experimentation alternate throughout with shots of Oxford life (street scenes, a cricket match, and so on), contrasting the normality with the bizarre isolation of the scientists in their project. The result is rather inconclusive in that the scientist, played by Dirk Bogarde, appears to triumph over his conditioning but doubts remain over Sharpey's original betrayal.

The fate of scientists working on secret projects links *The Mind Benders* with *The Ipcress File* of 1965, which opens with the news of a British nuclear scientist being kidnapped. The film clearly set out to counter the gratuitous glamour of Bond movies, not least through its protagonist Sergeant Palmer, played by Michael Caine, who is in intelligence on sufferance after black market activities in Berlin. Transferred by Ross to Dalby's section, the latter reads Palmer's description in his file as "insubordinate, insolent, a trickster, perhaps with criminal tendencies."

The film embeds its espionage action within the details of mid-1960s London life, starting with a sequence during the opening credits where Palmer wakes in an untidy flat filled with traces of the previous night's activity and slowly making himself freshly ground coffee. His kitchen is strikingly well equipped with copper pans and food emerges as a theme further distinguishing Palmer from Bond's preference for consumption over production (Beluga caviar and Dom Perignon). In one of the episodes with false suspense, when Palmer returns home early, he finds a female colleague who has searched his flat. Their cautious dialogue gives way to preparation for an omelet, offered in an attempted seduction which, at that point, doesn't happen. Later Palmer bumps into his superior Ross in a supermarket where an exchange over the relative merits of canned mushrooms thinly disguises Ross's message to give his prime loyalty to his department. A novelty in the mid-1960s, the setting has a cultural symbolism which Ross points out when he admits: "I don't really care for these American shopping methods. One has to move with the times I suppose." The film incorporates different contemporary business into the search for the kidnapper of the scientist Radcliffe. Palmer uses his police contacts to access Grantby's file, only to find three parking tickets. Using their location, the film then shows a parking meter running into excess until it is fed by Grantby's henchman who, in turn, leads Palmer to the science library where Grantby is working and thus starts the process of retrieving the scientist.

Ross's words above identify the film's complex engagement with modernity, achieved primarily through the many apparent parallels between Ross and the "passed-over major" Dalby. Both have parodically extreme military bearings; both tell Palmer to close their office doors; and they come to represent two poles in an institutional tension between departments rendered absurdly confusing when Palmer tells Courtney "you're working for Ross," whereupon she replies "I'm working for Dalby. *You're* working for Ross." When the two officers meet in Hyde Park, a military band is playing in the background and the two men seem temporarily identical as they march in step toward Ross's club for lunch. Each seems the very personification of old-school-tie imperial correctness but the film satirizes the elaborate bureaucracy central to Dalby's section, even when the reports have no content. Similarly, this section has to masquerade as a series of shabby businesses from "Dalby Domestic" to "Astra Fireworks" (the armory – little more than a storeroom) and "S.E.T.A. Commercial Television," another relative novelty at the time. The many commercial references connect ironically with the intrigue over the kidnapped scientist whose return involves "delivery arrangements" and which infuriates Dalby (apparently) because he proves to be "damaged goods," brainwashed to forget his research project. Though the film references Cold War themes, such as defection and the role of the CIA in assisting British intelligence, the action is contained within London and one of the most surreal moments occurs when Palmer escapes from an "Albanian" prison where he has been tortured, climbs a wall, and is suddenly confronted with a close-up of a London bus.

Any espionage film will set a high premium on observation but *The Ipcress File* weaves complex scenic variations through the use of visual obstructions and foregrounded objects (Nedomansky 2014). The former, in particular, whether the window of a telephone booth or the use of a pair of spectacles for their mirroring effect, constantly evoke the sheer difficulty of seeing, hence the appropriate detail that Palmer is short-sighted. At one point, he returns to his apartment to find the body of a CIA agent lying in his hall. The scene is shot from the ceiling through a lampshade, clearly not from Palmer's perspective, showing the body as a clear circular image, framed by the light but surrounded by darkness. As lighting is repeatedly associated with understanding, the image is posed as yet another enigma and, toward the end of the movie, as Dalby is speaking to Palmer over the telephone, his companion moves forward from behind a lamp to reveal himself as none other than Grantby.

The Ipcress File thus uses brainwashing initially to suggest that a double agent is working in British intelligence and then subjects the protagonist to its procedure as a test of Palmer's capacity for resistance. This famous sequence incorporates elements of the Hungarian Lajos Ruff's "Magic Room" where he was tortured and cue phrases similar to *The Manchurian Candidate*, and distorts both Palmer's visual perceptions and our perspective on him.[16] Even here, however, the film's main puzzle remains: who is the traitor? Dalby or Ross? In the denouement Palmer backs toward the camera, which then moves to and fro between these men, until he finally shoots Dalby. It remains one of the film's main ironies that traitor and patriot remain visually indistinguishable until the very end. As in *The Manchurian Candidate*, the imagery and personnel of the establishment prove to conceal traitors at their heart.

Notes

1. The CIA propaganda film *Small Town Espionage* (1960) played directly to this paranoia in showing a small town which was a "duplicate of what you would find all over the United States," except that it was a spy-training installation in the Ukraine.
2. "IT CAME FROM OUTER SPACE a story for films by Ray Bradbury," Universal International, September, 1952, in Albright 2004: 6 [non-sequential pagination].
3. Other titles considered by Bradbury were *Ground Zero* and *The Atomic Monster*.
4. In 1952, while he was working on the movie, Bradbury wrote a story called "A Matter of Taste" which describes an encounter between human astronauts and a spider-like creature. The latter is the narrator in a story that reverses the usual opposition in accounts of alien encounters. For commentary on this story, see Jonathan Eller, "Bradbury's Web of fear," in Albright 2004: 27–41.
5. Ray Bradbury, "Atomic Monster," Albright 2004: 34.
6. On the rather slim grounds that the role of the Martian leader was played by an African American, Michael Hardin has argued that the film explores anxieties over race (Hardin 1997). Barry K. Grant reads the film as representing "America's painful awakening at the dawn of the nuclear age and Cold War politics" (Grant 1987).
7. The last's words help politicize the subject when Sally states of Mysterious Mountain: "'Dad says he can't understand how the army missed building a base out there."
8. *The Brain Eaters* effectively halted Heinlein's plan for an adaptation. In *The Puppet Masters*, a small group of operatives spearheading the fight against the

aliens includes a female agent who uses her own sexuality to test whether humans have been transformed or not.

9. For an interpretation of the film as an attack on conformity, v. Gregory (1972). Cyndy Hendershot sees the film as an exploration of radiation anxiety (Hendershot 1999: 44-5). These different interpretations are summarized in Neil Badminton's examination of the film's indeterminacy (Badminton 2001).
10. This description does not gel with Finney's use of Churchillian rhetoric to describe how the townsfolk will fight the aliens on the beaches.
11. Apart from joking about the GIs' conditioning, Yen Lo is also quoting the most famous advertising slogan for Winston cigarettes, started in 1954.
12. The film's and Condon's source for information on McCarthy was the 1954 issue of *The Progressive Magazine*, "McCarthy: A Documented Record," which exposed his "numbers racket" constant search for publicity and which noted that McCarthy's "tactics are strikingly similar to those of the Communists" (*Progressive* 1954: 63).
13. In that respect the film reflects the insights offered in Vance Packard's *The Hidden Persuaders* (1957) which presented advertising as an Orwellian system of image manipulation. Though he does not use the term, Packard helped domesticate the notion of brainwashing.
14. For a comparison between the 1956 and 1984 movies, see Gottlieb (1995).
15. The model here was the experiments conducted by John C. Lilly which interested the CIA and other agencies for their potential application to interrogation. These same experiments formed the basis for the 1980 film *Altered States*. Sensory deprivation is used for interrogation in Tom Clancy's *The Cardinal of the Kremlin* (1988).
16. Ruff was subjected to elaborate "treatment" by the Hungarian secret police before he escaped to the West in 1956. He describes his experiences in *The Brainwashing Machine* (1959) where a "Magic Room" used psychedelic effects to destabilize his sense of reality.

Bibliography

"A.W." (1953), "*It Came From Outer Space* (1953). Look Out! The Space Boys Are Loose Again," *New York Times*, June 18, http://www.nytimes.com/movie/review?res=9B00EEDA143EE53BBC4052DFB0668388649EDE (last accessed April 7, 2016).

Albright, Don (ed.) (2004), *It Came From Outer Space*, by Ray Bradbury, Colorado Springs, CO: Gauntlet Publications.

Badminton, Neil (2001), "Pod Almighty!; or, Humanism, Posthumanism, and the Strange Case of *Invasion of the Body Snatchers*," *Textual Practice* 15.1, pp. 5–22.

Berg, Charles Ramirez (2011), "*The Manchurian Candidate*: Compromised Agency and Uncertain Causality," in Murray Pomerance and R. Barton Palmer (eds), *A Little Solitaire: John Frankenheimer and American Film*, New Brunswick, NJ: Rutgers University Press, pp. 29–47.

Biskind, Peter (2000), *Seeing is Believing. How Hollywood Taught Us to Stop Worrying and Love the Fifties*, London: Bloomsbury.

Condon, Richard [1959] (1975), *The Manchurian Candidate*, London: Michael Joseph.

Condon, Richard (1963), "'Manchurian Candidate' in Dallas," *The Nation*, December 28, pp. 449–50.

Erickson, Glenn (2002), "DVD Savant Part One: The Ultimate *Invaders from Mars* Savant Essay," *DVD Savant*, December 6, http://www.dvdtalk.com/dvdsavant/s96InvadersA.html (last accessed April 7, 2016).

Finney, Jack [1955] (1989), *Invasion of the Body Snatchers*, New York: Simon & Schuster.
Gottlieb, Erika (1995), "The Satirical Masks of Utopia and Dystopia: A Discussion of the Two Film Versions of Orwell's *Nineteen Eighty-Four*," *Texas Review* 16.1–4, pp. 83–94.
Grant, Barry K. (1987), "*Invaders from Mars* and the Science Fiction Film in the Age of Reagan," *CineAction!* 8, spring, pp. 77–83.
Grant, Barry K. (2010), *Invasion of the Body Snatchers*, London: Palgrave Macmillan.
Gregory, Charles T. (1972), "The Pod Society Versus the Rugged Individualists," *Journal of Popular Film* 1, pp. 3–14.
Hardin, Michael (1997), "Mapping Post-War Anxieties onto Space: *Invasion of the Body Snatchers* and *Invaders from Mars*," *Enculturation* 1.1 spring 1997, <http://enculturation.net/1_1/hardin.html/> (last accessed April 7, 2016).
Hendershot, Cyndy (1999), *Paranoia, the Bomb, and 1950s Science Fiction Films*, Bowling Green OH: Bowling Green State University Popular Press.
Latham, Rob (1995), "Subterranean Suburbia: Underneath the Smalltown Myth in the Two Versions of *Invaders from Mars*," *Science Fiction Studies* 22.2, July, pp. 198–208.
LaValley, Al (ed.) (1989), *Invasion of the Body Snatchers*, New Brunswick, NJ: Rutgers University Press.
McCarthy, Kevin and Ed Gorman (eds) (1999), *"They're Here . . ." Invasion of the Body Snatchers. A Tribute*, New York: Berkley Boulevard.
Marcus, Greil (2002), *The Manchurian Candidate*, London: British Film Institute.
Nedomansky, Vashi (2014), "The Cinematography of *The Ipcress File*," *VashiVisuals*, January 29, http://vashivisuals.com/cinematography-ipcress-file/ (last accessed April 7, 2016).
Patterson, William H. Jr. (2014), *Robert A. Heinlein: In Dialogue with His Century*, Vol. 2, New York: TOR.
Progressive, The (1954), *McCarthy: A Documented Record*, April, http://content.wisconsinhistory.org/cdm/ref/collection/tp/id/63567 (last accessed April 7, 2016).
Robin, Ron Theodore (2001), *The Making of the Cold War Enemy: Culture and Politics in the Military–Intellectual Complex*, Princeton NJ: Princeton University Press.
Sobchack, Vivian (2001), *Screening Space: The American Science Fiction Film*, 2nd edn, New Brunswick, NJ: Rutgers University Press.
Tobias, Scott (2000), "Interview: John Frankenheimer," *A.V. Club*, February 16, http://www.avclub.com/article/john-frankenheimer-13639 (last accessed April 7, 2016).
Warren, Bill (2010), *Keep Watching the Skies! American Science Fiction Movies of the Fifties*, 2 vols, Jefferson, NC: McFarland.
Young, Charles S. (1998), "Missing Action: POW Films, Brainwashing and the Korean War, 1954–1968," *Historical Journal of Film, Radio and Television* 18.1, pp. 49–74.

3. THE BERLIN CRISIS? PIFFL!: BILLY WILDER'S COLD WAR COMEDY, *ONE, TWO, THREE*

Ed Sikov

"So horribly sad. How is it I feel like laughing?" That's how an American agent reacts – presumably CIA, though never specified – in Alfred Hitchcock's 1959 thriller, *North by Northwest*. He's referring to the grotesque situation in which a New York advertising executive, Roger Thornhill (Cary Grant), finds himself after innocently wandering into a case of mistaken identity. This confusion of character culminates when he's standing next to a United Nations official at precisely the moment when a knife flies into the image and lands squarely in the official's back. The man drops to the ground, dead. Thornhill immediately pulls the knife out of the corpse's back and, holding it aloft as flashbulbs pop, ridiculously declares, "I didn't have anything to do with this!"

Thornhill's particular predicament is grim but no less funny for it, as the agent observes. But his reaction to Thornhill's awful situation says something surprising about a much larger issue – the American cultural psyche during the Cold War. One imagines – wrongly – that there was nothing funny about the threat of nuclear war that hovered over the nation, like an invisible mushroom cloud, from 1947 to 1991, the Cold War's most widely accepted brackets. The evidence suggests otherwise. Stanley Kubrick's black comedy *Dr. Strangelove: Or, How I Learned to Stop Worrying and Love the Bomb* (1964), is the most prominent example of how Hollywood examined United States–Soviet Union tensions during the period and found very good reasons to laugh.[1] Peter Sellers's spectacular performance as the eponymous nuclear physicist (one of the three roles he plays in the film) is so hilarious that one can see another cast member (Peter Bull) cracking up in the background of a shot that made it into the release print, Kubrick evidently deciding that Sellers's gestures and voice in that take were worth violating one of the basic tenets of classical Hollywood cinema – namely, that actors should not break character onscreen and so expose the means and forms of the film's construction.

One could argue that *almost every* comedy made during the Cold War is a Cold War comedy, especially during the 1950s and early 1960s, when paranoia reigned. Even when a film's ostensible subject has nothing to do with American–Soviet hostility, the culture that produced it was palpably tense and suspicious, and film comedies often reflected that jittery mentality. Nuclear annihilation was never far from people's minds. From the attacking mutant science fiction film to the popularization of heavy-duty tranquilizers, the 1950s – the heart of the Cold War – was a decade of widespread, often unacknowledged fear in America.[2] Just look at how often supposedly successful executives order cocktails onscreen in the 1950s and '60s. Sometimes they even keep the booze in their desk drawers to make sure that anti-anxiety medication is always close at hand.

Frank Tashlin's cartoonish farces (*Artists and Models*, 1954; *Hollywood or Bust*, 1955; *The Girl Can't Help It*, 1956; *Will Success Spoil Rock Hunter*, 1957) are hysterically funny in a clinical sense because their audiences were living lives of barely suppressed hysteria, and these audiences were hysterical, at least in part, because they knew they could be obliterated within hours if the Soviets launched a nuclear attack. Tashlin's comedies are Cold War comedies, too, despite their lack of explicit Cold War political content.

But of all the comedies of the Cold War period, two stand out as explicitly political –*Strangelove* and Billy Wilder's Berlin crisis comedy, *One, Two, Three* (1961). Just as funny if not nearly as dark as *Strangelove*, *One, Two, Three* has the particular virtue of having been written and shot concurrently with the real international crisis at its narrative core. Wilder began shooting the film on location in Berlin in June, 1961. By mid-August, East Germany closed the border, its troops were erecting barriers that would eventually become the Berlin Wall, and the flow of Germans from East to West halted. The run up to the crisis and the building of the wall coincided exactly with the writing of *One, Two, Three*'s screenplay and location shooting in Berlin, making the comedy especially germane as an example of Cold War American cinema. Wilder was shooting his film while East German soldiers and engineers were actually building the wall. How much timelier could a Cold War comedy be?

As is usually the case with his work, Wilder invests *One, Two, Three* with a practical, expedient, and comically cynical tone. Commenting on the potentially catastrophic confrontation between the world's two superpowers, a clash that sane people understood as edging humanity closer to nuclear war, Wilder tossed off one of his characteristic punchlines: "It seemed to me that the whole thing could have been straightened out if Oleg Cassini had sent Mrs. Khrushchev a dress."[3]

Wilder's Berlin

Billy Wilder was born in 1906 in Sucha Beskidzka, just south of Kraków. He was a German-speaking Jew living among Polish-speaking Poles in an empire ruled by Austro-Hungarian Roman Catholics in Vienna. His family moved to Vienna where he attended school and, forgoing a university degree, became a newspaper reporter. When Paul Whiteman and his jazz band passed through Vienna, Wilder, a jazz fanatic, acted as their tour guide despite the fact that the only English he knew were lyrics from popular music. The musicians found Wilder immensely entertaining and, when Whiteman and the band left for Berlin, Wilder left with them.

In stark contrast to formal, waltzy Vienna, Berlin was a hard-edged city full of hard-edged people. Wilder, an ambitious young man with an opportunistic streak, quickly felt at home there. He was as tough as the city was. He already had what was called a *Berliner Schnauze* – a Berlin lip, a sarcastic and cynical view of the world. In an interview with me, the agent Robert Lantz remembered Wilder as "a real snotty Berliner." Sensing that I might have misunderstood (I hadn't), Lantz quickly added, "And I mean that in the most complimentary sense!"[4] Lantz was surprised to learn that Wilder hadn't been born and raised there.

Wilder started his life in Berlin with nothing. He worked for a time as a gigolo escorting older women around a dance floor, and he wrote of his experiences so beautifully and engagingly in an autobiographical magazine article that suddenly he was in the Berlin literary scene's sights. One writing job led to another and soon he was writing screenplays. By the time he left for Paris and ultimately Hollywood, he had become a successful and respected screenwriter.

Wilder returned to Berlin – or what was left of it – soon after the end of World War II on assignment with the United States military: he was the production chief for the Film, Theater, and Music Control Section of the Psychological Warfare Division. His job was twofold: to edit what seemed like miles of concentration-camp footage into a feature-length film; and to devise propaganda films that would reeducate the defeated Germans without rubbing their noses in their loss. "It looked like the end of the world," he said of the city he loved. The destructive technology of World War II had no parallel and neither did its effects. The endless miles of gutted, firebombed buildings and rubble Wilder saw in Berlin had no meaningful point of comparison.

There was also the smell. "The summer of '45 was very, very hot – it was the hottest summer in Berlin that anyone could remember," he said. "Thousands of corpses must have lain under the wreckage; the stink in the heat was intolerable. The dead swam in the *Landwehrkanal*; in the vegetable gardens lay putrefying corpses."[5]

Wilder returned to Germany in 1947 to shoot location footage for *A Foreign Affair*, the first of his two comedies set in postwar Berlin. An early treatment for the film features this extraordinary description: "The city looked like a great hunk of burned Gorgonzola cheese on which rats had been gnawing. The rats were gone, and ants had taken over, putting some neatness into the ruins, piling the crumbs of destruction into tidy piles."[6] An editor recalled Wilder's violent reaction to something the editor had said offhandedly: "After viewing aerial shots of block after block of Berlin leveled to the ground, I remarked that I couldn't help feel sorry for the Germans. With that Billy jumped to his feet and yelled, 'To hell with those bastards! They burned most of my family in their damned ovens! I hope they burn in hell!'"[7]

In point of fact, Wilder was much more conflicted about the Germans. In *A Foreign Affair*, Johnny (John Lund) lusts for Erika (Marlene Dietrich) not despite the fact that she is a Nazi but *because* she is one:

> JOHNNY: What you Germans need is a better conscience.
> ERIKA: I have a good conscience. I have a new Führer now. *You*. [She raises her left arm in a Nazi salute.] Heil Johnny.
> JOHNNY: You heil me once more and I'll knock your teeth in.
> [They draw together in a sticky embrace.]
> ERIKA: You'd bruise your lips.
> JOHNNY: I ought to choke you a little. [He places his hands around her neck.] Break you in two. Build a fire under you, you blonde witch.
> [They kiss deeply and passionately.]

In the end, *A Foreign Affair* – which Wilder had originally conceived as a propaganda comedy – was banned in Germany. For one thing, Erika is entirely unrepentant about her Nazi past. For another, while Wilder gives Johnny a respectable reason for cuddling up to Erika (we learn, eventually, that he's trying to smoke out her lover, a former Gestapo leader, now a wanted war criminal), it's perfectly clear that his most urgent undercover mission occurs every night in her bed. "Crude, superficial, and insensible to certain responsibilities which the world situation, like it or not, has thrust on" Hollywood was how an American in charge of approving films for German distribution put it at the time: "Berlin's trials and tribulations are not the stuff of cheap comedy."

But they were. And the comedy was far from cheap.

One, Two, Three's Source

Writing in the Berlin newspaper *Tempo* in 1929, Wilder opined that Coca-Cola "tastes like burnt pneumatic tires."[8] Also in 1929, Ferenc Molnar's play *Egy-kettö-három* opened in Berlin as *Ein, Zwei, Drei*. A wild farce about an agitated capitalist, Norrison, and Lydia, the daughter of an important banking client, who hurls Norrison's life and career into chaos by falling in love with a socialist taxi driver. The actor Max Pallenberg, for whom Molnar had written the role, spat his lines furiously in a way that one contemporary critic compared to a machine gun. In other words, he was like a gangster on Benzedrine.

Ein, Zwei, Drei played out in one ferocious act which takes place in Norrison's office. The banker's daughter, Lydia, rushes in and announces not only that she has married the cabbie, Anton, but also that she is pregnant with his child. Terrified of losing her father as a client, Norrison works feverishly to turn Anton into a nobleman in the course of a single day. Tailors and shoe salesmen run in and out at such a frenzied pace that Molnar suggested that rooms in the set be separated by curtains, since the opening and closing of so many doors would have been unbearably loud. Anton takes an emotional beating by Norrison and by Lydia as well, and capitalism triumphs at the play's conclusion.

One, Two, Three's script, by Wilder and his cowriter, I. A. L. Diamond, begins with this description (or warning, or threat): "THIS PIECE MUST BE PLAYED MOLTO FURIOSO – AT A RAPID-FIRE, BREAKNECK TEMPO. SUGGESTED SPEED: 100 MILES AN HOUR ON THE CURVES – 140 MILES AN HOUR ON THE STRAIGHTAWAY"[9] The pace was practically the only thing Wilder and Diamond kept from Molnar's play. Characteristically, Wilder and his cowriter, Diamond, felt no need to stick to the playwright's script. Precious little of Molnar's dialogue remains intact in *One, Two, Three*. At one point in the screenplay, Scarlett (the renamed Lydia) asks MacNamara (formerly Norrison), "Why didn't you take better care of me?" When Wilder was shooting the scene, Pamela Tiffin, playing Scarlett, kept delivering the line too softly. "Pamela, dear," Billy said. "A little louder, please. We want to hear this line very clearly. It's the only line we've kept from the original play, and it's a very expensive one."[10]

Following the skeleton of Molnar's play, *One, Two, Three* concerns a command-spitting Coca-Cola executive in West Berlin who is forced to play host to his boss's hot-blooded, seventeen-year-old daughter who sneaks out of his house behind his back, crosses into East Berlin, and marries a communist student whose absurd name is Otto Piffl. Adding to the capitalist MacNamara's hyperactive agony is the fact that his wife discovers the mercenary affair he has been conducting with his secretary, the gum-chewing Ingeborg, and leaves him. MacNamara is trying all the while to crack the Iron Curtain market with the incompetent assistance of three Russian trade commissars. ("Napoleon blew it, Hitler blew it, but Coca-Cola's going to pull it off," he confidently predicts.) To top it all off, Scarlett's parents announce their imminent arrival from Atlanta, Scarlett declares that she's pregnant with Otto's baby, and a reporter shows up having sniffed out the story of an American teenager having married an East German.

MacNamara turns Otto into a suitable husband for Scarlett by paying off a destitute German nobleman – now reduced to being the men's room attendant at the Kempinski Hotel – and turning Piffl into the junior Count von Droste-Schattenburg. He outfits the communist-turned-aristocrat with a full wardrobe of men's formalwear and hires him as a Coke executive in the car on the way to the airport, where Scarlett's parents fly in on schedule. All of this occurs to the naggingly antsy tune of the Lenin Prize-winning Soviet composer Aram Khachaturian's "Sabre Dance."

Thirty-two years after *Ein, Zwei, Drei* opened in Berlin, Germany was torn in two – West Germany, allied with the United States and Europe, and East Germany, a protectorate of the Soviet Union. *Tempo*, the Jewish newspaper in which Wilder had compared the taste of Coke to burnt pneumatic tires, had been out of business for years, many of its readers gassed. The hungry young reporter had become a wealthy film director living in a Beverly Hills penthouse. The Americans and the Russians, formerly allies against the Germans, were now suspicious and inimical foes. American schoolchildren regularly heard sirens blaring through their schools as signals for terrifying air-raid drills. It appeared that the entire Free World was drinking Coca-Cola, and everyone on one side of the Iron Curtain sincerely believed that everyone on the other side thirsted for it helplessly, having to make do with a foul-tasting Soviet imitation. But, despite the shifting winds of politics, trade, art, and personal fortune, one thing hadn't changed: Billy Wilder still thought Coke tasted like burnt tires with fizz.

Casting

For the role of the manic capitalist, Wilder chose one of the most recognizable faces and voices in the world. *Public Enemy* (1931), *G-Men* (1935), *Angels with Dirty Faces* (1938), *The Roaring Twenties* (1939) *Yankee Doodle Dandy* (1941), *White Heat* (1949), *Mister Roberts* (1955), *Love Me or Leave Me* (1955), *The Gallant Hours* (1960) – James Cagney was a Hollywood giant. Like George Raft, Cagney could sport a machine gun and tap shoes with equal grace and credibility and, by 1961, he had been doing so for thirty years. A three-time Oscar nominee (he won once, for *Yankee Doodle Dandy*), Cagney knew his business well. In terms of working with the headstrong Wilder, this was an ominous sign.

For the role of Cagney's wife, essentially a wisecracking human caboose, Wilder and his team were initially stumped. At a casting meeting, Billy said something on the order of "I'm tired of clichéd typecasting – the same people in every film. Let's get someone whose face isn't familiar to moviegoers – a type like Arlene Francis." [PAUSE.] "In fact," said Billy, "why don't we get Arlene Francis?"[11] Best known for her good-natured appearances on the television game show *What's My Line?*, Francis's only film-acting roles had been in Robert Florey's *Murders in the Rue Morgue* in 1932 and small roles in *Stage Door Canteen* (1943) and *All My Sons* (1948). (Her appearance in *Murders in the Rue Morgue* is brief but lurid: she plays a prostitute whose corpse gets dumped in the Seine after Bela Lugosi bleeds her to death on a torture rack.) With her easygoing personality and television domesticity, Arlene Francis's casting in *One, Two, Three* is inspired. Was it pure coincidence that the mystery guest on *What's My Line?* on Sunday, May 15, 1960, was none other than Jimmy Cagney?

The familiarity of the leading actors is essential to *One, Two, Three*. With such recognizable faces, the stars of the film alleviated some of the anxiety American audiences may have felt about the divided Berlin. But the two stars weren't familiar to everyone. Wilder tells a suspect but funny story about this. According to Billy, he and his wife, Audrey, were dining at the home of Mr. and Mrs. William Goetz, Mrs. Goetz being the daughter of MGM's Louis B. Mayer. She asked Wilder what his new picture was and who would be playing the lead. Jimmy Cagney. "Who?" "*Jimmy Cagney!* You know, the little gangster who for years was in all those Warner Bros. . . ." Edith Mayer Goetz cut Wilder off: "Oh, Daddy didn't allow us to watch Warner Bros. pictures."[12]

Production

One, Two, Three was scheduled to shoot on location in Berlin in June, 1961, after which the company would move to Munich's Bavaria Studios for the interiors. Wilder assembled twenty-five key people for his production team, all of whom had worked with him before: Doane Harrison as associate producer and close advisor; Danny Mandell at the editing table; Milt Rice in charge of special effects; May Wale, the script supervisor; Danny Fapp, the camera operator, and others.[13] These were brisk, efficient men and women, and Wilder trusted them – more than the crusty writer–director ever let on. Alexandre Trauner designed the film's sets – a crisp, bland, modernist Coca-Cola Company office in West Berlin; the ballroom of a crummy East Berlin hotel; the interior of Cagney's and Francis's residence . . . It seemed at the beginning that *One, Two, Three* would be a relatively easy and straightforward shoot.

Also in June, 1961, Walter Ulbricht, the president of East Germany, told a Western newspaper that, no, despite the estimated 1.65 million East Germans who had already left for the West, his government had no intention of building a barrier between the eastern and western sectors of Berlin. The flood of immigrants from East to West grew into a raging torrent, and Wilder's timing seemed all the better. *One, Two, Three* had always been conceived as topical political humor. Now it was more topical than Wilder ever dreamed.

Originally, a voice-over narrator opened the film by explaining: "In February, 1945, with Hitler's legions crumbling under the relentless onslaught of the Allied Armies, the Big Three, meeting at Yalta, agreed on the partition of Germany and the joint occupation of Berlin. Subsequent events have proved that this decision was – to put it diplomatically – a boo-boo." Wilder ended up ditching the voice-over.

After a few days of filming *One, Two, Three*, Wilder asked Cagney if he had ever played anything so fast before. Cagney immediately replied that he had – *Boy Meets Girl* (1938), a comedy costarring Pat O'Brien. This was another bad sign. Cagney had despised playing everything at such rapid-fire, screwball speed and considered *Boy Meets Girl* one of the low points of his career. Cagney claimed that, when he saw the film, even he couldn't understand what he was saying.[14] Faced with Wilder's even more extreme pacing, Cagney was already annoyed. Only two days into his work on *One, Two, Three* he was telling people that he wanted to go home.

The Brandenburg Gate is Berlin's best-known monument. Its portals, through which vehicular traffic must squeeze on its way on to or away from the boulevard *Unter den Linden*, consist of a dozen weathered Doric columns, atop which the Goddess of Victory roosts along with her chariot and four stone horses. It's an elaborate heap with historical overtones. When Berlin was divided into sectors immediately after World War II, the Brandenburg Gate served as an easy point of bifurcation; the line was drawn a few yards to the west.

A symbol of Berlin's old imperial grandeur, its relatively recent ruin, its tenacious survival, and the geographical conflict of Wilder and Diamond's precarious farce, the Brandenburg Gate serves as the focal point of several sequences in *One, Two, Three* – most notably the crash site of a chase sequence involving MacNamara's sleek American limousine and the three Russian trade commissars' decrepit Moskvitch, which was supposed to self-destruct piece by piece and finally slam what remains of itself against one of the mighty Doric columns. In an earlier scene, too, Otto Piffl rides a motorbike through the gate from West to East. For these two sequences, Billy arranged to shoot on location at the gate itself. This, of course, required the permission of (at least) two governments. The West Germans were happy to oblige. The East Germans needed a little finessing but they, too, agreed. Initially.

Wilder's MO with the Communist authorities was reminiscent of his treatment of Bellevue Hospital's director for *The Lost Weekend* (1945). He told them the basic facts of the shots he wanted but left out a few choice details, in

Figure 3.1 Otto Ludwig Piffl riding his motorcycle toward Berlin's Brandenburg Gate in *One, Two, Three*

Figure 3.2 Piffl entering East Germany with a "Russki GO HOME" balloon on his motorcycle in *One, Two, Three*

particular the fact that Piffl's cycle has a "Russki Go Home" balloon inflating on its tailpipe. (When Bellevue's managing director saw *The Lost Weekend*, he was enraged at Wilder's depiction of his hospital and regretted ever having given Wilder permission to film there: "He showed me one script which I approved. Then he filmed a *different script*.")[15]

On a cloudy but shootable day in mid-July, the cast and crew departed from their headquarters at the Berlin Hilton for the location on the *Strasse des 17 Juni*, the broad boulevard in West Berlin that leads through the Brandenburg Gate onto *Unter den Linden*. Wilder rallied his troops: "Okay, get your steel helmets, everybody – we're going back to the Gate!"[16] A little later, with the camera rolling and the bright yellow balloon firmly attached to the bike, Horst Buchholz sped off toward the gate, a camera truck following him. A few shots were successfully taken but the weather turned for the worse and the sequence couldn't be completed that day. "It was Hitler's last revenge," said Wilder later, because, by the following morning, a regiment of uniformed East German police forbade him to shoot anything on their side of the border. They stood their ground at the gate, quite visibly, and monitored Wilder and his crew through powerful binoculars.

Lesser men would have been bullied. Not Wilder, who rehearsed the scene on his side of the frontier and sent a message to the East Germans on the other: since he was shooting toward the gate, he said, the East German officers were visible in the shot. This was fine with him, he added, but he was just afraid that international filmgoers would get the false impression that East Germany was a police state.

The officers scattered, and Wilder reopened negotiations to film the sequence the way he wanted from the angles he wanted, including those in East Berlin. The East Germans were willing to talk again but now they insisted on reading the script. "I wouldn't even show my script to President Kennedy," Wilder replied. They then refused to let him film at the gate. The price of *One, Two, Three* soared instantly higher as Trauner and his crew were forced to build a replica of the Brandenburg Gate at a studio in Munich. The cost of the new gate was either $100,000 or $200,000, depending on who reported it.[17]

"We got to Berlin the day they sealed off the Eastern sector and wouldn't let people come across the border," Wilder said a few years after the fact, bending history to make a snappier tale. "It was like making a picture in Pompeii with all the lava coming down. Khrushchev was even faster than me and Diamond."[18] Wilder's chronology is a little off but the mood he describes is not. On the night of August 12 and the early morning of the 13th, with location work on *One, Two, Three* not yet complete after a little over a month of shooting, the Soviets and their East German deputies sealed off the border and erected a makeshift barrier of barbed wire and cinder blocks. The 15-foot-high concrete walls, watchtowers, gun turrets, electric fences, and land mines came later. But the Berlin Wall was now effectively in place. Not only was the production of *One, Two, Three* thrown into turmoil, but the already fragile premise of the comedy suddenly became a great deal shakier. If Wilder wanted to make the most nervous comedy of his career, his timing couldn't have been better.

As Trauner remembered, "From that moment we knew that the film was commercially doomed. You couldn't joke about the Berlin problem: the subject had become too tragic. It's really too bad, because it's one of Wilder's greatest films."[19]

Tension in Berlin was extreme. Even before the wall went up Wilder was calling the city "Splitsville." Now families were forcibly separated from one another. Subway and surface-rail service between East and West was halted. Berliners wondered if the superpowers would use their divided city as an excuse to set off an atomic World War III. More disturbing to Wilder, perhaps, was the fact that he had to alter his screenplay: "We had to make continuous revisions to keep up with the headlines," he said later.[20]

Other exteriors were constructed in Munich as well as the gate, and the whole production shifted to Bavaria sooner than scheduled, just to be on the safe side of the international conflict. They hadn't been able to film on location at Tempelhof Airport, owing to the noise of real air traffic, so Trauner supervised the building of a replica Tempelhof in Munich. The *Unter den Linden* quarter of East Berlin – the embassy district, located on the first mile of the boulevard on the other side of the gate – had to be reconstructed as well though, in Wilder's mind, it still needed to be in ruins even though the East Germans had already renovated it as a showplace.

Wilder still hadn't filmed the final scene at the studio-reconstructed Templehof arrival gate when Horst Buchholz ran his motorcycle off the road and had to be hospitalized. The production shut down prematurely to give him time to recover, but because the Bavaria Studio sound stage on which Tempelhof was rebuilt was already booked for another production – John Huston's *Freud* (1962) – they had to take the set down and rebuild it again at the Goldwyn Studios in Hollywood where everyone reassembled weeks later. Buchholz's accident thus added $250,000 to the cost of *One, Two, Three*.[21]

For Wilder, *One, Two, Three* is as much a matter of conflicting styles of wit as it is a battle of ideologies. Wilder was impressed by what he saw as the Communists' complete lack of a sense of humor when he cowrote *Ninotchka* in 1939. (His cowriters were Charles Brackett and Walter Reisch.) It hadn't improved by 1961. Still, as in *Ninotchka*, Wilder draws individual comrades affectionately. Peripetchikoff, Borodenko, and Mishkin, the three Russian trade commissars, are the sons of *Ninotchka*'s Buljanoff, Iranoff, and Kopalski, and they are sufficiently mercenary to retain Wilder's respect even as he pokes fun at them.

Meanwhile, Cagney seemed content – on the surface. He equaled Wilder in bullheadedness but he kept his gripes to himself. Cagney was a consummate professional who recited his lines as often as Wilder wanted, rehearsed his gestures and blocking well, practiced tap dancing during the break, and made it a point to help Pamela Tiffin with her scenes.[22] Tiffin, young and inexperienced, was nervous to be working with a star of Cagney's stature, and Cagney, sensing her discomfort, patiently and generously coaxed her into a state of confidence.

Horst Buchholz, on the other hand, was a nagging problem for Cagney who took a quick dislike to the conceited young German. His contempt only grew as the filming proceeded. Cagney thought Buchholz was far too full of himself, especially for someone with so little experience. "I came close to knocking him on his ass," Cagney said later. One of the few things Cagney appreciated about Wilder was that he kept Buchholz in line himself, saving Cagney the need to follow through on his threat.

There was very little else about working with Wilder that Cagney found enjoyable. "Billy Wilder was more of a dictator than most of the others I worked with," Cagney said later. "He was overly bossy – full of noise, a pain. Still, we did a good picture together. I didn't learn until after we were done that he didn't like me, which was fine as far as I was concerned, because I certainly didn't like him. He didn't know how to let things *flow*, and that matters a great deal to me."[23] But Cagney kept his thoughts to himself even after *One, Two, Three* wrapped. His close friend Ralph Bellamy later described the gentlemanly way Cagney handled it: "He was not happy with Wilder at all, and the pace of the film got to him, too . . . When he finished, he came back and told me the experience had disturbed him, but he wasn't all that specific."[24]

When the production returned to Los Angeles to shoot the final scenes at the Goldwyn Studios, Cagney, who loved to sail for relaxation, loaned his yacht to some friends. They sent him a photo of themselves standing on the deck drinking a toast to their absent host; the photo was inscribed, "Thank God you are gainfully employed." On a break between setups, the star of sixty-one previous films over the course of thirty-one years was standing in the warm Southern California sunshine when an assistant director called for him. "We're ready for you now, Mr. Cagney," he said. "That's it, baby," Cagney thought to himself, and he never made another film until *Ragtime* (1981).[25]

One, Two, Three had been grueling for him. One shot in particular required fifty-two takes. Unfortunately, a reporter watched every last one of them. Cagney's MacNamara is spitting out dialogue while trying to select clothes for Buchholz's Piffl. The shot begins as a tailor wheels in a rack of suits and sport coats:

> MACNAMARA: "Now what do we have here?"
> TAILOR: "Very distinguished styles. All fabrics imported!"
> MACNAMARA: "They look more like they were *de*ported. [Grabbing the jackets, one by one:] Too loud, too quiet, alright but take the padding out of the shoulders, that's not bad . . . [in disbelief:] *belt in the back*!? I thought that went out with high button shoes!"
> SHOEMAKER: "High button shoes? I have some right here!"

> MACNAMARA: "Never mind! Take that stuff into the conference room! I want these ready in twenty-four hours!
> TAILOR: "Twenty-four hours?!"
> MACNAMARA: "And where's the morning coat and striped pants?"
> TAILOR: "My assistant is bringing them!"
> MACNAMARA: "Those I want fitted right away!"
> JEWELER: "*Schmuck*!"
> MACNAMARA: (threateningly) "*What did you say?*"
> JEWELER: "*Schmuck*! Jewelry!"
> MACNAMARA: "Oh."

Like Marilyn Monroe with her inability to memorize a simple line about bourbon in *Some Like It Hot* (1959), Cagney simply could not remember to say the "morning" in "And where's the morning coat and striped pants?" Over and over Wilder called for new takes, losing more of his temper each time. "Take it a little slower, Jimmy," Wilder said. "Let's try it again." On the eighteenth take, Cagney got it out, after which the jeweler failed to make his entrance on cue; thus no "*schmuck*." "*Damn it!*," Wilder roared. "*Too late!* You're supposed to come in on 'twenty-four hours!'" Wilder recovered his composure and said, "Let's go again. With emphasis, Jimmy." Cagney blew it once more. "Isn't it a lovely day?" he cried after take twenty-five.

On take fifty-two, everything worked. "Okay, print it," Wilder said in a rancid tone. But he still wasn't happy and insisted that he would have to reshoot it. "This is the worst day I've had in thirty-two years of making pictures. It's the *fohn*." The *what?*, a reporter asked. "The *fohn*," Wilder explained. "It's a wind that comes down from the Alps and drives everyone crazy. Really. People get depressed. Kill their wives. Commit suicide. Forget their lines."[26]

Wilder makes fun of Cagney's screen image, of course but, for Wilder, this kind of joke is a sign of respect. There's a grapefruit gag, straight from *Public Enemy*: the cuckoo clock plays "Yankee Doodle"; one of the MPs does a Cagney impersonation. Cagney references his own gangster image when things look particularly bleak for MacNamara: he cries, "Mother of Mercy! Is this the end of Rico?" just like Edward G. Robinson does in *Little Caesar* (1931). But these are just the obvious homages; the whole film is a tribute.

One, Two, Three is one of Wilder's most abrasive comedies. Adding to the tension of the film's political farce is a smarmy overlay of mercenary sex. Wilder even makes orthography dirty. MacNamara greets his secretary (Lilo Pulver) by calling her "Frau-lein Ingeborg." "It's *Fräulein*," she corrects – "*mit a umlaut!*" This gives MacNamara the chance to remark that he's looking forward to his wife's departure so he can have the "chance to brush up on the umlaut." When MacNamara escorts Ingeborg into the stunningly drab and dreary Grand Hotel Potemkin in East Berlin, he greets the three Russians with the remark, "If it isn't my old friends Hart, Schaffner, and Karl Marx." Mishkin immediately grabs Ingeborg's ass. "I said *Karl* Marx, not Groucho." All the while, Ingeborg remains only too happy to be pimped – first for the West, then for the East. She embraces MacNamara's scheme as enthusiastically as she embraces the married MacNamara himself. Without any hesitation whatsoever, she jumps up on the table at the Potemkin and dances a lurid routine with flaming shish-kebab skewers, all so that MacNamara will buy her a new dress. As a representation of the German national character, Ingeborg is not very flattering.

The ballroom, by the way, looks suspiciously like a Berlin dance hall of the 1920s – one that has, as they say, gone through the war. Two couples dance, adrift. One acts like a gigolo forced to sway his stone-faced partner around in order to earn small change; the other two, equally stone faced, are both women. The band's conductor, leading a rendition of the hit song – in 1922 – "Ja, Haben Wir Keine Bananen" ("Yes, We Have No Bananas") seems to have years of experience behind him and, indeed, he has: he's Friedrich Holländer, one of Wilder's émigré friends and the composer of some of the songs in *A Foreign Affair*.

As the scene progresses, the camera, at high angle, stares down from a considerable distance at an American executive calmly biding his time as three leering Russians go wild watching a busty West German woman wearing a loud, tight polka-dot dress shove her beautiful rear end in their faces while waving a whip. She cracks it on the table, showing them who's in control, MacNamara all the while patiently sitting there waiting for them to sell out. It's an accurate prediction. Under the paper-thin veneer of comedy, Wilder represents the Soviets as farcical nincompoops and the Germans as whores.

Capitalizing on their *Some Like It Hot* reputation, Wilder and Diamond added a subplot involving Schlemmer, MacNamara's assistant, donning Ingeborg's polka-dot dress in order to distract the three Russians, thereby giving MacNamara extra time to spirit Piffl out of the East. This leads to a nervous gag when Schlemmer returns to West Berlin utterly bedraggled, the dress in ruins. "Did you have any trouble getting out of East Berlin?," MacNamara asks. "No," Schlemmer responds, "but I had a little trouble in West Berlin. I was picked up by an American soldier in a Jeep. He was *very* fresh." One can only imagine because, even in the dress, Schlemmer looks nothing like a woman. Schlemmer cleans up the joke a little in his follow-up explanation: "Wanted to take my picture for something called *Playboy*," he explains unconvincingly.

"Sorry, sir," says Schlemmer later, pulling up his pants and running into MacNamara's office. "I had difficulty getting out the girdle." "Schlemmer!," MacNamara barks, "I want all those people out there to drop everything and stand by for orders. General alarm! Complete mobilization!" Schlemmer is thrilled: "Ah, like the good old days! *Yes, sir*!" Regimentation comes naturally to Wilder's Germans; when MacNamara enters a room full of Coca-Cola functionaries, they all snap to attention and rise to their feet in unison. "*Sitzenmachen*!" MacNamara roars, and the functionaries obey and sit down – also in unison. In Wilder's view, you can take Germany out of Nazism, but you can't take Nazism out of the Germans.

Later, when Schlemmer's old SS commander resurfaces in the form of a seemingly respectable West German journalist, Schlemmer automatically *heil*s him; Wilder was scarcely willing to let the Germans forget their own history. Wilder told the designer Ray Eames what one of the German actors in *One, Two, Three* had told him about the war. Wilder was fascinated: "He said to me, 'Billy, you know, during the war, we hid Jews.' And I said, 'You hid Jews?' 'Yes, we hid Jews.' 'And how many Jews did you hide?' 'Well, we only hid about two or three.' 'That's significant,'" Wilder replied, "because of all the Germans I talked to – how many Germans are there? – fifty million, forty million, something? That's 120 million Jews you hid."[27]

Wilder makes fun of the Germans and the Soviets but he doesn't spare Americans, either. Young American women may be as nubile as Ingeborg but in *One, Two, Three* they're a whole lot dumber. Played winningly by Pamela Tiffin, Scarlett is nevertheless an idiot. "You can forward my mail to American Express in Moscow," she confidently declares. "Do you realize that Otto spelled backwards is Otto?" In her finest moment, she casually executes her parents on her way out the door: "They're the ones I feel sorry for," she confides to MacNamara. "Otto says they'll have to be liquidated. Bye!"

Still, for all of Scarlett's inanity, MacNamara's cruelty, and the thoroughgoing prostitution of the West, Communism ultimately fares worse than capitalism in *One, Two, Three*. Never one to pocket a windfall for writing and directing a paean to peasants or a venerating tribute to the working class, Wilder is honest about his own sensibility. He respects the sellouts of the world:

> BORODENKO: "Well, comrades, what are we going to do? He's got it, we want it. Are we going to accept this blackmailing capitalist deal?"
> MISHKIN: "Let's take a vote."
> BORODENKO: "I vote yes!"
> MISHKIN: "I vote yes!"
> BORODENKO: "Two out of three – deal is on."
> PERIPETCHIKOFF: "Comrades, before you get in trouble I must warn you – I am not really from Soft-Drink Secretariat. I am undercover agent assigned to watch you."
> MISHKIN: "In that case, I vote no. Deal is off."
> PERIPETCHIKOFF: "But I vote yes!"
> BORODENKO: "Two out of three again. Deal is on!"

Making Fun of Torture

One might argue that certain subjects are inherently not funny and that it is impossible to employ them for comic purposes. Torture might seem to be on that list. But one particular scene in *One, Two, Three* gets at a deadly serious aspect of East Germany's history by means of farce. There is a stark difference between East and West in the film and in real life as well. The East German secret police, the Stasi, routinely tortured prisoners to extract confessions – an ugly, brutal fact about which there is no dispute. And the United States didn't torture people, at least not until the George W. Bush administration.

It's shocking, then, when – in the midst of this frenetic comedy – Wilder cuts to an interrogation room in the grim, imposing confines of the People's Police Station in East Berlin. The Stasi is holding Otto, arrested for carrying the absurd cuckoo clock that features Uncle Sam waving a flag to mark the hour to the tune of "Yankee Doodle Dandy"; the paper in which it's wrapped – a copy of the *Wall Street Journal*; and the "Russki Go Home" balloon that MacNamara has had fixed on the exhaust pipe of his motorcycle.

The visuals are forbidding: it's a drab room with a group of Stasi officers standing around Otto who is seated on a chair at a desk. A lone female officer sits at another desk on the side. She's wearing extra-thick eyeglasses that dehumanize her even more than the utterly blank expression on her face as she watches her fellow Stasi officers torture the prisoner. Holding his ears and screaming in agony and exhaustion, Otto breaks down. The secret police wring out a confession – a false confession, the type of confession that torture produces because the victim will eventually admit to anything to make the brutality stop. From the visuals alone, the East German police state isn't very funny.

But on the soundtrack is the supremely grating strains of Brian Hyland's inane hit record from 1960, "Itsy Bitsy Teenie Weenie Yellow Polkadot Bikini." It is this ludicrous song that Wilder's Stasi uses to extract Otto's confession. At first, he maintains his innocence as one of the officers shouts over the song and insists that he's an American spy. Otto collapses, exhausted, onto the desk, clutching his head in his hands and covering his ears. The Stasi officer pushes the desk away and grabs Otto by the hair, yanking him upright. There is nothing amusing about these images. Wilder pulls comedy out of the scene purely by way of the song.

An officer then speeds up the LP record from 33 rpm to 78 and, to top it off, he puts the record off center on the turntable. The already idiotic song becomes completely intolerable, and Otto quickly breaks under the pressure of having to listen to American culture at its worst. He confesses. Who could blame him?

Wilder captures Otto's confession in as close to a close-up as appears anywhere else in the film (with the exception of the final shot: a close-up of MacNamara looking straight at the camera, dumbfounded to have got a bottle of Pepsi from a Coke machine). It's a disturbing shot for precisely this reason; the viewer sees Otto's anguish at close range. The scene is both strikingly funny and strikingly not.

Conclusion

Wilder's moral vision hinges on expedience. His favorite characters are heroically glib. The little MacNamara boy is matter-of-fact about Scarlett's putative illness: "If she dies can I have my room back?" For Wilder, idealism isn't simply out of date. It's contemptible. "Maybe we should liquidate the whole human race and start all over again," Piffl cries in despair near the end. It's at this point that Wilder gives voice to his own concluding moral: "Look at it this way, kid," says MacNamara in close-up. "Any world that can produce the Taj Mahal, William Shakespeare, and Stripe Toothpaste can't be all bad."

One, Two, Three came in at a cost of $2,927,628. This was hardly excessive. Still, the picture did not make its money back. The domestic gross was less than $2.5 million, its foreign gross was only $1.6 million, and after all the advertising and distribution expenses were figured in, the Mirisch Company and United Artists were stuck for a loss of $1,568,500.[28] Jimmy Cagney never saw the film, and neither did most other potential audience members. The West Germans were particularly unamused. For some reason, the few who saw the film resented Wilder's treating most of the German characters as ex-Nazis. It was Wilder's first bomb since *The Spirit of St. Louis* (1957). "I happen to think Coca-Cola is funny," Wilder said later. "A lot of people didn't. Maybe that's why the picture bombed out. I still think it's funny. And when I drink it, it seems even funnier."[29]

In London for the British opening in early February, 1962, Wilder was defensive. "If there's anything I dislike more than being taken too lightly, it's being taken too seriously," he griped. "After every drama people say, 'What do you want to give us all this bitterness and gloom for? Why don't you go back to comedies instead?,' while after every comedy they say, 'Very nice, but isn't it now time for you to give us something really serious?'"[30] He confessed that he was worried that audiences just couldn't keep up with the frenzied pace of the film. Perhaps they simply didn't "have the stamina to pay such close attention continuously," he mused. Maybe, he said, his little "experiment" in speed went a step or two too far.[31] Some American reviewers applauded *One, Two, Three*; others were lukewarm at best. Stanley Kauffmann called the film a "political satire with an air of daring but without daring anything."[32] John Simon decried the "shallow, gratuitous cynicism which, somewhere in the back of Mr. Wilder's mind, seems to say, 'I laugh at the whole damned world – whether it's Shakespeare, striped tooth paste, or you.'" For Simon, this was wrong and immoral: "It's all right to laugh at striped tooth paste,"

Simon opined, "or us, or even Shakespeare, provided there is somewhere, at least by implication, something that one does not laugh at." (Simon may have been referring to his own critical *oeuvre*.) Pauline Kael was just disgusted and expressed her displeasure in an especially vulgar way, even for her: "*One, Two, Three* is overwrought, tasteless, and offensive – a comedy that pulls out laughs the way a catheter draws urine." Judging by the increasingly defensive tone he took whenever the subject of critics came up in the years to come, Wilder noticed these jabs and was far more hurt by them than one might expect, given his own abrasive nature.

There's a signal moment in *One, Two, Three* that sums up Wilder's take not only on the Berlin Crisis and the Cold War but on humanity as a whole. Piffl, in despair, cries, "Is *everybody* in this world corrupt?" "I don't know everybody," Borodenko replies with a shrug, It's amusing but glum. At the same time, when Piffl rushes into MacNamara's office in his boxer shorts, he declares, "I'm going to like this job! Do you know what the first thing is I'm going to do? I'm going to lead the workers down there in revolt!" "Put your pants on, Spartacus," replies MacNamara witheringly. As Mrs. MacNamara says when she learns that Scarlett's parents are about to arrive later that day, "Now *that's* funny."

Notes

1. Although *Dr. Strangelove* was mostly shot at Shepperton Studios in London, it was financed by Columbia Pictures, so it is a Hollywood film.
2. See my *Laughing Hysterically: American Screen Comedies of the 1950s* for a thorough treatment of this thesis.
3. Oleg Cassini was one of the glamorous Jacqueline Kennedy's favorite couturiers; Mrs. Krushchev was a frump. Anon. "Interview: Billy Wilder, *Playboy* 10, No. 6, June, 1963, p. 62.
4. Robert Lantz to ES, July 25, 1995.
5. Helmuth Karasek, *Billy Wilder: eine Nahaufnahme* (Hamburg: Hoffman und Campe, 1992), p. 310.
6. Margaret Herrick Library, Academy of Motion Picture Arts and Sciences (AMPAS), *A Foreign Affair* production file 1.
7. J. M. Woodcock, "The Name Dropper," *American Cinemeditor* 39, No. 4, winter 1989/1990, p. 15.
8. Billy Wilder, *Der Prinz von Wales geht auf Urlaub: Berliner Reportagen, Feuilletons unk Kritiken der zwanziger Jahre*, ed. Klaus Siebenhaar (Berlin: Fannet & Walz Verlag, 1996), p. 117; originally published as "Hallo, Herr Menjou?" *Tempo*, August 5, 1929.
9. State Historical Society of Wisconsin, Wisconsin Center for Film and Theater Research, I. A. L. Diamond Collection, Box 7, folder 4.
10. *Los Angeles Mirror*, September 2, 1961. Note: The line does appear more or less intact in Molnar's play; precious few others remain unchanged.
11. Arlene Francis, with Florence Rome, *Arlene Francis: A Memoir* (New York: Simon and Schuster, 1978), p. 169.
12. James Linville, "Billy Wilder: The Art of Screenwriting," *The Paris Review*, spring 1996, p. 67.

13. *Los Angeles Times*, July 14, 1961; *Sammlung Paul Kohner, Stiftung Deutsche Kinemathek*, h. ß – 88/1h – 6, file 3.
14. James Cagney, *Cagney by Cagney* (Garden City, NY: Doubleday and Co.), p. 155; Douglas Warren with James Cagney, *James Cagney: The Authorized Biography* (New York: St. Martin's Press), p. 120; *Los Angeles Mirror*, August 17, 1961.
15. Erskine Johnson, "Billy Wilder's Trail of Whims," *Los Angeles Mirror*, July 12, 1961.
16. *New York Times*, July 16, 1961.
17. *Los Angeles Mirror*, August 17, 1961; Joachim Eichhof, "Architekten betrügen das Auge," *Filmspiegel*, October 6, 1961.
18. *Playboy*, June, 1963, p. 62.
19. Alexander Trauner and Jean-Pierre Berthomé, *Alexander Trauner: Décors de cinéma* (Paris: Jade flammarion, 1988), p. 154.
20. *Playboy*, June, 1963, p. 62.
21. AMPAS, *One, Two, Three* clippings file; *One, Two, Three* press kit.
22. Francis, p. 172; Warren and Cagney, pp. 192–3; Cagney, p. 155.
23. Warren and Cagney, p. 244.
24. Timothy White, "Looking Backward: James Cagney's Armchair Tour of Fifty Years in Showbiz," *Rolling Stone*, February 18, 1982, p. 24.
25. Patrick McGilligan, *Cagney: The Actor as Auteur* (San Diego; A. S. Barnes and Co., 1982) p. 244.
26. *Los Angeles Mirror*, August 18, 1961.
27. John Neuhart interview with ES, December 4, 1997.
28. State Historical Society of Wisconsin, Wisconsin Center for Film and Theater Research, United Artists Collection, Box 5, folder 3.
29. Garson Kanin, *Hollywood* (New York: Viking Press), p. 185.
30. *London Times*, February 8, 1962.
31. *New York Times*, March 4, 1962, Sec. 2, p. 7.
32. *New Republic*, December 11, 1961; *Theatre Arts*, July, 1962; Pauline Kael, *I Lost It At the Movies* (Boston: Little Brown and Co., 1965), p. 150.

Filmography

Bacon, Lloyd, 1938: *Boy Meets Girl*.
Borzage, Frank, 1943: *Stage Door Canteen*.
Curtiz, Michael, 1938: *Angels with Dirty Faces*.
Curtiz, Michael, 1941: *Yankee Doodle Dandy*.
Florey, Robert, 1932: *Murders in the Rue Morgue*.
Ford, John and Mervyn LeRoy, 1955: *Mister Roberts*.
Hitchcock, Alfred, 1959: *North by Northwest*.
Houston, John, 1962: *Freud*.
Keighley, William, 1935: *G-Men*.
Kubrick, Stanley, 1964: *Dr. Strangelove: Or, How I Learned to Stop Worrying and Love the Bomb*.
LeRoy, Mervyn, 1931: *Little Caesar*.
Lubitsch, Ernst, 1939: *Ninotchka*.
Montgomery, Robert, 1960: *The Gallant Hours*.
Reis, Irving, 1948: *All My Sons*.
Tashlin, Frank, 1955: *Artists and Models*.
Tashlin, Frank, 1956: *The Girl Can't Help It*.
Tashlin, Frank, 1956: *Hollywood or Bust*.
Tashlin, Frank, 1957: *Will Success Spoil Rock Hunter?*

Vidor, Charles, 1955: *Love Me or Leave Me.*
Walsh, Raoul, 1939: *The Roaring Twenties.*
Walsh, Raoul, 1949: *White Heat.*
Wellman, William, 1931: *Public Enemy.*
Wilder, Billy, 1945: *The Lost Weekend.*
Wilder, Billy, 1948: *A Foreign Affair.*
Wilder, Billy, 1957: *The Spirit of St. Louis.*
Wilder, Billy, 1959: *Some Like It Hot.*
Wilder, Billy, 1961: *One, Two, Three.*

Bibliography

Anon. (June, 1963), "Interview: Billy Wilder, *Playboy.*
Cagney, James (1977), *Cagney by Cagney*, Garden City, NY: Doubleday and Co.
Eichhof, Joachim (1961), "Architekten betrügen das Auge," *Filmspiegel.*
Francis, Arlene with Florence Rome (1978), *Arlene Francis: A Memoir*, New York: Simon and Schuster.
Johnson, Erskine (1961), "Billy Wilder's Trail of Whims," *Los Angeles Mirror*, July 12.
Kael, Pauline (1965), *I Lost It At the Movies*, Boston: Little Brown and Co.
Kanin, Garson (1974), *Hollywood*, New York: Viking Press.
Karasek, Helmuth (1992), *Billy Wilder: eine Nahaufnahme*, Hamburg: Hoffman und Campe.
Linville, James (1996), "Billy Wilder: The Art of Screenwriting," *The Paris Review*, spring.
McGilligan, Patrick (1982), *Cagney: The Actor as Auteur*, San Diego; A. S. Barnes and Co.
Sikov, Ed (1994), *Laughing Hysterically: American Screen Comedies of the 1950s*, New York: Columbia University Press.
Sikov, Ed (1998), *On Sunset Boulevard: The Life and Times of Billy Wilder*, New York: Hyperion.
Trauner, Alexander and Jean-Pierre Berthomé (1988), *Alexander Trauner: Décors de cinéma*, Paris: Jade flammarion.
Warren, Douglas with James Cagney (1983), *James Cagney: The Authorized Biography*, New York: St. Martin's Press.
White, Timothy (1982), "Looking Backward: James Cagney's Armchair Tour of Fifty Years in Showbiz," *Rolling Stone*, February 18.
Wilder, Billy (1996), *Der Prinz von Wales geht auf Urlaub: Berliner Reportagen, Feuilletons unk Kritiken der zwanziger Jahre*, Berlin: Fannet & Walz Verlag.
Woodcock, J. M. (1989–1990) "The Name Dropper," *American Cinemeditor* 39, No. 4.

4. THE SMALL ADULT FILM: A PRESTIGE FORM OF COLD WAR CINEMA

R. Barton Palmer

Small Scale and Adult

Pressured by its upstart televisual rival (the new medium began full commercial operation in 1948), the American cinema in the initial decades of the Cold War found some success in a generally declining marketplace by exploring two production types that pushed the industry in quite opposite directions. Big-budget event films (the antecedent of contemporary tentpole [major] productions) made the most of then innovative wide-screen processes and color film stock and, to give an impression of "largeness," they also featured an expanded roster of name players and a running time so extended an intermission was often required. Small-scale, black-and-white, realist projects rivaled the similar international art films then doing profitable business in specialized urban venues. Both these forms of alternative cinema, which enjoyed growing reputations for being serious and prestigious releases, were, in the language of the exhibition trade, "sure seaters" or certain to fill auditoriums week in, week out (see Wilinsky).

It is no coincidence that the U.S. trend in small adult film production picked up steam in the early 1950s precisely when this niche end of the exhibition business began to enjoy a substantial boom owing to the unexpected popularity of foreign releases, especially from Italy. A significant change in audience taste was taking place, and there was a reaction among U.S. exhibitors (who promoted venues for screening art films from abroad) and producers who catered to this new fashion in their own way and in financial and institutional circumstances different from those under which foreign filmmakers operated (see Balio). This was the very same period when the social-problem film became an insistent, and prestige-claiming, presence on the nation's screens (see Cagle). Unfortunately, the prominent place that the social-problem film rightly claims in histories of the period has obscured the significance of small adult filmmaking, with which it shares some common features even if there are fundamental differences between the two domestic prestige (as opposed to entertainment) types, as this chapter will attempt to outline.

In contrast to the international art cinema, which was largely an auteurist phenomenon, small adult releases were usually literary adaptations, with their production linked closely to more outré Broadway and publishing fashions, a trend that can be traced to Elia Kazan's screening of Tennessee Williams's Broadway smash production, *A Streetcar Named Desire* (1951) (See Palmer/Bray). Hollywood was at first uninterested in the Pulitzer-Prize winning play because of its frank sexual themes but independent producer Charles Feldman took a chance on the property. *Streetcar* turned out to be both a huge box-office success and a prestige production that pushed filmmakers more toward literary sources that might pose representational challenges that, as the negotiations conducted by Feldman, Kazan, and Williams with Production Code Administration (PCA) officials demonstrated, could be handled. Like *Streetcar*, both the international art cinema and its domestic reflex presented themselves as "adult" in theme (this was their key marketing hook), prompting the loosening up of Production Code (which endured until 1968). Yet this process proceeded slowly and the domestic product did not catch up to the art cinema until the second half of the 1960s (see Lewis). By the end of the previous decade, "art cinema" had come to designate a niche product (mostly foreign) balanced uneasily between cinematic modernism and soft-core pornography; domestic production was to peak during the 1950s and early '60s. Still constrained by the fundamental Victorianism of the Code, American small-scale adult films never promoted erotic display and sex-symbol performers such as the so-called "bombshell" actresses from the Italian neorealist cinema (Sylvana Magnano, Gina Lollobrigida, and Sophia Loren). The French New Wave contributed the most famous performer/personality to this trend, with Brigitte Bardot achieving international notoriety as a sex kitten (in the era's misogynistic turn of phrase). Her Riviera romantic romp, *And God Created Woman* (1956), featured her in a bikini bathing suit, which immediately became a global fashion trend. Director Roger Vadim's initial foray into this kind of filmmaking proved to be the most profitable of all international art cinema releases in the U.S. even if the film's claims to be "art" in any substantial sense were risible (see Jobs 185–231).

Small-scale adult films were not sexy in the same sense. If the Williams property themed sex in innovative ways, including dramatizing the substantial discontents of "desire," *Streetcar* featured no nudity or even suggestive costumes, and its sexual situations were tamely inexplicit (even the story's notorious rape scene occurred almost entirely off camera). In promoting serious themes, particularly about intimate life and its complexities, the small adults were, in comparison with the standard Hollywood product, long on drama but short on action, spectacle, and glamour even when star players were involved playing against their established images in ways unusual for the industry (for example, in *The Catered Affair* [1956] Bette Davis donned a "fat suit" in order to incarnate a middle-aged housewife). Small adult films were often ostentatiously literary in the sense that they espoused the thematically rich realism of the postwar theater (including live television drama) and its novelistic counterparts. These films contact only rarely with cinematic (or literary) modernism, broadly defined. Instead, they are consonant with the broader, middlebrow movement within popular fiction of the period in which, as Gordon Hutner remarks, the representational concern is with "a rudimentary vision of some relative cohesiveness of American life, a shareable set of values and questions about the world in which middle-class Americans live" (Hutner 4).

The small adult film of the postwar era launched an enduring fashion, establishing a new form of prestige production for Hollywood, one that was taken up again in the auteur cinema of the 1970s renaissance and again, *mutatis mutandis*, in the independent cinema that emerged in the following decade. These films were realist in a sense just recently adopted by the industry. Prominent in them was a rich homage to the semidocumentary tradition that had whetted filmgoer interest in authentic settings during the war and after (see Palmer 2016). In terms of their themes and affect, the small adults, as I shall suggest in the second section of this chapter, reflect particularly powerful elements within the *mentalité* of Cold War America, marking an interesting rapprochement between "history" broadly considered and cultural production, and expressing serious doubts about the national culture, if not usually in terms that could be called political. Inevitably, the Cold War cinema embodied the structures of feeling of the period, particularly its paradoxical mixture of triumphalism and self-doubt, what Dana Polan refers to as the culture's fascination with "power," but susceptibility to "paranoia" (see Polan). The postwar era thus became, in historian William Graebner's formulation, a "culture of contingency" (Graebner 19–20). Americans had discovered, as theologian Reinhold Niebuhr told his fellows in 1952, that they were "the custodians of the ultimate weapon which perfectly embodies and symbolizes the moral ambiguity of physical warfare." Once invented, "the bomb" could not be renounced because no nation can justly dispense with the means to forestall a threatened destruction. And yet, if forced to use it, Niebuhr predicted, "we might insure our survival in a world in which it might be better not to be alive" (39). The national mood was not dominated, however, simply by nuclear dread and terror. Many commentators at the time also lamented the failure or abandonment of traditional notions about human purpose and virtue, prompting what Graebner terms a moral crisis, for "the seminal events of the forties seemed to confirm that humanity had, indeed, been set adrift from its ethical moorings" (19–20). For Niebuhr, the defeat of European fascism and eastern militarism was deeply ironic, calling into question the conventional pieties of the national creed. He opined that "we are the poorer for the global responsibilities which we bear. And the fulfillments of our desires are mixed with frustrations and vexations." Most frustrating, and morally puzzling, was the fact that "the paradise of our domestic security is suspended in a hell of global insecurity," undermining the "conviction of the perfect compatibility of virtue and prosperity which we have inherited from both our Calvinist and our Jeffersonian ancestors" (7). The small adults reflected this moral uncertainty.

A shortlist of significant productions from the era that can usefully be classified as small adult would include: *Death of a Salesman* (1951), *A Streetcar Named Desire* 1951), *Come Back, Little Sheba* (1952), *Blackboard Jungle* (1955), *The Rose Tattoo* (1955), *Patterns* (1955), *Marty* (1955), *The Rainmaker* (1956), *Storm Center* (1956), *The Catered Affair* (1956), *A Hatful of Rain* (1957), *Fear Strikes Out* (1957), *The Three Faces of Eve* (1957), *The Wrong Man* (1956), *12 Angry Men* (1957), *Sweet Smell of Success* (1957), *The Bachelor Party* (1957), *A Face in the Crowd* (1957), *No Down Payment* (1957 *The View from the Bridge* (1957), *Hot Spell* (1958), *The Diary of Anne Frank* (1958), *Middle of the Night* (1959), *Wild River* (1960), *The Hoodlum Priest* (1961), *The Hustler* (1961), *Days of Wine and Roses* (1962), *To Kill a Mockingbird* (1962), *Pressure Point* (1962), *David and Lisa* (1962), *All Fall Down* (1962), *The Birdman of Alcatraz* (1962), *Hud* (1963), *Baby the Rain Must Fall* (1965), *Mickey One* (1965), *The Pawnbroker* (1965), and *Patch of Blue* (1965). At least forty more films can be seen as part of this broadly defined production trend. What they most importantly share in common is the embrace of an antiestablishmentarian pessimism, with the bourgeois ideal of family life a frequent target (as in modern drama and fiction more generally). Filmmakers were sometimes forced to include unconvincing "happy" endings in order to satisfy the PCA because Hollywood's censors remained committed to the principle of "compensating moral value" when it came to the presentation of material that went against the values and practices of the social status quo.

And yet, even when complying with industry protocols, the makers of small adult films found ways to express a grimmer version of the national culture, especially its commitment to narrow visions of what might constitute "success." In terms of tone, small adult films constituted the intellectual other to another Cold War cinema type that likewise eschewed visual exuberance and star glamour. The social-problem film, as Chris Cagle describes it, offered narratives in the spirit of a "popular sociology," promoting a serious, ameliorist engagement with the social body as ever-developing forms of social science were then defining it (Cagle 6). Cagle recounts how the postwar social-problem film made a bid for prestige by dramatizing, in a broadly realist fashion, social issues then being raised in the public arena, especially as framed by news magazines such as *Reader's Digest* that gave prominence to an emerging "therapeutic culture" (see Sharp, especially 1–5; the various essays collected in Imber; and Rieff).

Deploying an affecting combination of "liberal thematic directness" and "left-wing allegorical resonance," social-problem films dramatized particular issues, such as juvenile delinquency, demands for conformity, teenage pregnancy, the loosening of family bonds, anti-Semitism, alcoholism, and drug addiction, promoting a progressivist *telos* (Cagle 13). The social-problem film eschewed thematizing discontents of a more intimate, inchoate, or intractable Durkheimian nature. These films do not occupy themselves with anomie, alienation, and despair, the complementary conditions of the moral torpor endemic in a post-Christian secular society which was exacerbated by new, as well as persistent, forms of economic and social inequality. But in Cold War culture there were significant developments that pointed in the opposite direction. William L. O'Neill, for example, concentrating on domestic life rather than on intellectual or ideological developments, argues that the first decade and a half of the postwar period can be termed "the years of confidence," and this assessment is echoed by others who emphasize the incredible prosperity the era witnessed, hitherto unexampled in the American experience, as a middle-class life, defined by home ownership and a bounty of consumer goods, was attained by a national (if largely white) majority.[1] If the social-problem films consistently imagined the brighter future thought of by many in American culture, a paralyzing torpor that was also widespread furnished many of the themes treated in the small adults.

Consider *Blackboard Jungle* (1955), based on the bestselling novel by Evan Hunter, which presents itself initially as an exploration of one of the decade's hot-button social issues, juvenile delinquency, by focusing on the problems of an inner-city school But continuing deep conflict between teachers and students reveals that the *ressentiment* of the latter toward the institution in which they are more or less confined has more sources (cultural, racial, economic, and generational) than can be addressed by the tough-love approach of the film's, Mr. Dadier (Glenn Ford), a somewhat reluctant convert to social reform on the local level. How is this impasse to be resolved? In the action-oriented tradition of the American cinema, with its investment in the display of physical prowess, *Blackboard Jungle* detours from the failure of public school to achieve a desired social engineering. The narrative climaxes with a fight between the most incorrigible member of the "hoods" in the class, Artie West

A PRESTIGE FORM OF COLD WAR CINEMA

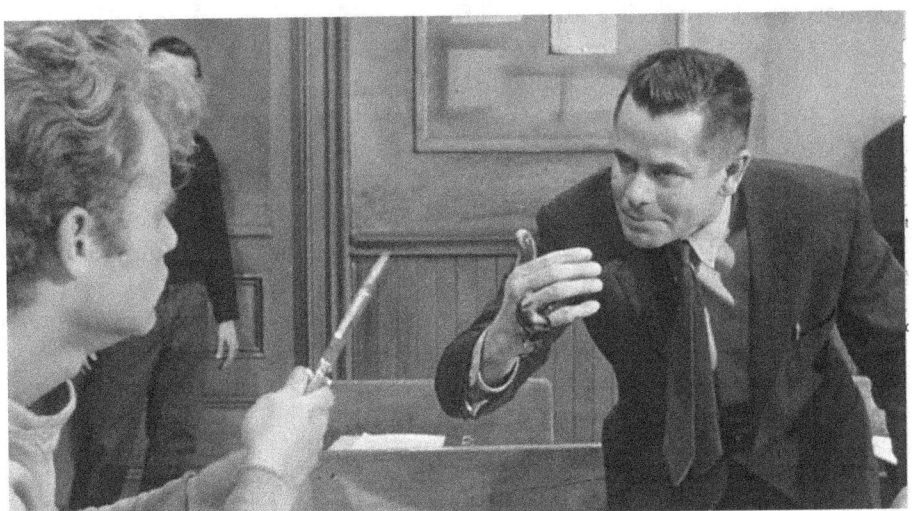

Figure 4.1 Teacher Richard Dadier (Glenn Ford) squares up against swtichblade-toting punk (Vic Morrow) in *Blackboard Jungle* (1955).

(Vic Morrow), and Dadier who is forced to fight for his life in a classroom meant for other things. Showing courage and fighting skill, the teacher disarms the young man of his switchblade, humiliating him in front of his friends. Yet nothing changes as a result of Dadier's triumph beyond the melancholy fact that he has finally demonstrated a quality primitive enough to earn the respect of his students. It is exactly the lesson about life that he would not have them learn but the dysfunctional public social space in which he attempts to purvey his intellectual skills (in the vain hope that education will make a difference) leaves him no choice. To be sure, Dadier does achieve some success with others in his charge, especially Gregory Miller (Sidney Poitier), but the film was sold on its promise to deliver sensational antisocial action (this high school is a "jungle") with a poster that showed a female teacher in the school library under attack from one of the students.

At the time, the discipline of sociology was then in the process of changing from the broad culturalism of earlier decades into a properly social "science," with signal publications like Gunnar Myrdal's 1944 *An American Dilemma* (financed by the Carnegie Foundation) sparking a lively debate about U.S. race relations. Public intellectuals, including such luminaries as C. Wright Mills, David Riesman, Erving Goffman, and Robert M. Lindner, were moved to write about similar issues for a broad middlebrow readership and not just their academic or professional colleagues.[2] Sometimes, as was the case with William H. Whyte's *The Organization Man* (1956), these books became legitimate bestsellers. Linder's *Must You Conform?* (1956) answered "no" to the question raised by its title and argued for informed, self-interested resistance to the social trend identified by Whyte, anticipating the criticism of the New Left in the 1960s of the so-called "establishment."

Like its parent discipline, the social-problem film assumes that some present social conditions self-evidently constitute problems in need of a solution on some level, be it individual or collective. Change is needed in society – so runs the implicit socialist politics of the genre whose remit can be understood as furthering the intellectual/moral energies of the therapeutic by translating them to the screen. Here, as Cagle puts it, was "a form of popular sociology marrying contemporary developments in American sociology to the new type of prestige filmmaking" in which seriousness and realism figured centrally (6). Such themes, it should be pointed out, could readily be accommodated to industry conventions, including building up the narrative around a pair of attractive star leads and the romantic connection that inevitably develops between them.

In general, the writers (of both original properties and scripts) as well as the directors of small adult films were not disposed to endorse the status quo. Even if they were not overtly left wing, small adult films often sharply critiqued national pieties (particularly the so-called "American dream" of successful self-fashioning), challenging the nation's flattering image of itself, while marking out the discontents of the supposedly empowering personal growth agendas pushed by the neo-Freudianism and Christian Positive Thinking movements that rose to cultural prominence during the early 1950s. If they were also controversial figures within their areas of practice, psychiatrist Erich Fromm and evangelist Norman Vincent Peale became key spokesmen for the gospel of energetic and commitment self-improvement, commanding large and appreciative readerships.[3] Dramatists and novelists saw a different postwar culture, one in which achieving self-fulfilling happiness might be more deceptive mirage than practical goal. This dialectic between different forms of Cold War cinema had ancient roots. In fact, it updated what is for Western culture the fundamental theological opposition of Augustine, promoting the notion of Original Sin, to Pelagius who argued that sinfulness was not of man's essence. Pelagianism acknowledges instead a divinely infused capacity for moral and spiritual self-improvement and, in the postwar era, its message found ready champions in the proliferating offices of psychiatrists or in the happy Christianity preached from revivalist pulpits and during the missionizing crusades sponsored by prominent evangelists such as Billy Graham.

Refusing enthusiastic engagement with either reformist or progressive agendas, small adult films partake of both a vague Augustinianism and the *Weltschmerz* of the later Freud, who acknowledged the powerful discontents, and thus individual dissatisfaction, on whose suppression civilization depends.[4] Like the film noir, a crime series with which it has some affinities, the small adult film customarily dramatized betrayal and failure in ways that were also then fashionable in serious theater and modernist fiction, and in the European art film as well. The pessimism of the small adults, especially evident in the refusal to provide conventionally happy endings, asks to be interpreted as a bid for prestige, and this supposition is easily confirmed by auteurist analyses of the directors involved. As Cagle observes of then developing industry trends, "in the postwar era, the prestige film had split between the popular prestige picture, often an epic spectacle, and the critical prestige picture, including the problem film and the literary melodrama" (29). To be sure, melodrama is the general category, with a long and varied history, with which the small adults show the most affinity. The particular affect of the small adult film series, however, reflects not only melodramatic protocols (including a focus on complex dynamics of family life), but also the preoccupation of United States Cold War culture with betrayal and the unraveling of once close relationships (a trend that *Streetcar*, with its box-office and critical success, may have been decisive in promoting).

Many, perhaps most, of the small-scale films of the era were directed by a younger generation of professionals. These include, most notably, Sidney Lumet, Robert Mulligan, Fielder Cook, Delbert Mann, Daniel Mann, Frank Perry, Jack Smight, and John Frankenheimer. Sojourners from other national cinemas, such as Guy Green, Peter Glenville, and John Schlesinger, also were active in the series. Interestingly, though they were meant to compete with what was being offered for free on the new medium, the era's small-scale films, almost always in black and white, reflected aesthetic/dramatic conventions then regnant in prime-time live televisual drama. Small-scale adult filmmakers also enjoyed strong connections to the contemporary Broadway theater and to live television theater, both of which were then flourishing with the rise to prominence of a new generation of important playwrights. These included: Tennessee Williams, Rod Serling, William Inge, Reginald Rose, Arthur Miller, and Edward Albee. All limned gloomy and crisis-ridden versions of modern life that often made it intact to the screen, giving the small adult film an aura of transgressive hopelessness. *Streetcar*'s Blanche (Vivien Leigh) descends at film's end into a psychosis that protects her from thinking about the sexual assault she suffered from her brother-in-law Stanley (Marlon Brando) who behaves out of a toxic mix of feelings, including anger at her demeaning pretensions, and goes relatively unpunished at the end, abandoned by his wife. In *Death of a Salesman*, based on the Arthur Miller Pulitzer-Prize winning Broadway smash hit, the paterfamilias Willy Loman (Fredric March) chooses suicide rather than face his own failures and betrayals, as well as the wreckage of his family life.

Doc Delaney (Burt Lancaster) is brought to face the mournful truth that his career has been a failure in William Inge's *Come Back, Little Sheba* while wife Lola (Shirley Booth) must endure a now loveless marriage with an alcoholic whose fleeting sobriety threatens her with unpredictable violence. Fielder Cook's film version of Rod Serling's television play *Patterns* depicts a dark vision of modern American business in which a profit-obsessed and heartless chief executive (Everett Sloane) and his operations manager (Van Heflin) resolve to wage a no-quarter-given struggle over how the company will treat its employees, customers, and shareholders. These are stories in which characters might come to a fuller self-knowledge but also face dead ends of one kind or another. They are not delivered to either a brighter world or to some more integrated and fulfilling sense of self. Reviewing *Patterns* for the *New York Times*, A. H. Weiler comments that the film offers a "frightening and often moving portrait of familiar and rare executives caught in mahogany-paneled 'jungles' with their teeth, hearts and minds bared," hardly the ordinary fare of Tinseltown melodrama (A. H. Weiler, "Patterns," *New York Times*, March 28, 1956 http://www.nytimes.com/movie/review?res=9401E0D81430E23BBC4051DFB566838D649EDE).

In contrast, therapeutic culture provides social-problem films with ready-made and, at least potentially positive, narrative trajectories. The genre offers a kind of socialist realism lite that is easily accommodated within the character-driven drama then standard in Hollywood. Consider one of the best-loved and admired of these productions: Elia Kazan's *Gentleman's Agreement* (1947), based on Laura Z. Hobson's novelistic exploration of anti-Semitism in the über-rich Fairfield County suburbs, a project pushed strongly by Fox production head Darryl F. Zanuck. Interestingly, the film finds its ending in a reconciliation between two attractive and upper-middle-class goyim. Magazine feature writer Phil Green (Gregory Peck) and Kathy Lacey (Dorothy McGuire) are lovers who figure centrally in the novel's investigative plot, which involves Green posing as Jewish in order to experience anti-Semitism for himself so that, as an outsider capable of being shocked, he can describe it from, as it were, the inside. Published for a huge national readership, Green's tale of suffering, so his earnest editor John Minify (Albert Dekker) predicts, will attract a broad readership and thus do much to ameliorate a problem that all involved agree is getting worse.

Phil's harsh condemnation of Kathy's unreflective sense of Gentile privilege leads to their breakup but he soon disavows this moral judgment when she shows clear evidence of unprejudiced good faith. This is a morally therapeutic turn that can be accounted for only by his influence. Kathy's anti-Semitism is of the mildest sort (a silent tolerance of anti-Jewish humor) but her passive collusion with illiberalism is exorcised by a minor adjustment of conscience once it is pointed out to her. With Phil's help, she comes to understand that, by failing to condemn such offensive humor, she is actually endorsing views she otherwise reprehends. Kathy's inner transformation leads to action as she commits to easing the social adjustment of a Jewish couple who have just moved into

A PRESTIGE FORM OF COLD WAR CINEMA

Figure 4.2 Philip Green (Gregory Peck) and Kathy Lacey (Dorothy McGuire) share uncomfortable silence after Philip reveals his plan to become a Jew in *Gentleman's Agreement* (1947).

a Fairfield county suburb (Darien, Connecticut) that had previously been kept *Judenfrei* by a "gentleman's agreement" between town residents and realtors. Only with Kathy's embrace of what the film defines as right thinking, and Phil's sanctimonious endorsement of that conversion, can the couple give in to mutual attraction and proceed with their planned marriage.

Gentleman's Agreement ignores how anti-Semitism is a collective, trans-subjective, and thoroughly international nexus of beliefs and practices, with a deeply rooted and murderous history whose horrific energies were then on very public display. The Nuremberg trials, which featured the sensational screening of footage of the Dachau concentration camp at the time of its American liberation, had ended with a mass execution of Nazi leaders (October 16, 1946) just as this Fox project was entering its final stages of production. In terms of its topic, many at the time were not reluctant to point out that the film had limited ambitions, as Bosley Crowther reviewing it for *The New York Times* observed. Phil's experience of anti-Semitism, he correctly points out, is "chiefly in the nature of petty bourgeois rebuffs, with no inquiry into the devious cultural mores from which they spring" ("Gentleman's Agreement" 12 November 12, 1947, http://www.nytimes.com/packages/html/movies/best-pictures/gentleman-re.html).

Even from this blinkered American perspective, the understanding promoted by Hobson and then of a cultural discontent is decidedly small beer. But the film offered as threatening an understanding of anti-Jewish sentiments and exclusionary practices as popular fiction and the emerging genre of the social-problem film would dare promote. Kazan's film gives the impression, as Cagle observes with no ironic sense of understatement, that anti-Semitism is "the accumulation of myriad interpersonal interactions, not confrontations between groups visualized collectively" (5). Indeed. And yet what perhaps matters is that the interpersonalization of this melancholy cultural condition permits it to be accommodated to the positive *telos* of therapeutic culture. The film offers the mirage of a solution ironically dependent on the self-satisfying liberalism of those who (like the bulk of the film's audience) actually have little or nothing at stake, and can afford, like Phil, to experience rejection and scorn at second hand, mindful that this calumny is actually misdirected.

Kathy is delivered from ethnic narrowmindedness while the larger society, exposed to the first-person tale of a (what else?) Gentile with whom identification is thereby eased, also gets the message, holding out the possibility of a broader transformation that lies beyond the ability of either film or novel to represent. Such was editor Minify's hope for the story Green agonized to write, and producer Zanuck's expectation for the film Kazan fashioned, with the help of the screenwriters, from Hobson's novel. In its earnestness, the film consciously consecrates itself as a mise en abîme for the process of awakening to injustice and the dispiriting experience of exclusionary practices that prompted its production (especially, the fact that Zanuck, though not a Jew, had been "mistakenly" turned down from membership to the restricted Los Angeles Country Club). Fox's bona fides in promoting this project was acknowledged when the Hollywood branch of B'Nai Brith International chose Zanuck as their "Man of the Year," testifying to his courage in bringing a serious problem out of the shadows and exposing the hurtful prejudice at its center. The largely Jewish Hollywood establishment had worried that the film would pick at the scab of anti-Semitic resentment of their success, arousing the hateful emotions it was committed to extirpating.

Unlike the tradition of engaged filmmaking represented by *Gentleman's Agreement*, the small adult film is disposed to display the resistance of cultural discontents to facile solutions of any kind, including the easily dismissed reformist gestures Kazan and Hobson here deploy, ascribing a power to missionary-style journalism that it only rarely has been shown to possess. Even when dealing with a troubling issue then more or less in the news, the small adult film of the period did not, at story's end, deliver filmgoers to a sense of satisfaction that progress had been made in lessening whatever threats had been exposed as threatening to happiness, both collective and individual. While the Ibsenian heritage of the modern theater includes the dramatization of collective ills (as particularly in *An Enemy of the People* [1882]), this dramatic tradition focuses more on *dépiautage*, as a series of confrontations "peels away" the inauthentic exterior layers of character as presented, revealing the "truth" of self. This dramaturgical method yields acting moments in which the yet-unexpressed inner finds itself transformed into something like a confession as mechanisms of suppression and reticence are whittled away by confrontation and bright shafts of self-insight. In realizing, and then admitting to Phil, that she has been complicit in giving polite cover to anti-Semitic calumny disguised as humor, Kathy has such a moment. The narrative treats her movement of conscience as a positive metonymy. What has emerged as problematic about her as a potential partner is resolved under the therapeutic stress of the interpersonal. Her "case" suggests that an informal movement of sorts opposing un-American prejudice might take shape, motored by the emotional cathexis Green's article makes available.

The small adult film puts such dramatic movement to very different thematic purposes. Fred Zinnemann's *A Hatful of Rain* (1957), based on the Broadway play by Michael V. Gazzo, makes clear how a trajectory of revelation need not be therapeutic. Instead, insight can simply yield a "what is, is" that connects to the tragedy, resistant to amelioration, at the essence of human experience. Johnny Pope (Don Murray) has returned home to New York City addicted to heroin after treatment for battlefield wounds suffered during service in Korea. He has hidden his habit (which is consuming most of the family budget) from his wife (Eva Marie Saint), while his brother Polo (Anthony Franciosa) has been helping him continue to purchase drugs as he loses one job after another. A visit by their father, John Sr. (Lloyd Nolan), complicates matters as Polo finds himself unable to hand over the $2,500 in savings he had promised him now that he has retired. John Sr. blames Polo for betraying his trust but the truth is that the money has been used to help pay down an escalating debt to Johnny's pusher. Celia has come to believe that Johnny is seeing another woman during the hours he spends away from his wife and child; she decides that divorce is the only answer and informs Johnny of her intentions.

The narrative climaxes with a moment of truth telling when Johnny, disgusted that his habit has driven a wedge between his father and brother while alienating him from Celia, confesses to his brother and wife, swearing to go cold turkey in order to end his heroin dependency. There is a more immediate threat and, in resolving it, the narrative provides no more than a false sense of resolution. Johnny's pusher, "Mother" (Henry Silva), has threatened to kill him if he does not get to work paying off his debt by taking up armed robbery. A temporary reprieve, however, is achieved at great cost to a family whose resources have almost all gone up Johnny's arm. Polo sells his car in order to pay off some of his brother's tab, happy to help because, in spite of himself, he has fallen in love with Celia and cannot stand to see her deprived of a husband who gives her some hope of a return to normalcy.

Relieved (if that is the right word) that Johnny's absence does not mean he is leaving her for another woman, Celia pledges her renewed commitment to their relationship. And yet, despite this renewed coupling, there seems little hope for their future. Her prediction that everything will be all right seems all wish and no reality. The family has no more resources, while their connections with one another are revealed as soured by betrayals or failures of different kinds. Johnny's belief that he can "beat" his addiction without treatment is pure self-deception. He has become thoroughly dependent on a powerful narcotic through no fault of his own but the film cannot imagine his misery as part of a more widespread social problem for which some solution can be found. Polo's affection for Celia, and hers for him, is uncovered during the crisis but has nowhere to go. It is a moment of false turning. John Sr.'s plans for retirement remain unfunded and he is now disappointed with both of his sons who, in his eyes, have been shown to be weak and unsuccessful. What the film delivers is no more than the hatful of rain of its title, which we might read as a metaphor for life itself. Certainly this family's collective cup of sorrow runneth over. Like other small adult films, Zinnemann's film reflects a sense of disillusionment with American life. Betrayals destroy trust, private feelings are aired to no useful purpose, the truth sets no one free, while no institution or social force emerges to halt the unraveling of those relationships that once gave life its purpose. That Johnny was decorated for his war service seems little more than a cruel joke in the light of the destructive consequences he suffers through no fault of his own or, indeed, of anyone else. *A Hatful of Rain* is not a film about drug addiction which never figures in it as an "issue"; instead, Zinnemann's subject here is the human condition, the central fact of which is arguably the random nature of misfortune.

With its terrifying Kafkaesque "real" story of an ordinary man wrongfully arrested and nearly imprisoned for a crime he did not commit, Alfred Hitchcock's *The Wrong Man* emerges as an archetypal film of the small adult series, illustrating how much a role chance, as opposed to intention, plays in determining the direction of individual lives. True to the literary traditions they transfer to the screen, the small adult narratives interrogate the efficacy of human action, often revealing as illusion the power we believe we possess to explain, transform, and restore. Like the Popes in *A Hatful of Rain*, the characters in these films often lose their trust in the persistence of the everyday. The key concept here, as William Graebner argues, is contingency.

On the international stage, a similar drama played out between the two powers without whose cooperation and sacrifice the wars against Germany and Japan could not have been brought to victorious conclusions. Cold War culture interestingly reflected the era's mournful, dangerous, and destructive politics, to which we now briefly turn.

Coda: A High Time, Wracked by Fearful Doubt

As a historical term of art, one that is quintessentially American, the Cold War refers to a series of escalating crises of global reach between the United States and the Soviet Union, along with their various allies and proxies. This nexus of conflicts began in the immediate postwar era and lasted until 1991, when the Soviet Union voted itself out of existence and the United States declared victory. Though he did not invent the term, in a short tract entitled simply *The Cold War* (1947), intended for a broad popular readership, American political commentator Walter Lippmann vigorously and successfully promoted the notion that, even though "the war" had ended, new hostilities, best expressed by a paradoxical label, had, as it were, "broken out."

The Soviets, Lippmann declared, had betrayed the promises made at the Yalta Conference (1945) and Western efforts needed to be directed toward forcing the withdrawal of the Red Army from Eastern Europe; the wait-and-see approach, which political adviser George Kennan called containment, was, in his view, simply inadequate, accepting a status quo that needed to be opposed vigorously. Most distressing, of course, was that this conflict set into opposition countries that had for more than three years cooperated successfully in waging a brutal, costly war against Nazi Germany and Imperial Japan (often forgotten is that a late-hour massive Soviet thrust on the Manchurian front, and not the atomic bomb, likely convinced the Japanese to surrender).

Together the United States and the Soviet Union had helped save the world from the fascist powers committed to its total domination. This was no mean feat, and yet it was one that only the Soviets, and not the Americans, were disposed to celebrate. In 1947, while Americans were reading Lippmann's call to arms, filmgoers in the Soviet Union, and throughout Europe and Asia, were viewing the Mosfilm production *Meeting at the Elbe*. This film memorialized the meeting of the two armies near the Elbe town of Torgau on April 25, 1945, an event effectively marking the defeat of Germany. Though it does not shrink from emphasizing the considerable Soviet triumph in winning what the Russians called the Great Patriotic War, *Meeting at the Elbe* offers a tribute to the courage and perseverance of both armies. An effective piece of propaganda, to be sure, the production also testified to the power of cooperation rather than conflict. It is of perhaps some interest that the fiftieth anniversary of the event was widely celebrated in the Russian federation, which even issued a memorial coin. Western countries, including the United States, saw no reason for official remembrance or even mournful recognition of an opportunity lost.

Fear, and its handmaiden distrust, dominate Lippmann's account of the status quo in postwar Europe, with the presumed Communist desire for world conquest simply replacing that of National Socialism. Perhaps speaking for widely shared anxieties, the pundit whips up public sentiment for yet another confrontation at a time when most Americans were in favor of the continuing demobilization of the vast forces that had been built up in order to win the war. Anticipating that an attack on Russia's military establishments might be necessary in order for the Red Army to be compelled to withdraw to pre-war borders, Lippmann argues that "the power of the United States to strike these vital centers ... be built up for the express purpose of giving weight to our policy of ending the military occupation of Europe" (59). Of course, a war that is cold is not a war in any meaningful sense of the term.

And yet ... The depressing notion that another war, albeit undeclared, had already begun was quickly adopted across American culture and then, to some degree, elsewhere in the West. This eagerness to proclaim a new state of hostilities, just as peace was settling in after the most disastrous war in history, might be seen as exemplifying the persecutory delusionism at the heart of paranoia. To be sure, paranoia was a prominent feature of the structure of feeling in postwar America, making itself particularly felt in the emergence and flourishing of the "paranoid thriller" (see Palmer 2006 for further discussion).

Shared by others in the political establishment (especially President Harry Truman and Secretary of State James Byrnes), the view of the Soviet Union as the most perfidious and dangerous of enemies prevailed in the country's political culture even though some of the most experienced Russia hands, especially former ambassador George Kennan, warned that surrendering to this darkest of interpretations of Stalin's intentions posed a long-term threat to American security (see Messer, Kennan 1954 and 1958). In 1946 Kennan played something of a tragic role in the way that believing there was a "cold war" took hold in the United States government and subsequently in the larger culture. He had warned in the famous "Long Telegram" sent from his office in Moscow that the Russians were suffering from "a traditional sense of insecurity" and that their efforts to compete with the capitalist powers and, if possible, undermine them, should be contained (for full text see http://nsarchive.gwu.edu/coldwar/documents/episode-1/kennan.htm). But he had also maintained that the United States should "approach calmly and with good heart the problem of how to deal with Russia" (Long Telegram). Misunderstandings, and an American sense of "insecurity," matched by similar Soviet anxieties about American intentions, soon led to the notion of undeclared belligerence Lippmann popularized in his bestselling book. Americans were quickly mobilized and, not for the first time, to be anti-Red and to view as contingent the peace that many of their countrymen had recently died in order to achieve. What seemed to be a looming threat reinforced, even as it gave geopolitical shape to, a pessimism that had been on prominent display in the national culture beginning in the early 1940s, even before the Soviet Union and United States were forced into an alliance opposing Germany which had invaded the Soviet Union the previous June and then, in the wake of the Japanese assault on Pearl Harbor, declared war on the United States (11 December 1941).

That pessimism did not dissipate even with the overwhelming triumph of American arms and, on the domestic front, an economic boom that brought hitherto unimaginable prosperity. "Fables of virtue struggling to maintain itself in a hostile environment that reflect a profound disillusionment with American idealism," is how historian Nick Smedley characterizes what he calls the "cult of failure" preached in the 1930s and '40s by leading American writers (Ernest Hemingway, Nathanael West, Dashiell Hammett, John Steinbeck, Clifford Odets, F. Scott Fitzgerald, and many others), as well as in much middle-brow fiction (28). Eager to promote projects that, in a film culture becoming ever more sophisticated, could be valued as "art," the industry cooperated in transferring this "cult of failure" to the nation's screens in the first Cold War decades, with a series of productions that could, and often were, regarded as prestigious, even if, or perhaps because, they embodied much of the gloomy uncertainty then very much abroad in American life.

Notes

1. William L. O'Neill, *American High: The Years of Confidence, 1945–1960* (New York: Free Press, 1960). A similar view is offered by Joseph C. Goulden, *The Best Years, 1945–50* (New York: Atheneum, 1976). Of works written at the time expressing an unapologetic optimism in the American future, none, perhaps, was more popular or influential than Eric Johnston's *America Unlimited* (New York: Doubleday, 1944) who observed that "We Americans are optimists . . . It is one of our spiritual dimensions, and therefore stronger than any statistics . . . Defeatism does not suit our national character. We yield to it only rarely and briefly" (15).
2. See, for example, Herbert Aptheker's *The Negro People in America* (1946) which offers a Marxist critique of Myrdal's analysis. For an example of a text central to the earlier understanding in the United States of the discipline of sociology, see Richard Livingstone, (ed.) *The Legacy of Greece* (Oxford: Oxford University Press).
3. Neo-Freudianism in general abandons Freud's emphasis on "instinct," broadly considered as the shaping force of individual human destiny, for the influence of "culture." He was criticized as a result for having abandoned the radical force of Freud's insights for traditional forms of idealist ethics – see in particular, Herbert Marcuse, *Eros and Civilization*.
4. Augustine's melancholy recognition of human limitation found during the postwar era an eloquent spokesman in theologian Reinhold Niebuhr in his *The Irony of American History*. For Niebuhr, the defeat of European fascism and eastern militarism was deeply ironic, calling into question the conventional pieties of the national creed. He opined that "we are the poorer for the global responsibilities which we bear. And the fulfillments of our desires are mixed with frustrations and vexations." Most frustrating, and morally puzzling, was the fact that "the paradise of our domestic security is suspended in a hell of global insecurity," undermining the "conviction of the perfect compatibility of virtue and prosperity which we have inherited from both our Calvinist and our Jeffersonian ancestors" (7).

Bibliography

Balio, Tino (2010), *The Foreign Film Renaissance on American Screens: 1946–1973*, Madison, WI: University of Wisconsin Press.
Cagle, Chris (2016), *Sociology on Film: Postwar Hollywood's Prestige Commodity*, New Brunswick, NJ: Rutgers University Press.
Graebner, William S. (1991), *The Age of Doubt: American Thought and Culture in the 1940s*, New York: Twayne.
Hutner, Gordon (2011), *What America Read: Taste, Class, and the Novel, 1920–1960*, Chapel Hill, NC: University of North Carolina Press.
Imber, Jonathan, ed. (2004), *Therapeutic Culture: Triumph and Defeat*, New York: Routledge.
Jobs, Richard Ivan (2007), *Riding the New Wave: Youth and the Transformation of France after the Second World War*, Stanford, CA: Stanford University Press.
Kennan, George (1954), *Realities of American Foreign Policy*, Princeton, NJ: Princeton University Press.
Kennan, George (1958), *The Decision to Intervene*, Princeton, NJ: Princeton University Press.
Lewis, Jon, (2000), *Hollywood v. Hard Core: How the Struggle Over Censorship Created the Modern Film Industry*, New York: New York University Press.
Lippmann, Walter, (1947), *The Cold War*, New York: Harper & Row.
Messer, Robert L. (1982), *The End of an Alliance: James Byrnes, Roosevelt, Truman, and the Origins of the Cold War*, Chapel Hill, NC: University of North Carolina Press.
Niebuuhr, Reinhold (1952), *The Irony of American History*, New York: Charles Scribner's Sons.
Palmer, R. Barton (2006), "The Hitchcock Romance and the 70s Paranoid Thriller," in Boyd, David and R. Barton Palmer (eds), *After Hitchcock*, Austin, TX: University of Texas Press, pp. 85–108.
Palmer, R. Barton (2016), *Shot on Location: Postwar American Cinema and the Exploration of Real Place*, New Brunswick, NJ: Rutgers University Press.
Palmer, R. Barton and William Robert Bray (2009), *Hollywood's Tennessee: the Williams Films and Postwar America*, Austin, TX: University of Texas Press.
Polan, Dana (1990), *Power and Paranoia: History, Narrative, and the American Cinema, 1940–50*, New York: Columbia University Press.
Rieff, Phillip (1966), *The Triumph of the Therapeutic*, New York: Harper & Row.
Sharp, Joanne P. (2000), *Condensing the Cold War: Reader's Digest and American Identity*, Minneapolis, MN: University of Minnesota Press.
Smedley, Nick (2011), *A Divided World: Hollywood Cinema and Emigré Directors in the Era of Roosevelt and Hitler, 1933–1948*, London: Intellect Books.
Wilinsky, Barbara (2001), *Sure Seaters: the Emergence of Art House Cinema*, Minneapolis, MN: University of Minnesota Press.

5. "I'M LUCKY – I HAD RICH PARENTS": DISABILITY AND CLASS IN THE POSTWAR BIOPIC GENRE

Martin F. Norden

Facing an uncertain future in the years following World War II, the Hollywood studios embarked on several strategies that they hoped would lure audiences away from their new leisure activities and back into movie theaters. From his perch as resident film critic for the *New York Times*, Bosley Crowther identified one of the earliest tactics: the development of a genre that featured stories loosely based on the lives of then-famous celebrities. "The makers of Hollywood's films are nowadays doing something which they usually avoided in years gone by," he declared in January 1946. "They are frankly making many movies about real-life personalities." As Crowther further noted, the American film industry had begun moving away from a *roman-à-clef* approach to current biography (or a *cinéma-à-clef* approach, perhaps) in favor of a more straightforward one. "Hollywood has entered a phase wherein it strives to give [the] illusion of actuality to many of its stories of contemporary life," he wrote, "and so it is making film biographies of living persons (or those but recently deceased) with personal identifications freely and proudly proclaimed."[1] Simply put, the classic Hollywood biographical film, or "biopic," had been reborn.

Building on the decidedly mixed tradition of biographical films produced during the war years,[2] the studios created a range of adulatory tributes to veterans and civilians alike who had recently been in the public eye or perhaps still were. Often laden with splashy production numbers, the biopics featured a general storyline that the studios thought would appeal to postwar audiences, particularly disabled veterans and their families: a larger-than-life personage struggling to "overcome" a disabling circumstance while at or nearing the height of his/her career. The figures and films in this strand included composer Cole Porter in *Night and Day* (1946), professional baseball player Monty Stratton in *The Stratton Story* (1949), pop singer Jane Froman in *With a Song in My Heart* (1952), opera diva Marjorie Lawrence in *Interrupted Melody* (1955), naval captain John Hoskins in *The Eternal Sea* (1955), naval lieutenant commander Frank "Spig" Wead in *The Wings of Eagles* (1957), and pre-presidential Franklin Roosevelt in *Sunrise at Campobello* (1960). In each case, the lead character undergoes a life-changing disabling circumstance only to make a comeback that the filmmakers framed as unambiguously heroic and inspirational. Often populated with Hollywood "A"-list actors such as John Wayne, Cary Grant, and James Stewart, the films imply that the same extraordinary determination that got their characters to the top of their professions led to their eventual "triumph" over their debilitating conditions.

This chapter examines the narrative and thematic concerns of this core group of Hollywood biographical films as they played out from the mid-1940s to the early 1960s, a time that biopic scholar George Custen has characterized as the last major period of the Hollywood biographical film.[3] It will also examine the biopics' decline following the success of *The Miracle Worker* in 1962 and the rise of disability-themed films during the 1960s and '70s that took a very different turn from the biopics by depicting the lives of ordinary people with disabling circumstances.

A brief word needs to be said about this chapter's general approach to the post-World War II biopics: a disability studies perspective. Disability studies is a relatively young discipline that locates the impaired human body as the site of often conflicting discourses. Among its concerns is the portrayal of people with disabilities (PWDs) in popular culture, and it addresses this concern through an interrogation of disability representations – a reading of them "against the grain," so to speak – in order to uncover their submerged attitudes, assumptions, and agendas.

Disability studies scholars have soundly rejected the paradigm that has structured the thinking on disability since the latter part of the nineteenth century: the medical model, which privileges physicians and other health-care practitioners while treating disability as an individual's physical and psychological problem to be overcome. These scholars have instead embraced the social model, which takes the view that a person's disabled status is a sociocultural construct. Far from regarding PWDs as tough-luck, physically flawed individuals who only need the right attitude to succeed, disability studies scholars contextualize them as members of a political minority that has historically endured widespread ableist bigotry, paternalism, and indifference. They draw an important distinction between "impairment" and "disability" as leading disability studies scholar Rosemarie Garland-Thomson has observed:

["Impairment"] is a term that disability scholars and activists use to denote functional limitation. "Disability," on the other hand, is a term we use to describe the system of representation that produces discriminatory attitudes and barriers to full integration. In essence, "impairment" and "illness" are about bodily differences, whereas "disability" is about the social and political context in which our bodies operate. The distinction is much the same as the one that scholars often draw between "sex" and "gender."[4]

Guided by the belief that society relies heavily on the popular culture that surrounds it for information about disability, this chapter's examination of postwar biopics draws on a disability studies sensibility. It follows a general perspective that I have articulated elsewhere: namely, that a mainstream society will employ various channels of discourse, such as films, to define the issues, and these actions have historically included the positioning of PWDs as outliers with low social approval. The Hollywood studios, catering to the needs of the dominant culture with which it is interwoven, have "Otherized" PWDs in various ways: as fear-mongering villains; as embodiments of pitiable childlike innocence who deserve to be cured; as comic troublemakers; or, in the case of the films under scrutiny here, as awe-inspiring figures placed up on pedestals. At the expense of the country's PWD minority, the resulting films have had the effect of allaying the dominant culture's collective guilt, fears, and uncertainties about disability while reinforcing its cohesion.[5]

A key disability studies text that informs this study of postwar biopics is Paul Darke's "Understanding Cinematic Representation of Disability" which posits that the struggling-to-overcome-a-disability film, or what Darke calls the "normality drama," is a genre in and of itself. Including both patently fictive films and putatively historical (but often no less fictive) ones such as biopics, normality dramas typically assert in no uncertain terms that all will be neatly resolved once the lead characters have "triumphed" over their disabling circumstances. As Darke wrote, "The normality drama initially, and superficially, represents disorder and chaos – abnormality – so that order and stability can be created in the denouement of the narrative thrust, thereby providing both entertainment and a simple resolution to the highly complex social 'problem' of abnormality and disability."[6] Anchored in the medical model tradition, the normality drama places the burden of "overcoming" squarely on the shoulders of the individual while glossing over – or, far more typically, ignoring – such social concerns as discrimination, prejudice, class difference, issues of access and transportation, and inequalities of educational and employment opportunities.

If we accept Darke's argument that such films indeed constitute a genre, we can make the case that the films discussed in this chapter sit at the intersection of two genres: the biography and the normality drama. Put another way, we might argue that the films are integral members of a hybrid genre: the disability-themed biopic. By uncovering the workings of these films, I hope readers will be in a better position to understand the general Hollywood "take" on disability during the postwar period and, as "oppositional readers," will see the need for resisting the films' questionable messages.

General Characteristics

The postwar biopics cover a range of high-visibility occupations and personal stories, many of which are related directly or indirectly to World War II. All the represented figures had lived through the war and some of their war-related experiences were laced into the films. As Bosley Crowther further observed in his 1946 essay, the studios were taking full advantage of the spate of recent personal narratives published in newspapers, magazines, and ghosted autobiographies. "This trend toward the 'living biography' has been encouraged, in part, by the wealth of personality stories which have come out of the war," he wrote. "The dozens of thrilling real-life dramas which have been generously reported in the press have provided a new source of legend."[7] As we shall see, however, the similarities among the films extended far beyond the films' wartime context to include issues such as disability, class, race, sexual orientation, and, as Crowther's use of the word "legend" would suggest, a particular narrative pattern.

The most obvious among the films' overlapping concerns is fame; their characters are often quite famous and at, or heading toward, the apex of their careers. In other words, the figures are not ordinary people at all but inhabit worlds far removed from the circumstances of most audience members. For example, *Interrupted Melody*'s Marjorie Lawrence (Eleanor Parker) is a globetrotting operatic soprano renowned for her Wagnerian interpretations, while *With a Song in My Heart* details the extensive stage, nightclub, and radio career and volunteer work of the popular Missouri-born chanteuse Jane Froman (Susan Hayward).

Some of the films show their characters before they entered the international spotlight, such as *Night and Day*'s representation of Cole Porter (Cary Grant) as a college student, *Interrupted Melody*'s portrayal of Marjorie Lawrence as a worker on her family's sheep farm, and *Sunrise at Campobello*'s imaging of Franklin Roosevelt (Ralph Bellamy) during his pre-gubernatorial and pre-presidential years. A strong sense of inevitability envelops these films, however; there's no question that the characters' reputations preceded them and that the filmmakers played upon audiences' prior knowledge of these figures and who they became. The filmmakers often had the actors play the characters in their pre-fame days essentially the same way as in their later years: that is, as if they

Figure 5.1 Franklin Roosevelt (Ralph Bellamy) charms his daughter Anna (Zina Bethune) with a story in *Sunrise at Campobello* (1960).

were already famous. For example, *Night and Day* director Michael Curtiz had Cary Grant play Cole Porter with the same panache at all stages of Cole's adult life including his years at Yale, even though Grant, at age forty-two, was rather long in the tooth to be playing a college student. Similarly, Ralph Bellamy played *Sunrise at Campobello*'s Franklin Roosevelt with mannerisms associated with the latter's presidential years, such as speaking with a cigarette holder protruding at a jaunty angle from his mouth, even though the film was set in the early 1920s. This point was not lost on film critic Crowther who, in a 1960 *New York Times* review, generally praised *Campobello* but complained about Bellamy's "tendency to overdo some of the famous Roosevelt expressions – at least, more famous in later years than the ones of his early political probing represented here."[8] In addition, Bellamy's dyed hair did little to obscure the fact that he, at age fifty-six, was closer in age to FDR during the latter's White House years than during the time period covered in the film.

Another major characteristic of these films is that their characters' impairments are all related to mobility: the partial or complete loss of leg function. Furthermore, the impairments are not genetically based; instead, the characters acquired them through injury or sudden illness, and only as adults. For example, *The Stratton Story*'s Monty Stratton (James Stewart) accidentally shoots himself in the leg during a hunting trip on his family's farm in 1938, jeopardizing his career as a top pitcher for the Chicago White Sox, while Cole Porter is thrown from a horse spooked by lightning late in *Night and Day*, undergoes more than two dozen surgeries, and gets about on crutches or in a wheelchair. Jane Froman, en route to a United Service Organizations tour in Europe in early 1943, endures a horrific accident; her plane crashes into the Tagus River near Lisbon, leaving her with a nearly severed left leg, a compound fracture in her right leg, and multiple fractures in her right arm. Marjorie Lawrence and FDR both contract poliomyelitis, she while in the midst of a global opera tour and he while vacationing with his family on Campobello Island in New Brunswick, Canada. In *The Eternal Sea*, John Hoskins (Sterling Hayden) loses a leg in a shipboard accident during the military engagement at Leyte Gulf, while *The Wings of Eagles*' Frank Wead (John Wayne), an accomplished Navy pilot who tirelessly promoted U.S. military naval aviation, becomes paralyzed after a fall down a flight of stairs at his home.

Not all of the disabling circumstances were directly related to World War II but all were refracted, in a sense, through the prism of the war. For instance, Monty Stratton, who eventually returned to professional baseball following the amputation of his severely injured right leg, was not a war veteran but the actor who played him, James Stewart, was a highly decorated bomber pilot who had flown numerous combat missions over Europe only a few years before. The presence of the iconic Stewart, one of Hollywood's most famous veterans, made it exceptionally easy for audiences to ascribe a veteran-like quality to the Stratton persona he played.

Following its character's acquisition of the impairment, each film then addresses the key "normality" narrative ingredients observed by Paul Darke: the characters' despair, struggle, and ultimate "triumph" with the help of significant others. An extended case in point is *Interrupted Melody*, which tells the story of Australian diva Marjorie Lawrence, whose "melody" is "interrupted" when she collapses during a rehearsal in Mexico City in 1941. Upon learning that she has polio, she becomes extremely depressed and resists all therapeutic suggestions offered by her husband Thomas King (Glenn Ford), an American physician. When he says he only wants to help, she cuts him off with "You're a doctor – help me to die." Later, after Thomas thwarts a suicide attempt by Marjorie, the filmmakers had her utter an explanation that reflects the typical Hollywood perspective on characters with severe impairments. "I can't go on anymore," she says to her husband. "Not like this. It's no marriage, no life, nothing! I can't give you anything – home, children, family." He counters her intense, suicidal self-loathing with the magical words that solve almost anything in Hollywood movies: "But I love you."

Though Marjorie eventually comes around to the belief that life remains worth living, she stubbornly refuses to sing in public anymore. That perspective changes, too, after an army doctor asks her to perform for the benefit of disabled veterans at a nearby hospital. She initially declines, citing her use of a wheelchair. "Well, you see, I – I'm in this thing all the time," she says. After

Figure 5.2 Marjorie Lawrence (Eleanor Parker) sings "Over the Rainbow" for disabled World War II veterans in *Interrupted Melody* (1955).

reflecting on the physician's brief but compelling response – "So are a lot of the boys" – Marjorie accepts his invitation. In the very next scene, she wheels herself among the disabled vets while warbling the familiar Harold Arlen–E. Y. Harburg ballad "Over the Rainbow," and she finds the experience so rewarding that she eventually returns to the operatic stage. The film's final shot, which shows her standing and basking in the adoration of the Metropolitan Opera audience after her comeback performance, leaves no doubt that she has "triumphed."

Issues of class, race, and sexual orientation go largely unaddressed in the biopics. The films seldom if ever imply that their characters, all of whom are endowed with the privileged status of white heterosexuality,[9] are socially or financially disadvantaged in any significant way either before or after their accidents/illnesses; indeed, the characters typically enjoy high socioeconomic standing. Some, like Cole Porter and Franklin Roosevelt, were born into wealthy families, graduated from elitist schools (Yale and Harvard, respectively), and speak with cultured accents, while others, who come from less privileged backgrounds, are reasonably well off as result of their successful careers. For example, *Interrupted Melody* underscores the point that Marjorie Lawrence rose from humble beginnings as a farm girl in Deans Marsh, Victoria, just as *The Stratton Story* notes Monty Stratton's early experiences as a Texas farm boy. In short, the characters were either born into wealth, reached a comfortable standard of living as a result of their life's work, or both. Though the trappings of upper-class life may be amply on display (such as the Porter family mansion replete with African American servants in *Night and Day*), the films do not explore the topic of class in any meaningful way; instead, the characters' privileged class status, just like their race and sexual orientation, is treated as a given. There is seldom any sense that the characters have to struggle financially in their post-disablement lives; medical and surgical treatment, hospital stays, rehabilitation, and so on, just happen seemingly without regard to their enormous expense. In other words, the films do not imply that the financial burden associated with PWD status – a burden that very much includes a dearth of meaningful employment opportunities and the distinct possibility of a life of poverty – is of any concern to the characters. "I have no personal complaints," says Franklin Roosevelt to his mother Sara Delano Roosevelt (Ann Shoemaker) in *Sunrise at Campobello*. "I'm lucky – I had rich parents."

Another issue is the almost complete lack of discrimination and other social ills typically encountered by PWDs. Day-to-day concerns, such as prejudice, lack of universal access, inadequate transportation, and so on, seldom, if ever, rear their ugly heads in these productions. The only thing that comes close is the social disapproval of the characters' status as PWDs, and it is often handled subtly – that is, under the guise of pity. In no way do the films attempt to address or explore this disapproval on a critical basis; it is simply another unspoken "given."

On the questions of class and prejudice, it is well worth comparing the postwar biographic films with a disabled-veteran biopic produced during the war: *Pride of the Marines* (1945). This Warner Bros. film reconstructs the experiences of Al Schmid (John Garfield), a Philadelphia steelworker who enlisted two days after Pearl Harbor and was blinded by a Japanese grenade during Guadalcanal.[10] Though technically a postwar film (it was released on August 24, 1945, a mere nine days after the Japanese surrender), *Pride* was written and produced during the war and reflects progressive sentiments characteristic of Hollywood at the time. It differs from the later biopics in two key respects: it dwells on the experiences of a lower-class "average Joe" kind of character, and it addresses discrimination against PWDs. In particular, it explicitly compares ableism with anti-Semitism. Consider the following dialogue spoken by Lee Diamond (Dane Clark) to Al, his blinded friend and fellow veteran:

> Sure, there'll be guys who won't hire you even when they know you can handle a job. There's guys that won't hire me because my name is Diamond instead of Jones. 'Cause I celebrate Passover instead of Easter. Do you see what I mean? You and me, we need the same kind of world; we need a country to live in where nobody gets booted around for any reason.

Yet, in the new cautious and conservative era of the late 1945s and 1950s, when the U.S. House Committee on Un-American Activities investigated what it believed was leftist subversion in Hollywood, such pleas for tolerance and understanding quickly vanished. The blacklisting of progressive-minded Hollywood personnel, such as *Pride of the Marines*' lead actor John Garfield and principal screenwriter Albert Maltz, had a chilling effect on the film industry. Warner Bros. production head Jack Warner may have had *Pride* in mind when he proclaimed in 1945 that he was through making films about "the little man,"[11] by implication preferring instead to create lavish productions like his studio's *Night and Day* that centered on famous, well-to-do people.

In their lack of attention to discrimination, class, and related issues, the postwar biopics were hardly different from many disability-themed fictional films produced before the war. A key factor which distinguishes them from the pre-war films, however, is the question of cure; the postwar biopics do not feature their lead characters cured of their impairments while many 1920s and '30s films did. The newer films reflected a major Hollywood shift in thinking about disability. For pre-war film producers, the promise of a harmonious life for disabled characters coded as "good" frequently included the guarantee of a cure. (Villainous disabled characters such as the many played by Lon Chaney during the 1920s were, of course, a different matter; they would usually be dead by the end of the film or ejected from the narrative in some other way.) Plying their craft at a time when serious injury or illness was sometimes tantamount to a death sentence, these earlier filmmakers were uncomfortable with the idea that good people might live out the rest of their lives with permanent impairments. To them, "goodness" and "disability" were incompatible concepts; if "goodness" was the dominant quality of the characters, then the "disability" factor needed to be effaced by the end of the films. By taking the easy and sentimental way out and rewarding the characters with a one-way ticket back to able-bodied society in the form of a cure, the filmmakers conveniently skirted the long-term implications of permanent impairment. By the post-World War II period, when PWDs were living longer lives as a result of medical and surgical advancements, the facile and completely restorative cure had become an increasingly untenable and unnecessary narrative proposition. The postwar filmmakers, perhaps realizing that audiences were not buying the concept of cure anymore if they ever did, jettisoned the idea in short order.

The postwar biopics, however, frequently offered a rather questionable strategy in place of the obsolete concept of the miracle cure: the inclusion of a climactic scene in which the disabled character "passes" as able-bodied while performing in front of an audience. *Interrupted Melody* shows Marjorie Lawrence dramatically standing up and taking a few steps at the climax of her comeback performance in Wagner's *Tristan und Isolde*,[12] for instance, while an audience of service people applauds when Jane Froman enthusiastically throws away her crutches before launching into a medley of patriotic tunes in *With a Song in My Heart*. In another example, *Sunrise at Campobello* concludes with Franklin Roosevelt rising from his wheelchair and taking ten long lonely steps to the podium at the 1924 Democratic National Convention in Madison Square Garden to deliver a nominating speech on behalf of Al Smith. The noisy convention venue grows dead silent as FDR, using crutches, walks toward the podium; after he arrives, his son James (Tim Considine) surreptitiously removes the mobility appliances. The film's final shot is a lingering view of Franklin standing tall behind the podium unencumbered by any mobility aids, and the film concludes before he actually delivers his speech. Dore Schary, the film's screenwriter and producer, attributed overwhelming importance to the scene. "This was the moment that was to affect the entire world," he proclaimed, "because this was the moment at which Roosevelt returned to politics." In actuality, however, FDR did not walk to the podium unassisted, as the film implies.[13] Conceptually and perhaps uncoincidentally, this concluding shot is identical to the final shot of *Interrupted Melody*; in each case, the camera pulls back from the now-standing heroic figure who soaks up the tumultuous applause from an enthusiastic audience.

Not every biopic featured an explicit "passing" scene. For instance, *The Wings of Eagles*' Frank Wead, a World War I veteran who helped develop United States naval air power during the 1920s and had a second career as an author of books, short stories, magazine articles, and screenplays, does walk a few steps but with the help of supportive friends. Nevertheless, all of the films imply that the characters must liberate themselves from their wheelchairs in order to be judged as having fully returned to their respective fields. Indeed, Dore Schary said as much about Franklin Roosevelt in his comment on *Sunrise at Campobello*'s concluding scene, noted above. For Hollywood, wheelchairs symbolized a kind of powerlessness and confinement at odds with the sense of "heroic overcoming" the studios were trying to convey.[14] An additional and unstated message is that, *sans* wheelchairs, the newly liberated and invigorated figures would not be burdens on society.

A case in point that illustrates both the low social approval of PWDs and several "passing" strategies is the concluding set of scenes of *Night and Day*. Cole Porter, having been shown using a wheelchair after his surgeries, has returned to his alma mater to perform with a college chorus and string orchestra. His estranged wife Linda (Alexis Smith) belatedly arrives at the Yale concert hall and eagerly looks toward the stage. The camera slowly dollies in on Linda's face, and then the film cuts to show the object of her gaze: Cole, photographed from the rear and in long shot, as he slowly ascends the stage's steps with the aid of canes. The film cuts back to a close-up of Linda's face, which has disappointment written all over it. Lest the audience miss the point, the filmmakers had a deep shadow quickly envelop her face as she watches; it is a dark moment for her, figuratively and literally. Moments later, Cole, seated at a grand piano while he, the chorus, and the orchestra are about to

Figure 5.3 Cole Porter (Cary Grant) is surprised to see his wife in the audience during a Yale concert performance in *Night and Day* (1946).

perform the title tune, spies Linda in the audience. The camera moves away from Cole to show the chorus and orchestra but, when it pivots back to the piano seconds later, he is nowhere to be seen; the filmmakers had him exit off-camera to meet Linda alone outside the building. In other words, the filmmakers did not want the audience to witness the spectacle of a less than fully able-bodied Cole getting up and moving away from the piano. It's a kind of "invisible" passing, not unlike the frequent stage-managing of Franklin Roosevelt's news media appearances to avoid showing his use of a wheelchair during his presidential years. Once Cole and Linda are outside the concert hall, the filmmakers presented a more conventional passing scene; the characters walk toward each other – Cole barely needing his canes – and embrace in an emotional moment designed to assure Linda and the audience that Cole has fully "returned."

The filmmakers behind the military-themed productions *The Eternal Sea* and *The Wings of Eagles* did not seem particularly interested in creating the illusion of passing but their films imply more strongly than the others that the central characters have been symbolically disempowered and need to be "remasculinized," perhaps to show that patriarchal values had not been permanently weakened during the war. These two films, both produced in the mid-1950s, celebrated a Cold War neo-heroism; John Hoskins eventually reaches the rank of admiral and serves in the Korean War despite having lost a leg during World War II, while the paralyzed Frank Wead returns to the ranks as a naval tactician after Pearl Harbor and eventually sees action against Japanese forces. In other words, the films suggest that it's not enough for the disabled veterans to be reintegrated into American society in gratitude for their service, as they were in such prominent wartime biopics as *Thirty Seconds Over Tokyo* (1944) and *Pride of the Marines*. Instead, the vets have to prove their mettle – or prove it again, perhaps – by going back on active duty and simultaneously showing that they will not be burdens on society. In this regard, *The Eternal Sea* and *The Wings of Eagles* are no different from the other postwar biopics in that their central characters resume their high-profile careers following their "triumphs."

Contextual Considerations

What are we to make of these representations? What kind of messages do they seem to be sending? Superficially, the films suggest that their central figures are heroes and heroines in whom audiences should take national pride; they reflect mainstream American values (even if one of the characters – Marjorie Lawrence – wasn't an American but was played by one). A closer reading, however, suggests a number of other things adumbrated below.

The Hollywood studios were quite aware of the influx of disabled veterans coming back to the States during and immediately following the war, and it is reasonably clear that they wanted to make films that presented a "buck up" message and taught a lesson. As we have seen, though, the resulting biopics did not feature average people who were now disabled; instead, the message seemed to be rooted in a pedestalization that asked viewers to be inspired by, and learn from, the examples of famous people. Indeed, *The Stratton Story* concludes with an off-screen narrator intoning the sentence "He stands as an inspiration to all of us," the phrase "he stands" taking on a special meaning not only for this particular film but also for the entire strand of biopics of which it is a part. A comment by Bosley Crowther at the end of his biopics article, that Hollywood "endeavors to give us the exquisite power to see ourselves (or our fellow mortals) in the glamorous stereotypes of make-believe,"[15] seems particularly applicable to disabled veterans. It is well worth noting that several films – *Night and Day*, *With a Song in My Heart*, *Interrupted Melody*, *The Eternal Sea*, perhaps others – have disabled veterans among the central character's onlookers, including a few who have small speaking roles. While watching Cole mount the concert stage near the end of *Night and Day*, for instance, one disabled vet in the audience turns to another and asks, "What are you thinking about? He did all right, didn't he?" In a moment meant to represent an epiphany, the second vet pauses and then gratefully replies "Yeah" before the twosome turn their attention back to Cole. In a sense, these minor characters served as surrogates for disabled veterans watching the films. The studios clearly wanted a second order of viewing to take place; disabled vets in the audience would watch and presumably identify with the disabled vets on screen who, in turn, admiringly watch the larger-than-life characters transition back to "normal" life.

Reflecting a new conservatism in the wake of the Cold War, the films implied that PWDs should not rely on government or society in general for help. The message seemed to be that, if you are a PWD, you are mostly on your own and have only the people in your immediate orbit – family, friends, neighbors, physicians, nurses, physical therapists – willing and able to provide support. In this regard, the films arguably took a key element of the American mythos, the notion of rugged individualism, and distorted it in the name of a conservative agenda: keeping PWDs off of public support and making little if

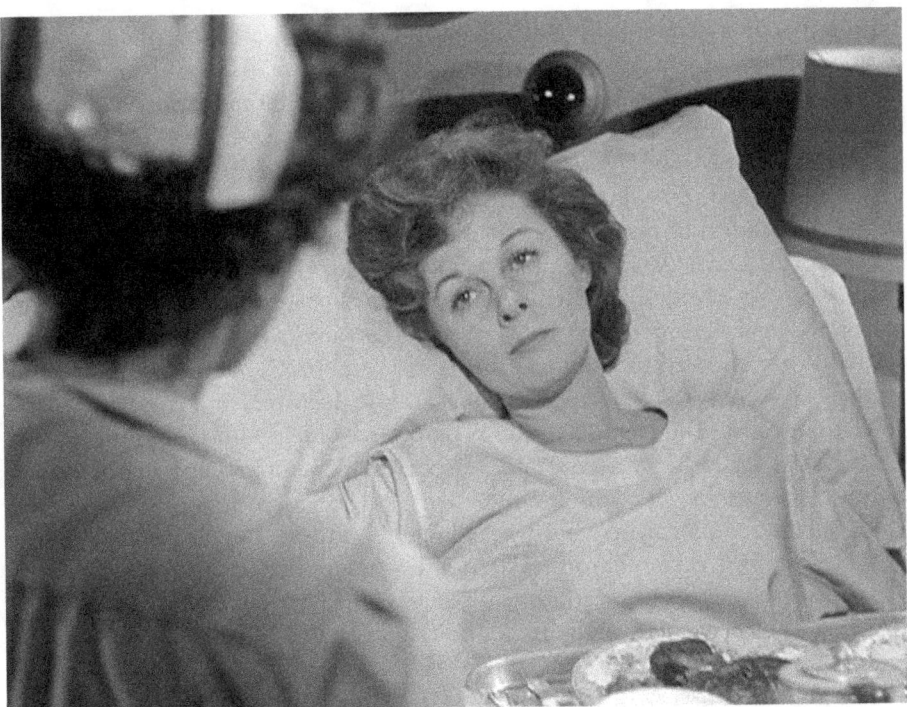

Figure 5.4 "You haven't got what it takes – guts!": Jane Froman (Susan Hayward) receives a reprimand from her nurse in *With a Song in My Heart* (1952).

any effort to compel society to accommodate their quotidian needs and enforce their civil rights.

Another concern is the extent to which the PWDs themselves participated in the films based on their lives. None of them played themselves, though Jane Froman did provide the vocalizations that were spiritedly lip-synced by Susan Hayward in *With a Song in My Heart*; instead, able-bodied actors played the disabled characters, a phenomenon that many in the disability community have likened to white actors in blackface playing African Americans. Though the PWDs may have served as consultants, they typically had little if any say on the final versions of the films that supposedly told their life stories. As an example, *Interrupted Melody* screenwriters William Ludwig and Sonia Levien made a point of interviewing Marjorie Lawrence for their script but the singer later expressed dissatisfaction with the film, saying it did not accurately represent her life.[16] And, as George Custen has observed, Cole Porter signed an agreement with Warner Bros. that gave the studio absolute freedom to fictionalize his life experiences, which it did.[17]

A Winding Down

The arrival of several key films in the early 1960s suggested that the formulaic biopic/normality drama was rapidly coming to a close. The first, *The Miracle Worker*, represented a major break with the other biopics discussed in this chapter. Though its lead character, Helen Keller (Patty Duke), acquired her impairments from a non-genetic source, just like the other figures, and became world renowned, the film shows her only during her pre-fame days; there's no representation of her adult years and no semi-obligatory passing scene. In other words, Helen wasn't already well known for something else, as were the other biopic celebrities. In a sense, the *Miracle Worker* filmmakers flipped the essential narrative; their film implied that the same extraordinary spirit and tenacity that allowed the youthful Helen to "triumph" over her impairments led her to become world famous (as an author, lecturer, and social activist – roles that go unvisualized in the film but were widely known by audiences), rather than the other way around. Also unlike the characters in the earlier biopics, she was a very young child – only nineteen months old – when she acquired her impairments, both of which, blindness and deafness, differed notably from the other characters' loss of leg function. With the war gradually receding into the country's collective memory, the studios began moving away from contemporary figures with mobility-associated impairments that were related to, or coincided with, the global conflict.

The arrival of a very different film – *Dr. Strangelove, or How I Learned to Stop Worrying and Love the Bomb* – in 1964 seemed to sound the death knell for this variant of the biographical film. Though not a biopic, *Dr. Strangelove* exhibits several similarities to the disability-themed postwar biographical film. Most notably, it features a world-class figure who happens to be disabled: the title character (Peter Sellers), an expert on global political affairs and weaponry development, who uses a wheelchair and sports a bionic arm that has the unsettling tendency to choke its owner or give Nazi salutes. Dr. Strangelove also performs a "passing" act at the film's conclusion; with the world on the brink of nuclear annihilation, he rises dramatically from his wheelchair and takes a few halting steps. "Mein Führer! I can walk!" he exclaims to U.S. President Merkin Muffley (also played by Sellers). Best remembered as a satire on Cold War geopolitics, *Dr. Strangelove* in its own "strange" way is also a parody of the normality drama with its larger-than-life individual who triumphs over his disability, albeit mere seconds before the film concludes with a montage of atomic bomb blasts.

Parodies often suggest that the genres with which they are associated have come to the end of their current cycle, and *Dr. Strangelove* is no exception. The kind of biopic discussed in this chapter began fading fast after its approximately fifteen-year run, to be replaced by a different type of disability-themed production: the fictional film that featured ordinary and sometimes impoverished people who happen to be disabled. Exemplary films, all of which are beyond the scope of this chapter, include *A Patch of Blue* (1965), *The Heart Is a Lonely Hunter* (1968), *Midnight Cowboy* (1969), *Tell Me That You Love Me, Junie Moon* (1970), *Butterflies Are Free* (1972), and *Coming Home* (1978). Produced outside of the rapidly collapsing Hollywood studio system and informed by the increasing societal attention to civil rights, discrimination, poverty, and the divisive war in Vietnam, these 1960s and '70s films portrayed situations vastly different from those of the post-World War II biopics. The movie industry occasionally returned to the disability-themed biopic during the 1970s with such films as *The Other Side of the Mountain* (1975) and *The Other Side of the Mountain Part II* (1978), both of which focused on Olympic hopeful Jill Kinmont (Marilyn Hassett) who was seriously injured in a skiing accident, and the made-for-television production *Wilma* (1977), on Olympic sprinter Wilma Rudolph (Shirley Jo Finney), who had contracted polio as a child, but such films had essentially run their course.

Concluding Thoughts

Presumably designed to be inspirational, the biopics discussed in this chapter promoted the unfortunate message that disabilities are personal medical problems, not social constructs or identity factors; in other words, the films conflated "impairment" and "disability" as disability studies scholars have defined the terms. The biopics heavily imply that a major dissonance exists between a person's PWD status – which typically bears low social approval – and a high level of fame and accomplishment. The films would have their audiences believe that these factors are contradictory and cannot coexist, and thus the normality drama pattern suggested by Paul Darke plays itself out. In addition, the biopics seldom if ever addressed issues related to prejudice, civil rights, access, transportation, and so on, and completely failed to acknowledge the poverty and joblessness faced by so many PWDs. Finally, the movies seemed to say that, to succeed, people with disabilities need only follow the tough-love admonitions of the people around them and develop the "right attitude."

With a Song in My Heart offers a powerful illustration of this last point. When Jane Froman laments post-injury that "I'll never be a normal woman again," her personal nurse Clancy (Thelma Ritter) delivers a stern rebuke intended to get under the singer's skin; she declares that Jane still has her voice and face but doesn't have guts. Needless to say, the hectoring works. The implied message of this film and the other biopics to PWDs in the audience was clear; if they ignore the advice of the physicians and other able-bodied people in their lives and do not make that lonely and heroic effort to "conquer" their impairments, they are failures.

I base this last observation on the work of Irving Kenneth Zola and Stella Young, both of whom wrote in depth about the lived experience of PWDs. Zola was one of the earliest disability studies scholars to identify the mixed messages embedded in what he termed "the great achievement syndrome" conveyed in disability-themed biopics and other biographical texts. As he noted in 1982:

> In almost all the success stories that get to the public there is a dual message. The first one is very important—that just because we have polio, cancer, or multiple sclerosis, or have limited use of our eyes, ears, mouth, or limbs, our lives are *not* over. We can still learn, be happy, be lovers, spouses, parents, and even achieve great deeds. It is the second message which I have recently begun to abhor. It states that if a Franklin Delano Roosevelt and a Wilma Rudolph could *overcome* their handicaps, so could and should all the disabled. And if we fail, it's our problem, our personality defect, our weakness [emphasis in original text].[18]

In an addendum to his 1982 book, Zola pinpointed the disconnect between these narrative vehicles and the everyday experiences of PWDs:

> All this further masks what chronic illness and disability are all about. For our lives or even our adaptations do not center around one single activity or physical achievement but around many individual and complex ones. Our daily living is not filled with dramatic accomplishments but with mundane ones. And most of all, our physical difficulties are not tempo-

rary ones to be overcome once-and-for-all but ones we must face again and again for the rest of our lives. That's what chronic means![19]

Going a step further, we might say that the biopics qualify as early examples of "inspiration porn," a term made famous by disability activist Stella Young in a 2012 *Ramp Up* webzine editorial for the Australian Broadcasting Corp. Though Young was referring mainly to the depictions of PWDs doing perfectly ordinary things, her comments readily apply to the biopics. For example, she suggested that inspiration porn exists "so that non-disabled people can put their worries into perspective." Some of her comments echo those of Irving Zola:

> Inspiration porn shames people with disabilities. It says that if we fail to be happy, to smile and to live lives that make those around us feel good, it's because we're not trying hard enough. Our attitude is just not positive enough. It's our fault. Not to mention what it means for people whose disabilities are not visible, like people with chronic or mental illness, who often battle the assumption that it's all about attitude. And we're not allowed to be angry and upset, because then we'd be "bad" disabled people. We wouldn't be doing our very best to "overcome" our disabilities.[20]

Though the postwar biopics commendably show their main characters getting on with life after a major traumatic event in their lives, the paths they take to reach that point are at best problematic as I hope this chapter has shown. The challenge for today's audiences is to recognize that these films are not just period pieces that reflect antiquated views but that their messages still coincide with some people's perceptions of the disabled experience and of the "proper" attitudes that PWDs should cultivate to succeed.

Notes

1. Bosley Crowther, 'Living Biographies, Hollywood Style,' *New York Times*, January 20, 1946, section 6, p. 24.
2. The wartime biopics, which included *Young Tom Edison* (1940), *Edison, the Man* (1940), *Sergeant York* (1941), *The Pride of the Yankees* (1942), *Yankee Doodle Dandy* (1942), *Thirty Seconds Over Tokyo* (1944), *Wilson* (1944), and *Pride of the Marines* (1945), ran hot and cold at the box office. Among the disappointments were *Young Tom Edison*, which featured MGM star Mickey Rooney as the famed inventor early in life, and *Wilson*, Darryl Zanuck's tribute to Woodrow Wilson, which garnered five Oscars but tanked at the box office. Audiences seemed little interested in the lives of people from an earlier era, though some of these films had considerable propaganda value during World War II. The films with disability themes listed above are discussed in Martin F. Norden, *The Cinema of Isolation: A History of Physical Disability in the Movies* (New Brunswick, NJ: Rutgers University Press, 1994), pp. 148–62 *passim*, p. 188.

3. George F. Custen, *Bio/Pics: How Hollywood Constructed Public History* (New Brunswick, NJ: Rutgers University Press, 1992), p. 2.
4. Rosemarie Garland-Thomson, "The FDR Memorial: Who Speaks From the Wheelchair?" *Chronicle of Higher Education,* January 26, 2001, p. B11.
5. Norden, pp. 1–6.
6. Paul Darke, "Understanding Cinematic Representations of Disability," in Tom Shakespeare (ed.), *The Disability Reader: Social Science Perspectives* (London: Cassell, 1998), p. 184.
7. Crowther, p. 24.
8. Bosley Crowther, "Screen: Intimate Portrait," *New York Times,* September 29, 1960, p. 32.
9. The famously gay Cole Porter would ordinarily have been an exception but the *Night and Day* filmmakers removed all overt traces of his sexual orientation.
10. For a comparison of the film with the historical record of Al Schmid's life, see David A. Gerber, "In Search of Al Schmid: War Hero, Blinded Veteran, Everyman," *Journal of American Studies,* 29, April 1995, pp. 1–32.
11. Warner quoted in Gordon Kahn, *Hollywood on Trial: The Story of the 10 Who Were Indicted* (New York: Boni & Gaer, 1948), p. 11. As Kahn, a blacklisted screenwriter, sardonically noted of Warner on the same page, "it can be said that he has kept his word."
12. To accentuate the poignancy of the moment, the filmmakers included a mirroring gesture in a cutaway shot. Upon witnessing Marjorie's climactic rise, her husband Thomas, seated backstage, stands up, too.
13. Schary quoted in Murray Schumach, "Democrats 'See' 1924 Convention," *New York Times,* April 21, 1960, p. 24. Eyewitness accounts indicate that FDR, using crutches, was escorted to the podium. For example, see John Stuart, "Roosevelt Nearly Names Al Smith," *New York Sun,* June 26, 1924, p. 14.
14. There are, of course, exceptions to this general rule. For example, Lionel Barrymore, an actor who used a wheelchair during the latter stages of his career, exuded considerable power and authority in just about every film in which he appeared. See Norden, pp. 145–8.
15. Crowther, "Living Biographies," p. 46.
16. Barbara Jamison, "Biography Boom," *New York Times,* May 8, 1955, section 2, p. 5; Helga M. Griffin, "Lawrence, Marjorie Florence," in Bede Nairn and Geoffrey Serle (eds), *Australian Dictionary of Biography,* Vol. 10: *1891–1939, Lat–Ner,* (Melbourne: Melbourne University Press, 1986), p. 15.
17. Custen, p. 119.
18. Irving Kenneth Zola, *Missing Pieces: A Chronicle of Living with a Disability* (Philadelphia: Temple University Press, 1982), pp. 204–5.
19. Irving Kenneth Zola, "Communication Barriers Between the Worlds of 'Able Bodiedness' and 'Disability,'" *Australian Disability Review* 1, no. 3 (1988), p. 31.
20. Stella Young, 'We're Not Here for Your Inspiration,' *Ramp Up,* Australian Broadcasting Corp., July 3, 2012. http://www.abc.net.au/news/2012-07-03/young-inspiration-porn/4107006.

Filmography

Ashby, Hal, 1978: *Coming Home.*
Auer, John, 1955: *The Eternal Sea.*
Bernhardt, Curtis, 1955: *Interrupted Melody.*
Brown, Clarence, 1940: *Edison, the Man.*
Curtiz, Michael, 1946: *Night and Day.*

Daves, Delmer, 1945: *Pride of the Marines.*
Donehue, Vincent, 1960: *Sunrise at Campobello.*
Ford, John, 1957: *The Wings of Eagles.*
Green, Guy, 1965: *A Patch of Blue.*
Greenspan, Bud, 1977: *Wilma.*
Hawks, Howard, 1941: *Sergeant York.*
Katselas, Milton, 1972: *Butterflies Are Free.*
King, Henry, 1944: *Wilson.*
Kubrick, Stanley, 1964: *Dr. Strangelove, or How I Learned to Stop Worrying and Love the Bomb.*
Lang, Walter, 1952: *With a Song in My Heart.*
LeRoy, Mervyn, 1944: *Thirty Seconds Over Tokyo.*
Miller, Robert Ellis, 1968: *The Heart Is a Lonely Hunter.*
Peerce, Larry, 1975: *The Other Side of the Mountain.*
Peerce, Larry, 1978: *The Other Side of the Mountain Part II.*
Penn, Arthur, 1962: *The Miracle Worker.*
Preminger, Otto, 1970: *Tell Me That You Love Me, Junie Moon.*
Schlesinger, John, 1969: *Midnight Cowboy.*
Taurog, Norman, 1940: *Young Tom Edison.*
Wood, Sam, 1942: *The Pride of the Yankees.*
Wood, Sam, 1949: *The Stratton Story.*

Bibliography

Crowther, Bosley (1946), "Living Biographies, Hollywood Style," *New York Times*, January 20, section 6, pp. 24 and 46.

Crowther, Bosley (1960), "Screen: Intimate Portrait," *New York Times*, September, p. 32.

Custen, George F. (1992), *Bio/Pics: How Hollywood Constructed Public History*, New Brunswick, NJ: Rutgers University Press.

Darke, Paul A. (1998), "Understanding Cinematic Representation of Disability," in Tom Shakespeare (ed.), *The Disability Reader: Social Science Perspectives*, London: Cassell, pp. 181–97.

Garland-Thomson, Rosemarie (2001), "The FDR Memorial: Who Speaks From the Wheelchair?," *Chronicle of Higher Education*, January 26, p. B11.

Gerber, David A. (1995), "In Search of Al Schmid: War Hero, Blinded Veteran, Everyman," *Journal of American Studies*, 29, April, pp. 1–32.

Griffin, Helga M. (1986), "Lawrence, Marjorie Florence," in Bede Nairn and Geoffrey Serle (eds), *Australian Dictionary of Biography*, Vol. 10: *1891–1939, Lat–Ner*, Melbourne: Melbourne University Press, pp. 14–15.

Jamison, Barbara (1955), "Biography Boom," *New York Times*, May 8, section 2, p. 5.

Kahn, Gordon (1948), *Hollywood on Trial: The Story of the 10 Who Were Indicted*, New York: Boni & Gaer.

Norden, Martin F. (1994), *The Cinema of Isolation: A History of Physical Disability in the Movies*, New Brunswick, NJ: Rutgers University Press.

Schumach, Murray (1960), "Democrats 'See' 1924 Convention," *New York Times*, April 21, p. 24.

Stuart, John (1924), "Roosevelt Nearly Names Al Smith," *New York Sun*, June 26, p. 14.

Young, Stella (2012), "We're Not Here for Your Inspiration," *Ramp Up*, Australian Broadcasting Corp., July 3, [http://www.abc.net.au/news/2012-07-03/young-inspiration-porn/4107006].

Zola, Irving Kenneth (1982), *Missing Pieces: A Chronicle of Living with a Disability*, Philadelphia: Temple University Press.

Zola, Irving Kenneth (1988), "Communication Barriers Between the Worlds of 'Able Bodiedness' and "Disability,'" *Australian Disability Review* 1, 3, pp. 29–32.

6. ROGUE NATION, 1954: HISTORY, CLASS CONSCIOUSNESS, AND THE "ROGUE COP" FILM

Robert Miklitsch

> Surely this is not the best of possible worlds since we can easily conceive of possible worlds that are better.
>
> Gottfried Wilhelm Leibniz, *Theodicy*

In 1954 the hydrogen bomb or H-bomb – 2,250 times as powerful as the atom bomb that was dropped on Hiroshima – was exploded at Bikini atoll in the Pacific; Wisconsin Senator Joseph McCarthy was condemned by the United States Senate, at the time only the fourth person in its history to be so censured; and the U.S. Supreme Court ruled that "separate facilities [for Negroes] are inherently unequal," outlawing segregation in public schools.[1]

If the "outstanding feature of the crime film" in 1950s America "was its focalization of the audience through the perspective of the cop,"[2] Fritz Lang's *The Big Heat* (1953) can be said to dramatize the period's racial and atomic structures of feeling even as it indexes one of the dominant subgenres of the '50s crime film: the syndicate film.[3] The syndicate film, in turn, can be said to represent the "criminal-cop moment of the McCarthyite crime film"[4] in which the nationwide "combine" exposed by the Kefauver Committee is the domestic other of the "red menace," itself understood as the Big Other. From this dual perspective, the "rogue cop" film can be said to promote the individual against the totalizing forces of Cold War society which is epitomized, in the political and criminal spheres, by pervasive corruption. The prototype here is *The Racket*, John Cromwell's 1951 remake of Lewis Milestone's 1928 picture where Captain McQuigg (Robert Mitchum) is the "rogue cop" double of "rogue gangster" Nick Scanlon (Robert Ryan) and where McQuigg, like Scanlon, is an anachronism in a "post-war corporate world" in which "old-style civic duty" is opposed to the slave-wage, alienated labor of the cop on the street.[5]

A slightly different dynamic, one infused by personal vengeance, obtains in *The Big Heat*. In his reading of Lang's film, Tom Gunning observes that "in some of the strongest films of the 50s" the rogue cop "affirms an ideal justice untrammeled by official corruption or incompetence, but he also risks becoming indistinguishable from the gangster he fights."[6] The narrative must therefore "resolve the cop's quest not only by defeating the gangster but with a renunciation of violence."[7] While this is an accurate description of *The Big Heat*, it does not really do justice to *The Big Combo* (1950), the other "rogue cop" picture that Gunning invokes. Leonard Diamond (Cornel Wilde) in Joseph Lewis's film is certainly zealous about rooting out the criminal element but his disgust of the underworld, as embodied in the figure of mob boss Mr. Brown (Richard Conte), is arguably motivated by his homosocial envy of the racketeer's "high society" moll, Susan Lowell (Jean Wallace).

In fact, though *The Racket* and *The Big Heat* are representative, not to say classic examples of the genre, the "rogue cop" film cannot be reduced, topically speaking, to either vigilante violence or governmental corruption. As in any (sub-) genre, the protagonist's motivation tends to be more complex than not. Consider, for instance, one of the seminal "rogue cop" films, *Where the Sidewalk Ends*. In Otto Preminger's 1950 picture, Mark Dixon's (Dana Andrews) treatment of criminal suspects is marked by physical violence and grim self-righteousness but his crusading behavior derives less from his idealism than from the fact that his own father was a mobster. (In this, he's not unlike Jim McLeod [Kirk Douglas] in William Wyler's *Detective Story* [1951].) If other policemen, like Jim Wilson in Nicholas Ray's *On Dangerous Ground* (1952), suffer from the occupational hazards of the job, burn-out verging on unbalance, still others such as Ed Cullen (Lee J. Cobb) in Felix Feist's *The Man Who Cheated Himself* (1951), Paul Sheridan (Fred MacMurray) in Richard Quine's *Pushover* (1954), and Cal Bruner (Steve Cochran) in Don Siegel's *Private Hell 36* (1954) are driven by sex or, in the paradigmatic case of Webb Garwood (Van Heflin) in Joseph Losey's *The Prowler* (1951), sex *and* money.[8]

One cannot perhaps emphasize the last meme – call it capital – enough. Thus, if it's true that in 1950s Hollywood cinema "cultural politics shifted away from working-class concerns," it's also true that the "protagonists of the now dominant police procedural" who "surveyed and policed the neighborhoods" were nonetheless anxious about their place in the pecking order in an age when Americans were fast becoming "status seekers."[9] William McGivern's novels – from *Shield for Murder* (1951) and *The Big Heat* (1953) to *Rogue Cop* (1954) and *Odds against Tomorrow* (1957) – are especially significant in this regard since the métier of his protagonists tends to be law enforcement and the milieu of his fiction proletarian.

While the film adaptations of *Rogue Cop* and *Shield for Murder* are not as well known as *The Big Heat* and Robert Wise's *Odds against Tomorrow* (1959), the first-mentioned McGivern novels and adaptations are provocative in their own right, not only shedding shadow, as it were, on the "rogue cop" genre but also on the contentious issue of class in mid-century Cold War America. For instance, *Rogue Cop* mobilizes the familiar and familial trope of two brothers – one a veteran, one a rookie; one bad, one good – in order to explore the lure of easy money for law-enforcement officers trying to live on sixty-five dollars a week. Whereas Rowland's film depicts the protagonist's abrupt volte-face and eventual redemption, however, *Shield for Murder* tracks a detective who, embittered at being on the outside of the high life, goes from bad to worse when he murders a bookie and steals his payoff in order to pursue the American Dream in the form of a suburban tract home. In fact, the protagonist's ignominious death in Edmond O'Brien and Howard W. Koch's film gives the lie to the received wisdom about the glorification of law and order in the 1950s crime film; not so incidentally, it also calls into question the middle-class-based consensus of the Cold War, as if the rogue cop were an inverted or displaced symptom of the "red" or alien other in all of us.

Prologue: Castle

McGivern's *Rogue Cop* opens with police detectives playing cards to kill time until the "murder, knifings, and shootings would bring the game to an end."[10] At the card table, Detective Sergeant Mike Carmody is dealing, his "big clean hands spraying the cards about with expert speed": "Everything about him looked hard and expensive, his gray flannel suit had cost two hundred dollars and was superbly fitted" (10). The "tell" here, though subtle, is the dissonance between the "clean" hands and the "expensive," two-hundred-dollar suit.

Not unlike Larry Gordon and Vince Stone in *The Big Heat*, Carmody lives in an apartment building with a doorman and canopied entrance in a "three-room suite on a premium floor high above the city's noise and dust" (54). In other words, Carmody's hands are clean but the closet in his bedroom suggests it's because they're manicured:

> A dozen suits faced him in a neat row and there was a line of glossy shoes with wooden blocks inside them in a rack on the floor. On either side of the suits were cedar-lined drawers filled with shirts, socks and underwear, and smaller trays containing cuff links, tie-clips, handkerchiefs, a wallet and cigarette cases. Carmody took out a blue gabardine suit,

a white shirt and a pair of cordovan shoes which had been shined and rubbed until they were nearly black. (56–7)

If the blue suit points up Carmody's occupation as a detective, the "gabardine" cloth, like the row of suits and "premium" apartment, not to mention the "nearly black" shoes, are a hint that the police department isn't his only employer.

Early in the novel, Carmody is summoned to the apartment of one of his employers, big-time "gambler and racketeer" Dan Beaumonte. Before Beaumonte and his partner Ackerman arrive, Mike admires the view with Beaumonte's girlfriend Nancy: "The city was beautiful now, the lights spreading over it like an immense sparkling carpet. On the twenty-fifth floor of a massive building which overlooked the park and a long curving stretch of the river. Like a castle, Carmody thought. With a safe view of the slaves" (18). The architectural resemblance between Carmody's and Beaumonte's apartments is not accidental. Unlike Barney Noland (Edmond O'Brien) in *Shield for Murder*, Mike doesn't have to steal from a bookie to purchase a tract home in Castle Heights; he's already made it by being a sergeant detective *and*, as Beaumonte later describes what he does for Ackerman, keeping an "eye on the bookies."

The "big boys" want to see Carmody because Mike's "kid" brother, Eddie, a rookie cop, just witnessed Delaney, one of Beaumonte and Ackerman's hoods, standing over a dead man. The bad news is that he got away. BEAUMONTE: "If [Eddie] had killed the bastard right there, he'd have done us a favor" (23). The good news – at least for the syndicate – is that there's still time for Mike to talk to Eddie before he's scheduled to testify at the trial. "If your brother doesn't play ball," Beaumonte warns, "we'll have to handle it our way." The only problem is that Eddie, unlike his older brother, doesn't wear two-hundred-dollar gabardine suits or live in a castle overlooking the river. In other words, he doesn't mind being down in the "noise and dust" of the city. He's happy, in Mike's twisted terms, to be a slave.

Rogue Cop: "A Houseful of Taxes"

Scripted by Sidney Boehm, Roy Rowland's *Rogue Cop* is one in a series of "dark crime films" produced by MGM in the 1950s. The first part of the opening credit sequence – a montage of police activities (a prowl car, a cop walking his beat, an officer typing a report) – is photographed in the bright, high-key lighting associated at the time with Metro. Suddenly, in conjunction with the producer Nicholas Nayfack's and director Roy Rowland's names, it's night, a cruiser's racing down an avenue toward the camera, and we're plunged – via a strung-out, kerchiefed woman rushing down the street – into the swirling chaos of the dark city.

The woman, who's just exited a burlesque house, enters a Penny Arcade where she's surveilled by "Wrinkles" Fallon (Peter Brocco) who's pretending to be looking through a kinescope. After another man in a dark suit enters a telephone booth, then exits, the woman goes into the booth, pockets the drugs, and deposits some money. As the man's retrieving the money, however, Fallon sticks him with a knife, "You're through working my territory." Though Eddie Kelvaney (Steve Forrest) stops Fallon as he's leaving the arcade – his car is "over-parked" – when a woman screams and a man rushes out of the arcade shouting "A man's been stabbed!" Eddie's momentarily distracted and Fallon drives off.

Cut to a police station as Detective Sid Myers (Robert Ellenstein) strolls into the back room – a poker game is in progress – where he announces that Eddie had Fallon with the "meat in his mouth, but didn't know he was the killer." One of the card-playing detectives makes a big raise and Detective Chris Kelvaney (Robert Taylor) remarks, "Won't get rich changing the rules in the middle of a deal," to which the chided detective responds, "is that how you got rich? Following the rules?" Meanwhile, Myers, who has been bartering with another one of the card-playing detectives for his sandwich, takes out his coin purse and carefully extracts thirty-five cents.

The above, seemingly mundane sequence is important for two reasons. First, it sets up an opposition between the "poor" detectives, Myers in particular, and the "rich" Kelvaney. Second, in the novel, Carmody knows that he has the winning hand but folds, reflecting as he does, "Myers, pulling in his money triumphantly now, was like most cops, brave, honest, and dumb" (12). The fact that in the film Kelvaney plays the winning hand – significantly, kings – and pockets the cash indicates that he's not only taking money from the syndicate but from his fellow, poorly paid detectives.

Later, after Eddie, with Chris's help, identifies Fallon in a lineup, the two Kelvaneys burst into a pool hall where they bust up another poker game and arrest "Wrinkles," an act that underscores the older brother's bond with his younger brother and his tenuous but residual affiliation with the other "brothers" in the police department. As soon as Chris returns to the police station, however, he takes a phone call from Beaumonte (George Raft) and is ordered to meet him at the racetrack. While Beaumonte's ensconced in an upscale restaurant populated with, as he tells his lush girlfriend Nancy Corlane (Anne Francis), "refined people" – he's watching a race with a pair of binoculars – he issues another, non-negotiable order: that Eddie can't make the identification because, as we later learn, Fallon has a photograph in his possession that could incriminate Beaumonte. For Eddie's troubles (it'll cost him his job), he'll be paid the tidy sum of $15,000. Chris reluctantly agrees to talk to his brother and, as he's departing, Beaumonte offers him his winnings from the race. Although Chris declines ("Not this time"), the similarity of the "racetrack" scene with the previous, "poker" one is striking. Earlier, while playing cards, Kelvaney was perfectly willing to take money from his fellow detectives. Now the rules of the game have changed: because he's not willing to gamble with his brother Eddie's life, he's starting to have second thoughts about working for Beaumonte and Ackerman (Robert F. Simon).

In *Shield for Murder* Barney Nolan shoots a bookie in the back and steals the $25,000 payoff for a bet to purchase a suburban tract home for his fiancée. In *Rogue Cop* all Eddie Kelvaney has to do is "square the beef" and he'll be able to afford, like his big brother, sharp suits and a river-view apartment. In fact, not unlike Barney, Eddie's thinking about asking his singer girlfriend Karen Stephanson (Janet Leigh) to get married. At a bar where he's waiting for her to get off from work and where his brother has come to talk to him about Beaumonte's "offer," Chris reminds him that "marriage is tough on sixty-five dollars a week." If he changes his story, though, he'll get "more money than [he] can save in a lifetime pulling police boxes." Though Eddie allows that he may be "dumb," he prefers, true to his father's ideals, to "stick with the ribbon clerks."

As in *Shield for Murder*, the locations in *Rogue Cop* elucidate the characters' class status and aspirations. Beaumonte's apartment – the balcony of which, as in the novel, looks out over the city ("Like living high in a castle," Nancy muses) – is spacious and expensively furnished. While Kelvaney's one-bedroom apartment is more compact, it's lavishly decorated in the most contemporary, "masculine" style, including a cocktail table with a polished ice bucket and a chrome-and-glass seltzer bottle that gleams in the light. Karen Stephanson's place is, by contrast, "cozy," as Chris notes when he first sees it. A studio apartment, it's softly lit and white, like the color of Karen's negligée. If Chris's dark suit and brusque manner – "I know who you are and what league you played in" – clash with the dominant tonality of the room, which is light like Karen's hair and the blond maple furniture, her fold-out bed and lingerie also code her as a "good bad girl." In fact, Chris, having previously met her when she was living in Miami, knows that she was seriously involved with a gangster there named Frankie Nimo. When, however, Karen protests, Chris kisses her – initially, against her will – to prove that they're the "same kind of dirt."

The brownstone where Chris grew up and where he's arranged to talk to Eddie again about changing his story is the last interior location we're introduced to and it's arguably the most significant one in *Rogue Cop* not simply because it reflects their father's Irish, Old World values but because Eddie still lives there. In McGivern's novel, as soon as Carmody returns to the old neighborhood, he thinks: "He had lived in this neighborhood until he was twenty-seven, increasingly bored by the middle-class monotony of the people" (71). His reaction is even more pronounced once he enters his father's house: "he hated the uncertainty and guilt this shabby, middle-class world produced in him" (72).

For Carmody, the house is associated with his father's "immutable categories of conduct" (72) – about, that is to say, his father's uncompromising notions of right and wrong. Consequently, once Chris went to work for Beaumonte and "learned that his job could be made to pay off like a rigged slot machine," his father couldn't conceal his disdain about the "source of the money" as well as the "new convertible, the good clothes, the expensive vacations" (72).

In the film, the interior of the brownstone, decorated with plant stands and a player piano, overstuffed loveseat and flower-print wallpaper, isn't "shabby," it's Victorian. The only anomaly is a series of framed newspaper articles on the wall: PATROLMAN KELVANEY CAPTURES BANDITS/KELVANEY CITED – MADE DETECTIVE/KELVANEY IS MADE DETECTIVE SERGEANT. Like his father, Eddie once admired his older brother – "I'm the kid who used to hang around when you were on traffic and watch you blow the whistle and wave your arms" – until one day, in a locker-room, "in the old 27th precinct," another cop said to him about Chris, "Kid, your brother's got the right idea, take it big or don't take it at all."

The turning point in *Rogue Cop* occurs in the immediate wake of Chris's unsuccessful appeal to his younger brother's worst instincts. When Chris subsequently shows up at Beaumonte's apartment at the appointed hour without Eddie and having lied about his brother being on board, the big boys decide to cut him loose. Johnny Stark (Alan Hale, Jr.), Beaumonte's bodyguard, is escorting him to the door when Chris coldcocks "Stumblebum" and, in the extended fight that follows, the two men trash the apartment. Though the brawl abruptly ends when Chris hits Johnny in the windpipe with his forearm, Beaumonte exclaims, "No stupid jerk like your brother is gonna louse us up!" In response, Chris slaps Beaumonte across the face; then, when Beaumonte's about to take a swing, punches him in the gut, sending him to the floor gasping for air and holding his stomach. Nancy, who's stewed to the gills, adds insult to injury –"Daddy got a tummy ache? Big man kick you back to the gutter?" – before she unceremoniously dumps a bucket of ice on his head.

If "Kelvaney's fight with Beaumonte is his first brush with physical violence," the irony is that "it takes place in the mobster's luxurious apartment, so that as Kelvaney breaks up his expensive furniture he is also destroying the basis of his own insular mentality."[11] Actually, Kelvaney's first brush with physical violence happens at his father's house when his brother Eddie punches him after Chris throws Karen Stephanson's relationship with Nimo in his face. Kelvaney also initiates the fight with Johnny. The three punches, however, are linked: while Eddie's punch compels Chris to reconsider his relationship with the syndicate, Chris's coldcock of Johnny is intended not simply to disarm "Stumblebum" but to provoke Beaumonte into reacting. Therefore, if Chris's "self-justification for being on the syndicate payroll is a personal distaste for the brutality of everyday police work" – if, in short, "he uses his money to

Figure 6.1 Chris Carmody (Robert Taylor) about to pay off newsstand stoolie Selma (Olive Cary) in fotobusta for *Rogue Cop* (1954).

insulate himself from what he sees as sordid and demeaning"[12] – the "street" fight at Beaumonte's apartment is a sign that he's ready to get down and dirty again.

Chris is sitting at the bar at the Fanfare Club nursing a drink and nervously trying to locate Eddie's whereabouts when he receives a reprieve. Beaumonte, who's lounging at his apartment in a smoking jacket and toying with a match cover, telephones to relate that Kelvaney has another forty-eight hours to get his brother to change his mind. In the middle of the night, however, a disheveled Nancy shows up at Chris's apartment – she's been "worked over" by Fanzo's men (it's implied that she's been raped, perhaps repeatedly) – and Chris learns that Eddie has been "shot down in the street": "two bullets in the back," execution-style. It's only after Eddie dies and Chris is face to face with his body in the morgue (Father Ahern arrives while he's there to administer "last rites") that Chris confesses to Lieutenant Bardeman (Roy Barcroft) that he's a "crooked cop": "Those are dirty words, but they fit." Though Inspector Cassidy (Robert Burton) asks for his badge, District Attorney Powell (Carleton Young) is convinced by Kelvaney's argument that because he's on the inside, he's the only one who can bring down the syndicate: "I've got a witness who can give you every man, every date, every payoff." POWELL: "Who is he?" KELVANEY: "Me."

HISTORY, CLASS CONSCIOUSNESS, AND THE "ROGUE COP" FILM

As in the opening montage of *Rogue Cop*, Rowland's film is premised on a high contrast between "Kelvaney's world and that of the streets."[13] In other words, if Kelvaney is initially seen in "well-lit rooms, relaxed and groomed as he goes through a charade of police work," "Eddie is photographed on his night beat, cautiously patrolling neighborhoods of cheap bars and flophouses separated by dark alleyways."[14] Chris begins the hard work of being a police detective again by talking to Selma (Olive Carey), a grizzled old woman who works at a newsstand and who, like Moe (Thelma Ritter) in *Pickup on South Street* (1953), is a "stoolie." (The first time that we see Kelvaney talking to Selma, he's paging through a glamour magazine; the second time, he's perusing one called *Crime*.) In exchange for $5,000 – Chris writes an IOU for the money and she shrewdly insists that he postdate the note in case he ends up dead – Selma gives him the address of the West Coast "hatchet man," Joey Langley (Vince Edwards), who killed his brother. She agrees, moreover, to get the word out to Beaumonte's stoolies that he's on his way to pick up Langley.

Chris is walking to his car, the camera tracking in reverse as he passes bars and billboards ("The Bam Girl"), pawnshops and storefronts ("Cut Rate Records"), when he sees Sid Myers who has been ordered to shadow him. Myers knows exactly what Chris is thinking: "Sid Myers, another dumb cop who waits around in his thirty-buck suit of clothes until it's time to collect his pension." Kelvaney, though, has begun to mend his ways, "Maybe I even wish I was a cop with a thirty-buck suit." More importantly, when Sid learns that he has a chance to apprehend a cop killer, he agrees to work with him. The two men proceed to the basement of the syndicate's billiards room where they learn that Beaumonte and Ackerman appear to have taken the bait and where Chris, using his badge and his former "crooked" relation to Beaumonte ("I work for Dan, I'm a cop"), tricks and arrests Langley.

As Chris and Sid are taking Langley away – the setting is a silent, deserted, rain-slick street at night – the headlights of a car parked in the shadows across the way suddenly come on. In the subsequent sequence, which transposes the action from the tasteful, well-tended interior of Beaumonte's high-rise apartment to the "noise and dirt" of the streets, Chris shoots Ackerman at point-blank range before Beaumonte shoots and gravely wounds him. Beaumonte's frantically trying to start his car when Sid, who's also been wounded, steals up to the passenger-side window and – again, at point-blank range – shoots and kills him.

Rogue Cop ends on a not unambiguous note: with Sid, his arm in a sling, at his side, Chris Kelvaney lies like a corpse on a gurney as the ambulance disappears into the night. The ambiguity, relative to other "rogue cop" films, is apropos. While Kelvaney redeems himself by setting a trap in which he knows he may be killed, unlike Bannion (Glenn Ford) at the end of *The Big Heat*, he's not actively back on the force and, if he survives, he may well be going to jail. At the same time, the conclusion of *Rogue Cop* can be said to effect a happy ending, however qualified, as it represents an affirmation of the solid, middle-class values associated with his father, his brother, and Sidney Myers. Previously, right before Eddie was about to introduce him to Karen at the Fanfare, Chris reminded him to "tell her about the Kelvaneys and the Kings of Ireland": "We Kelvaneys owned a dozen castles." Eddie's reply – "I never met a Mick whose family didn't own one or two" – wryly undercuts his brother's aristocratic claim. In America, there are no kings, popular music aside, and the Kelvaneys, as their father's brownstone demonstrates, do not own a castle. Hence the only other framed item on the wall in Patrick Kelvaney's living room is a certificate from the Statewide Consolidated Gas Company where he slaved his whole life for, as Chris snidely puts it when he's arguing with Eddie, "fifty bucks a week."

In the last economic instance, the mise-en-scène of the penultimate sequence of *Rogue Cop* – VALUABLE FRONTAGE FOR LEASE – is unusually evocative, recollecting as it does the ending of *Shield for Murder*. That Beaumonte's hitman is hiding out there suggests that this "frontage" is not in fact "valuable"; that the syndicate, as McGivern puts it, is "squeezing the heart out of the [city] for its own profit" (136). In the novel, Lieutenant Wilson tries to explain to Kelvaney that the syndicate's days are numbered:

> The city's changing . . . defense plants have come into this town in the last few years and the men running them pay a houseful of taxes. And they want value from them. Parks, schools, things like that. They don't want bookies and brothels and bars. Neither do the unions. And when you get the unions working on the men who run the companies you get a clout that can stand up to Ackerman and Beaumonte. (81)

McGivern here appears to be invoking the historic accords between capital and labor that were enacted in the 1950s and that were the catalyst for the rise of the middle class in the United States in the same period. "Houseful of taxes" is, in this historical context, a rich locution. If you're fortunate to own, say, a detached, single-family home, you're also obliged to pay taxes on it, albeit – if you're middle class – rather less than a "houseful." In return (and this is the social contract), you get parks and schools and cops – in the best of all possible worlds, *good* parks and schools and cops.

Prologue: Dirt

In *Shield for Murder*, McGivern elaborates on Barney Nolan's past – in particular, the forbidding, urban environment in which he grew up: "Nolan had been born in the section of Philadelphia called Brewerytown and had grown up fighting the Jews from Strawberry Hill and the Italians that came from South Philly . . . Nolan's father, a brawling, blustering laborer, championed Barney's fights, and threatened to beat him senseless if he ever took any dirt from what he called the foreign element."[15]

In the novel, we also learn how Barney became a policeman, and this backstory – necessarily elided in the film – is tangled up not with "reform" elections, as it is in *The Big Heat*, but "ward" politics:

> his break came in the '34 Mayoralty campaign, when the Ward Leader had been genuinely worried for the first time in twenty-nine years. Barney had weighed one-ninety then, had a minor reputation as a street brawler; and used his physical endowments to chase the Democratic canvassers off the street. He put two of them in Jefferson Hospital, and pretty soon the Democrats were afraid to step into the ward. (71–2)

As compensation for his intimidating tactics, the Ward Leader advised Barney to "take the exams for the police department" and "six months later he received his appointment" (72). Then he "accidentally got in right with old Mike O'Neill" – he let O'Neill's brother go after stopping him for drunk driving and running a red light – and the "fluke had landed him on the detective force" (72). He was with "Foot Traffic," a beat cop, for ten years and then in Germantown, "a monotonous dead end," for six more before he was transferred to Center City (30). But even in Center City, Barney's on the outside looking in:

> Everybody had money, but there wasn't a chance for him to get at it. Some cops, just a few to be sure, were in on the take from the night-club owners, racket men, and gamblers, but not Nolan. He had lived on the fringes of a set that enjoyed easy money, easy living and easy women . . . He had gone along as usual on forty-eight dollars a week; and, as usual, the smart people had written him off as another dumb cop. (30)

The last part of this passage recalls Webb Garwood's lacerating description of himself at the beginning of *The Prowler* – before, that is, he gets smart and kills Mr. Gilvray (Emerson Tracy). Like Garwood before he goes rogue, Barney Nolan is a good, "clean" cop – at least in terms of corruption – yet he can't help thinking about the fast set: the easy money and women and living. And, like a lot of noir characters, he's laboring under the yoke of Necessity: 'Luck, fate, God's will . . . What was it that jerked him around like the dummy on the end of a string?' (72–3).

Shield for Murder: Castle Heights

Directed by noir stalwart Edmond O'Brien and producer Howard W. Koch, *Shield for Murder* opens not with God but Barney Nolan jerking the string and turning the Wheel of Fortune. In the first, pre-credit sequence in the film, Barney strides down the street before slipping into the shadow of a doorway to screw a silencer on to the barrel of his revolver. Kirk Martin, a bookie, stands on the curb talking to two men in a car. Once Martin concludes his business, he's walking away when Barney catches up with him and, throwing an arm around his shoulder like an anchor, steers him into a dark alley. Martin, terrified, offers Barney more and more money to let him go, but Nolan's been tipped off that the bookie has $25,000 on him. Barney promptly shoots Martin in the back, then, after unscrewing the silencer from the handgun and rifling through the bookie's jacket pockets for the money, screams "Stop or I'll shoot!" before firing his gun twice into the air. Unknown to him, an elderly, deaf and dumb man, Ernest Sternmueller (David Hughes), has seen everything from a high apartment window that looks out on to the alley. As passersby crowd noisily into the alley, the film cuts to the title: *SHIELD FOR MURDER*.

In McGivern's novel, the narrator makes note of bookie Dave Fiest's "slender, neatly tailored back" (5). Later, Barney remembers that the first time he met Fiest, he was wearing a "beautiful, light-weight gabardine [suit] with hand-stitched lapels; and when [he] waved for drinks, he'd seen the flash of gold cuff links and a diamond ring" (35). Like Vince Stone (Lee Marvin) in *The Big Heat*, Fiest's clothes and accessories signify his membership in the fast, smart set. One difference between McGivern's novel and the film, however, is that, in the book, Barney doesn't know how much money the bookie has on him; he just knows that "Fiest, like all bookies, carried his assets in a liquid form and close at hand" (26). The difference is important because, whereas in the novel, Fate still has a hand in Nolan's fortunes, in the film, Barney already knows that the money – "the payoff on a big bet" (26) – belongs to Packy Reed (Hugh Sanders), a small-time mobster who is principled when it comes to his money: which is to say, he'll want it back on the pain of death.

Another difference between the novel and film is that, while Barney's antagonist in McGivern's book is newspaper reporter Mark Brewster, in O'Brien and Koch's picture Brewster (John Agar) is a young, fellow detective who's Nolan's protégé. Though there's an investigative reporter in the film as well, Cabot (Herb Butterfield), the investigation is conducted by Brewster who, despite his affection for Barney, is determined to follow the case where it leads him, even if it means taking down his mentor. In fact, Brewster's investigation is mediated, as in McGivern's novel, by Nolan's girlfriend who, like Mark, wants to believe that Barney's not guilty of murdering a man in cold blood just for the money.

In the novel Barney's girlfriend, Linda – Patty Winters (Marla English) in the film – is central to McGivern's exploration of the politics of class as well as Nolan's desire forever to change his proletarian station in life – to be on the inside looking out. Linda's a singer at the Simba, a "fashionable nightclub" with an "elegantly dressed doorman and a green-and-white canopy that extended from the club's double-glass doors to the street" (27). If the Simba is an object of Barney's class resentment – 'He saw [the politicians and racket men], night after night, sitting around ... and heard them talking about big days at the track, watched them pick up fifty dollar dinner checks, listened to their stories of money, women, vacations" (33–4) – Linda's not only a "good girl" but the embodiment of a different, entirely better class of people and way of life. The opposite of everything that's dark and dirty and mean, Linda's a fantasy come to life, a dream wish reflected in Barney's first, pristine vision of her: "She was wearing a white net gown with a billowing skirt, and her finely molded shoulders were bare. Her skin was lightly tanned, and he had never seen anyone in his life who looked so shining and lovely and clean" (31).

For Barney, Linda's also a revenant, a sublimated reminder of his past impoverished and bruising life. Before he dropped out of school, he had admired a girl in chemistry class "who wore soft wool sweaters, tweed skirts, and even a string of pearls" (50).

> She came from a family with money, obviously, because she lived in Haddington and, just as obviously, she was a high-class sort of girl. She represented a type Nolan had never known at all, but one which he instinctively resented ... However, the ambivalence of his relationship to her was such that while resenting her and hating her he also wanted her to be his girl. (50–1)

In McGivern's *Shield for Murder*, as in *The Big Heat*, issues of class are imbricated with issues of race. In high school Barney worked "setting pins in his neighborhood bowling alley"; however, he hated the job "because most of the regular pin boys were colored, and Nolan's father had always warned him against working with colored people. It gave them ideas, his father said, with mysterious emphasis on the word ideas" (51).

For Barney, Linda is the ultimate embodiment of white society and femininity, her "lightly tanned" skin a signifier – by virtue of the fact that it's a function of choice, not nature – of her superior, unblemished class status. She therefore represents a chance to redeem an incident that occurred in the past. One day, having purchased a gardenia with the money from his pin-setting job, Barney asked the Haddington girl out and, when she refused, grabbed her by her finely molded shoulders and, "in a frightening rage," "shook her until the books she was carrying tumbled to the floor" (51). Though the chemistry teacher, who was one of Barney's "few heroes," berated him and made him clean up after class that afternoon, what really "hurt was being treated like a criminal because he had presumed to date a little bitch from the fancy section of Haddington" (52). If Patty as Linda reincarnated motivates Barney to buck the system, his cold-blooded killing of the bookie is the moment when he irrevocably crosses the line from being a violent but, technically speaking, "clean" cop to an irrepressibly bad one.

While Linda in McGivern's novel is a "good bad girl," if only because she's a singer at the Simba and, for Mark at least, because she's dating Barney, in the film Patty's the "good girl" as ingénue. Barney has just gotten her a job at the Blackout club when he sees her dressed as a cigarette girl in a strapless, black satin corset with a sweetheart neckline. After grabbing the owner by his lapels, Barney barks, "Haven't gotten enough legs here? Gotta put her in a peep show!" Nolan's intemperate behavior is reminiscent of Johnny Farrell's (Glenn Ford) in *Gilda* (1944) when he drags the eponymous character off the floor after her striptease, although the only thing that Patty does to displease Barney is put on a Playboy Bunny costume minus the white collar, cuffs, and cotton tail.

Patty's completely bewildered by her beau's unpredictable and violent behavior ("What makes you hate like that?") but Barney promises that "things are gonna be different": "You'll see in a minute. Think I'm gonna be a cop forever?" As proof, he drives Patty out to a new housing development in the suburbs called Castle Heights to show her a "model home" that's "all furnished" and "ready to go." (The set decorator is Alfred E. Spencer.) It's dark and, after turning on the lights and flooding the interior of the house, he takes her on a guided tour, proudly pointing out the living room, complete with cabinet television; a dining room, the table already set with plates, silverware, cups, and saucers; a guest bath; a master bedroom; and, best yet, a "Beauty Queen Kitchen." About the last regal space, Barney enthuses like a salesman, "Everything's automatic. Electric garbage disposal. Dishwasher. Up here we have an electrical stove, three burners." Patty chimes in "Special cooker," at which point Barney picks up his pitch: "And there's a frigerator, deep freeze. Rotisse-a-mat." Then, while Patty toasts an imaginary guest with one of the cups and lies down on the couch, kicking off her heels, Barney steals outside where he buries the twenty-five grand in some dirt. Later, as he's dropping Patty off at her apartment building, two of Packy Reed's hoods, in the guise of private detectives, Fat Michaels (Claude Atkins) and Laddie O'Neil (Larry Ryle), inform Nolan that the boss wants to see him. Barney leaves to see Packy but not before he drops Patty off at her apartment where he tells her: "sleep tight and dream about our little house."

Although the "model home" scene is an invention of the screenwriters, John C. Higgins and Richard Alan Simmons, it's a brilliant evocation of the mid-century middle-class suburban dream. A "tract home" in "Castle Heights" may be an oxymoron but, for Barney Nolan – haunted by the Haddington girl and, as Cabot says about one of the cops with "too little money in [his] pockets" – it's to die for. In other words, as Patty later laments to Mark, "he wants to carry me through the door with a ring on my finger." Then, with his girl by his side and an "automatic," appliance-rich, ready-to-move-in home, Barney will, at long last, have realized his dream of leaving the mean streets behind for the good, middle-class, suburban life. However, as with the high-angle shot of the ribbon cross that decorates the top of the Garwoods' wedding car in *The Prowler*, when Barney retrieves the key for the model home that the real-estate agent has left for him, the tight shot of the couple imprisoned behind a crisscross of white clapboards portends that Barney's dream is a trap.

In fact, the Wheel of Fortune has already begun to turn. First, the deaf-and-dumb witness shows up at the police station with a letter detailing the crime he witnessed and, though Barney's able to intercept him, he's later forced to confront the man at his apartment. As in *Where the Sidewalk Ends*, the man accidentally dies when he hits his head as Barney pushes him. To make the man's death look like an accident, Barney drags his body out of the room and throws it down the stairs, an act that makes Nolan seem less like a hot-tempered but essentially good cop like Mark Dixon in *Where the Sidewalk Ends* than a seriously crazed ex-con like Tommy Udo (Richard Widmark) in *Kiss of Death* (1947).

To unwind, Barney retreats to an Italian restaurant where he meets a blonde woman named Beth (Carolyn Jones) who, as he puts it in the novel, "let a man do anything to [her] as long as he filled [her] up with booze first." But when he notices a bruise on her arm, he becomes disgusted and calls Patty, who relays that Packy Reed's goons have just tried to force their way into her apartment. Apoplectic (not unlike Bannion in *The Big Heat* after the obscene phone call to his wife), Barney telephones Reed. Cut to Barney and Beth eating a spaghetti dinner. (While she's busy cleaning her plate, Barney, who hasn't even touched his, removes his revolver from his holster and slips it into his jacket.) The big plates of pasta with red sauce and meatballs echo the elegantly set table at the model home as well as Barney's bitter description of himself in McGivern's novel after Linda has asked him whether Dave Fiest, the bookie he killed, was married and had a family: "I'm a cop, a meat-ball cop from South Philly" (44).

Barney has told Packy that he'll return the money but, when Reed's "private detectives" arrive, instead of handing it over, he pistol-whips Michaels and O'Neil and, as the jazz music on the radio spikes, beats them to a pulp. (For its time, circa 1954, the scene is startling, at once graphic, extended, and surreal: see, for example, the alabaster-white "comedy" masks that look down, grinning, from the wall.) Watching Barney's over-the-top violence, a woman screams; Beth covers her face with her hands; a man, a strand of spaghetti trailing from his mouth, recoils in horror; and the matronly Italian-American proprietor shouts, "Somebody call the police!" "You had the police," Barney, deadpan, replies as he strolls out the door.

Earlier, in a seemingly throwaway scene, Beth uses the mirror behind the bar to teach Barney how to look tough. After repositioning the cigarette in his hand, she tells him: "Now take a puff, square your shoulder, narrow your eyes." It's an odd, parodic moment that self-reflexively foregrounds the film's cognizance of its own belatedness and intimates that Barney's abuse of the deaf-and-dumb man's body was an aberration – that, like Mark Dixon in *Where the Sidewalk Ends*, Barney may not be as bad as he seems. Barney, however, to quote Gus Burke (Robert Burton) on Bannion after the fiery death of his wife, is "on a hate binge." Thus, when Barney returns to his apartment and Brewster tries to take him in (Mark has in the meantime discovered another draft of the deaf-and-dumb man's letter), he knocks the gun out of Mark's hand before, after momentarily considering shooting him, hitting him over the head with the butt of his gun. Then, when Patty won't run off with him – she asks him if he took Packy's money and he asks her, in turn, if she's been talking to Mark – he slaps her across the face.

In McGivern's novel, Barney doesn't hit Linda; he shoots her because, having given her the money to hide, he thinks she's double-crossed him: "He fired a shot and saw her spin as if struck by a giant fist, and then he waited ... until he saw the blood spreading through her robe" (216). Right before he shoots her, though, he goes to the bathroom to wash his face and pauses to gaze at the "bottle of cologne and perfumes and jars of cold cream and bath salts": "The bottles were pretty, and their contents looked gay and colorful. Everything about the immaculate bathroom was her, he thought: clean, dainty, precious" (212). Linda's bathroom is an intimate, feminine space and, as such, a refuge from his hypermasculine world, a sordid, coarse, cheap one in which Barney has, from the very beginning, had to make his way. Earlier, defending Barney to Mark Brewster, Linda says about him: "Barney's made a symbol of me. He's put me on a ridiculous pedestal. He's got me confused with success and security and love, and all the things he's missed in life" (172–3).

While Captain Gunnarson (Emile Meyer) has concluded that the bookie Kirk Martin's death was a matter of "blue murder," he also believes that, as Mark Brewster reflects in the novel, "bad cops are nobody's business but the police department's" (13). Confronted with the evidence of Barney's crimes, Gunnarson, addressing the assembled detectives in his office, is forced to admit that Barney is a "maniac wearing a city shield" and surmises: 'When this story breaks ... [e]very police officer in the country will get dirty looks and dirty words ... If he gets away, they'll laugh at us. If we nail him, they'll hate us. Go out and rub your faces in the mud." The following wide-shot of Barney standing outside a laundry, the word "CLEANED" clearly visible in the background, couldn't be more ironic: Barney's shield is not tarnished – it's black, like Kelvaney's shoes.

Barney's watching from the shadows of the laundry when a motorcycle cop rides up to a call box to get the report. After the officer speeds off, Barney goes over and listens to the APB:

> The homicide suspect at large is Barney Nolan, detective lieutenant attached to university precinct. He may be driving precinct detective car 8. His description: 5'11", 200 lbs., male Caucasian, 36 years of age, wearing a brown suit, brown shoes, possibly tan topcoat, brown hat. This man is armed and dangerous, probably psycho. Use caution.

In a continuation of the film's play on appearances (when Reed's "private detectives" previously appeared at the police station, Brewster queried "Cops?" and Cabot answered "Robbers"), Barney throws his hat and trench coat into a garbage can and, disappearing into a basement, re-emerges as a patrolman. (Earlier, at the bar, when Beth wondered where Barney's uniform was, he responded, "Home in the basement, in mothballs.") Barney is surreptitiously trying to return to his apartment when a policeman on a stakeout approaches him and asks, "Are you the beat cop?" Barney's uniform is not simply a disguise; it's a sign of regression and, like Webb Garwood at the end of *The Prowler*, he's not moving forward, he's going backward, fast.

Caught between the police and Packy Reed, Barney arranges to meet a man named Manning (Richard Cutting) who claims that he can get him out of the country. However, in the upside-down world in which Barney presently finds himself – he's hiding out in another basement with a "friend," "The Professor," who's studying for an exam that night – everybody's a wise guy. When Barney asks the "friend" if he knows how to talk, "The Professor" complains: "I got an exam tonight. Night school at my age isn't easy. Business administration's a very difficult subject." And when Manning finally arrives, he takes one look at Barney and quips, "That's quite a deal, a detective dressed in a patrolman's uniform." Still, for "fifteen grand," Manning promises to deliver the goods: "US passport, charter plane to Cuba, airline tickets to Buenos Aires." Though Barney doesn't have the cash on him, he agrees to pay off one of Manning's men at a gymnasium.

In the locker room at a local high school, Barney makes the exchange but Packy's goon, O'Neil – his head covered with bandages like Claude Mulvihill's in *Chinatown* (1974) after Jake Gittes (Jack Nicholson) has just smashed his head against a gate – realizes that the envelope is stuffed with newspaper slips, not money. The ensuing shoot-out, which takes place in a public swimming pool where men and women in bathing suits scurry from the whizzing bullets, unfolds like some absurdist play and comments, like Barney's

Figure 6.2 Barney Nolan (Edmond O'Brien) with the loot in *Shield for Murder* (1954).

demented behavior in the bar, on his utter disregard for human life. Reverting at one point to training, he drops to a crouch and, taking direct aim at O'Neil, drops him. In *The Prowler* Bud Crocker (John Maxwell) says to Webb that a policeman's job is not to protect things but people. Now, having given up for good on people, Barney returns to the model tract home that he showed Patty to get the only thing that means anything to him in his rapidly downward-spiraling life: money.

In McGivern's novel, Barney, after watching Mark Brewster exit Linda's apartment and having attempted to run him down, drives through the "middle-class residential streets of the city . . . with no destination in mind": "Outside the sun was shining and wind sang clearly in the trees. Kids from a nearby school ran along the streets shouting to each other and the policeman at the intersection" (148). If this impossibly idyllic vision of suburbia, one in which policemen are an integral part of the good life, is the "exterior" complement to the felicitous portrait of the middle-class *interieur* in *The Big Heat*, both films nevertheless suggest that such happiness is as elusive as the wind singing in the trees.

Barney, bleeding profusely from a shoulder wound and with the police in hot pursuit, races out to the new, tract-home development located on the outskirts of the city. Like Webb Garwood at the end of *The Prowler*, Barney scrambles up one hillside of dirt, then another until, after exchanging fire with two officers, he digs the cache of money out of its hiding place, his not-so-angelic face twisted into a lunatic grimace. Then, with the money in one hand, his revolver in the other, Barney staggers to the front of the house where he stops next to a sign: CASTLE HEIGHTS TRACT HOMES. When the headlights of the police cruisers lined up across the street suddenly flood the "lawn" with light, Barney goes down, 1930s gangster style, in a hail of bullets, the money littering the dirt like dead leaves.

In McGivern's novel Barney, who's hiding out in the city, decides to escape to Mexico and dreams of seeing Linda there: "He could see her in a white dress, her arms and legs browned by the sun, coming across a hotel lobby to him with the bright quick smile on her face" (235). This passage, which uncannily conjures the famous Mexican cantina scene in *Out of the Past* (1947) when Jeff Markham (Robert Mitchum) sees Kathie Moffat (Jane Greer) coming toward him out of the sunlight, confirms just how idealized the "first" Linda – "the bright and smiling one ... who had stroked his head when he was drunk and ready to explode" (232) – has become in Barney's mind.

Later, after catching a private flight to Richmond, Barney boards another plane to Dallas where, as he waits for it to take off, he has another vision of Linda: "happy and smiling, coming to him somewhere, sometime, in Mexico" (247–8). In the seat directly behind him is a "paunchy little man" named Tommy with a briefcase, who's been hired by Espizito, the South Philly racketeer to whom Barney owes the 25 Gs, to take care of Barney somewhere between Dallas and Mexico: "[Tommy] looked at his watch as the plane taxied down the runway. Time for forty winks before they reached Dallas. Settling himself comfortably, he glanced once at the back of Barney's head, and then closed his eyes. The plane climbed into the night" (248). In McGivern's novel, Barney is fatally subject not to "the big heat," the institutional forces of law and order, but the merciless law of the syndicate pictured in 1950s gangster noirs such as *New York Confidential* (1955) and *The Brothers Rico* (1957). In the end, his mind's eye on the heavenly Linda, he never sees it coming.

At the end of O'Brien and Koch's take on McGivern's novel, Barney, the badge and uniform notwithstanding, is not a policeman – he's a psycho-killer costumed as a cop. The fact that he dies like a gangster in a blaze of glory on the bare dirt outside his dream home, rather than somewhere between Dallas and Mexico, highlights the film's critique, like *The Prowler*'s, of the "myth of suburbia" and the American middle class.[16] Despite its persistence, this ostensibly equal-opportunity dream is not, as Barney belatedly learns, accessible to everyone.

Epilogue: The Thin Blue Line

Despite its reputation for gloss, MGM, the studio "with more stars than there are in heaven," produced a number of crime films in the 1950s, including the seminal American heist film, John Huston's *Asphalt Jungle* (1950), the late noir musical, Nicholas Ray's *Party Girl* (1958), and rather less high-profile features such as John Sturges's *Mystery Street* (1950) starring Ricardo Montalban, Leslie Kardos's *The Strip* (1951) starring Mickey Rooney, and Tay Garnett's domestic melodrama, *Cause for Alarm* (1951) starring Loretta Young. If this "mini-series of thrillers" is an anomaly of sorts, the dark crime pictures released by Allied Artists would appear, despite the generic consonance, to represent the diametrical opposite of those made at MGM under Dore Shary.[17]

Although Allied Artists was initially formed as a subsidiary of prototypical Poverty Row studio Monogram in 1946, it continued to "grind out low-budget fare" in the 1950s as evidenced by – to cite a handful of lurid titles – *Murder without Tears* (1953), *Blonde Sinner* (1956), *The Come On* (1956), *The Deadliest Sin* (1956), and *Teenage Doll* (1959).[18] At the same time, just as MGM released a number of now obscure "mellers" in the 1950s such as *Dial 1119* (1950), *The Sellout* (1952), *Jeopardy* (1953), *Shadow in the Window* (1957), and *Nowhere to Go* (1959),[19] Allied Artists, which was committed under the executive purview of Steve Broidy to making both higher-budget and higher-quality films, was responsible for two classic A/B 1950s noirs, *The Big Combo* and Phil Karlson's *The Phenix City Story* (1955).

The respective personas of MGM and Allied Artists are reflected in the leading actors of *Rogue Cop* and *Shield for Murder*: while Robert Taylor, "The Man with the Perfect Profile," was a "top romantic star" and one of the "principal players" at the "Tiffany" studio, Edmond O'Brien, with his "stocky build, pudgy features, and heavy jowls," not to mention propensity for "ham," albeit savory "ham," was destined for character roles.[20] The difference between the two studios is visible, moreover, at the level of style. On one hand, the director of photography for *Rogue Cop*, John Seitz, was nominated for an Academy Award for his cinematography on the film and was one of the most celebrated cameramen of the classical period. (He also invented, among other things, the matte shot.) On the other hand, Gordon Avil, after lensing King Vidor's *Hallelujah* (1930) and *The Champ* (1931), spent the rest of his career working on programmers and, later in life, in television. Seitz's black-and-white cinematography in *Rogue Cop* is, as is to be expected, beautifully lit and composed but relatively free from shadows and chiaroscuro. Compared to Seitz's, Avil's photography is less accomplished. Yet, despite the fact that Seitz is associated with film noir (he shot *Double Indemnity* [1944] and *Sunset Boulevard* [1950] as well as numerous other "thrillers"), Avil's photography in *Shield for Murder* is arguably more expressive. Consider, for example, the choker close-ups of Barney's puffy, sweat-stained face in which his eyes are bugged out and his pompadour has flopped against his forehead like a deflated soufflé.

Given all this, it's not especially surprising that *Shield for Murder* is darker, both visually and thematically, than *Rogue Cop* or that its ending is decidedly more ambiguous. In the dénouement to *Rogue Cop*, set in an ambulance as it races, siren blaring, toward a hospital, Chris Carmody, haunted by "all the things [he'll] never get to tell Eddie," says to Sid Myers that he's a "lot like [his brother]": "A better cop than I'll ever be." Chris then asks for his forgiveness, a request that not only underlines Sid's status as Eddie's surrogate and Chris's symbolic reconciliation with his brothers in blue but the Judeo-Christian ethos and teleology of the film.

By contrast, the ending of *Shield for Murder* cuts from a high-angle shot of Barney Nolan – his bloodied hand outstretched as if, in death, he's still grasping for the money scattered next to his corpse – to a low-angle shot of a phalanx of policemen approaching the tract home. Once the men have collectively appraised the scene, Mark Brewster gets down on one knee and, while the score segues from a bluesy riff to a dramatic swell, he removes the "shield" from Barney's uniform. As Mark stares at the badge cupped in his hand, Gunnarson tells Cabot, "Write his story good." Though there's no doubt about the captain's grammar – it's bad – the meaning of his directive is ambiguous: is his imperative aesthetic, as in "Write a good story," or political, as in "Make it right."

Early on in *Shield for Murder* Cabot refers to the police as a "one big secret society" and, when Mark Brewster refuses to shed any light on the Kirk Martin killing ("No story. What is done is done"), Cabot laments that his story will get "buried behind a girdle ad." It's no secret, though, that Cabot believes that Barney was different from the other good, if "impure," men on the police force who, as he explains to Mark, "don't have to kill and beat up [people] just for kicks." In fact, as he's all too well aware and reminds Mark, "Last year Nolan killed two hungry wetbacks in a market burglary. Three years ago it was that tramp on Sullivan Street."

In McGivern's novel Mark doesn't have to be reminded. In Germantown he talks to a detective named Jerry Spiegel who "had made the mistake of knocking off too many protected handbooks in the downtown area and had been sent to Germantown to reflect on his sins" (58):

> I was working with [Nolan] the night he killed those two colored boys. We come in from different ends of the alley, see, and I get to 'em first. They were scared silly. I calmed 'em down, and then along comes that Nolan with his gun out and swearing like a wild man. The kids were edgy anyway and bolted. Nolan dropped 'em both with shots in the back. (63)

Later, at the Center City station, Barney, after interrogating Brewster about where he's been, accuses him of being a "snoop." Barney's getting ready to take a swing at him when a sergeant, then a lieutenant, break it up.

Mark proceeds downstairs to the call room where the day's hearings are about to begin and where it's crowded with "vags and drunks," cops and bondsmen, claimants and defendants, lawyers and witnesses (127). A black man named Jeremiah Green, dressed in "incredibly tattered clothes" with "no address" (127), has been brought in for being drunk and walking the streets with a brick. The magistrate asks Jeremiah what the brick is for:

> "Fo de rat."
> There was a murmur of laughter, and the Negro bobbed his head and smiled tentatively.
> "What rat?"
> The magistrate, who had a reputation for wit, leaned back in his chair and regarded the Negro with raised eyebrows.
> "De rat is where I sleep."
> "I thought you told the House Sergeant you had no address?"
> "*It* ain't got any address, Jedge. It's a box and I move it 'round. The rat comes in the hole, and I'se chockin' it wit de brick." (128)

McGivern records Mark's disenchantment, a disillusionment that no amount of Leibniz can ameliorate: "He felt tired and depressed, partly because of the brush with Nolan, and partly because people like the old Negro always made him wonder what in hell was wrong with the best of all possible worlds" (128).

Notes

1. I'm drawing here on *The Unicorn Book of 1954*, ed. Joseph L. Morse (New York: Unicorn Books, 1954).
2. Dennis Broe, *Film Noir, American Workers, and Postwar Hollywood* (Gainesville, FL: University Press of Florida, 2009), p. 93.
3. On the syndicate film, see my "Gangster Noir" (forthcoming) which examines *The Phenix City Story* (1955) and *The Brothers Rico* (1957) as well as *711 Ocean Drive* (1950), *The Enforcer* (1951), *The Captive City* (1952), and *The Big Combo* (1955).
4. Broe, *Film Noir*, p. 87.
5. Fran Mason, *American Gangster Cinema* (Basingstoke: Palgrave Macmillan, 2002), pp. 112 and 111.
6. Tom Gunning, *The Films of Fritz Lang: Allegories of Vision and Modernity* (Chicago: University of Chicago Press, 2000), p. 423.
7. Ibid., p. 423.
8. On this aspect of the "rogue cop" film, see Frank Krutnik, *In a Lonely Street: Film Noir, Genre, Masculinity* (London: Routledge, 1991), p. 193.
9. Broe, *Film Noir*, p. 81.

10. William P. McGivern, *Rogue Cop* (New York: Dodd, Mead & Company, 1954), p. 9.
11. Alain Silver, "*Rogue Cop*," in Alain Silver and Elizabeth Ward (eds), *Film Noir: An Encyclopedic Reference to the American Style* (Woodstock, NY: Overlook, 1992), p. 246.
12. Ibid., p. 245.
13. Ibid., p. 245.
14. Ibid., p. 245.
15. William P. McGivern, *Shield for Murder* (New York: Dodd, Mead & Company, 1951), pp. 70–1.
16. Carl Macek, "*Shield for Murder*", in *Film Noir*, p. 256.
17. Robert Porfirio, "*Mystery Street*", in *Film Noir*, p. 194.
18. Arthur Lyons, *Death on the Cheap* (New York: Da Capo, 2000), p. 48. See also the appendix, "B Noirs Listed by Year and by Studio", pp. 180–1.
19. For a list of B crime films released by Allied Artists, see ibid., pp. 180–1.
20. Ephraim Katz, *The Film Encyclopedia* (New York: HarperCollins, 2008), pp. 1400 and 1072 respectively.

Filmography

Asher, William, 1957: *The Shadow on the Window*.
Beaudine, William, 1953: *Murder without Tears*.
Birdwell, Russell, 1956: *The Come On*.
Cromwell, John, 1951: *The Racket*.
Corman, Roger, 1957: *Teenage Doll*.
Feist, Felix, 1951: *The Man Who Cheated Himself*.
Fuller, Samuel, 1953: *Pickup on South Street*.
Garnett, Tay, 1951: *Cause for Alarm*.
Hathaway, Henry, 1947: *Kiss of Death*.
Holt, Seth, 1959: *Nowhere to Go*.
Hughes, Ken, 1955: *The Deadliest Sin*.
Huston, John, 1950: *The Asphalt Jungle*.
Kardos, Leslie, 1951: *The Strip*.
Karlson, Phil, 1957: *The Brothers Rico*.
Karlson, Phil, 1955: *The Phenix City Story*.
Lang, Fritz, 1953: *The Big Heat*.
Lewis, Joseph, 1955: *The Big Combo*.
Losey, Joseph, 1951: *The Prowler*.
Mayer, Gerald, 1950: *Dial 1119*.
Mayer, Gerald, 1952: *The Sellout*.
Milestone, Lewis, 1928: *The Racket*.
O'Brien, Edmond and Howard W. Koch, 1954: *Shield for Murder*.
Preminger, Otto, 1951: *Where the Sidewalk Ends*.
Quine, Richard, 1954: *The Pushover*.
Ray, Nicholas, 1952: *On Dangerous Ground*.
Ray, Nicholas, 1958: *Party Girl*.
Rowland, Roy, 1954: *Rogue Cop*.
Siegel, Don, 1954: *Private Hell 36*.
Sturges, John, 1953: *Jeopardy*.
Sturges, John, 1950: *Mystery Street*.
Thompson, J. Lee, 1956: *Blonde Sinner*.
Tourneur, Jacques, 1947: *Out of the Past*.

Vidor, King, 1931: *The Champ*.
Vidor, King, 1930: *Hallelujah*.
Wilder, Billy, 1944: *Double Indemnity*.
Wilder, Billy, 1950: *Sunset Boulevard*.
Wise, Robert, 1959: *Odds against Tomorrow*.

BIBLIOGRAPHY

Broe, Dennis (2009), *Film Noir, American Workers, and Postwar Hollywood*, Gainesville, FL: University Press of Florida.
Gunning, Tom (2000), *The Films of Fritz Lang: Allegories of Vision and Modernity*, Chicago: University of Chicago Press.
Katz, Ephraim (2008), *The Film Encyclopedia*, New York: HarperCollins.
Lyons, Arthur (2000), *Death on the Cheap*, New York: Da Capo.
Macek, Carl (1992), 'Shield for Murder', in Alain Silver and Elizabeth Ward (eds), *Film Noir: An Encyclopedic Reference to the American Style*, Woodstock, NY: Overlook.
McGivern, William P. (1951), *Shield for Murder*. New York: Dodd, Mead & Company.
McGivern, William P. (1954), *Rogue Cop*, New York: Dodd, Mead & Company.
Mason, Fran (2002), *American Gangster Cinema*, Basingstoke: Palgrave Macmillan.
Morse, Joseph L. (1954). *The Unicorn Book of 1954*, New York: Unicorn Books.
Porfirio, Robert (1992), "Mystery Street," in Alain Silver and Elizabeth Ward (eds), *Film Noir: An Encyclopedic Reference to the American Style*, Woodstock, NY: Overlook.
Silver, Alain (1992), "*Rogue Cop*," in Alain Silver and Elizabeth Ward (eds), *Film Noir: An Encyclopedic Reference to the American Style*, Woodstock, NY: Overlook.

7. INTERNAL ENMITY: HOLLYWOOD'S FRAGILE HOME STORIES IN THE 1950s AND 1960s

Elisabeth Bronfen

As Michael Wood notes in his discussion of the myths Hollywood came up with in the 1940s and 1950s so as to negotiate actual dilemmas, "America is not so much a home for anyone as a universal dream of home, a wish whose attraction depends upon its remaining at the level of a wish."[1] Applying this notion of home as a vaunted ideal to the anxieties engendered by the Cold War on the home front, it is further worth noting that any solution Hollywood films come up with to contain these fears can be only imaginary because, as Wood adds, if there were a real solution then there would be no need for mythic narratives. When, in turn, genre films at the time, and particularly the melodrama, make dramaturgic use of concrete homes to represent the idea of protection and comfort, these houses refer to a personal sense of belonging even as they also stand in for the nation as the geopolitical community whose safety one must be willing to protect at all costs. Under Senator Joe McCarthy's witch-hunt against alleged Communist spies and sympathizers in the United States government and elsewhere, the Cold War not only turned into a domestic issue, rendering clear the fragility of any American dream of home. Rather, the logic of antagonism on which this international conflict was predicated also transformed into a struggle within. The simple opposition between "we" and 'them' transformed into the far more differentiated opposition of "we v. us," in the context of which the home emerged as a contested site. In what Richard Hofstadter called "a paranoid style in American politics," an anxious hyper-vigilance fostering the collective fantasy that subversive elements where living everywhere, undetected, ready to contaminate or attack their unsuspecting fellow men, underscored not only a crisis of national security but also of the home as its most effective cultural trope.²

As point of departure for my discussion of the way Hollywood came to shape this imaginary threat to the nation as a subversion of the family by enemies within, I have chosen Joseph Weisberg's *The Americans*. The retrospective look at Cold War culture, which this television series offers, conceives of the house which the Soviet undercover agents, Philip and Elizabeth Jennings, inhabit in Falls Church explicitly as the stage for a struggle that renders both this home and the American homeland "uncanny." Sigmund Freud coined the term so as to analyze the distress called forth when the ordinary suddenly becomes strange, unsettling any sense of psychic certitude.³ His formulation of a disturbance of the ordinary can, however, also be fruitfully applied to a discussion of the malaise on which Cold War culture thrives, given that the German word *heimlich* refers both to something familiar and something secret; to a clandestine core at the heart of the ordinary. In the case of the Jennings, one might surmise: while this couple represents a clandestine foreign body in an allegedly safe neighborhood, the fact that FBI agent Stan Beeman, working in counterintelligence, moves into a house across the street from them signals that what on the surface looks like a secure neighborhood is nothing other than a cover-up. In other words, in *The Americans*, the familiar is quite explicitly rendered strange because something repressed is shown to have resurfaced, namely the political Other that was meant to be safely lodged on the other side of the Iron Curtain. At the same time, in that we know the Jennings to be spies, while no one else seems to be able to tell, the television show also offers a particular spin on the Cold War culture of paranoia. The Jennings are adroit not only at a perfect mimicry of the ordinary, middle-class family. In that the disguises they put on during their missions offer an equally convincing performance of what a wide array of urbanites, living in Washington, D.C. in the early 1980s, look like, their deft masquerading of Americans renders visible the intangibility of an internal enemy that has appropriated to perfection the appearance of its adversary.

Their home base is equally duplicitous. On the surface, their house looks exactly like all the other homes in their neighborhood while, in fact, it is here that their espionage is planned and carried out. Next to the washing machine in the cellar is a secret closet, sheltering their costumes, their weapons, as well as the technical equipment they use to contact their handler. While Elizabeth and Philip's bedroom is the obvious site for clandestine conversations, whenever the telephone rings and they are given a new assignment, their double life even pervades the kitchen, normally thought of as the hearth of the home. Above all, the mother, who in post-World War II Hollywood was meant to assert the myth of an intact domesticity, is the more aggressively patriotic of the two secret agents. And yet, while Elizabeth conspires to undermine her children's allegiance to the United States, Philip entertains fantasies of defection. As such, he renders the distinction between enemy and friend even more complicated in that he has, himself, become infected with America as the dream of home. Furthermore, with the Beemans living across the street from the Jennings, their home transforms into a domestic battle zone in yet another sense. Befitting a culture in which everything is under suspicion, what appear to be neighborly exchanges between the two families could be a cover for mutual surveillance. Indeed, at the end of the first season, Stan, who has noticed that Philip's car is the same make as the one in which a Soviet double agent was abducted, actually breaks into their garage one night. Though he finds nothing because Elizabeth has already removed all traces of their hostage, the friendship between him and this couple, sustained throughout the next three seasons, is predicated on uncertainty: has he guessed who his neighbors are and is waiting for them to make a mistake? Does he deny what he wishes not to acknowledge because he has grown fond of them? Or is he successfully duped by the Jennings because their con game is such a perfect facade of an American home?

By looking back at the last years of the Cold War through the lens of the political consequences we know them to have had, what *The Americans* draws our attention to is that even, if the home, in the name of which one fights, is a political myth that must remain at the level of fantasy, the illusion of security it promises is itself predicated on the invocation of an internal threat that *can never* but also *must never* be fully contained. If there were no sign of threat, then the vast effort of containment would not be necessary. As such, owing to the cult of domesticity propagated by Cold War culture, the domestic space turned into a contested site where the inability to stabilize the distinction between the other and the same, on which this logic of containment was predicated, was repeatedly addressed *and* repeatedly propagated.[4] As this chapter will argue, during the 1950s and '60s, the Hollywood melodrama emerged as one of the key genres in which America was able to explain its anxieties and dreams to itself. It did so by lodging the concerns of Cold War containment in home stories, revolving around an uncanny instability at the heart of the of family, that is, the very ideal meant to guarantee national security and international peace. Formations of internal strangeness inside private homes came *to reflect* and *reflect on* the permeability of national borders as well. At the same time, many of these melodramas refigure cultural preoccupations into shapes even while they don't necessarily tame them. Rather, they contain them in the double sense of the word: controlling and restraining anxieties even while comprising and accommodating them. When, in revisiting these melodramas, we privilege the fissures in the mythic solutions they offer, rather than the ideology they seemingly purport, what we notice is a double voicing inherent to the mutual implication of private home and nation. Family narratives revolving around an enmity within think about domestic security in terms of personal crisis threatening the quotidian life of the characters even while the resolution discovered by each text also serves as a trope for the possibility of a political solution.

Bringing the War Home

Leo McCarey's anti-communist film, *My Son John* (1952) quite explicitly brings the Cold War home in the figure of a young, left-wing intellectual who has infiltrated the government.[5] John Jefferson embodies the alien within, however, not only because, by assisting a Soviet courier, he threatens national security. Upon his return home, the acerbic irony he deploys to signal his detachment from the values of his middle-American parents, is also read by them as a form of mental alienation. While John openly opposes the father, who immediately suspects him of being "a Commie," a deeper intimacy connects him to his mother Lucille. She, in turn, is the one who, owing to his strange behavior, actually spies on him, who listens in on his conversations with others, who interrogates him hoping to elicit a confession and even threatens to expose him to the F.B.I. At the same time, driven by nostalgia, she repeatedly reminds John, who now appears to her as an uncanny double of himself, of the happy boy with whom she used to play. If, as the film's title suggests, in her ability to control her son, the mother is the key player, she also emerges, however, as a deeply ambivalent figure. In the course of the film it becomes increasingly difficult to decide whether John's alienness is only a symptom of the political climate or also a reflection on the home that shaped him.

Indeed, in that the film offers a psychological explanation for the appeals of Communism, conceiving John's political leanings as his Oedipal struggle with his parents, the very home meant to provide the solution emerges as the source of the problem. As Michael Rogin puts it, the film "located the threat to the free man less in the alien Communist state than in his loving mother."[6] Excessive maternal care, the fulcrum of the cult of domesticity, emerges as a mirror inversion of the perfidious influence and surveillance of the Communist Other. The threat the home poses absorbs the political threat. Once the son has rendered visible the internal instability of the home, the figure presiding over it is also made responsible for his alienation from the very political and religious values she espouses. If the mother emerges as the unwitting cause for her son's breach in national security, the political climate of the Cold War in general (and not just the appeal of left-wing politics) is what ultimately destroys this home, fundamentally severing the bond between parents and child.

The narrative resolution, in turn, hinges on a further aspect of the uncanny. The son ultimately decides to do the "one decent thing" open to him and, having just been awarded an honorary degree of law, he uses the speech he is scheduled to give to the graduating class to warn them about the dangerous lure of the Communist movement. Yet, because the actor, Robert Walker, had died during production, his character, John, had to be killed off as well. After making a tape recording of the self-accusation in which John calls himself a traitor, he dies in a car crash spearheaded by Soviet agents. In the final shot of the film, the dead son's recorded voice delivers his confession regarding his defiance of the values of his home from beyond the grave. The lectern on the darkened stage is empty, while a spotlight draws the attention of all those present at the commencement ceremony to the tape recorder transmitting this disembodied voice. The son, targeted by the F.B.I. as an internal enemy, turns into a martyr of the very cause that had entrapped him. He speaks with the authority that death lends any storyteller. Yet, against the manifest intention of the film's director, McCarey, a retrospective gaze can uncover a second, far more ambivalent meaning in the performance of this spectral doubling of the alien within. If John can make his confession only as a dead person, the effect is also a cinematic trick. On-screen, the man retracting his political views is simultaneously present and absent as a ghost of himself. The evidence is given in absentia, undermining the very containment it is meant to support because the body of the man speaking is missing.

Stephanie Coontz has argued that the notion of the nuclear family, providing physical shelter and emotional protection from the dangers of the outside world, was not only an invention of the 1950s. In fact, during this time, many Americans were far more aware of the violence or quiet misery beneath the polished facades of what was conceived as a mark of middle-class status than later retrospectives suggest.[7] With the postwar period fostering an upward mobility for men even while reintroducing domesticity for women, the American family may have been homeward bound but also bound to the home in such a containing manner to render this an ambiguous dream.[8] Decisive for my discussion is the fact that many Cold War melodramas themselves already belie this subsequent nostalgia for a safer, more intact past that actually never existed. In these films, the home as site where personal needs could be fulfilled in face of an outside threat, is rarely without internal fault lines, making it vulnerable to external threats even while placing pressures on family life from within.

The films I have chosen to explore this internal enmity all focus on a disruption of the three positions necessary to maintain this emotional bond: the fallibility of paternal authority, the challenge of maternal self-empowerment, and generational conflict. While *The Man in the Gray Flannel Suit* (1956) and *Autumn Leaves* (1956) focus on war memories rendering the home uncanny, *Half Angel* (1951) refutes the ideal of feminine domesticity which, in *The Desperate Hours* (1955) and *Something Wild* (1961), can only be regenerated through violence. While *The Bad Seed* (1956) revolves around a seemingly perfect child who, in fact, belies the role of obedient offspring, *The Bigamist*

(1953) and *The Swimmer* (1968) focus on the father who fails in his paternal role, engendering a complete break with what might be called home bondage. Thus, where, in *The Americans* and *My Son John*, those who render the home uncanny are explicit political subversives, these melodramas give shape to the concerns of Cold War culture by having recourse to the rhetoric of displacement. The threat to national security is re-encoded as a family affair. Forced to engage with internal frictions, rendering visible that something is wrong with the very bonds that hold the family together, at issue is the question whether the home can be recuperated? Can a couple, separated by discord, come together again? Can the family overcome its internal differences so as to face the outside enemy once more reunited? And what must be sacrificed for the family to become home bound once more?

Traces of War

A self-evident displacement for bringing the Cold War home is the veteran of an earlier war, unable to cast off his war memories. In *The Man in the Gray Flannel Suit*, discontent in the home is explicitly linked by the mother, Betsy Rath, to the fact that, ever since the war, she feels her husband Tom has changed. During a conversation in their kitchen, she begins by ranting against the suburban house they are currently inhabiting, calling it "a graveyard of everything we used to talk about – happiness, fun, ambition – and I want to get out of it." To press her point, she adds that this house has not been a happy one ever since the war. Though Tom tells her to stop harping on a war which has been over for ten years and is thus gone and forgotten, she slyly retorts: "I don't believe it, not for you anyway." The flashback that soon follows reveals that he is, indeed, an uncanny double of the citizen soldier who enlisted, not only because of the destruction of human life which, in the name of the homeland, he was compelled to participate in. Maria, an Italian woman with whom he had a brief affair in Rome before shipping out to the Pacific, also inhabits this home as a spectral foreign body, producing a distance between him and his American family. Precisely because he has kept this other woman secret, Betsy has the canny sense that he is not sharing all of himself with her, perceiving him at times as an alien in their midst. Like McCarey's anxious mother, she, too, wants to find out what it is that has changed him, hoping to resurrect in him the spirited resolve he used to have.

Tom thus finds himself split between a past that continues to haunt him and a present, burdened by his wife's ambitions. While she wants him to have a job that will allow him once again to fight for something, his war past seems to have curtailed his willingness to take the risks necessary for the upward mobility to which she aspires. Even when his calm self-reliance lands him a promising job in the public relations office of a powerful philanthropist, he remains divided against himself. Unable to assume the position of a stabilizing paternal authority, he inadvertently splits apart the home they share. Resolving this division involves bringing out into the open the secret he has sought to cover up. When the sergeant who was with him in Rome finally reveals that Maria had his child, an honest conversation with his wife proves to be the only way Tom can straighten out their home troubles. In their bedroom Betsy is finally able to extort the confession from her husband that will prove her suspicions correct.

In hindsight, this can be seen as an inversion of the HUAC hearings which, at the time, were hovering on the edges of all seeking after truth regarding past alliances. By sharing with her his wish publicly to acknowledge his son in Rome, enmity is transformed into a shared bond with the foreign woman who has been the source of their division. By asking from Betsy "some kind of understanding," Tom is proposing a definition of marriage that would be sustainable in the face of all external pressures in the future. She is to accept that his love for another woman was the response to the terror and hopelessness of an experience of war she, as someone who wasn't in a battle zone, can never really know. She is to trust – and therein lies the imaginary solution to the culture of paranoia this film reflects – a marriage that includes the open admission of infidelity and the responsibility for an illegitimate child. The fact that Betsy is the one who suggests setting up a trust fund for this boy enacts a different form of containment. If her discontent served to bring to light what was causing a disturbance of the home, her acceptance of her husband's fallibility not only allows the couple to be reunited. By engaging in an act of mercy she has come to accommodate the spectral rival disturbing her home, even while finding an articulation of her ambitions more conducive to her husband.

In *Autumn Leaves*, produced in the same year, the traumatized veteran brings war into a home that was not intact to begin with. The dark shadows on the walls of the apartment in Cedar Court where Milly Wetherby lives attest to a disturbance of her domestic life even before she meets Burt Hanson. While she was younger, her filial duties to her bedridden father had made marriage impossible, so that now, middle aged, she not only lives alone but has found it necessary to turn her apartment into her home office as well. Though, owing to the age difference, Milly is, from the start, cautious about this romance, she consents to marry the former army sergeant who showers her with gifts, only to discover that, like Nunally's hero, he is keeping secrets from her. He has only recently been divorced from a wife who, as figure of the repressed other, has returned for him to sign the settlement papers. His lying, regarding not only his true involvement on the Pacific war front but also false claims regarding his promotion at work, is, in turn, certifiably pathological. His bouts of memory loss make it impossible for him to remember what he has said and done. Unclear to the end, however, is whether his mental alienation is a form of war neurosis and thus a reflection on the destruction of human life in the war that just ended in Korea. Or whether the intermittent amnesia attacks that leave him utterly incapacitated, are his psychic revolt against the fact that his first wife, who had betrayed him with his father, is now also seeking to dispossess him of his mother's estate.

Once Milly's suspicions about the truth of what he has been telling her have become aroused, her home turns into the site of a far more visceral domestic struggle than in *The Man in the Gray Flannel Suit*, rendering visible the contradictions between the various displacements at issue. Is he lying to her in retaliation for the secrets kept from him by his first wife? Or is the violence he commits against her, smashing her hand with her typewriter, a symptom of the prejudice against single working women prevalent at the time? Has she brought this fracture of her home on to herself, as an expression of her own discontent with herself as the breadwinner in this marriage? Or is this attack in her home the emergency she requires to assert her agency belatedly against the demands of the ailing father of her youth? As in the other films discussed, her response – and in this she mirrors the 1950s culture of paranoia – is surveillance and interrogation. Milly forces Burt to confront his past although, significantly, the confession she is finally able to extort from him covers up his war trauma with family drama. The result is a nervous breakdown which reduces him to infantilism and forces her to have him committed to an institution that treats his schizophrenia with shock therapy; a different form of torture.

In *Autumn Leaves*, excessive influence of the self-reliant woman thus gives focus to the far less tangible anxieties revolving around political domestic enmity, even as, because this maternal love corresponds to Burt's neurotic need, it also proves to be its cure. When Milly goes to pick him up at the hospital, Burt is able to overcome her last remaining uncertainty with the candor of his newly rediscovered love. Taking her into his arms, he can return home with her. What was lurking beneath the surface of their union can now, having been addressed, once more be contained. Stanley Cavell argues that, in Hollywood cinema, the "covenant of marriage is a miniature of the covenant of the commonwealth." The reunion of a couple, separated because they had not yet understood the terms for the mutual acknowledgement that would allow them to share a "meet and happy conversation" with each other, can be taken as a trope for the successful recuperation of a trust in America as the community worth participating in.[9] As in Nunally's melodrama, the remarriage at the end of *Autumn Leaves* offers an imaginary solution to Cold War's culture with internal enmity that puts the onus on the restoration of individual happiness.

Feminine Domesticity Reloaded

Other films explore the uncanniness of home by bringing into focus how the cult of domesticity makes the heroine a hostage *in* and *of* the home. In *Half Angel* she proves to be an uncanny double of herself. Nurse Nora Gilpin, still living with her father, a dotty botanist, keeps putting off the engagement to the dull organization man, Tim, who is courting her. While, during the daytime, she corresponds to the stereotype of the demure and restrained 1950s bride-to-be, there is a psychic conflict hidden within her, involving her childhood sweetheart, the lawyer John Raymond, who seems to have forgotten all about her. At night, her hope that she might jog his memory, brings out that other side of herself she is unable fully to repress. In contrast to *Autumn Leaves*, this struggle within herself does not take the form of schizophrenia but simply that of the love-sick sleepwalker who forgets during the day what she does at night. Yet the unfinished business Nora attends to at night is as personal as it is collective. The woman who will allow nothing to get in the way of her pursuit of the man she wants recalls the empowerment of women on the home front during World War II. This claim to self-determination is what the 1950s working woman, waiting to become home bound by marriage, was meant to deny herself. What produces domestic disturbance in *Half Angel* is thus the return of two phantoms of the past: the adolescent Nora, as yet unrestrained in pursuing her romantic dream, as well as the heroine of the sophisticated comedies of the 1930s and '40s, resilient and resourceful in articulating her desire. Nora's first scene of transformation underscores how an assertive sexual drive, lurking beneath the surface of 1950s docility, successfully breaks through. Having chosen a green silk dress as her instrument of seduction, the somnambulist undoes the ribbon around the neck to produce a décolletage more typical of the fashion of the previous decade and uses it instead to accentuate her waist. With this uncanny appearance, which brings the past back into the present, Nora is able to make Raymond fall in love with her again.

The domestic struggle that ensues is based on the fact that the memory loss of her diurnal self is a desperate attempt to avoid facing the raucous fun her nocturnal doppelgänger has. At day she fights not against some past that is harmful to her (as is the case with the traumatized veteran) but rather against something which she, in pursuit of romantic happiness, cannot afford *not* know. In her effort to repudiate this insight, Nora turns her father's house into the scene of an enemy assault, culminating in the night before the wedding with Tim, which she hopes will contain her unruly unconscious desires once and for all. So as to protect herself both from herself as well as the lovelorn Raymond, keeping a close watch on her activities from his position on the other side of the street, she tries to barricade her bedroom. Yet the nocturnal Nora will not be contained and, escaping through the window, induces

Raymond to marry her immediately. The next morning, Nora, finding herself asleep next to her newlywed husband, runs away from the truth of her desire one last time. While her diurnal self still hopes to go through with the marriage to Tim (which would make her a bigamist), Raymond manages to interrupt the ceremony at the last minute. The fact that the moment Nora sees him she faints not only allows her repressed self to win the day but also attests to the resilience of this internal alien. When Nora finally acknowledges Raymond in public, she is in a state of trance from which, through the final moments of the film, she never wakes up. The tables have turn and it is now the diurnal self of repressed sexuality that has come to be contained. The vows that are renewed celebrate a wacky triumph of the return of the past which, as a deflection from the political realities of the early 1950s, can be taken as a quasi-nostalgic imaginary resolution for the time before the Cold War started.

While Wyler's *The Desperate Hours* also has recourse to the confidence of the World War II home front, it reintroduces this military past into the paranoia of Cold War culture in a far more explicit manner. Initially, nothing seems to trouble the home of Ellie Hilliard. Once her husband and her children have left her alone to do her morning chores, however, Glenn Griffin and two other men, who have just broken out of prison, force their way into her house, taking her hostage. If this criminal assault is conceived in terms of a military invasion, with drum taps accompanying their arrival, the result is strangely invigorating to the entire Hilliard family. One could read Glenn as the mother's symptom, rendering manifest what was hidden beneath the allegedly happy home she is mistress of; namely that her domesticity is, in fact, a trap. Yet it is also the case that, in so far as the presence of these bank robbers renders Ellie's housewife existence uncanny, this brings out her prior more resilient home-front self which, comparable to Nora in *Half-Angel*, she has been compelled to repress since World War II ended. When, at the end of the day, her family returns, they seem to be at the mercy of their aggressors, forced to comply with their orders. Indeed, as a form of class reversal, Ellie and her daughter are now the servants of men who have never lived in a middle-class house like theirs, cooking for them and attending to their needs. And yet, as though the family needed precisely such a state of emergency, they come together as a fighting unit in their effort to defend this home. Indeed, in that the gangster figure had come to serve as another self-evident example for the enemy within, Glenn's attack on the American home, which in war-effort films, such as *Since You Went Away*, was considered an unconquerable fortress, cannot only be seen as a continuation of war with other means. Rather, in that in this case the internal enemy is tangible, the house becomes the scene of battle where a very clear and unequivocal line can be drawn between friend and foe.

In this domestic war zone it is above all, however, the father who is revitalized, as he resiliently puts up resistance. Once he has managed to escape and join up with the police, Dan C. Hilliard is finally able to cast off his current civilian role as a banker and become again what he once was, a war hero. Fighting this particular public enemy so as to restore peace to his home, he also stands in for an effort to eradicate those who threaten national security in general. By analogy, Glenn, the deviant, criminal citizen, is recast as an enemy of the state. When the police finally arrive, they surround the house, pointing their guns at all possible exits. Dan watches his house, now under attack from the inside as well as from the outside, through his neighbor's attic window. The wooden arches visually evoke the window in a bomber plane, rendering his house at the center as the chosen target of a military mission.[10] To underscore the fact that this is more than a city police affair, the FBI agent is the one who allows Dan to re-enter his home and use a ruse worthy of the best wartime strategy to force the last remaining criminal outside. Fully in line with the logic of the sacrificial victim, the execution of Glenn on the front lawn of the Hilliard home is not only justified. The violence rejuvenates the family as well. It is as though, along with the gangster, all that had implicitly been troubling this family has also been destroyed. As Dan, reunited with his family, re-enters a home seemingly cleansed of all danger, the lights in the house go on again. Only one detail mars this restoration. The telltale bicycle that had drawn the gangsters to this particular house in the first place, because it meant a nuclear family was living there, is still lying on the front yard. There could be another assault.

Figure 7.1 Attack on the Hilliard home in *The Desperate Hours* (1955).

Jack Garfein also gestures towards a militarization of domestic strife at the beginning of *Something Wild*. During the credit sequence, light bulbs on a billboard offer up the sentence fragment, "dimmed by military action," so as to gesture toward an unspecified sense of war hovering around the edges of this story about a rape victim. In contrast to the other films discussed so far, however, a concern with internal enmity is reshaped into a discussion of urban decay. Though Mary Ann does not confide in her mother after the assault, the awkward behavior of her daughter elicits from Mrs. Robinson the confession that, owing to the rise in crime, she no longer feels at home in their Brooklyn neighborhood. If the rape scene represents one form of domestic violence, it draws into focus another war zone as well, namely the world of those who have been pushed to the margins of 1950s middle-class upward mobility. Rather than displacing the political anxieties of Cold War culture onto the economically dispossessed, Garfein's film reverses the argument: an obsession with political enemies outside and within draws attention away from those who have been left behind in the war waged by capitalism against all those who are no longer profitable.

Estranged from her ordinary world, Mary Ann leaves her home and moves into a squalid room in a tenement building where she finds herself surrounded by vagabonds, sleeping on benches, literally homeless. Then, unable to regain her footing in a city that remains utterly threatening to her, she tries to jump off a bridge but is hindered by the car mechanic, Mike, who insists on taking her to his basement apartment. Offering her shelter and nourishment in his stark home, he also locks the door when he leaves so that she cannot escape. Having left a familiar neighborhood, which was no longer a site of protection and moved through the completely unfamiliar detritus of the lower East Side, Mary Ann thus lands in a home where she is the hostage of a stranger who is himself a splice between rescuer and assailant. As such, his home becomes the scene for working through the prior assault that had rendered her homeless, drawing out retaliatory violence in her as well. Their first night together, while protecting herself against Mike's drunken sexual advances, Mary Ann kicks out his left eye. Though she remains his hostage for several more days, she has proven herself no longer to being a passive victim and instead able to assert her resistance against his will to dominate her. Their domestic struggle is complicated, however, by the fact that to justify why he won't let her leave, despite her violence against him, he explains: "you are my last chance." The bars on the windows she looks out forlornly when she is alone underscore that this home is a prison, and yet, as the place she is trapped in because the man who has saved her can not afford to relinquish her, it also sets the scene for a spiritual redemption they can bring about only *for* and *with* each other.

Although, when Mike proposes marriage, she defiantly rebukes him, once she realizes that, upon leaving his home in hurt frustration, he has forgotten to lock the door, necessity turns into choice. As she wanders through Manhattan, free again to go wherever she pleases, the city is no longer the scene of danger and destitution, serving instead as the backdrop for her rebirth. Her decision to return to him is one she makes for herself. In response to the uncertainty with which he greets her when she once more enters his home, she asserts: "I came back for you." The marriage these two people enter into at the end of *Something Wild* is an expression of radical hope, born out of a will to accept the fallibility of the other. When, many months later, Mary Ann writes to her mother, she is herself pregnant. In response to Mrs. Robinson's perplexity at hearing from her daughter only now, Mary Ann explains: "this is my home, this is my husband, this is where my life is." And while her mother initially won't understand, asking her repeatedly when she is coming home, the daughter uses this final struggle to assert her right to declare what she considers to be home for her. The rite of passage that began with her rape culminates in her achieving a state of adulthood which must include a mutual acknowledgement between daughter and mother. In the penultimate shot of the film, Mary Ann, locked into a tearful embrace with her mother, reaches for her husband's hand and smiles at him. In a lap dissolve, her radiant face then melds with the bridge she tried to jump from. The internal antagonism, on which this home is predicated, is contained and sustained by the sentimental bond forged between the three.

Figure 7.2 Mary Ann's bridge to tomorrow in *Something Wild* (1961).

Unruly Children, Failing Fathers

A different version of the momism of Cold War culture which, as Michael Rogin argues, "locates the problem in the very family that was suppose to provide the solution," can be found in *The Bad Seed*.[11] This film suggests that perhaps the most terrifying, undetected alien within might be the perfect child whose sweet appearance dupes those adults around her who want to be taken in because their trust in youthful innocence serves as an apotropaic charm against the threat the outside world poses. Rhoda Penmark, an adroit liar, for whom murder is the solution to all domestic conflicts, serves as a particularly vicious mirror for the fantasy of political subversives, living undetected in the midst of honest American citizens, because she uses flawless obedience to cover up her killer instinct. Here, too, the actual military conflict the United States was involved in is invoked obliquely and, as such, functions as the backdrop for the eruption of family violence in the home. Early on in the film, as the father, Colonel Kenneth Penmark, having been called off to Washington, D.C., takes leave of his family, the landlady, who lives upstairs from them, jokingly declares: "Do something about not having a war, will you, I'm not ready to be turned into a piece of chalk just yet." At the end of the film, in an act of quasi-divine retribution, the killer child, on to whom the threat of nuclear war has been displaced, will instead be struck down by lightning and incinerated.

External punishment is necessary because the mother, Christine, does not succeed in containing her daughter once she realizes that Rhoda not only killed the boy who was awarded the medal for penmanship she had hoped to receive but has also done away with the handyman Leroy because he has found the cleats-studded shoes she used as her murder weapon. The notion of an enemy within takes on a double meaning in *The Bad Seed*, however, in that Christine herself is haunted by nightmares that make her strange to herself. When she confronts her father with her suspicion that there is something uncanny about her daughter, Richard Bravo offers a confession she interprets as a conviction of herself. It proves her to be the unwitting source of the internal enmity that has erupted in her home. Her real mother, she discovers, was a serial killer who had abandoned her daughter on a farm while fleeing from the police. It was there that Richard Bravo found Christine while covering the story for a Chicago paper and, taken in with her sweet appearance, had adopted her on the spot. While the father staunchly refuses to believe that murder is a hereditary trait, Christine grows ever more suspicious that her daughter has inherited a complete lack of remorse or guilt from her. Like the mother in *My Son John*, she spies on her, searches her room, and interrogates her until she is finally able to extort a confession to a series of killings. *The Bad Seed* thus offers yet another interpretation of the Cold War fantasy that an internal enemy, if skilled at camouflage, cannot easily be discovered. Rhoda is able to perform the role of virtuous child so convincingly precisely because she was born morally blind. The notion of the innocent child is thus debunked as a superb con game. Like McCarey's melodrama, this film, however, also poses the question: what kind of a family produces a bad seed that looks like a perfectly sweet little girl but can, if provoked, turn into an angry uncontrolled monster within seconds?

In contrast to Lucille Jefferson, Christine not only places the blame on herself for having mothered this alien child but also feels compelled to bear the responsibility for this fatal deed. The emotional quandary into which this places her leaves her facing a false choice. Should she protect her daughter at all cost? Or is she bound by the law to betray her (much as those before the House Committee on Un-American Activities were called upon to do)? The solution *The Bad Seed* comes up with is far more duplicitous than McCarey's melodrama. Embracing the idea that the disturbance which has disrupted her home since her husband went away, in fact, implicates both daughter and mother, Christine opts for a double sacrifice. She gives her daughter a lethal dosage of sleeping pills and then tries to shoot herself.

The fact that she doesn't succeed can be read as the film's discovery that there can be no neat solution of internal enmity.[12] Rhoda is finally killed off when lightning strikes the boathouse she has gone to at night. She had wanted to retrieve the medal her mother hid there so as to dispose of all evidence linking her daughter to the murder of the little boy. Christine, in turn, wakes up from her coma but is prevented from making her confession. Although, when her husband telephones the hospital, she wants to tell him everything, he insists – as yet another oblique reference to the clandestinity fostered by Cold War culture – that they must not talk about it now. The close-up of her silenced face suggests that, like the nightmare images of her mother, this forbidden knowledge will come to haunt the home she, upon her convalescence, will be bound to again. Yet a further ambivalence mars the reunion of this couple over the dead body of their killer child. Her father was not the only one to insist that the cause for a child proving to be a moral bad seed must be environmental not hereditary. If, then, Rhoda's evil is a response to the Cold War milieu she grew up in, her killing reflects a political culture that produces the very aliens it seeks to eradicate. As a symptom of this logic, Rhoda may have disappeared but the problem she gave shape to remains unresolved.

While, in the *Bad Seed*, the father remains oblivious to the alien force that has rendered his home uncanny, and with this blindness displays, albeit unwittingly, his own fallibility as figure of authority, *The Bigamist* revolves around a man whose failure as a husband ends in a court case that puts him on trial. And, while in *The Man in the Gray Flannel Suit*, the father is spiritually torn between his suburban American home and the wartime lover he left behind in Rome, Harry/Harrison Graham literally lives in two homes – the elegant apartment he shares with his official wife, Eve Graham in San Francisco, and the house he inhabits with his clandestine wife, Phyllis Martin (along with his illegitimate son) in Los Angeles. This double life renders both homes uncanny, even as it destabilizes his paternal authority. Each home is haunted by his life with the other woman about whom neither wife knows anything. Indeed, analogous to the undercover agent, this traveling salesman is strained by the deception he must sustain so as to prevent each of his wives from even suspecting the existence of the other. Ironically, his bigamy comes out into the open because he and Eve have decided to adopt a child. The man from the agency in charge of their case, Mr. Jordan, proceeds with an investigation that, too, is shaped by Cold War concerns. Though on the surface, the Grahams seem to be the perfect couple for adopting a child, Mr. Jordan feels compelled to check everything. While sitting in the kitchen with Harry, he addresses the fact that he spends much time in Los Angeles on business and asks for "the names of some of the people down there with whom you work." Deviously he pulls a small black notebook out of his left jacket pocket and then proceeds to explain, "it is all routine nothing more than that."

The concern on Harry's face, in turn, further invokes memories of similar tactics on the part of the FBI agents working in the name of HUAC. Indeed, as Mr. Jordan goes down to Los Angeles in an effort to gather more information, his surveillance becomes increasingly more sinister. The camera repeatedly focuses on the piercing gaze he casts on the world, constantly in search of one clue that will confirm the suspicion driving his inquiry. Following up on the names he has been given, he seems almost disappointed when the assessment of his suspect is favorable. Then again he gets positively excited at any information the people at the office out of which Harry works supply that suggests something may be wrong after all about the man he is investigating. His suspicion pays off when he finds a paperknife on Harry's desk bearing the name Harrison Graham, under which he is also listed in the Los Angeles telephone book. The confession Jordan extorts from him once he has found him living in this other home does not produce the understanding Harry had hoped for. Nevertheless, Jordan doesn't call the police, explaining that, although he both despises and pities him, he almost wishes him luck. Instead, Harry is arrested shortly after having returned to his home in San Francisco, with Eve, standing on the balcony of her apartment, tearfully watching him being taken away by two men.

By turning himself in, Harry destroys both marriages. The peculiar irony of the case, as the judge notes during his trial, is that his crime consisted in doing the right thing by marrying Phyllis when he discovered she was pregnant, even if this very act also meant a betrayal of both women he claims to love. The fact that the judge goes on to explain that bigamy strikes at the root of American society, can be read as a final reference to the domestic struggle sustaining Cold War culture. If the covenant of marriage is a miniature of the covenant of the nation, a man united with two women represents a breach in the allegiance to only one flag that American patriotism demands. The judge's closing statement addresses the quandary now facing this basically decent salesman in terms of a forfeiture of home. Conceding that he may well have loved both women, the judge adds: "I also suspect that he may now have lost them both." Having been found out publicly, the issue isn't which woman he chooses to go back to but rather which one might take him back. While it is clear that the decision is theirs, the film leaves open which choice they will make. Phyllis is the first to rise from her seat and leave once the court is adjourned. Eve, in turn, hesitates on the threshold and turns back to look at her husband. As Harry is led away, she remains there, leaning on the doorframe. A successful recuperation of her home, like the reunion of nation in the face of the split allegiance in its midst, remains suspended; a possibility that might, or might not, still be achievable.

If *The Bigamist* ends with a hero, uncertain which home, if any, he may be returning to, *The Swimmer* focuses on a father who has already lost his home but refuses to acknowledge this fact. One late summer morning, Ned Merrill suddenly appears at a friend's pool and, looking out across the valley, comes up with a project to sustain the dream he has regarding his own prowess. He notices that there is a string of pools that go clear across the county all the way to the recreation center pool where, just a bit further up the hill, his house stands. As a tribute to his wife, he wants to call the river these pools form the Lucinda River. The mantra sustaining him throughout the day is the claim: "I can swim home." What initially looks like a playful take on the Emersonian notion of self-reliance becomes progressively more somber. With each new neighbor he meets, it becomes ever more clear that Ned is in a state of denial, holding on to a dream of home to which no reality corresponds. Indeed, his swim from pool to pool is meant to cover up the fact that, owing to the failure of his business, he has been forced to give up this residence. He has become a stranger to some of his former friends, a *persona non grata* to others, in debt with shopkeepers and his daughters' object of ridicule. The limp and the shiver he develops as the day progresses serve as a bodily symptom of this fallibility, even while his resistance against this impairment signifies the force of his dream. That his story, like the others discussed in this chapter, serves as a trope for the state of the nation is invoked when his former lover, Shirley, mockingly reminds him of how troubled his family life had been while they were having their affair, calls the place she could never come visit his "house on a hill."

The more he holds on to images of past happiness, the more the people who confront him contradict this nostalgia. As such, he emerges as the foreign body among them, rendering visible a fissure in the collective dream regarding the sustainability of prosperity and security holding together this county in Connecticut. He represents internal enmity in part because he has failed or disappointed some of the members of this community, in part because, owing to his refusal to accept the truth of his failure, he uses violence against those who rebuke him or tell him facts about his family life that contradict the vaulted ideal of home he is clinging to at all cost. He also puts on display a crisis in paternal authority in that, because he is dressed in nothing more than his swimsuit, his vulnerable bare body is a warning to others that their situation, too, could be precarious. The fact that his real estate is in his wife's name, even while she was also the one to sell off their possessions, draws into focus the role gender plays in his domestic struggle. Lucinda and her daughters, we are led to understand, have no illusions about their changed prospects. Indeed, the coverup Ned performs, as he staunchly holds on to the need to swim home, is, above all, a form of self-dupery. The uncanniness he introduces into each of the homes he visits emerges from the fact that he is a double of himself. The image of the successful business man and loving father, to which he clings, is a spectral self hovering over the reality of his ruin.

When he finally reaches his home it has not only begun to rain. The house has also clearly been abandoned. The gate is rusty, the driveway overgrown, the tennis court in disrepair. Yet, even in the face of this manifest evidence of failure, Ned remains the resilient American hero who will not relinquish his memories of past happiness regardless of his current situation. As he walks up to his front door, the steps covered with broken branches, he hears the spectral laughter of his daughters playing tennis. Finding the front door locked, he persists in trying to force his way in until he realizes that he is irrevocably shut out from the very home on which his blind optimism was predicated. Forced finally to acknowledge what he can not afford not to know, he remains caught on the threshold in a huddled position, weeping helplessly, sheltered only by the wall framing the door. If the attraction of Ned's dream of home remains to the end on the level of a wish, this no longer serves an anticipation of what might yet be achieved, personally and collectively. Rather, in the year of the Tet Offensive, when the American public, forced to recognize the resilience and capabilities of the North Vietnamese, began to launch their own opposition to this war on the home front, *The Swimmer* proposes a dream of home revolving around the ruin of this vaunted ideal. The paternal position is not restored, as in *The Man in the Gray Flannel Suit* or *Autumn Leaves*, nor is the couple reunited as in *The Desperate Hours* or *The Bad Seed*. No remarriage is achieved as in *Half-Angel* to provide consolation regarding the couple formation as miniature standing in for the nation. Instead, the final shot of the film arrests the fallible father in a freeze frame, utterly alone in his arrogant individualism, reduced to his bare life, melding him into the image of detritus that is his home.

Figure 7.3 Ned arrested in the frame of his home ruin in *The Swimmer* (1968).

Coda

At one moment in the romantic comedy, *That Funny Feeling*, Tom Milford, a successful publisher, rushes into a phone booth on 62nd Street, just across from his apartment. An elderly woman is already standing there, hoping to enter it herself. Gently but firmly he takes the dime she has just extracted from her purse to make her own call and uses it himself. Several passersby gather around the enraged woman who begins embellishing her tale by turning it into a story of violent assault. Then one of them explains: "It's the Russians. They're sprinkling something around, makes everybody crazy." This is both the logical conclusion and, at the same time, a playful inversion of all the strategies of displacement discussed in this essay. A Russian attempt at interfering with the everyday life in Manhattan serves as a catchall explanation for whatever disturbances may be occurring. For the comic turn of events, this intangible, ubiquitous political threat thus serves as a cover for the concrete takeover of the hero's home by Joan Howell, a striving actress who cleans his apartment when he is away. Displacing the threat of a nuclear confrontation between the two superpowers into a love story, *That Funny Feeling* revolves around the collisions between these two people as they, at first, literally keep crashing into each other and then embark on a love affair that culminates in a battle of wits. The cause for this struggle is the fact that the apartment Joan shares with a roommate is too small for her to entertain Tom. She thus decides to usurp the home of the client she has never met, calling it her own, even while unaware that Tom is, in fact, that very man.

If, thus, on a latent level, the confusion Joan causes allows her to be read as a subversive agent on the romantic home front, the manifest reason for her agitation is of an economic nature. At the same time, her lack of a comfortable home does turn her into an imposter comparable to an undercover agent when, upon taking Tom to the home she has occupied, she claims to be Joan Milford because that is the name on the door. The irony, of course, is that, she has not only rendered Tom homeless, compelled to seek shelter with a friend. By assuming his last name and moving into his apartment, she also anticipates what the conclusion of any romantic comedy must be: the achievement of marriage. If, in turn, it not only takes mutual deception and surveillance but even a police raid on the apartment for the couple to finally come together, this debunks the myth of home as a place of comfort and security. The proposal scene, on which this couple's future happiness is predicated, significantly takes place in the police van taking them to the station. Their collisions and conflicts may have successfully been resolved but, through the end, they are not home bound. To suggest that all this disturbance at home is the result of something the Russians are sprinkling around is telling. When an external political threat can be normalized into domestic wackiness, it loses all touch of paranoia. That, too, is an imaginary resolution to actual conflicts but one that leaves the future once more open.

Notes

1. Michael Wood, *America in the Movies* (New York: Columbia University Press, 1975), p. 42.
2. See Richard Hofstadter, *The Paranoid Style in American Politics and Other Essays* (New York: Random House 1952), p. 3–41.
3. Sigmund Freud, "The Uncanny" (1919), *The Standard Edition 17* (London: Hogarth Press 1955), p. 220.
4. See Alan Nadel. *Containment Culture. American Narratives, Postmodernism, and the Atomic Age* (Durham, NC and London: Duke University Press 1995), p. 20.
5. J. Hoberman, *An Army of Phantoms: American Movies and the Making of the Cold War* (New York: The New Press 2011) notes that while John's terminal irony signals that he has clearly gone wrong, the question that above all the film addresses is "what sort of American family produces an Alger Hiss?" p. 193.
6. Michael Rogin, "Kiss me Deadly: Communism, Motherhood, and Cold War Movies, " *Ronald Reagan: The Movie* (Berkeley: University of California Press 1987) p. 252.
7. See Stephanie Coontz, *The Way We Never Were. American Families and the Nostalgia Trip* (New York: Basic Books 1992).
8. As Elaine Tyler May argues in *Homeward Bound: American Families in the Cold War Era* (New York: Basic Books 1988), the ideology of domestic containment and Cold War militancy rose and fell together. If, initially the turn to the home was the response to the threat of nuclear war, by the mid-1960s Cold War tensions had given way to culture wars, with the baby-boom generation reconsidering the cult of domesticity.
9. Stanley Cavell, *Pursuits of Happiness. The Hollywood Comedy of Remarriage* (Cambridge, MA: Harvard University Press 1981), p. 151.

10. *The Desperate Hours* plays with genre memory concerning the World War II war film, not least because of the star, Frederic March, who had already played a banker, returning from a bomber unit in William Wyler's *The Best Years of Our Lives* (1946). For a discussion of the crime film as a continuation of war with other means, see also Elisabeth Bronfen, *Specters of War: Hollywood's Engagement with Military Conflict* (New Brunswick, NJ: Rutgers University Press 2012); pp. 196–213.
11. Rogin, ibid., p. 252.
12. While in the novel by William March, the mother does die, leaving Rhoda undiscovered and now also unhindered in her freedom to kill, the film had to reverse this solution in compliance with the Hays Production Code.

Filmography

Aldrich, Robert, 1956: *Autumn Leaves*.
Garfein, Jack, 1961: *Something Wild*.
Johnson, Nunnaly, 1956: *The Man in the Gray Flannel Suit*.
LeRoy, Mervyn, 1956. *Bad Seed*.
Lupino, Ida, 1953: *The Bigamist*.
McCarey, Leo, 1952: *My Son John*.
Perry, Frank (and Sydney Pollack uncredited), 1968: *The Swimmer*.
Sale, Richard, 1951: *Half Angel*.
Thorpe, Richard, 1965: *That Funny Feeling*.
Weisberg, Joseph, 2013: *The Americans*, Season One.
Wyler, William, 1955: *The Desperate Hours*.

Bibliography

Biskind, Peter (1983), *Seeing is Believing, or How Hollywood Taught Us to Stop Worrying and Love the 50s*, New York: Henry Holt and Co.
Bronfen, Elisabeth (2001), *Home in Hollywood: The Imaginary Geography of Cinema*, New York: Columbia University Press.
Coontz, Stephanie (1992), *The Way We Never Were: American Families and the Nostalgia Trap*, New York: Basic Books.
Foreman, Joel, ed. (1997), *The Other Fifties: Interrogating Midcentury American Icons*, Champaign, University of Illinois Press.
Halberstam, David (1993), *The Fifties*, New York: Ballantine Books.
Hoberman, J. (2011), *An Army of Phantoms: American Movies and the Making of the Cold War*, New York: The New Press.
Nadel, Alan (1995), *Containment Culture. American Narratives, Postmodernism, and the Atomic Age*, Durham, NC: Duke University Press.
Rogin, Michael (1987), *Ronald Reagan, the Movie and Other Episodes in Political Demonolog*, Berkeley: University of California Press.
Tyler May, Elaine (2008), *Homeward Bound. American Families in the Cold War Era*, New York Basic Books.
Young, Paul (2006), *The Cinema Dreams its Rivals: Media Fantasy Films from Radio to the Internet*, Minneapolis: University of Minnesota Press
Wood, Michael (1975), *American in the Movies*.

8. SUBURBAN SUBLIME

Homer B. Pettey

In 1947, Abraham Levitt, along with his sons, transformed rural grazing land in Nassau County on Long Island into the tract-home, planned community of Levittown which would become a symbol of American middle-class values. The postwar invasion, really a mass white immigration of returning GIs to the suburbs, prompted Hollywood to develop a new cinema of distraction. Middle-class suburbia offered a fertile landscape on which to stage broad physical farces of upward mobility and all of its diversions and headaches – disastrous renovations, unruly appliances, financial woes, and the ever-present threat of adultery. Marriage, as both a social contract and amorous exploit, redefined modern gender roles through a series of comic vignettes on middle-class existence in these films. Central to all of these suburban romps were the visual distractions of mid-century modern architecture, interior design and its lively palette, and contemporary women's fashions from *Vogue* and *Harper's Bazaar*, all of which serve as pleasant diversions from toils and troubles of modern life. In these visual pleasures can be found an accepted system of consumption based upon economic and class identification. These suburban comedies, then, offer the visual enchantment of American modernity and gloss over its discontents.

Though patterned after Jack Benny's successful parody *George Washington Slept Here* (1942), even popular stars Cary Grant and Myrna Loy could not save *Mr. Blandings Builds his Dream House* (1948) from losing a quarter of a million dollars in its first run in 1948. That year also signaled the beginning of the Cold War with the Berlin Blockade. Two years later, *Father of the Bride*

(1950) would make six million dollars, nearly six times its production budget, probably because its tale of suburban excess held up a mirror to the foibles of the burgeoning American middle class. That film would start a trend in moneymaking suburban comedies for Hollywood throughout the 1950s and '60s, producing what can be classified as a *film cycle*. Even the most modest box-office returns proved profitable because audiences flocked to see gently absurd reflections of their own imagined lives. Profits ranged from three million for *Rally Round the Flag, Boys!* in 1958 to over twenty million a decade later for *Yours, Mine and Ours* (1968), twenty times its production budget. Even somewhat satirically dark films, such as *The Gazebo* (1959) and *Bachelor in Paradise* (1961), made reasonable, if small, profits. Into the 1980s, suburban comedies, often rehashing gender-role narratives and visual detractions from the 1950s and '60s cycle, had very successful runs, such as *Mr. Mom* making over sixty million and *The Money Pit* (1986) making over fifty million at the box office. By the fall of the Berlin Wall, the last Cold War suburban comedy, the very dark *Parents* (1989), like *Mr. Blandings Builds His Dream House* at the beginning of this cycle, lost considerably at the box office, to the tune of two million dollars. Still, this suburban comedy cycle during the Cold War held tremendous visual appeal and distraction for American audiences as much as it provided critiques of suburban life. Recognizing familiar space, place, and materiality certainly contributed to these comic reflections of a changing America.

Frederick Law Olmsted, among other landscape architects, set guidelines in the late nineteenth century for the layout of suburbia. Roads needed to be "curvilinear, designed not to run through the natural surroundings but to fit into them"; sidewalks had to be attractive to the eye as much as the "large, well-planted spaces between the sidewalk and the homes"; "generous provision for parks and recreation areas" where the democratic principles for people of "all classes" to assemble; and, neighborhood covenants would ensure that the aesthetic vision prevailed over the gaudy and inappropriate displays so much a part of American consumerism.[1] These suburbs formed a new American immigration of white middle-class families. Redistribution of new economic immigrants to this new American space occurred as a kind of invasion, a popular motif for any movement – military seizures, foreign agencies, aliens from outer space – in the Cold War period. In 1960, the Campanelli brothers descended upon Schaumberg, Illinois with their modified L-shaped ranch homes, proudly announcing in their ad campaign "New England's No. 1 Home Builder INVADES Chicagoland" and showing Archibald MacNeal Willard's *Spirit of '76* revolutionary drummer and two fife players marching in the street outside the home.[2] William H. Whyte, in *The Organization Man*, drew the analogy between the movement to the suburbs and immigration to illustrate the psychological hazards of disappointment awaiting this "social revolution" of the middle class: "In somewhat the same way that Americanization affected succeeding waves of immigrants, acclimatization to the middle class will lessen the feeling of social vulnerability that can turn these newcomers ugly."[3] Many suburban comedies rely upon the alien presence – bachelor, new family, new kid on the block – as a premise for suspicious, usually slapstick antics.

Of course, other covenants persisted to keep racial segregation a cornerstone of suburban life, such as those omitting African Americans, Asian Americans, and Jewish Americans. The suburban comedy of the Cold War era had a racial, ethnic, or cultural surveillance aspect to it, even if it were not explicit or overt in the narrative, because absence of racial groups living in the suburbs documents these covenants as part of film. In many ways, suburban films depicted accurately the political reality of America:

> By the 1960s, most whites were property owners, concentrated in all-white communities that were separated from – and in the case of suburbs, viewed as sanctuaries from – urban, minority communities. Most whites were convinced that the spatial and socioeconomic segregation of the metropolis was purely the result of free market forces.[4]

Racial minorities hardly counted for all marginalized figures in the developing suburban marketplace. For example, among executives for the New Levittown, whose planners tried to shake off the image of cookie-cutters housing designs, concerns arose about blue-collar workers whom "Levitt officials worriedly called 'marginal' buyers, people who could not really afford the house but were able to take it because no down payment had been required under Veteran Administration mortgage insurance regulations."[5] (Prophecies of the 2008 housing crisis in sub-prime mortgages to come.) There occurred a radical shift in suburban demographics that marginalization had never counted on, the creation of stratified suburban communities. The urban persistence theory, that initial economic and racial status continued over time for a suburb, did not coincide with the life-cycle shifts for suburban housing projects which saw a pattern, according to Hoover and Vernon (1962), of "development, transition, down-grading, thinning-out, and renewal," which can, to some degree, account for "edgeless cities, exurbs, and various subcenters that have emerged on a grand scale" since the 1970s that produced low-income and minority suburbs.[6]

Housing starts, almost exclusively for whites, achieved incredible growth in the early postwar years: "In 1949 alone, there were 1.4 million housing starts, and in 1950, another 1.9 million, more than three times the prewar record."[7] This dramatic increase in homes also meant a sharp rise in energy use, especially with the appeal of labor-saving appliances designed for the new lifestyle of suburbia. The all-electric household became the standard in

America, and corporations planned for the future with time-saving gadgets. In 1957, Whirlpool created a traveling show, the "Miracle Kitchen," which had a microwave oven, combo washer and dryer, mobile dishwasher, mobile floor sweeper, close-circuit television, as well as "automatic food preparation devices ... a hot-and-cold beverage dispenser" that made the kitchen a control center for the home.[8] West Bend produced *Flavo-matic* percolators, the *Electric Ovenette* and the *Electric Bean Pot*. General Electric had a *Rotisserie Oven*, Presto, the *Electric Pressure Cooker*, and Sunbeam, the *Automatic Waffle Baker*. Dormeyer's Spring Carnival of Values offered the *Fri-Way Electric Skillet*. Oster put out its *Juicer–Slicer–Shredder* as well as *Electric Meat Grinder*, *Electric Ice Crusher*, and *Electric Knife and Scissors Sharpener*. General Electric *Stratoliner range*, named for the Boeing plane, had push-button settings and an automatic timer. In the 1950s, the sales of built-in electric ranges jumped from fifty-seven million dollars to twice that sum by mid-decade, as did clothes dryers which "reached $217 million in 1955 and soared to $252 million in 1956"; dishwashers reached sales of ninety million in 1955 and one hundred sixteen million in 1956, and electric skillets, "a particularly fifties innovation that is rarely used today," nearly matched dishwashers with over one hundred ten million in sales.[9] International Harvester produced refrigerators that it claimed were "femineered" and others whose doors could be decorated with the same cloth pattern as the kitchen drapery – Scots plaid being quite popular. Built-in freezers, deepfreezes, and Frigidaire's and Gibson's self-defrosting units were all the rage in the postwar era. Most kitchen appliance companies offered a portable electric mixer. Of course, the surface of counters were Formica: "It's a joy in the kitchen, because it won't stain, crack, or chip, resists heat up to 310 °F and is wiped clean with a damp cloth."[10]

Commercialism and suburbia conjoined in the Cold War period, particularly for the new housewife emerging in the age of time-saving devices. *The Thrill of It All!* (1963) has wealthy ad executive Gardiner Farleigh (Edward Andrews) and his now pregnant wife (Arlene Francis) repay their obstetrician, Dr. Gerald Boyer (James Garner) and his wife, Beverly (Doris Day) with a dinner party. The gathering turns out to be the family meal with the patriarch, old Farleigh (Reginald Owen), a soap company tycoon, who becomes charmed by Beverly's home-spun anecdotes about her daughter wanting her hair shampooed with his *Happy Soap*. Beverly's honest approach and innocent stammering before the camera prove to be a successful market segmentation scheme, akin to the one that Wendell Smith proposed in the mid-1950s as an alternative to mass market competition which "advanced a new axiom of marketing, whether applied to cigarettes or refrigerators: homogeneity of buyers within a segmented market, heterogeneity between segmented markets."[11] For *Happy Soap*, changing half-nude, sudsy starlet, Spot Checker, for suburban doctor's wife Beverly proved a windfall because the psychographics – the emotions, gender, and economic circumstances – of consumers shifted from male businessmen to housewives, the new segment of consumers. Beverly's commercial success, over one hundred thousand dollars per year, outpaces her physician husband. Tensions mount as Beverly's long hours at the studio conflict with the doctor's hours, to the point that Dr. Boyer has his own words of advice for housewives to find fulfillment outside the home come back to haunt him. The film intersperses arrivals and departures of Dr. and Mrs. Boyer, each missing the other on the way out or in, with Beverly's soap ads on television. Beverly has become as much a product as the soap itself, the exemplary suburban woman. Finally, the good doctor causes a minor traffic accident when he sees Beverly's image on a billboard as she kisses a bar of *Happy Soap*, the commercial cuckolding by his commodified wife. To surprise Beverly for her new success selling *Happy Detergent*, the company installs a swimming pool in the backyard which, of course, Dr. Boyer drives his convertible into. As he leaves the house in fury, he kicks over a pyramid of *Happy Detergent* boxes into the pool – and then, the fun begins – suds everywhere! In a reversal of Beverly's market segmentation, Dr. Boyer targets his wife with his own branding, this time as hints of an affair with his office nurse. As will be evident, hints of adultery often form the narrative arc of suburban comedies. He has a photo taken of them indulging in champagne at a restaurant and tops off the charade with putting telltale lipstick on his white shirt collar. Of course, housewife Beverly finds the shirt as she is about to do the washing with *Happy* Soap – the irony as fitting as Dr. Boyer's reversal of the marketing scheme. After helping her husband deliver Mrs. Farleigh's baby in the back of the Rolls-Royce in a traffic jam, Beverly returns to the stability of housewifery, a logical conclusion to suburban product placement – Beverly the housewife, with the emphasis on *house*.

Sunset magazine promoted the ranch house, which marked off living spaces into zones:

> In the center might be the kitchen, bathrooms, and utility room, for plumbing cohesion; farthest from the bedrooms were the living room and study. One-story living meant less separation. A new room off the kitchen, called the den, was geared to relaxing with the children.
> The concept of the open kitchen – a radical idea – liberated the housewife moving the kitchen from a far-off station to the center of the house and by removing walls that separated it so that it could flow into the den or living room or dining area.[12]

The spacious quality of the open floor plan of the ranch house afforded the new nuclear family time to be together as a unit. Pony walls, which did not go to the ceiling, but had a pass-through, "kept even a partially enclosed kitchen

Figure 8.1 Dr. Boyer (James Garner) unwittingly drives his convertible into the new swimming pool that his wife Beverly (Doris Day) forgot to mention in *The Thrill of It All* (1963).

more open and allowed it to share light with adjoining rooms – an internal window in effect."[13] So essential in the housing market, construction companies began to include branded appliances in sales pitches.

In *Progressive Architecture*, companies producing new materials for the home found abundant advertising space as well as commentary. For example, Kimpreg plastic surfacing, in its full page ad, announced that "a new material with new advantages," among them "Permanent Surfacing" of a "themosetting phenolic resin laminate ... that defies parasites, decay and extreme temperatures ... is washable, insoluble, stainproof."[14] Donning a checkered dress, stylish hat, and black-and-white pumps, a suburban housewife pushes a button on her dashboard and opens her garage door: "With indications of a growing demand for this outstanding convenience in post-war homes, we urge you to investigate the distinctive features of the *Barber-Colman Radio Control*."[15] Those elicited to investigate this product are architects, not home buyers. Ingersol Utility Unit, a full home electrical, heating, and plumbing plan with fixtures and appliances, urged builders to follow the model set by successful firms:

> Pictured here are a few of the 182 comfortable homes built during the past year by John R. Worthman, Inc., in Ft. Wayne, Indiana. These and similar homes are an ideal answer to the current housing shortage. Each

of 35 Worthman homes now under construction is being speeded to completion, thanks to the Ingersol Utility Unit.[16]

To persuade architects and builders of the best product for the newest home design, the ranch house, Ceco Steel offered the "Picture Window of Steel": more than just beautiful, it had utility with "controlled ventilation" to "capture and control every stray breeze" and required no specific framing, but were "*stock* windows."[17] These products appealed to architects and builders for cost efficiency. Because the war made available numerous innovative products in lighting, plastics, and laminates, the marketplace rapidly transformed as architects fretted that they increasingly "ceded the high ground of technological expertise to engineers, industrial designers, or the manufacturers themselves."[18] Of course, for suburbia, architects for ranch-model houses became almost superfluous.

In 1947–8, Joseph McCarthy presided over the five-month Senate Joint Committee Study and Investigation of Housing and ran it as an arm of suburban contractors, planners, financiers, and relators:

> McCarthy mounted a well coordinated publicity campaign. He used a hefty cut of the committee's $100,000 budget to hire a staff from the New York public relations firm of Bell, Jones, and Taylor, whose other clients included, not coincidentally, the National Association of Home Builders, the U.S. Savings and Loan League, and the National Association of Real Estate Boards.[19]

Spurred on by nationalistic protection of returning World War II veterans, by a conservative distaste for public housing, and by a capitalist vision of expanding housing markets – this Senate committee gave the go-ahead for widespread postwar suburban development, such as Levittown. Each year after World War II, single-family homes increased tenfold in annual construction from 114,000 in 1944 to over one million in each successful year until the 1.6 million high point in 1950.[20] For lending agencies, mortgage companies, builders, and real-estate companies, the American Dream would come true with the advent of suburbia.

In its inaugural issue of January 1952, *House + Home* discussed the economic significance of home building in the United States which, in 1950 alone, had grossed as much as the entire automotive industry with a production rate of over one million new houses each year:

> The invention which made this new home-building possible is a new financing plan worked out in partnership with government. Under this plan millions of families have been able to buy new homes with little or

no down payment at a monthly cost cheaper than rent. Equally important, thousands of builders have been able to finance million-dollar housing developments on government-guaranteed advance commitments for mortgages. So well has this plan worked that in six years the total cost to taxpayers for creating a whole industry has been less than the cost of price support for a single year's crop of potatoes! Home building is thus an outstanding example of government & industry co-operation.[21]

A decade later, *House + Home* reported several disturbing trends in the American Dream market. First of all, the Veterans' Administration put up "12,000 loans totaling $100 million for sale," which the VA acquired "after the original GI purchaser defaulted."[22] The fourth quarter of 1961 ended, according to the Mortgage Bankers Association, with a record number of mortgage delinquencies, the VA contributing the "highest percentage of problem loans."[23] Additionally, foreclosures, according to Home Loan Bank statistics, "shot up 42%" with a "total of 73,640 foreclosures" that almost matched the number in 1940.[24] Ironically, the page extensions of these reports in *House + Home* sat between full-page ads of suburban housewives in party dresses before the new Tappan dishwasher and compact stove top with oven.

Mr. Blandings Builds His Dream House (1948) chronicles another American postwar suburban fantasy, the Do-It-Yourself hobbyist movement turned loose upon the fixer-upper dwelling. They must raze their pre-Revolutionary house to the ground, hire an architect to design their perfect home, and wait interminably as mishaps and construction problems plague the project. The well-digger charges exorbitant rates by the foot and seems incapable of finding water. The collection of contractors and construction workers have their own vision for the house which slowly evolves away from the sublime manse that the Blandings once envisioned. The novel, *Mr. Blandings Builds His Dream House* (1946), concludes with the couple finally moving in to their long-constructed home only to find light switches not working properly, loud humming florescent lights, window hardware that does not function, bathroom linoleum that no longer adheres to the floor and unvarnished paint mixtures that now allow for fingerprints to mar every wall. As he drifts off to sleep, Mr. Blandings unconsciously consoles himself with a solution to suburban home ownership: "Miles away, on Bald Mountain, in the midst of Surrogate Acres, beneath an uninsulated roof which creaked slightly now and then under the growing snow load of a winter storm, Mr. Blandings smiled uneasily in his sleep. He was dreaming that his house was on fire."[25]

The film script for *The Money Pit* (1986) includes the usual suburban domestic disasters that accompany home ownership, with the typical Hollywood physical comedy of the inept middle-class male facing home repairs:

Figure 8.2 The Blandings (Cary Grant and Myrna Loy) watch their classic home being brought down in order to build their dream home in *Mr. Blandings Builds His Dream House* (1948).

> INT. HOUSE – ENTRY HALL – DAY
> On the THIRD KNOCK the door (beautiful eighteenth-century mahogany) comes off its thirty-five cent hinges and crashes to the floor, destroying the boxes of dishes, household wares and most important the entire hard liquor supply. Those who cannot identify Walter's form through the cloud of dust may recognize him by his cough. He enters the house.<EXT/>

Or, when Anna screams at the dark, furry animal she pulls up in the defunct dumbwaiter and Walter in an act of comic heroism fails because the house is set dead against him:

> INT. ENTRY HALL AND STAIRCASE – DAY
> Walter races up the stairs to the rescue. As he reaches the midway point, the top of the step begins to give and detach from the landing. With Walter's next few steps, it gives completely and the whole staircase collapses. Walter makes a desperate leap and manages to grab onto the landing from which he now hangs. Walter's scream and the crash of the staircase cause Anna to stop screaming.[26]

The comedy of errors that plague renovations of the suburban house becomes a feature of these films. *Please Don't Eat the Daisies* (1960) chronicles David Niven and Doris Day following the typical urban to suburban move, with its own problems of transforming a bleak Gothic into a livable, family home. Doris Day, plucky as usual, takes on the challenges of remodeling and soon the place has a House Beautiful decor, with some minor mishaps along the way. Not so simply done in Jean Kerr's book, however. At the end of "How to decorate in one easy breakdown," Kerr explains that, even though a necessity for housewives, the results of redecorating the home may not turn out as one had hoped:

> In due time you will have selected material for your slipcovers, picked out a darker color for the drapes and a lighter color for the walls, and dropped the whole confusing assortment at the upholsterer's. One day seven months later everything arrives, and it's beautiful, beautiful--or maybe it isn't. You can always do it over again in eighteen or nineteen years.[27]

The Gazebo (1959), a very dark comedy, reverses this house-humiliating-the-owner trend of most suburban comedies. Instead, the owner, Elliott Nash (Glenn Ford), a television writer of murder mysteries, tries to destroy the house bit by bit, at least enough to convince his ranch-home-loving wife Nell (Debbie Reynolds) to sell to buyers offering $50,000 in cash. In a montage sequence, Nash reconfigures the plumbing so that when Nell turns on the bathroom sink faucet, the toilet becomes a fountain; Nash loosens the front door knob; he rewrites the fuse box to create outages; he tightens the recloser atop the kitchen door, so that Nell can barely open it; and he takes the sliding glass door off its track, so that Nell's only egress is a very tight squeeze. The reason for selling the house is that Nash needs money to pay off a blackmailer who claims to have nude photographs of his Broadway musical actress wife. Nell gives Nash a present of a gazebo whose foundation will become the perfect spot for Nash to hide the body of the blackmailer, whom he tries to kill by using one of his own television plots. The gazebo, then, becomes a mausoleum to middle-class morality and married life gone awry.

With the creation of suburbia, however, came social criticism of syndromes of conformity, mind-numbing existence, and rampant consumerism. David Riesman, in *The Lonely Crowd*, summed up the problems created for the suburban housewife in this existence:

> Many suburbanites, not to speak of farm wives, are much worse off. The husband drives to work in the only car and leaves his wife a prisoner at home with the small children, the telephone, and the radio or television. Such women can easily become so uninteresting that they will remain psychological prisoners even when the physical and economic handicaps to their mobility are removed. And this privatization in turn limits the friendship choices and increases the guilts of everyone else.[28]

This deprivation led to a form of social and psychological alienation, according to the persistent suburban myth of the times. This myth produced the myth of the bored housewife who seeks out a lover or becomes part of the swingers. John Keats's devastating critique of housing developments as new slums, *The Crack in the Picture Window*, also contributed to this suburban myth about neurotic housewives left alone by their daily absent, commuting husbands: "On the middle level, where most people have been married for, say seven years, there's apt to be the affair with the women in the car pool."[29] Suburban superconformity induces tedium and sexual restlessness in domesticity, so goes the myth.

This myth fostered an entire subgenre of smut, such as Orrie Hitt's *Suburban Sin* with the tagline of "Infidelity was a way of life with the split-level dwellers!" or his *Sexurbia County*. Jason Swiven's *Pampered Women* used as its come-on "A suburb of attractive, restless women – ripe for the suave charm of a man whose specialty was seduction," and for its second printing gave the sociological insight which read more like a singles ad: "An outspoken novel that dares to discuss a major problem – Unhappy women bored with their husbands seeking new love and excitement!" Its cover illustration showed a fully clothed man reclining on a double bed with a seated red-headed woman in her white bra, panties, and high heels as her negligée opens. J. X. Williams's *Suburban Wanton* offered on its cover the biblical injunction that "She coveted any man except her husband!" Alex Carter's novel of restless immorality, *The Games She Played*, promised that "The entire suburb was her private bedroom!" All of these sleaze-reads offered new meaning to the term "bedroom" community. The mid-1960s produced sexploitation films with low budgets and yet curiously moral endings often devoted to suburban adulterous affairs and swinging, with titles such as *Sin in the Suburbs* (1964) and *The Swap and How they Make It* (1966), both directed by the prolific Joe Sarno, known for his soft-core work, such as *Confessions of a Young American Housewife* (1974). Just as Reisman and Keats hinted about fidgety, not frigid housewives, so Sarno exploited the suburbs as the domain of very willing and very domineering *stray*-at-home wives. While much not-seen extramarital sexual activity fills these 1960s films, they conclude with couples returning to their marriages, almost as though the excursion into the realms of sin and depravity had brought them back to moral values.

Such a myth certainly finds its way into mainstream Hollywood productions, with the bored, yet always eager women down the street ready for some extramarital excitement. Many of these films flirt with adultery themes but only titillate with no dalliances occurring. *Bachelor in Paradise* (1961) finds sexual and sensualist writer Adam J. Niles (Bob Hope), owing to IRS tax reasons, having to hide out in Paradise Valley, California, a newly constructed subdivision whose welcoming sign reads like a quintessential suburbs ad: Paradise Valley. Ultra-Modern Homes. 2 & 3 bedrooms with gas kitchens. There, in his pink ranch house, whose interior decoration he sarcastically calls "early Disneyland," he can observe the domestic rituals of married suburban housewives for his new book, *How The Americans Live*. In voice-over, Adam dictates his observations, most of them in line with critics of suburban life, especially about gender divisions: "And during the period from sunup to sundown, the typical American community is completely matriarchal, dominated entirely by females, a no-man's-land more foreboding than Scythia, home of the Amazons." He invites the neighborhood women for discussion groups at his home about reviving romance and sexual seduction of husbands which becomes the source for scandals, including his being named in three divorce cases. Fortunately, Niles has won over Rosemary Howard, the subdivision's realty secretary (Lana Turner), who persuades the judge of Niles's innocence. Of course, nothing untoward ever happens in Paradise Valley and marriage becomes the natural and moral solution for Niles and Rosemary.

The male version of the suburban comedy of adultery includes the bedroom satire directed by Gene Kelly *A Guide for the Married Man* (1967), in which Paul Manning (Walter Matthau) discovers that his friend Ed (Robert Morse) has been having affairs for some time. Through a series of instructional vignettes, acted out by Hollywood regulars from Jack Benny, Sid Caesar, Joey Bishop to Lucille Ball, Jane Mansfield, Terry-Thomas, and Wally Cox, Paul learns from Ed, Ph.D. "doctor of philandering" as the trailer claims, how to cheat on one's wife without getting caught. Of course, when Paul's moment of truth arrives, the shady motel where he has brought a rich divorcee (Elaine Devry) for an assignation erupts when wailing sirens announce vice detectives breaking down a room's door to expose Ed and not-his-wife Irma Johnson (Sue Anne Landon) fully compromised. In a panic of fidelity, Paul flees back to the arms of his faithful and shapely wife Ruth (Inge Stevens). The humor of this middle-aged male fantasy, with the camera acting as the male libido for close-ups of breasts, legs, and hips, relies upon Ruth shown in suggestive states of undress, sometimes clad in a bikini, a leotard, or only a towel, and Paul's bored inattentiveness. This nod-wink-wolf whistle suburban farce concludes in a similar manner to Joe Sarno's sexploitation films, with the couple reunited after sin.

In *Mr. Mom* (1983), recently laid-off Ford Motor Company automotive engineer, Jack Butler (Michael Keaton), becomes a stay-at-home father with all the problems of suburban life. Both *Bachelor in Paradise* and *Mr. Mom* share a common media misandry concerning the abandoned male in the household, where washing machines produce *The Blob*-like unending and engulfing billows of suds. Jack, an engineer mind you, cannot control a simple vacuum cleaner, for comic effect referred to as "Jaws." Of course, he eventually becomes proficient at household tasks but not effective at avoiding the persistent amorous intentions of his neighbor Joan (Ann Jillian) whose habit of thrusting her cleavage into Jack's face punctuates the sexual humor. At one point in the script, Jack, having given up on his appearance and chores, watches *Now, Voyager* on television and slips into a dream of an assignation with the buxom Joan, only to be interrupted by his now ad executive wife, Caroline (Teri Garr) with pistol and silencer in hand. Jack tries to wrestle the gun from Caroline's hand, which goes off wounding him, but not before he offers an explanation to Caroline's "What got into you, Jack?" which is straight out of Reisman's and Keats's view of suburban domesticity: "The boredom, the repetition, the days flowing one into the next, the loneliness."[30] The film's conclusion involves Joan slipping into the bed Jack shares with Caroline but Joan's sexual trap becomes her own snare when Caroline returns early from a business trip. Of course, the suburban comedy formula resolves all issues of housewrecking and monogamy: Joan leaves before Jack can be intimate, Jack and Caroline reunite, Caroline returns to motherhood that she sorely misses, and Jack gets his old job back.

In *Neighbors* (1981), Earl Keese's (John Belushi) quiet, suburban cul-de-sac existence ends when Vic (Dan Aykroyd) and his seductress wife, Ramona (Cathy Moriarty), move in next door. Frustrated by their noise, lunatic behavior, and intrusiveness, Earl's sanity nearly shatters in one very odd evening. His wife (Kathy Walker) and daughter (Lauren-Marie Taylor) offer him no solace or aid, which induces more paranoia and alienation in Earl. While still having no actual adultery, *Neighbors* rejects the return to normalcy model of other suburban comedies. His wife takes off with a wealthy Native American while his daughter runs away with a tow-trucker. In the end, Earl joins Vic and Ramona on their new road-trip adventure away from the responsibilities of suburbia while his house becomes engulfed in flames, a visual homage to the conclusion of *Mr. Blandings Builds His Dream House*. As the threesome drive away, Earl comments, always keeping the Mrs. in mind, "Enid never did like coming home to a dark house." *Neighbors* satires the sleazy sexploitation genre as much as suburban comedies. Audiences found the formula for these comedies quiet appealing, as their box offices attest: *Bachelor in Paradise* cleared over a million dollars for MGM; *Mr. Mom* achieved an annual domestic gross of over sixty million for Twentieth Century-Fox; and, *Neighbors* grossed almost thirty million dollars domestically for Columbia (Weekend Box Office).

Two suburban comedies nearly a decade apart focus upon adultery as a subtext for social commentary, *Rally 'Round the Flag Boys!* (1958) and *The Graduate* (1967). Adapted from Max Shulman's suburban Cold War humorous novel, *Rally 'Round the Flag Boys!* combines suburban village middle-class hanky-panky with guided missiles. The film's kooky plot pits bored commuter Harry Bannerman (Paul Newman) as P.R. man for the Pentagon to insure the construction of a new military base installation in the Connecticut suburb of

Putnam's Landing against his obsessively civic-conscious wife Grace (Joanne Woodward), leader of the committee against the base. With the domestic battle lines drawn, the novel also follows the bored television-widow Angela who wants a divorce but knows too well the uxuorial code of Cold War suburbia that an "unfettered adult female was regarded, at the very best as a second class citizen, and in the case of one as decorative as Angela, as an enemy agent."[31] Angela, however, realizes that her "great untapped reservoir of wifelinesss" granted her a messianic duty to free "dozens of discontented husbands, men who found their wives inadequate, unsympathetic, even hostile" (72–3):

> Angela rose and paced. She had never before analyzed things in quite this way. It sure put a new face on the situation. Taking somebody's husband – somebody's *discontented* husband, that it – was not thievery; it was *liberation!* Like John Brown going into Harper's Ferry, kind of. Angela smiled, pleased with the notion of herself as Old Pottawatamie. And it wasn't so far-fetched either, thought she with a righteous nod. Wasn't she, too, going on a slave raid? Wasn't she going to find a man in bondage and set him free? Of course she was. That was *exactly* what she was going to do – release a poor captive, sever his shackles, unyoke his shoulders, heal his welts, and guide his faltering feet down Freedom Road! (73)

Shulman's double-edged humor captures the Civil Rights Act of 1957 by which Congress supported African American freedom in voting and reinforced the antisegregation *Brown* decision of 1954, as it does the Hungarian revolt for liberation in 1956. Of interest, Shulman published chapter versions of this novel for *Good Housekeeping* in 1954 and 1957. After surveying the landscape, Angela settles on Harry Bannerman. In the film, Harry and the aggressive Angela (Joan Collins) have a series of coitus interested, but interruptus: first at the train station when she drives him home in her appropriately passion-red convertible; next, when she plies Harry with whiskey to the point that he swings from the foyer chandelier as primal man; and, in his Washington, D.C. hotel, only to be caught by surprise by the now frisky let's-do-it-like-we-used-to wife Grace. The splitting up of the Bannermans continues after the ill-fated and wholly unhistorical Pilgrims Pageant, an embarrassment for Grace. Harry tracks down the now U. S. Army fatigue-donning Grace to Control Room 1 of the missile installation. To profess his undying love, he grabs the fleeing Grace by her pants top, holds her in mid-air from her buttocks, as she pulls on the control levers with both hands, a position readily understood. Finally, when all is forgiven, Harry lifts her and plants her on "The Button" before planting his kiss, thereby launching the symbolic, phallic rocket. *Rally 'Round the Flag Boys!* (1958) made a million six for Twentieth Century-Fox.

At the end of the Cold War period, suburban comedies take on dark twists, not about adultery, but about the obsession with surveillance and rooting out antisocial activity. Shot obviously on the back lot at Universal Studios, *The Burbs* (1989) revives the 1950s sociological distrust of suburban conformity with Ray Peterson (Tom Hanks) and his neighbors, Art Weingartner (Rick Ducommun) and crazed veteran Lieutenant Mark Rumsfield (Bruce Dern), surveilling their suspicious East European neighbors, the Klopecks. The cul-de-sac vigilantes suspect the Klopecks of being a murder cult, with the ocular proof of their strange digging-up of their backyard during a rain storm, driving down their short driveway to put trash out on the street, and creating strange emanations of light from their basement each night. Their not-so-funny investigations result in their burning the Klopeck place to the ground. While it turns out that they were correct, when a trunkload of skulls are discovered as police, firefighters, and Emergency Medical Technicians arrive on the scene, Ray had previously explained why all of this disastrous behavior occurred – suburban mania:

> RAY: Remember what you were saying about people in the 'burbs going nuts, Art? Guys like Skip who mow their lawn for the eight hundredth time and then snap? That's *us*! It's not *them*! *We're* the crazy ones! *We're* the ones that see things that aren't there! We live in these houses that are all the same on these streets that are all the same! And we have the same jobs and the same cars and the same friends! And we get so conditioned to the same routine that as soon as someone different moves onto the block, we *lose* it! And we run around vaulting fences and peeking in windows and throwing garbage in the street and setting fires and acting suspicious and paranoid! *We're* the lunatics, Art! *Not* them! *Us!* [32]

Ray's indictment of suburban conformity might well fit Cold War hysteria, except that the problem is homegrown, not foreign. This form of self-criticism reasserts the basic assumption of these Cold War comedies that living in suburbia produces not just complacency and ultraconformity but also patterns of insanity and deviancy. Reading *The Burbs* as an indictment of Cold War mentality misses the point of these comedies. To one degree or another, these suburban comedies satirize American values and treat lunacy as a kind of American normalcy. This all-too-familiar cinematic formula certainly delighted audiences, as attested to by *The Burbs* doubling its budget outlay of eighteen million dollars in domestic box-office returns.

Parents (1989), directed by Bob Balaban, serves as a tonic to those saccharine 1950s–60s television family situation comedies about the innocuous travails of middle-class existence in the suburbs, such as *The Donna Reed Show*, *Leave It To Beaver*, and *Father Knows Best*. *Parents* in some ways represents the quintessential suburban comedy, even if a very dark satire, especially during the closing years of the Cold War. The film begins as a black-and-white close-up moves from lips to eyes to reveal Michael Laemie (Bryan Madorsky) with a cold, distraught expression, à la Hitchcock's *Vertigo* opening credits. It dissolves to an overhead sweeping shot of a Levittown-like suburb, which cuts to an overhead panning vista shot of home after home across the land, and then cuts to the grille (a visual pun) of a 1950s Oldsmobile. All the while, "Cerezo Rosa" ("Cherry Pink," the 1950s *couleur de jour*) by Perez Prado blares as background score. The film's closing credit sequence plays Sheb Wooley's "The Purple People Eater" as a final sardonic note.

The Laemies, Nick and Lily (Randy Quaid and Mary Beth Hurt) have moved into a split-level ranch house with a carport that follows the general pattern of the period. The interior decor showcases mid-century modern designs. Just off the entrance with its wooden étagère to the right across from the short steps to the split-level bedrooms, the living room expands in an open plan that reveals the kitchen and the dining area. In the corner created by the low entrance wall and vertical board separation slats stands the television cabinet and a Rockwell accent chair. Against the central living room gray stone interior wall separation resides a dark, cloth-covered platform couch with several bright colored throw pillows, a tall tree floor lamp, and before them, a sculpted boomerang coffee table. Adjacent to the matching gray stone fireplace on the outer wall, in the far corner stands a wooden hi-fi console cabinet, above which hang a large, white, paper, geodesic ceiling lamp and a Calder-like, suspended, wire-and-black sheet metal mobile. In the dining area, a circular table with Eames-style vortex side chairs rest beneath a pull-down drum pendant ceiling light and, for decoration, irregular atomic radioactive black waves on the white wallpaper match the blue waves on floor-to-ceiling drapes for the sliding glass doors.

The nerve center of this suburban home remains the kitchen with a classic, white, louvered-shutter pantry door, a double sink with disposal, white cabinetry, plastic sliding opaque paneled storage cabinetry above the sink, pendant white ceiling lamps, and deep blood-red countertop throughout. It is equipped with the latest conventional, labor-saving appliances: white top-freezer, upright refrigerator (the large white spacious, coffin-like chest freezer sequestered in an alcove room off the kitchen), metal blender, white Mixmaster, two-slice toaster, practical large oven with four-top range used to warm the parents' favorite dish – leftovers. The basement, referred to by the father Nick as "the Cellar," has a bare-bones, two-by-four staircase and, against a cement-block wall, stands the multitiered wine rank where he keeps his middle-class Château Margaux that goes so well with red meat. The Laemies dress appropriately for the era, Nick often in a yellow cardigan at meals and Lily with in a black shrug over a white, small-collared blouse with a belted full print skirt and petticoats, and high heels. The couple love to barbecue together, as shown in several

Figure 8.3 Parents (Randy Quaid and Mary Beth Hurt) barbecuing some fresh meat for dinner in *Parents* (1989).

shots through the film with an aproned Nick wielding a long-handled salt shaker as Lily douses sporadic flames from the large foregrounded grill stacked with unidentifiable slabs of meat. House, furnishings, and attires bespeak the typical suburban couple; something is eating at young Michael, however – he thinks his parents are cannibals. When Nick tries to force a bite of meat on his problem-eater son, young Michael stabs his father and that sets off a chain reaction of dark comedy that eventuates in the parents' deaths and the ranch house engulfed in flames. Like the ending of *Mr. Blandings builds his Dream House*, *Parents* reveals the alienating effects of suburban consumption.

During the Cold War era, no racially based suburban comedy appeared. Carl Franklin's *Devil in a Blue Dress* (1995), however, attests to an even earlier creation of a minority subcenter with World War II veteran Easy Rawlins (Denzel Washington) entering a dangerous missing person case in order to pay the mortgage on his house located just off Central Avenue in Los Angeles. This post-Cold War film, like Walter Mosely's novel, differs substantially from the social comedies of white suburbia. Here, Easy Rawlins finds his home a liminal sanctuary, easily invaded by Los Angeles Police Department detectives, dangerous white gangsters, and violent African American thugs. While a neo-noir, *Devil in a Blue Dress* does provide a sociohistorical account of simultaneous African American economic disenfranchisement and mobility that would continue into the suburbs in the 1990s.

Suburban comedies did not broach the serious economic effects of suburban growth during the Cold War. Suburbia remained a sublime place in the imagination of the American viewing public. The post-Cold War period, however, brought home several types of disastrous declines for retailers, consumers, and homeowners. With the shift to purchasing on-line and retailers losing touch with their customers, such as in the failures of Sears, Wards, and K-Mart, the center hub of suburbia – the mall became moribund. Dan Bell's series *Dead Malls* reveals the economic transformation and devastation to suburban towns with the closure of most storefronts in what had been the product of Late and Post-Cold War America – the giant, supermalls with anchor upscale branded stores, food courts, theaters, and local businesses and franchises. After the Berlin Wall fell, more malls dotted the American landscape in the 1990s, only to fall into disuse and decay within twenty years, in much the same way as scores of suburban communities did after 2008. No suburban comedy has yet to take on this dark subject matter. Perhaps none ever will.

Notes

1. Robert M. Fogelson, *Bourgeois Nightmares – Suburbia, 1870–1930* (New Haven, CT: Yale University Press, 2005): pp. 41–2.
2. Barbara Miller Lane, *Houses For a New World – Builders and Buyers in American Suburbs, 1945–1965* (Princeton, NJ: Princeton University Press, 2015): p. 179.
3. William H. Whyte, Jr., *The Organization Man* (New York: Simon and Schuster, 1956): p. 310.
4. David M. P. Freund, *Colored Property: State Policy and White Racial Politics in Suburban America* (Chicago: University of Chicago Press, 2007): p. 385.
5. Herbert J. Gans, *The Levittowners: Ways of Life and Politics in a New Suburban Community* (1967; New York: Columbia University Pres, 1982): p. 9.
6. Bernadette Hanlon, *Once the American Dream: Inner-Ring Suburbs of the Metropolitan United States* (Philadelphia: Temple University Press, 2010): pp. 43, 46.
7. Carroll Pursell, *Technology in Postwar America: A History* (New York: Columbia University Press, 2007): p. 22.
8. Brian S. Alexander, *Atomic Kitchen: Gadgets and Inventions for Yesterday's Cook* (Portland, OR: Collectors Press, 2004): p. 33.
9. Bill Yenne, *Going Home to the Fifties* (San Francisco: Last Gasp, 2002): pp. 63, 64.
10. Lesley Hoskins, *Fiftiestyle: home decorations and furnishings from the 1950s* (London: Middlesex University Press): p. 50.
11. Lizabeth Cohen, *A Consumers' Republic: The Politics of Mass Consumption in Postwar America* (New York: Vintage Books, 2003): p. 295.
12. Katherine Ann Samon, *Ranch House Style* (New York: Clarkson Potter, 2003): p. 21.
13. Michelle Gringeri-Brown, *Atomic Ranch: Design Ideas for Stylish Ranch Homes* (Salt Lake City: Gibbs Smith Publisher, 2006): p. 48.
14. *Progressive Architecture (Pencil Points)* (January 1947): p. 9.
15. *Progressive Architecture (Pencil Points)* (February 1947): p. 12.
16. *Progressive Architecture (Pencil Points)* (May 1947): p. 4.
17. *Progressive Architecture (Pencil Points)* (October 1947): pp. 6–7.
18. Philip Nobel, "Who Built Mr. Blandings' Dream House?" in *Architecture*

and Film, ed. Mark Lamster, (New York: Princeton University Press, 2000): p. 75.
19. Rosalyn Baxandall and Elizabeth Ewen, *Picture Windows – How the Suburbs Happened* (New York: Basic Books, 2000): p. 90.
20. Kenneth T. Jackson, *Crabgrass Frontier – The Suburbanization of the United States* (New York: Oxford University Press, 1985): p. 233. Jackson also mentions how consolidation in the house-starts market took place at this time: "As early as 1949, fully 70 percent of new homes were constructed by only 10 percent of the firms (a percentage that would reamin roughly stable for the next three decades)" (p. 233).
21. "What Lies Ahead for Home Building," *House + Home – the magazine of building* (January 1952): p. 138.
22. "VA to sell loans," *House + Home – the magazine of building* (May 1962): p. 51.
23. "Delinquencies reach peak," *House + Home – the magazine of building* (May 1962): p. 51.
24. "Foreclosures at 21-year high," *House+Home – the magazine of building* (May 1962): p. 51.
25. Eric Hodgins, *Mr. Blandings Builds His Dream House* (1974; New York: Simon & Schuster, 1946): p. 228.
26. David Giler, *The Money Pit*, story and screenplay (December 4, 1979 through draft revisions January 18, 1985): p. 38, shot 39; 43, shot 50.
27. Jean Kerr, *Please Don't Eat the Daisies* (Garden City, NY: Doubleday & Company, Inc., 1957): pp. 59–60.
28. David Riesman, *The Lonely Crowd: A study of the changing American character* (New Haven, CT: Yale University Press, 1969): p. 282.
29. John Keats, *The Crack in the Picture Window* (New York: Ballantine Books, 1956): p. 125.
30. John Hughes, *Mr. Mom* (Eighth Draft, January 24, 1983): p. 72, shot 163B.
31. Max Shulman, *Rally 'Round the Flag, Boys!* (Garden City, NY: Doubleday & Company, 1958): p. 71.
32. Dana Olsen, *The Burbs* (Composite Draft April 15, 1988): p. 114, shot 306.

FILMOGRAPHY

Arnold, Jack, 1961: *Bachelor in Paradise*.
Balaban, Bob, 1989: *Parents*.
Benjamin, Richard, 1986: *The Money Pit*.
Dante, Joe, 1989: *The Burbs*.
Dragoti, Stan, 1983: *Mr. Mom*.
Jewison, Norman, 1963: *The Thrill of It All!*.
Marshall, George, 1959: *The Gazebo*.
McCarey, Leo, 1958: *Rally 'Round the Flag, Boys!*.
Pasternak, Joe, 1960: *Please Don't Eat the Daisies*.
Potter, H. C., 1948: *Mr. Blandings builds his Dream House*.

9. DOMESTIC CONTAINMENT FOR WHOM? GENDERED AND RACIAL VARIATIONS ON COLD WAR MODERNITY IN THE APARTMENT PLOT

Pamela Robertson Wojcik

An apartment plot is a film in which the apartment figures as a central device. This means that the apartment is more than setting but motivates or shapes the narrative in some key way. Famous apartment plots include *Rear Window* (Hitchcock, 1954), *In a Lonely Place* (Ray, 1950), *An American in Paris* (Minnelli, 1951), *How to Marry a Millionaire* (Negulesco, 1953), *Pillow Talk* (Gordon, 1959), *Bells are Ringing* (Minnelli, 1960), *Barefoot in the Park* (Saks, 1967), *Wait Until Dark* (Young, 1967), *The Odd Couple* (Saks, 1968), and *Rosemary's Baby* (Polanski, 1968). Though none of these films is typically taken to be reflective of the Cold War – *In a Lonely Place* might be an exception in its depiction of paranoia and friends distrusting friends – this chapter discusses the apartment plot as a Cold War genre.

My book, *The Apartment Plot: Urban Living in American Film and Popular Culture, 1945 to 1975* argued for an understanding of the apartment plot as genre and, without naming it as a Cold War genre, focused on films made within the Cold War era.[1] Yet, the apartment plot is not invented in 1945 and is not exclusive to the American context. In *Apartment Stories: City and Home in Nineteenth-Century Paris and London*, Sharon Marcus locates a cycle of apartment plots in nineteenth-century British and French novels.[2] In film, Abram Room's *Bed and Sofa* (1927) offers an early Russian apartment plot in which a housing shortage leads to an adulterous *ménage à trois*. *Hands Across the Table* (Leisen, 1935) shows two gold-diggers – one female (Carole Lombard) and one male (Fred MacMurray) – sharing quarters while each searches for a rich prospect. Early musicals, such as *Sunny Side Up* (Butler,

1929) and *Gold Diggers of 1933* (Berkeley, 1933), revolve around female apartment roommates who date and marry rich men. The genre includes art cinema films such as *Ali: Fear Eats the Soul* (Fassbinder, 1974) and *Jeanne Dielman, 23 Quai du Commerce, 1080 Bruxelles* (Akerman, 1975). And the apartment plot extends well beyond the Cold War era, notably in television shows such as *Three's Company* (1977), *Seinfeld* (1990), *Melrose Place* (1992), *Frasier* (1993), *Friends* (1994), *Will and Grace* (1998), *Two and a Half Men* (2003), *How I Met Your Mother* (2005), *Rules of Engagement* (2007) and *Don't Trust the B— in Apt. 23* (2012). Nonetheless, the cinematic apartment plot in America seems to reach its pinnacle in the mid-twentieth century, and the apartment functions as a particularly privileged site for representing an important alternative to dominant discourses of and about mid-twentieth-century America. Thus, I argue that we can characterize a Cold War cycle of the apartment plot.

For the most part, the apartment plot does not directly engage the subset of political issues central to the Cold War, such as anti-Communist rhetoric or nuclear fear. Instead, the Cold War apartment plot navigates dominant mid-century discourses around domesticity and urbanism. The nineteenth-century variant emerged in a time and in places where apartment living was essentially being invented. The apartment plot in mid-century American film, by contrast, surfaces roughly a century after the development of apartment houses. The meaning and status of the apartment, however, are crucially up for grabs in this period, as the ideals of suburban living and private home ownership dominate the cultural imagination. Therefore, the mid-century American apartment plot needs to be viewed in relation to various discourses on family, home, and suburbia. But it is precisely the dominance of those discourses, both during the period and retrospectively, in accounts of the period that have rendered the apartment plot virtually invisible.

Lynn Spigel offers a summary description of the dominant view of the American 1950s as "a time when domesticity was a central preoccupation of the burgeoning middle class:"

> During and after the war, the marriage rate rose to record heights; of those who came of age, 96.4 percent of the female and 94.1 percent of the male population married – and at younger ages than ever before. The baby boom, which began during the war and lasted through 1964, reversed declining birthrates of previous decades, creating a revitalization of the nuclear family as a basic social construct. The resurgence of the family unit was met with a new model for living – the prefabricated suburban tract home, so affordable that young middle class couples, and, at times lower middle class, blue collar workers, could purchase their piece of the American dream ... Popular media also participated in the

cultural revitalization of domesticity, taking the white middle-class suburban home as their favored model of family bliss.[3]

This description brings together key elements of the 1950s ideal – the white, heterosexual middle class, rising marriage rates, the baby boom, and suburban living – and claims that popular culture fed this ideal. James Harvey puts it simply, "The movies, like their audience, were moving to the suburbs."[4]

Elaine Tyler May extends this analysis of the 1950s to incorporate Cold War politics into our understanding of the suburban home. In particular, May argues that the suburban home of 1950s reflected and refracted Cold War policies of "containment," United States ambassador George Kennan's 1947 term for American foreign policy apropos the Soviet bloc:

> In the domestic versions of containment, the "sphere of influence" was the home. Within its walls, potentially dangerous social forces of the new age might be tamed, where they could contribute to the secure and fulfilling life to which postwar women and men aspired ... More than merely a metaphor for the cold war on the homefront, containment aptly describes the way in which public policy, personal behavior, and even political values were focused in the home.[5]

While acknowledging that the "traditional" family of the 1950s represented a newly constructed ideal, without deep roots in the past, May nonetheless views it, and the suburban ideal that goes along with it, as overriding: "In the postwar years, Americans found that viable alternatives to the prevailing family norm were virtually unavailable. Because of the political, ideological, and institutional developments that converged at the time, young adults were indeed homeward bound, but they were also bound to the home."[6]

To be sure, the fifties witnessed a huge boom in suburban development and cities felt the effects of white flight. Nevertheless, apartment living was a "viable alternative" to prevailing norms and the only real choice for many people left out of the suburban imaginary, including single and divorced people, African Americans, working-class whites, ethnic minorities, and gay people. Apartments were, as well, the preferred option for many married, middle-class families with urban or bohemian tastes. While some percentage of films and other media were perhaps "taking the white middle-class suburban home as their favored model of family bliss,"[7] as Spigel says, an equal number were troubling the waters of the suburban ideal – think of *Mr. Blandings Builds His Dream House* (Potter, 1948), *Rebel Without a Cause* (Ray, 1955), *All That Heaven Allows*, *Please Don't Eat the Daisies*, or *Bachelor in Paradise* (Arnold, 1961). And very many films were representing the alternative of urban apartment living, sometimes in collusion with the dominant suburban ideology, sometimes in opposition to it, and sometimes without any direct reference to, or acknowledgement of, it.

The apartment plot can be seen as a correlative of the suburban domestic ideology of the period. The suburban, after all, requires the urban for its definition. The suburb needs the city to center itself, as a site for commuting, as what is proximate, and as its antithesis. Similarly, the ideal definition of home – as privately owned single-family home – requires a notion of the apartment, rental units, multiple dwellings, subdivided homes and tenements. And, obviously, heterosexual family ideals depend upon the opposing examples of the single, divorced, childless, and gay.

More than just providing a counterweight to suburban fantasies, though, the apartment plot maintains and celebrates the urban against the forces of suburbia, against containment, and against the destruction of the city. I have argued that the apartment plot produces a philosophy of urbanism. Here, I want to designate that philosophy of urbanism as a form of vernacular modernism. I take the term vernacular modernism from Miriam Hansen's scattered writings on the subject. To summarize briefly, the concept of vernacular modernism suggests an engagement with modernity, rather than a style. Rather than a mere reflection *of* modernity, vernacular modernism must, in some way, reflect *upon* modernity. Hansen writes: "The question was, and continues to be, how particular film practices can be productively understood as *responding* – and making sensually graspable our responses – to the set of technological, economic, social and perceptual transformations associated with the term modernity."[8] Instead of modernist style, then, vernacular modernism functions as a mode that navigates the experience of modernity. Cinema, in Hansen's words, was "the single most inclusive cultural horizon in which the traumatic effects of modernity were reflected, rejected, or disavowed, transmuted or negotiated,"[9] a means to articulate fantasies and anxieties about modernity.

The Cold War cycle of apartment plots serve to transmute and negotiate the traumatic effects of Cold War modernity. Cold War modernity can be seen as consisting not only of increased alienation, paranoia, and containment culture but also changing ideas of the urban, consumerism, and the postwar postindustrial knowledge economy. While the emphasis on encounter and contact in the apartment plot can be seen as a counter to the alienation and paranoia of the Cold War, my emphasis here is more on the way in which the apartment plot mediates the effects of containment, the urban, consumerism, and the new economy. Against models of containment, the apartment plot provides a release valve for what can't be contained – sexual desire, delimited gender roles, queerness, racial divisions, and so on – at the same time that it ultimately serves the dominant ideology by making the urban experience seem temporary, at least for some. Space and place are imbricated by discourses of gender, status, race, and class and, therefore, the philosophy of urbanism available to urban residents is housed within systems of power and privilege related to one's identity. In relation to the modern Cold War economy, the apartment plot figures access to the philosophy of urbanism via these systems of privilege. In this sense, the apartment plot might be seen as conspiratorial, justifying heterosexual closure, the taming of the feminine, and the deracialization of urban space. At the same time, it helps uncover and recall alternatives to overly rigid ideologies of borders and containment, family and home.

Playboy Modernism

One subset of the apartment plot revolves around the figure of the playboy and the bachelor pad. The image of the bachelor pad signals a very particular urban fantasy or philosophy of urbanism tied to sexuality and masculine ideals. Both the connotative codes of a playboy lifestyle and the attendant philosophy of playboy urbanism come to the fore in mid-twentieth-century America, primarily through *Playboy* magazine which began publishing in 1953. As I have discussed elsewhere, in *Playboy*'s imagining and in the apartment plot, the bachelor pad reflects a particular philosophy of urbanism that links the urban with sophistication, consumption and seduction, and pits that against the suburban which is associated with marriage and emasculation.[10]

In part, the playboy represents the epitome of success in Cold War modernity: he is what has come to be called a knowledge professional.[11] The new middle class, defined through managerial or knowledge work, absorbs and appropriates "formerly excluded groups such as artists and other creative professional ... into the center of the labor market" thus forming a creative class.[12] In *Pillow Talk* (Gordon, 1959), playboy Brad Allen (Rock Hudson) works as a songwriter. In *Lover Come Back* (Mann, 1961), Rock Hudson's character Jerry Webster is an advertising executive. In *The Tender Trap* (Walters, 1955), Charlie Reader (Frank Sinatra) works as a theatrical agent. In *That Funny Feeling* (Thorpe, 1965) and *If a Man Answers* (Levin, 1962) Bobby Darren plays, respectively, a publishing executive and commercial photographer. Each of these men has achieved financial success and has cultural capital. Unlike the stereotypical "organization man" or "man in a grey flannel suit," they exert individual control over their work and creative process and are not trapped in a corporate environment.

Moreover, the playboy engages in consumerism and leisure activities that underpin notions of success in the Cold War era. His apartment is defined through his consumption of modern art and modern furniture, a mix of rich textures and earthy colors, open spaces for easy flow, a bar, and high-tech entertainment technologies, including hi-fi and a system of electronic switches that enable the playboy to impress, dominate, and control female guests. In *Pillow Talk*, for example, Brad Allen's apartment contains all the features

Figure 9.1 Jan Morrow (Doris Day) on the party line with Brad Allen (Rock Hudson) in his *Playboy*-style apartment in *Pillow Talk* (1959).

of the stereotypical bachelor pad: numerous modern paintings hung densely on the wall; contrasting textures with one exposed red-brick wall and others covered in a nubby beige fabric; a fireplace; an earthy color scheme with dusty reds, brown, and beige punctuated with a few bright-red cushions.

The apartment flaunts a piano which marks Brad's status as a member of the creative class and his ability to work at home. Most hilariously, the apartment displays the playboy's technologized domination and control via a system of electronic switches that turn down the lights, turn on the phonograph, lock the door, and open a sofa bed. In *Come Blow My Horn* (Yorkin, 1963), Alan Baker's (Frank Sinatra) Manhattan apartment features a black, brown, and white color scheme, with bold touches of red, that set off a mirrored bar, modern art, modern furniture – including a giant curved white couch and red leather director's chairs – and giant windows overlooking the skyline view from the twentieth floor. Dark interior railings and a sunken conversation area serve to partition, but not close off, the space, enhancing the room's porousness and flow. Brass fixtures, wood panels, glass surfaces, marble statues, tile floors and shag carpeting create the vital juxtaposition of textures. Signs of masculine sophistication lurk in leather-bound books, scales of justice, candelabra, and a classical bust. Accoutrements for entertaining include two fireplaces, a gaming table, a large television, and a hi-fi. The mise-en-scène of these apartments serves as a shorthand to links these spaces to a playboy lifestyle of easy access to women, parties, leisure activities, and financial success.

At the same time as the playboy epitomizes some aspects of Cold War ideology, the playboy troubles the dominant ideology regarding sex and gender roles and family. The bachelor pad is marked as avowedly masculine; but, on the other hand, it requires the man to take on stereotypically feminine interests in consumption, decorating, hosting, and cooking. The bachelor pad is determinedly heterosexual but vulnerable to queer influences and suspicions (the term "confirmed" bachelor was code for someone perceived as gay). The bachelor pad seemingly intersects with ideologies of containment, insofar as it situates the single man's identity and lifestyle in the home, but it troubles the idea of containment by envisioning the urban home as a public, social, porous, and permeable space, a space of encounter rather than retreat from the world.

Moreover, the figure of the playboy directly challenges the necessity for marriage, monogamy, and reproduction. For example, in *Pillow Talk*, Brad Allen explicitly enunciates an antimarriage philosophy:

> Before a man gets married, he's, uh, like a tree in the forest . . . then, he's chopped down, his branches are cut off, he's stripped of his bark . . . Then this tree is taken to the mill. And when it comes out, it's no longer a tree. It's a vanity table, a breakfast nook, baby crib, and the newspaper that lines the family garbage can.

This analysis paints the man's subjection to marriage as a form of castration, his "branches" cut. More tellingly, it uses the metaphor of furniture and decor. In Brad's rendering, the married man is transformed from his natural state, a tree, to a domestic fabrication, furniture. In *If a Man Answers*, when Eugene first meets Chantal (Sandra Dee) she tells him her last name is "only temporary" until marriage; and when they meet again she tells him that marriage is "the ideal state for men." Eugene's reply echoes the *Playboy* philosophy. He tells her that, as a New Yorker, he has access to hundreds of restaurants, can easily hire a maid, and has phone numbers for 111 models in his little black book.

Bachelor pad films, however, do not valorize the playboy's status as a permanent condition but represent his status and, thus, his residence in the bachelor pad, as temporary or under pressure from women. By films' end, Brad in *Pillow Talk*, Eugene in *If a Man Answers*, Charlie in *The Tender Trap*, and other playboys are all married or engaged, under what Steven Cohan calls the "taming of the bachelor" scenario.[13] As the playboy is tamed, his apartment is also redecorated or abandoned; and, therefore, his consumerist tendencies – his furniture, his art, his technology – are shifted from purposes of leisure and seduction towards reproduction and family. Rather than mark him as oppositional to corporate culture, or as urban and sophisticated, his creative work gets subsumed into the logic of breadwinning.

As George Wagner suggests in relation to readers of *Playboy* magazine, the spectator of the bachelor pad variant of the apartment plot was as likely as not a married man, not himself a swinging bachelor. Like *Playboy*'s idealized blueprint for bachelor pads, films such as *Pillow Talk* provided "a private fantasy

Figure 9.2 Chantal Stacy (Sandra Dee) enters photographer Eugene Wright's (Bobby Darin) apartment in *If a Man Answers* (1962) and begins the taming process.

escape for the man whose home had been appropriated as the domain of wife and family and whose office was the site of a definitive reality – the wage ... the playboy acquired a fantasized mobility because he was a bachelor."[14] The bachelor pad apartment plot is thus a fantasy space that functions like a mirror, allowing the married or suburban man to see reflected an idealized version of himself. To escape his confinement in the domestic suburban home, he can identify with the projected idealized image of himself as a bachelor and attain fantasy feelings of mastery. At the same time, his projection of himself into that other space produces a potentially bifurcated self, a dual identity or identities – married/single, suburban/urban, emasculated/predatory, monogamous/promiscuous, and so on. Thus, providing a fantasy of freedom, on the one hand, and a confirmation of domestic ideals, on the other, the playboy films serves to mediate the effects of Cold War modernity, to provide a space to reflect, transmute, and mediate the anxieties attendant upon contemporary ideologies of domesticity and manhood.

Bohemian Modernity

Like films centered on a playboy, apartment plots focused on single girls also negotiate the effects of Cold War modernity. In the apartment plot, the single girl, like the playboy, offers a counterweight to the stereotypical image of the suburban housewife, and provides a fantasy of a temporary reprieve from what Betty Friedan described as "the feminine mystique."[15] The figure of the working single girl in the apartment plot complicates our understanding of the Cold War era by troubling the associations between women, suburbia, home, and domesticity. The single girl's apartment represents an alternative private sphere for women, a space that challenges the association between women and domesticity and that enables women to create a transitive or liminal identity away from their family home, prior to – and, sometimes, rather than – entering marriage.

The single girl apartment plot dovetails in many ways with what Joan Dideon described in a 1960 article for *Mademoiselle* as "The Great Reprieve":

> However myriad the reasons that draw the young to New York, there is often this common thread, this feeling that the future can be postponed, forgotten about for a few years and picked up later, still intact and brighter than ever. Make no mistakes: what they have in mind is a sabbatical, not a break with anything; their intentions, however vague, have more to do with exploration than with rebellion, more to do with making themselves "ready" for something than with splashing in the Plaza fountain.[16]

In Dideon's account, the single girl in New York is "above all, uncommitted."[17] Dideon suggests that single girls are not seeking marriage but want instead to "prolong the period when they can experiment, mess around, make mistakes."[18] The urban "reprieve" offers girls a "leave of absence" in which they can avoid "the gentle pressure" to marry. Though temporary, the "reprieve" Dideon describes is nonetheless transitive – during this period, young women grow and change. According to Dideon, urban life enables girls to reinvent themselves, "to start over, to make mistakes and erase them."[19] Sexual knowledge, especially, marks the urban single girl as "unconventional." The anonymity and privacy of the city allow a young woman to experiment with sex, try out various non-marital relationships, and even new sexual identities. Often equated with losing one's virginity, these sexual "experiments" and "mistakes" are, presumably, like virginity itself, transformative but invisible.

Similar to the playboy, the single girl in the apartment plot can be seen as providing an alternative model for women resistant to the dominant ideologies of gender and family, a fantasy of non-conformity. At the same time, the single-girl narratives expose the gendered limitations of that fantasy, as the woman's ability to navigate the urban single life is seen as restricted by her reduced and dependent role in the new economy. In a consideration of different "tenants" of the apartment plot, not surprisingly, single male tenants tend, on the whole, to have a higher social status, more economic power, greater cultural power, and easier access to consumer goods than their female counterparts. Whereas the stereotypical bachelor in the apartment plot is figured as a playboy who lives in a well-furnished apartment with high-tech gadgets, modern paintings, and modern furniture, and who works in the culture/entertainment industry, the stereotypical single girl is taken to be a more itinerant bohemian figure, less competent to navigate the new economy.

In terms of work, the single girl's status is lower than that of her male counterpart. While the playboy is usually a successful member of the creative class, the single girl works in more lowly jobs, sometimes within the culture industry and sometimes on the fringe. In *That Funny Feeling*, Joan is an aspiring actress but works as a maid to support herself. Gloria Graham plays an aspiring actress in *In a Lonely Place*. In *Cactus Flower* (Saks, 1969), Goldie Hawn's character Toni works in a record store. In *Bells are Ringing*, Judy Holliday plays a receptionist at an answering service whose clients are mainly creative professionals. *Breakfast at Tiffany's* (Edwards, 1961) and *Klute* (Pakula, 1971) both feature call girls, and *Any Wednesday* (Miller, 1966) showcases a kept woman.

Whether or not she is associated with artistic or intellectual life, the single girl's apartment in the 1950s and 1960s is most often represented as a bohemian space. There are instances of well-appointed career-girl apartments, like Doris Day's in *Pillow Talk*, Lauren Bacall's in *Designing Woman* (Minnelli, 1957), or Natalie Wood's in *Sex and the Single Girl* (Quine, 1964), but they tend to be seen as inappropriate and the woman as castrating or frigid. Most often, the girl's apartment is represented as inexpensive, inadequate, underfurnished, cramped, messy, or eccentric. In *That Funny Feeling*, for example, roommates Joan (Sandra Dee) and Audrey (Nita Talbot) share a tiny, one-bedroom apartment. The bedroom is so small and cramped – with sewing machine, radio, old dolls and stuffed animals – that Audrey can't open the drawers to her bureau or the door to the kitchen without rearranging furniture. They are so close to their neighbor's apartment that *his* alarm clock wakes *them*, then they bang on their wall with shoes to wake *him*. To make coffee, Audrey must shout to neighbor Luther (Larry Storch) to turn off his shower. In *How to Marry a Millionaire*, the three roommates (Lauren Bacall, Marilyn Monroe, and Betty Grable) are so poor that they must sell furniture in the apartment they sublet, eventually living with just one small chair and telephone table. In *Breakfast at Tiffany's*, Holly Golightly (Audrey Hepburn) lives in an underfurnished one-bedroom apartment with one legless plastic sofa, a phonograph, a suitcase on the floor, empty kitchen, empty bookshelves, and blank white walls.

The bohemian girl's apartment bears an inverse relation to the consumerism of both the suburban home and the bachelor pad: the single girl runs her apartment by economy. Unlike the suburban woman, the single girl doesn't order her life with modern domestic technologies. Unlike her urban male counterpart, the single girl cannot afford to decorate her apartment in high-tech designer modern style. In what Helen Gurley Brown refers to in *Sex and the Single Girl* as "the Greenwich Village approach," the girl can "make everything gay and colorful and warm and cozy, and no single item of furniture or refurbishing costs more than ten dollars." [20] Even for the sophisticated woman aiming to go beyond the bohemian apartment, Brown advises buying secondhand furniture at thrift shops, the Salvation Army, Junior League, and so on.[21] In *Any Wednesday*, when the married Mrs. Cleves (Rosemary Murphy) sees the apartment of Ellen Gordon (Jane Fonda), she proclaims it: "Overdone, diffuse, bizarre. Obviously done by someone insecure." But Ellen defends the thrift-store expertise required to furnish with such decorative touches as church candlesticks, plastic flowers coming out of a gramophone nailed to the wall, a Cigar Store Indian turned into a lamp, white wrought-iron chairs, Tiffany lamps and hurricane lamps: "I spent years scouring 3rd Avenue, the Salvation Army and auctions."

As a liminal and transitive space, the bohemian apartment needs to be considered not only in spatial terms but also in its temporality. Via the mechanism of place, the bohemian apartment signifies a time in a woman's life, an ephemeral moment. Just as the playboy is tamed, the single girl usually ends the film married or engaged; and she moves out of her apartment and either into a man's apartment or, as often, to the suburbs. The bohemian apartment thus registers as modern not only in its opposition to notions of home but in its contingency and temporality. The single girl who inhabits the apartment is "modern," neither by virtue of producing modern art, nor in her affiliation with modernist design or modern technologies, but in the way she organizes her domestic and private life. She rejects traditional conceptions of femininity and tries on "new" identities, related to urbanism, work, and sexuality. Her modernity, however, is a temporary condition, an identity she inhabits only as long as she inhabits the apartment. Rather than a permanent rupture (with tradition, home, stability), modernity can be understood, in this case, as a temporary displacement, an experience of limited duration, and a space one enters and exits at will.

African American Modernity

Within the apartment plot and within African American cinema, until recently, representations of the African American apartment are rare, exceptions to the rule. As Paula Massood suggests, African American characters and films are deeply associated with the urban; however, while certain genres, such as the black-cast musical and blaxploitation, represent the city, they tend to represent public spaces such as nightclubs, bars, streets, and corners, not domestic spaces.[22] When African American film and representations do show domestic urban life, black characters are usually shown living not in apartments per se but in tenements or projects in the ghetto, and especially Harlem. Black urban life, then, exists outside the usual arena of the apartment plot which generally situates characters in Greenwich Village, the Upper East Side, or the Upper West Side.

The apartment plot's elision of race is all the more surprising given the size of the mid-twentieth-century black urban population. From the Great Migration forward, African Americans moved north in ever increasing numbers.[23] At the same time, through practices such as redlining (in which mortgage companies put a red line through black applications, thus denying them mortgages) African Americans were prevented from moving into most suburbs and thus restricted to cities.[24] The segregation and concentration of black populations in the ghetto enable the white population, and white representations of the city, to ignore or avoid black areas. Though black populations are at once highlighted as a causal feature of urban blight and fears of the urban, and thus key to mid-century suburban discourse, they are, at the same time, segregated from the dominant white urban population in ghettos. The black ghetto has a ghostly presence, as a space that haunts the white imagination but remains invisible to most white people. Thus, while the expansion of suburbs in the 1950s and forward is often attributed to "white flight" away from increasingly black cities, the apartment plot most often draws attention to the vitality and promise of urban life for white populations by emphasizing those areas of the city that house primarily white people.

The very few Cold War apartment plots with black characters map the city differently and deliberately from white apartment plots: they emphasize the way in which the city establishes boundaries and restrictions between neighborhoods and peoples, and the way in which neighborhood and housing don't just shape but limit one's experience of the city. Where white apartment plots enact a form of containment with respect to race, and especially blackness, the black apartment plot speaks more directly to a tension between mobility and containment as a feature of black urban living. The black apartment plot, then, portrays the city as not merely divided by neighborhood but with a deep understanding that the specifics of neighborhood and housing type are always already determined by race, class, and status.

African American apartment plots expose the privilege underpinning white apartment plots. White apartment plots, featuring playboys and bohemian girls, represent suburban living as a choice: the suburbs are seen as a space that represents a character's acquiescence to mainstream ideals of home and family, or a space one refuses or exits to escape or avoid those ideals. In African American films, the suburbs are not a choice: the suburbs are represented as a wholly white space that blocks black access.[25]

A Raisin in the Sun (Petrie, 1961) offers a particularly stark delineation of the ways in which black life chances are blocked by white suburban communities. Lorraine Hansberry's play *A Raisin in the Sun*, and the film adaptation of it, stem partly from Hansberry's own family experience with restrictive covenants. As with her family experience, Hansberry's text moves the Younger family out of a black tenement and into a white neighborhood. This move goes against the wishes of the white residents, represented by the Clybourn Park Improvement Association, a protectionist group that tries to buy their home back from them. Arguing that "race prejudice simply doesn't enter into it," Mr. Linder (John Fiedler) of the Clybourn Park Improvement Association makes clear that like should stay with like and that the Youngers are perceived not as neighbors but as a "community problem."[26]

In what comes to be the dominant mode of representing the suburban/ urban divide in black films, the white neighborhood in *A Raisin in the Sun* is contrasted to the tenement through a contrasting light versus dark mise-en-scène. In the white neighborhood, we see the sun shining on bright sidewalks, showing the shade from trees. This serves to emphasize the suburban access to nature and contrasts with the dark tenement where there is not enough sunlight for plants to grow. We see the suburban neighborhood only in the daytime whereas we see the tenement throughout the day and evening. When we see the interior of the three-bedroom house that Mrs. Younger (Claudia McNeil) has purchased, it has clean, white-painted walls with light streaming through the windows. By contrast, we see only the tenement interior; it seems, therefore, to be a closed space, removed from the outside world. It has dark and dirty walls. The tenement has three sets of windows. One, off Walter's (Sidney Poitier) bedroom, looks out on to the street but we never see the view. Instead, our eyes focus on the view from the kitchen window, a view into an airshaft. This window provides no light. Rather than the outdoors, it shows interior walls of the tenement and neighbors' hanging clothes. This view emphasizes the enclosed quality of the space. The third set of windows are *faux* windows that look into the tenement hall – one of these is the top half of the door and the other an internal window, presumably built to allow more airflow between apartments.[27] These windows have frosted glass, and a lace design in gold foil, as well as curtains. Thus, these windows, too, emphasize the window's function as barrier more than aperture.

Despite being an enclosed space, the tenement affords the Youngers little or no privacy. The Youngers share a bathroom with their neighbors and are, presumably, visible to them through the airshaft windows. Moreover, the Youngers have no privacy from one another. The tenement has one small bedroom off the kitchen that the mother and sister Beneatha (Diana Sands) share, and another room, separated from the kitchen/living room by pocket doors, where Walter and his wife Ruth (Ruby Dee) sleep. Walter's son Travis (Stephen Perry) sleeps on the couch in the living room. The family all share a bureau in the living room. Visitors, such as Beneatha's boyfriends, Asagai (Ivan

Dixon) and George Murchison (Louis Gossett, Jr.) must be entertained with the family looking on, or with the family hiding in Walter and Ruth's bedroom during the visit to bestow the illusion of privacy. Where *A Raisin in the Sun* deals with issues of access to the suburbs as plot, *Claudine* (Berry, 1974) employs the suburbs more as a shorthand for racial division. In *Claudine*, the main character, played by Diahann Caroll, meets Rupert "Roop" (James Earl Jones) in the white suburbs in Westchester County where she works as a maid and he works as a garbage man. This shows that both Claudine and Roop work for white people and that the white people have no understanding of, or interest in, their lives. It further establishes that they must leave their community to work. The opening credits of the film show Claudine walking down a Harlem street with six children, three on either side of her, spanning the sidewalk. The children peel away one by one with a kiss, leaving Claudine to board her bus for work. Then we see Claudine's long commute by bus to a wealthy suburb where she and other black maids travel on the back of the bus to a pristine, tree-lined roundabout, each exiting toward a different point of the suburban circle. The suburban setting then generates the chance meeting between Claudine and Roop as they do not meet in the city where they live but in the suburbs where both work. The film departs from the suburban setting, however, and focuses on their romance in an apartment plot situated in their respective Harlem apartments. As an apartment plot, the film deploys themes of porousness, proximity, density, and contact but it filters those themes through poverty and racism.

In *Claudine*, the two main characters each inhabits an apartment, not tenements, but those apartments are located in Harlem and are not middle-class apartments so much as the apartments of the working poor. Claudine's apartment at 139 Edgecomb Avenue is in an attractive four-story limestone six-flat. She lives on the second floor in a railroad flat with living room, bedroom, kitchen and bathroom. The space is clean and tidy but crowded. Six kids and Claudine all share the space, with beds jammed in the bedroom, a room between the kitchen and living room with no door. The apartment has a television and stereo, and a few appliances. Characters have no privacy.

Roop's apartment reflects his bachelor status but also his poverty. He lives in a large building with a large entryway. His building is inhabited by numerous prostitutes, all of whom know Roop by name – a more realistic twist of the bachelor pad fantasy of free-and-easy access to women in apartments. Roop's unkempt bachelor quarters consist of two adjoining rooms with no wall between, a small kitchen and a bathroom. Roop has a television in the center of his living room – a more modest form of entertainment technology than in white playboy films. Along with such bachelor touches as a zebra-pattern chair, throw pillows, and daybed in the living area, Roop has African woodcuts and a Black Panther poster of a raised fist that invokes a black nationalist critique. Roop's apartment also has a mouse – one he knows well and has named Millhouse.

In these films, the characters have access only to tenements and apartments in the ghetto. And, unlike their white counterparts in the apartment plot, they are not participants in the knowledge economy. Like those of the bohemian girls, their jobs are lowly but, whereas the girls' jobs were often determined by gender, jobs here are imbricated by both race and gender. In *A Raisin in the Sun*, Walter Younger works as a chauffeur for a rich white man. As mentioned above, Claudine is a maid for a white woman – her work enabling the white woman's success as a housewife and mother in the suburbs – and Roop is a garbage man.

Both *A Raisin in the Sun* and *Claudine* underscore ways in which race delimits opportunities. *A Raisin in the Sun* not only shows the insidious effects of redlining but also points to inequities in housing costs between white and black neighborhoods. The main reason Mrs. Younger buys a home in Clybourn Park is cost. Houses in the white neighborhood are cheaper than "them houses they built for colored people out in them areas." Thus, it takes more money for a black family to purchase a home in the neighborhoods relegated to them, and then neighborhood associations and other discriminatory practices block their access to cheaper housing.[28]

Claudine points to the ways in which white government institutions create and perpetuate many of the problems the black family faces. Claudine says she is married to "Mr. Welfare," and astutely critiques a system that will only give her money to support her kids only if : 1. she does not work (and thus forces her to practice deceit when she works or be accused of being lazy if she does not); and 2. does not marry (thus forcing her to remain a single mother). Claudine views her life chances as curtailed: "Shitty neighborhood and the shitty school and the shitty world. No matter what I do." Roop also critiques the system that keeps him away from his kids. Roop is served for "willful neglect" of his kids. He pays support out of his salary as a garbage man but "they" say it is not enough and garnish his wages. Unable to afford his rent on such meager pay, Roop considers running away to a new city with a new identity, suggesting that the father's abandonment of his kids is caused, in part, by unfair practices.

Not only Claudine and Roop's role as parents but also their relationship to one another are boxed in by the welfare system. At the outset, their relationship is subject to surveillance. Most nights, Claudine asks Roop to drive her home so that nosy neighbors won't report their romance to the welfare people because, if there is a man in her life, Claudine risks losing benefits. In addition, Claudine must conceal any gifts from Roop because they will be counted as "income." This includes items he takes off the garbage truck as well as beer he brings to her house for dinner. Not only do neighbors report gossip about

Claudine but a social worker routinely visits her house unannounced to check up on her. This emphasizes how vulnerable Claudine is to institutional forces and how the porousness of apartment living takes on a menacing Big Brother quality under welfare. More than anything, Claudine and Roop are subject to the arcane bureaucracy of the welfare system. When they decide to get married, they visit the welfare office to find out the rules. They discover that welfare promotes living together over marriage. If Roop moves in but does not marry Claudine, he will be listed as a non-recipient and she will lose her welfare but still get money for her kids. If they marry, however, she loses benefits and he takes responsibility for her kids. If he loses his job, he is required to go on welfare. Thus, their best bet is for Roop to move in but conceal that fact.

As these brief examples suggest, African American apartment plots are not merely variations on the genre but trouble many of the assumptions that underpin the Cold War cycle of apartment plots. Rather than a question of lifestyle, they pitch the urban/suburban debate as one of race and exclusionary practices. These films stitch the ideals of the Cold War era – ideals related to domesticity and family as well as to the urban – to discourses of poverty and racism to reveal their underside.

Conclusion

Revisionist histories have complicated somewhat our understanding of containment culture – to showcase the many ways in which women did not conform to the domestic ideal, for example.[29] A consideration of the Cold War apartment plot as a form of vernacular modernism shows that containment, and all its attendant ideologies and components, was *always* contested, questioned, and negotiated. The Cold War cycle of apartment plots responds to the conditions of Cold War modernity and makes "sensually graspable"[30] our responses to the changes and expectations of the era. In different ways, the playboys' resistance to marriage, the single girl's exploration of sex outside marriage, and the African American film's articulation of the limited access and lack of privilege afforded black urbanites would have served, then, as a means of transmuting and negotiating the anxieties and fantasies of Cold War modernity. And now, from our vantage, they provide an archive of discontent, a way of recalling the tensions, uncertainties, and discomforts of the period.

Notes

1. Pamela Robertson Wojcik, *The Apartment Plot: Urban Living in American Film and Popular Culture, 1945 to 1975* (Durham, NC: Duke University Press, 2010).
2. Sharon Marcus, *Apartment Stories: City and Home in Nineteenth-Century Paris and London* (Berkeley: University of California Press, 1999).

3. Lynn Spigel, *Make Room for TV: Television and the Family Ideal in Postwar America* (Chicago: University of Chicago Press, 1992), p. 33.
4. James Harvey, *Movie Love in the Fifties* (New York: Da Capo Press, 2001), p.74.
5. Elaine Tyler May, *Homeward Bound: American Families in the Cold War Era* (New York: Basic Books, 1988), p. 14.
6. Ibid., p. 15.
7. Spigel, *Make Room for TV*, p. 33.
8. Miriam Bratu Hansen, "Tracking Cinema on a Global Scale," in Mark Wollaeger and Matt Eatough (eds), *The Oxford Handbook of Global Modernisms* (New York: Oxford University Press, 2012), p. 608.
9. Miriam Bratu Hansen, "The Mass Production of the Senses: Classical Cinema as Vernacular Modernism," in Christine Gledhill and Linda Williams (eds), *Reinventing Film Studies* (New York: Oxford University Press, 2000) pp. 341–2.
10. Wojcik, *The Apartment Plot*, p. 88 ff.
11. My thinking on the link between the apartment plot and the knowledge economy was inspired by Elizabeth Patton's paper, "Who Has Rights to the City?: Televisual Place-making, Urbanism, and Early Depictions of Single Working Women in the City," which she presented at Console-ing Passions, University of Notre Dame 2016. See also David Bell, *The Coming of Post-Industrial Society: A Venture in Social Forecasting* (New York: Basic Books, 1973) and Richard Florida, *The Rise of the Creative Class* (New York: Basic Books, 2003).
12. Patton, "Who Has Rights?"
13. Steven Cohan, *Masked Men: Masculinity and Movies in the Fifties* (Bloomington, IN: Indiana University Press, 1997), p. 275.
14. George Wagner, "The Lair of the Bachelor," in Debra L. Coleman, Elizabeth Ann Danze and Carol Jane Henderson (eds), *Architecture and Feminism* (Princeton, NJ: Princeton Architectural Press, 1996), p. 195.
15. Betty Friedan, *The Feminine Mystique*, original publication 1963, (New York: W. W. Norton & Company, 2001).
16. Joan Dideon, "The Great Reprieve," *Mademoiselle* (February 1961), p. 150.
17. Ibid., p. 103.
18. Ibid.
19. Ibid., p. 148.
20. Helen Gurley Brown, *Sex and the Single Girl*, original publication 1962 (Fort Lee, NJ: Barricade Books, 2003), p. 125.
21. Ibid., p. 131.
22. Paula J. Massood, *Black City Cinema: African American Urban Experiences in Film* (Philadelphia, PA: Temple University Press, 2003).
23. St. Clair Drake and Horace R. Cayton, *Black Metropolis: A Study of Negro Life in a Northern City*, (Chicago: University of Chicago Press, 1993), pp. 31–98.
24. Ibid., pp. 174–5. See also Robert M. Fogelson, *Bourgeois Nightmares: Suburbia, 1870–1930* (New Haven, CT: Yale University Press, 2005) and Elizabeth Moore, "I Sold a House to a Negro: Florida Real Estate Broker Loses Her License in Brave Fight for Racial Desegregation," *Ebony* (October 1963), pp. 92–100.
25. In his book on suburban Los Angeles, Eric Avila charts "the formation of a new 'white' identity," via suburban development. He suggests that, "as *black* became increasingly synonymous with *urban*," "public policy and private practices enforced a spatial distinction between 'black' cities and 'white' suburbs," or, borrowing from George Clinton, "chocolate cities and vanilla suburbs." Eric Avila, *Popular Culture in the Age of White Flight: Fear and Fantasy in Suburban Los Angeles* (Berkeley: University of California Press, 2004), p. 5.
26. According to the DVD booklet, shooting on location in Chicago proved problematic

as the film mirrored the text's "community problem." According to producer David Susskind, "We ran into some bigotry in scouting locations. Houses that we wanted to use became unavailable when the owners learned what the film was about ... We shot one sequence in a white neighborhood, and then heard the woman who lives there was receiving threatening phone calls. Since she was seven-months pregnant, we pulled out."

27. At the Tenement Museum in New York's Lower East Side, visitors discover that tenements often had internal windows separating the kitchen and bedroom, or living room, as well as windows into the airshaft, to allow airflow in summer. Rather than just cut holes in the walls, landlords built proper windows, presumably so that they could close the windows and block cold air in winter. These windows were often decorated with curtains and made to look like windows to the outside.
28. For a real-world account of these practices in action, see Moore.
29. See, for example, Joanne Myerowitz (ed), *Not June Cleaver: Women and Gender in Postwar America, 1945 to 1960* (Philadelphia, PA: Temple University Press, 1994) and Stephanie Coontz, *The Way We Never Were: American Families and the Nostalgia Trap* (New York: Basic Books, 1993).
30. Hansen, "Tracking Cinema," p. 608.

10. SUCCESS AND THE SINGLE GIRL: URBAN ROMANCES OF WORKING WOMEN

Jennifer Lei Jenkins

At the dawn of the twentieth century, Theodore Dreiser published *Sister Carrie*, a country-mouse Cinderella story that followed Carrie Meeber from rural Wisconsin to Chicago to make her fortune in the big city. Carrie's career involves trading up through a series of men until she finds independence as a New York actress, fully capitalizing on her skill at artifice that she uses to survive. Carrie's upward mobility is based on her ability to play a scene with whomever can help her and she ends the novel with neither regret nor self-awareness. Her career path is wholly determined by urbanism and the advantage she takes of the anonymity and opportunity afforded to country girls who can learn city ways quickly. *Sister Carrie* is at heart a reimagining of *Moll Flanders*, updated for a modern audience and stripped of its redemptive conclusion by the realities of American secularism. As such, the novel defines one plotline or trope of the career girl in the city.

By mid-century, U.S. women had served in auxiliary, support, and military capacities in two world wars, gained the right to vote, embraced coeducational college, and explored myriad jobs that had not been available to their mothers and grandmothers a half century before. During World War II, sociologists fretted about the reconfigured gender dynamic as women took wartime jobs, such as in this report from 1944: "It seems reasonably clear that the white-collar jobs for women – teaching, secretarial work, and various kinds of merchandizing jobs – were enabled to attract and hold workers at low wages because of the social respectability attached to them. When the war made it equally respectable and somewhat more profitable to make airplanes, women deserted the old occupations in droves with the present embarrassing results for schools, offices, and stores. Whether the prestige of the old occupations will be restored with the coming of peace we cannot be certain."[1] Some of the earlier "white-collar jobs" of the interwar period absorbed postwar women workers but the skills and paychecks of wartime work led many young women to reject respectable but low-paid jobs. Girls sought careers and brought education and experience to the workplace. Cinema – both studio production and educational film – reflected this seachange in labor demographics. As the United States entered the Cold War era, GI Joe film narratives were balanced by tales of young women's conquest of the corporate jungle through smarts, spunk, and sartorial élan. Two pairs of films, released twenty-five years apart, bookend the career-woman genre as it emerged in the years between the end of World War II and the fall of the Berlin Wall, while the motif of the working girl infiltrated diverse genres from comedy to drama to the musical in the period.

While rarely the chosen entertainment genre, educational films nonetheless spoke early and often to captive high-school audiences about work options for the modern girl. Postwar social hygiene films for young women positioned office work as a meaningful holding-pen for girls between high school and marriage. These 16 mm films, produced by a robust industry of educational filmmakers who worked from immediately after the war until the advent of consumer-grade video equipment, were designed to inculcate postwar mores about gender, work, and coupling in high-school students across the nation. The message to girls was always one of deference: to gendered notions of work, to corporate culture, to potential mates. As Megan Stemm-Wade explains in her study of postwar classroom films, "[the representative film] *Office Courtesy* shows us that if Barbara can have the right submissive, pleasant attitude at work, she will be successful at remaining in that position until she can be married" (Stemm-Wade, 624). In this world, work is a means to an end rather than an end in itself. In the entertainment sector, this plotline was replaced by that of the career girl, a narrative that would grow in the second half of the twentieth century to dominate media portrayals of young women.

Broader popular culture, ever mindful of new markets, quickly embraced narratives that celebrated the successful career girl in the city. As Lisa Parks has shown, television's early investment in the "working girl sitcom" echoed the message of educational films by mythologizing office work as a likely career for postwar women, the earliest of whom often had surrendered better-paid jobs to returning veterans. Parks's study of three television sitcoms from 1952 to 1957 traces the secretarial career path to marriage and motherhood: marriage to the junior executive (*My Friend Irma* and *Meet Millie*), or motherhood of the senior executive (*Private Secretary*).[2] Indeed, the small screen cultivated the career woman early on, with pioneering series such as the classroom-based *Our Miss Brooks* (CBS, 1948–57). At the height of the Cold War, workplace comedies and dramedies, such as those featuring housekeeper *Hazel* (NBC, 1961–5; CBS, 1966), African American nurse *Julia* (NBC, 1968–71), nurse and black, actress and temp *That Girl* (ABC, 1966–71), and television producer on *The Mary Tyler Moore Show* (CBS, 1970–7) became television staples. These television plotlines, which established the tropes of the now prevalent workplace comedy, moved fluidly between small and large screens. Then, as now, small-screen storylines could directly influence cinema output, and vice versa.[3] Hollywood embraced the divorced or widowed working woman as a staple of melodrama weepies and as a comic *buffo* in the fish-out-of-water workplace farce. Somewhere between these poles of the tragic self-sacrificing working mother and the ditzy gamine falls the working girl with clear goals which include an interesting job and financial and social independence. By the final two decades of the Cold War, the "working girl" motif had spawned a distinct subgenre of women's films that drew upon elements of farce, revenge tragedy, and romantic comedy.

Released three years apart, *It Should Happen to You* (1954) and *Desk Set* (1957) develop the marriage versus career plot in interesting crossover ways. Each among the twenty-five top-grossing films for its year, both films featured strong female protagonists who were defined by their careers or career goals. Rather than heralding a new wave of women's films, however, these two working-girl stories are distinctive for their conventionality. They do not announce themselves as anything other than workaday romantic comedies. Yet each in its way follows a storyline that moves from *Sister Carrie* across the century on the peplums of working women.

George Cukor's *It Should Happen To You* (1954)[4] presents a cautionary fable of the girl in the city. Gladys Glover (Judy Holliday) moves to New York from Binghamton ("that's upstate New York") to make "a name for herself," as Garson Kanin's working script was titled. The narrative begins with a lost job. After being fired as a girdle model for an excess ¾ inch, Gladys takes to Central Park to consider her options. On a very hot day in the park, she encounters a variety of New York types who dismiss and mock her as a "nut." Much of this activity is filmed by Pete Sheppard (introducing Jack Lemmon), a freelance documentarian capturing slice-of-life shots in Central Park. His in-camera montage of passing feet on sidewalks, reminiscent of the opening of *Strangers on a Train*, is interrupted by a pair of stockinged but shoeless women's feet that walk into frame. Pete is intrigued by Gladys's face (and her habit of taking her shoes off to think) and they strike up a conversation in which she tells him about her failed modeling career and her decision this day to reconsider life in the city. The choices, as she sees it, are to return home "to work in the shoe factory and marry the first man that asks. Or the second. And then, good-bye, name for yourself" or to do away with herself. She doesn't feel like suicide on this day – it's too hot – and Pete advises her to make her luck:

"Not only where there's a will there's way, but where there's a way there's a will." Gladys's way home leads her to exit the Park at Columbus Circle where she sees a billboard for hire: the will. A fantasy insert turns the billboard into a screen onto which Gladys projects her quest for fame, literally making a name for herself in letters 10 feet high.

Her will to fame leads her straight to the advertising agent who leases her the billboard for three months. This arrangement begins Gladys's career as an unknown and then known celebrity. The Adams Soap Company, which has always rented that space, seeks to trade the Columbus Circle billboard for six others around town, and deploys not-so-squeaky-clean soap scion Evan Adams III (Peter Lawford) to bend Gladys to their corporate, and his sexual, will. Feeding her hunger for fame, Adams takes Gladys on glamour dates and offers her a modeling contract as the new face of Adams Soap. In this deal, Gladys's face (but not her name) will grace all Adams Soap billboards and print advertisements while her name will appear "all over the place" on signage in Manhattan. Even the fateful ¾ inch becomes a boon as she moves from modeling soap to being the before-and-after model for a diet tonic once her persona as the Adams Soap Girl is known. Thus begins Gladys's career of being herself.

Cukor will devote comic sequences of the film to Gladys's adventures at work but the film's core narrative is the marriage plot. Pete pursues Gladys from their first meeting, even moving in down the hall at her boarding house on West 63rd Street. He attempts to balance her quest for individual fame with a persistent and clear message about coupling. During a friendly evening at the local tavern, the television plays the nightly news while Pete and Gladys sit together at the piano crooning the film's signature song, "Let's Fall in Love," a Harold Arlen–Ted Koehler standard from 1933. The message is pure Pete: "We might have been meant for each other/ To be or not to be, let our hearts discover/ Let's fall in love/ Why shouldn't we fall in love?"[5] The newscaster's voice interrupts their reverie, asking why this name "Gladys Glover" is all over New York – like Kilroy. That query leads to a television spot, skyrocketing publicity, and the realization of Pete's fears of her being touted as a "freak" and a "goofball." Gladys, not just her name but her person, appears in more and more publicity materials, four television appearances in one week and a subsequent contract from Adams Soap to be the "Average American Girl" in their latest advertising campaign.

Gladys, starstruck with herself, breaks dates and falls briefly under the spell of playboy Adams. Unlike Sister Carrie, however, she is unable to trade up: her sense of autonomy, no less than her laser-sharp focus on her career of Being Somebody, keeps her from becoming Adams's mistress. Pete, meanwhile, attempts to redirect Gladys by inviting her on class-appropriate dates: to the corner bar, on walks in New York, and to meet his parents in New Jersey. Pete

URBAN ROMANCES OF WORKING WOMEN

also maintains a running campaign to protect Gladys from herself, cautioning discretion rather than overexposure. *It Should Happen To You* promotes the narrative that a career can turn a girl's head in ways that only marriage can turn it back.

Indeed, Cukor literalizes the head-turning motif when Adams picks up Gladys for an after-work date and she asks him to drive around and around Columbus Circle, absently answering his banter while keeping her eyes firmly on the prize: her name on the 40-foot billboard. From Adams's sporty convertible, Gladys becomes the postwar *flâneuse*, described by Anne Friedberg as "wandering through urban space ... [following] patterns of distracted observation and dreamlike reverie."[6] Only when he turns off toward their supper-club destination does her attention revert to Adams and, even then, her conversation is career driven. Columbus Circle serves as a kind of autopanopticon, a vantage point from which Gladys's self-construction may be viewed for herself and from the car. This externalized affirmation of her success in meeting her goal of making her name known both reflects and projects her desire for publicity.

The career-girl film often includes some balance of scenes at work and scenes at home, thereby renegotiating for the modern era the doctrine of separate spheres that dominated nineteenth-century working life in the popular imagination.[7] In *It Should Happen to You,* more than half the film's scenes occur in domestic venues: Gladys's apartment, the boarding house public spaces,

Figure 10.1 Gladys Glover sign in Columbus Circle in *It Should Happen To You* (1954).

185

Pete's apartment, or Adams's bachelor pad. A key scene of domesticity occurs when Gladys, dressed in her work clothes covered by a frilly, ironed apron, cooks lamb chops for Pete. The homeliness of Gladys's chintz-appointed apartment and the relaxed familiarity between the couple suggest that the marriage plot is proceeding apace and that her career will soon be domestic. Until ... Gladys persistently turns the dinner conversation to the location of her signs. Pete argues strenuously against this quest for notoriety, saying that fitting in is better than trying to stand out. This oblique invocation of the doctrine of social conformity appears here not as social engineering or a government plot but as a factor in courtship and coupling. He frets that he won't be able to get her attention until "the bubble bursts." Pete's point that "everyone can't rise above the crowd" carries the implication that acceptance of "real life ... here on earth" entails acceptance of social norms, marriage – and him. Notably, he doesn't ask her to give up her job, as that would mean her leaving the city – and him. This conversation develops as a reversal of the woman jealous of her mate's career but it is not played for broad comedy. There is a hint of pending sadness. Their differing views of her work threaten to doom the relationship, a problem which Pete sees as all hers. Yet publicity is her career.

Pete ultimately concedes defeat in the medium of Gladys's message: the screen. He leaves a 16 mm projector threaded up with his farewell *oeuvre*. On a billboard-shaped screen, his film runs, the opening credit a frame containing another "Gladys" message: "Good-By Gladys." In order to watch Pete's film, Gladys must pull down the shades, thus obscuring her view of one of her signs. She must fully focus on Pete's message for the first time in their relationship. This intimate, domestic scene of Pete's confession of love and dejection marks the turning point of Gladys's career. Once she has embraced the small-scale projection of herself, framed by Pete's camera and affection, she can no longer pursue fame as cravenly as before.

Her public appearances ultimately lead to a meltdown at a military dedication where, surrounded by admiring servicemen, Gladys collapses under the weight of being an ideal. She realizes what Pete has said all along, that "it isn't just making a name ... the thing is making a name stand for something." Refusing to have a plane named after her, Gladys sinks her career as a celebrity by redirecting the public gaze to the men in the military who are "one of the crowd." This eleventh-hour deferral to the proper (military, patriotic) objects of publicity ends Gladys's career as a publicity seeker and begins her career as a wife. Her final screen projection is skywritten, and the first name listed is not her own: "Pete Call Gladys Please ..."

This taming-of-the-screwball story fulfills the early postwar narrative that work is a place to wait for marriage. Since Gladys's work is primarily being herself, her work journey functions as a kind of *bildungsroman*, shaping her character into an appropriate state for marriage. The final scene captures the newly married Shepherds driving west; they spot a billboard to lease and Gladys asserts that she sees "absolutely nothing" and turns her gaze to her husband. In this narrative, work is not an end in itself.

An unspoken subtext of moving-image depictions of working-gal screen narratives is that the women shown on-screen were doubly employed: as workers within the world of the film or television show, and as working actresses within the production. Held up to female media consumers as gender icons and role models by the studio system's publicity machine, actresses appeared on-screen as working women, and in fan and movie magazines as "real life" women balancing career and family obligations. Judy Holliday early on established herself as a tough negotiator and controller of her own image despite having William Morris representation. Riding the wave of attention from her Oscar for *Born Yesterday*, Holliday bargained for and won a profitable contract for the "straw hat" tour of *Dream Girls* in the summer of 1951. Her contract called for $5,000 and 50 per cent of the gross over a $10,000 break-point for each venue. *Variety* reported "The film star is figured to have snared $27,000 in four weeks of performances." [8] It was also widely reported that she flatly refused the role of Lorelei Lee in *Gentlemen Prefer Blondes*, believing that it would typecast her "further and forever as a 'dumb blonde.'"[9] *Variety* is careful to note that Columbia's willingness to let the Gentlemen project go has nothing to do with HUAC glances in Holliday's direction. Holliday's management of her own image and career underscores the career-gal role to come, three years later, in *It Should Happen*. Unlike an older generation of actresses, such as Joan Crawford, Barbara Stanwyck, and Celeste Holm, Holliday kept press attention on the work and made little effort to feed fan magazines' hunger for personal interviews and home-life photo shoots. The exception in the previous generation was Katharine Hepburn who, early in her career, eschewed personal details in interviews and focused on the work: "It can have nothing to do with the good or bad performance I give in my next picture."[10] She held to that principle throughout her career.

Desk Set (1957)[11] is more centrally a workplace comedy than *It Should Happen to You* with all but one scene staged in the Reference Department of the Federal Broadcasting Company in New York. The department is fully staffed by women, led by Bunny Watson (Katharine Hepburn) who has "a college education and after that a library course at Columbia. I was going to take a Ph.D. but I ran out of money." Her team includes two experienced reference specialists, Miss Peg Costello (Joan Blondell) and Miss Sylvia Blair (Dina Merrill) and the neophyte Ruthie (Sue Randall) who is learning the ropes. The proscenium set of this research library is wholly legible, left to right, with the hallway entrance screen-left, staff desks facing each other, center, and Bunny's glass-walled office, screen-right. Stacks fill the middle and rear of the set, with a mezzanine continuing the stacks. The set and *mise-en-scène* create an open-book backdrop for the events of the plot.

While the setting is a research library, it is also an arm of the television industry, and these female staff are dressed accordingly. Indeed, the research staff are as well turned out and tuned in to the fashion of the day as any New York career women: no dowdy librarians here. The romance subplot involving Bunny and junior executive Mike Cutler (Gig Young) is marked by two distinct items of raiment: a dress for the country-club dance and a bathrobe with hand-embroidered initials. Setting the tone for subsequent career girl comedies, *Desk Set* sets the fashion bar high.[12] These smart working women are also smartly dressed in a variety of outfits that indicate their professional status as well as their personalities.[13] Ruthie, the youngest member of the team, begins the film one step up from a bobby-soxer, with straight skirt and sweater set – but pumps to denote her transition from saddle shoes to the work world. She will come to dress more like Sylvia as the narrative unfolds and she learns her job. Sylvia wears classic New Look-inspired full skirts and short jackets or sweater sets. She smokes, and carries a gold lighter. Her jewelry is tasteful and discreet: she seems to be from money. Peg, the baseball expert and reluctant singleton, wears form-fitting sheaths and "wiggle" dresses in dark colors. Bunny, the intellectual and style center of the film, wears professional jackets and skirts or dresses imbued with Hepburn's personal style: raised collars, cinched waists, tweed. Her signature piece is a calf-length swing coat that reverses from red to black (green?), with contrast cuffs and collar. The implication of this attention to costume is clearly that these working women know clothes and have the money to buy them. Designed by Charles Le Maire, whose portfolio included draping working women in *All About Eve* (1955) and *The Seven Year Itch* (1957), the costumes here reflect the economic reality of career girls in the late 1950s. They could afford and enjoyed wearing stylish clothes that reflected their status, independence, and buying power. Even Ruthie, lowest in pay grade, pursues a "little black velvet strapless number" on sale at I. Magnin in a surreptitious phone call before the coffee break. Clothes-talk comes a clear second to the job, however. Bunny enters the narrative with a box from Bonwit's, asking if she's late and reporting that she was on site until 10.30 the night before and at IBM by 9 this morning for a demonstration of the EMERAC computer. Only a few scenes later does the dress emerge, and then only in her private (though glass-walled) office.

The Jeanne Henry plot of Woman-against-Machine consumes the major arc of the story, with a romantic subplot involving Bunny, Mike, and the efficiency expert and computer engineer, Charles Sumner (Spencer Tracy). The domestic subplot is where the real conflicts occur because Mike has spent the seven years of their relationship on his corporate rise, using Bunny as a private editing service, information bank, and cheerleader. And occasional date, when convenient. Bunny and Sumner are far more intellectually matched, and seem to share an understanding of the world from the start. He's an MIT-trained engineer whose socks don't match and she's a Columbia-trained librarian with a talent for word problems and puzzles, and a compendious memory for verse as well as general and specific knowledge and where to find both.

When Sumner and Bunny get caught in the rain on a Friday-night commute, we get to see the private space of a career woman in New York. Bunny's apartment is spacious and well appointed: clearly the home of a woman who has money to spend on creature comforts. At 75th and Lexington, she lives in the respectable Upper East Side, not the bohemian Upper West Side nor the Columbia campus environs. Her job at Rockefeller Center clearly affords her the lifestyle of a successful working woman, certainly one more comfortable that her schoolteacher parents could afford. As Pamela Robertson Wojcik reports in her study of apartment films, "the Upper East Side is relatively more fashionable and wealthy than the Upper West Side. But, both the Upper East Side and the Upper West Side feature characters who operate within commercial artistic or intellectual professions."[14] Bunny has Degas and Watteau prints on the bedroom wall, an oil painting over the fireplace, no chintz anywhere, simple (double) bedspread, books on the nightstand and on the table by the bed. The large living room has bookshelves, reading chairs and lamps, a Chinese figure lamp, a Picasso print over the couch. The setting is precisely the postwar comfortable elegance that became highly prized at the millennium.

Bunny and Sumner have dinner on a card table with tablecloth, china, and silver, seated on upholstered armchairs on the edge of the living room. This companionable dinner marks the turning point in the career-marriage plot. As with the similar set piece in *It Should Happen to You*, the conversation about the meal segues into discussion of work matters. Bunny grills Sumner about his pending report on the Research Department's efficiencies. Summer notes that "You and EMERAC have something in common: you're single-minded. You go on relentlessly trying to get the answer to whatever it is you're trying to get the answer to." Unlike Pete Shepherd trying to dissuade Gladys from her quest for fame, Sumner simply observes and makes friendly conversation. Even in this intimate setting, these two people are colleagues and adults, and would not indulge in the spatting of younger people. The unreliable Mike arrives to find them both in bathrobes and assumes the worst; Bunny takes umbrage at his assumption that she'd be alone. The fact that Sumner is wearing a bathrobe meant as Mike's Christmas present further complicates matters. It is worth noting that this domestic scene does not appear in the original play script, and was added by the Ephrons for the film adaptation. By 1957, the at-home scene had clearly become a career-girl genre convention.

The ensuing competition between the Research staff and EMERAC (and her fussy nanny, Miss Warriner [Neva Patterson]) plays out as a battle of mind

Figure 10.2 Peg Costello (Joan Blondell), Sylvia Blair (Dina Merrill), Ruthie Saylor (Sue Randall), and Bunny Watson (Katharine Hepburn) in front of EMERAC in *Desk Set* (1957).

versus machine. The four librarians can multitask while the mainframe cannot. Data are simply not enough; nuanced knowledge of information and context can be added only by humans. Miss Warriner smugly attempts to field all calls to the Research Department by feeding questions to "Emmy" and discovers that subject expertise (and four people to answer the phone) trumps punch-cards every time. The computer confuses Corfu with "curfew" and reviews of *King Solomon's Mines* with information about the Watusi, and goes out of control, belching smoke and beeping sounds. A hairpin from Bunny finally shuts it off.

The domestic situation resolves when ambitious junior exec Mike wants Bunny to follow him to California, with no regard for her career whatsoever. Sumner, the computer scientist, is a far better match for Bunny, and the film resolves their antithesis with a synthesis of her mind and his machine. *Desk Set* ultimately champions the career woman: not one of the research staff leaves to marry, and not one considers another line of work.

Desk Set's inauguration of the computer age heralds change to come, and not just for women researchers. The decade of the 1960s began with a trifecta of female empowerment: in 1960, the birth-control pill was approved for contraceptive use in the United States; in 1962, Helen Gurley Brown's advice book, *Sex and the Single Girl*,[15] sold two million copies in three weeks and expanded to thirty-five countries; in 1963, Betty Friedan published *The Feminine Mystique*, a study of unfulfilled housewives that sold one million copies in 1964 and went on to be a cornerstone of Equal Rights Amendment- (ERA)-era feminism. While Brown's and Friedan's books addressed different generations, both sought to give voice and strength to women in, or returning to, the workforce. Brown encouraged young women to make the most of career opportunities, to save and spend according to one's goals, and to seek pleasure without apology or deference. Friedan, whose research was based on her Smith College class of 1942, interviewed educated women of privilege who had followed the cultural rules of their day about marriage, motherhood, and subservience to a single-career family model. Reaching their forties and fifties, these women were reentering public life as widows and divorcees. Their daughters were Brown's audience but, in truth, both generations would be expanding the work force by decade's end.[16]

Hollywood eagerly explored and exploited this seachange in American work culture. Friedan's sociological study would filter into madness melodramas, such as *Diary of a Mad Housewife* (1970) and *A Woman Under the Influence* (1974), while Brown's sisterly advice sparked a new kind of workplace comedy, focused on the single woman on the rise. As Barbara Ehrenreich and Deirdre English reported, "The 'single girl' who burst into the media in the early sixties corresponded to a new social reality: the single woman, divorced or never-married, who lived alone and supported herself ... They were secretaries, stewardesses, social workers, 'gal Fridays,' and 'assistants' of various kinds in publishing houses, banks, department stores, etc."[17] Such were the jobs and workplaces that began appearing on screens across America.

Comic strips also contributed to the construction of the career girl in the popular imagination. *Apartment 3-G* ran as a daily and Sunday strip from 1961 to 2015, and followed the career and romantic adventures of three girls (3-G) in the big city. A blonde, a brunette, and a redhead, the three worked in a variety of period-appropriate office jobs and negotiated the big city under the watchful eye of neighbor Aristotle Papagoras.

Shepherd Mead's 1952 satirical self-help novel, *How to Succeed in Business Without Really Trying* (original title: *The Dastard's Guide to Fame and Fortune*) could counter *Sex and the Single Girl*. The book spent twelve weeks on the bestseller list and inspired the 1961 Broadway musical that won seven Tonys, the 1962 Pulitzer Prize for Drama, and made Robert Morse a star. The 1967 United Artists film condenses and refines the longer Broadway show and showcases Bob Fosse's choreography. The story of a window-washer who rises through pluck and luck to become Chairman of the Board plays out the same marriage plot as *It Should Happen to You*, with protagonist genders reversed and in a corporate setting. J. Pierpont Finch (Robert Morse), armed with the eponymous book, literally runs into the president of World-Wide Wickets and parlays that collision into a mail-room job. On his first morning, he meets chipper secretary Rosemary Pilkington (Michelle Lee) who becomes his cheerleader and moral compass. This reversal of the formula of *It Should Happen to You* skews more closely to the gender-normative character roles of male junior exec and female support staff but also offers a comic-cynical view of United States corporate culture. (Like *Desk Set*, the film credits a business machine giant, in this case 3-M Company, for "office copying equipment.") While *Desk Set* only references Mondrian in the opening credits as a gameboard backdrop with miniature computer playing pieces, *How to Succeed*'s art design fully inhabits the Mondrian color blocks and grids for its corporate layout and women's costumes. These working girls reflect the modern, progressive corporate culture that rebuilt the world after World War II – with or without wickets.

Rosemary serves as guide and moral interpreter of corporate culture, an on-the-ground source in counterpoint to the "Book Voice" advice for manipulating the capitalist system. As staged, the workplace is clearly a boys-and-girls venue, with well-defined boundaries of power and agency. As one of three functioning female staff, Rosemary inhabits the career-girl role along with Smitty (Kay Reynolds) and the chairman's assistant Miss Jones (Ruth Kobart). The steno and typist pool is filled with young women who arrive at work and spend the time between 9 a.m. and coffee break doing their nails, hair, and makeup at their desks. Another kind of corporate career girl appears in the shape of Hedy La Rue (Maureen Arthur), the fully upholstered 39-22-38 object of executive leering. Under the protection of the company president, Hedy's physical presence and lack of work skills are a surefire career killer for the junior executive to whom she is assigned. Her arrival prompts the management message song, "A Secretary is not a Toy," the first ensemble number which combines male junior execs and the typing pool in a full song-and-dance memo from Human Resources: "A secretary is not a toy/ No my boy/ Not a toy to fondle and dandle/ And playfully handle/ In search of some puerile joy." The female ensemble chimes in, "A secretary is not to be/ Used for play therapy ... Her pad ... / Is to write in,/ And not spend the night in."[18] Punctuated by rhythmic typing sounds and carriage-return bells, this clearly Fosse-inflected number combines chassés and jetés, soft shoe to accompany scribbles in steno pads, and finger snapping to underscore the jazz dimension of corporate ballet. The message of the song, that the female staff are not there for male employees' amusement, lends surprising agency to the female "corps de clerks."

This film's depiction of working women promotes the corporation as a benevolent father figure, watching over his "children" from the penthouse president's office. Rosemary is the means to Ponty's rise to the top, always in counterpoint to the sexpot Hedy. All problems disappear when Hedy is foisted upon the chairman of the board, making way for Ponty to succeed and Rosemary to take her place beside him in the chairman's office atop the corporate cathedral. Again, work exists as a holding pen for coupling.

At the same time that corporate fortunes were rising ever upward in vertical skyscrapers and profit graphs, a sector of the female workforce garnered significant attention from Hollywood for horizontal profits. Films such as *The Apartment* (1960), *Breakfast at Tiffany's* (1961), *Sweet Charity* (1969), and the tragic *Butterfield 8* (1960) followed party girls with "no visible means of support"[19] in the gray economy of the 1960s. (They set a trajectory that led to *Pretty Woman*, the highest grossing film of 1990.) The pillow-trade films of the 1960s were rarely Cinderella stories and, while marketed as romantic comedies, often had very dark undertones of abuse and suicide to counter the cheerful optimism of these Cold War-era Sister Carries.

"Don't You Find Being a Woman in the 80s Complicated?"

Another pair of films released thirty years later revises the depictions of working women in *It Should Happen to You* and *Desk Set*. The United States Census Bureau reported in 1960 – the closest count to the release of *Desk Set* – that 22,402,000 women worked, of whom 3,518,000 were "other" in terms of marital status. The vast majority of working women tallied in the 1960 census, 13,620,000, were married women. By contrast, in 1980, the total female labor force was 45,487,000, or 51.1 percent of the workforce. Of that number, 8,643,000 women were classified as "other": widowed, divorced, or separated – nearly equal to the number of married women in the workforce.[20] This cultural landscape sets the backdrop for career woman comedies of the final decade of the Cold War period.

Colin Higgins's *9 to 5* (1980)[21] combines the enemy-within plot of *Desk Set* with updated characters in a bad-boss revenge fantasy for the Equal Rights Amendment (ERA) era. The Bunny Watson role has been demoted from department head to "senior office supervisor" who reports to a credit-stealing male executive (Dabney Coleman), albeit one who is no love object whatsoever. A widow with four children and an aging parent to support, Violet Newstead (Lily Tomlin) has trained a string of male executives who get promoted above her. Like Bunny Watson, she is quick-witted, a fierce defender of her female cohort, and fashionable within her means. We learn that her lost promotions are attributed to her lack of a college degree, masking the entrenched sexism within Consolidated Industries, the megacorporation that is the setting for this cautionary tale. Peg Costello, the buxom baseball expert of *Desk Set*, is reinvented as the executive's secretary, Doralee (Dolly Parton). Southern, bleached blonde, and sweet natured, Doralee is an object of lust for Mr. Hart and of contempt for the female workforce because of her perceived sexual involvement with the boss. Neophyte Judy Bernly (Jane Fonda), a newly divorced housewife, takes a job in the very role that ended her marriage: secretary. This trio differ from the women of *Desk Set* in that they do not bring professional education to the job, and they really need these jobs in ways that the Federal Broadcasting Company's librarians do not. The economic boom of the postwar period has given way to the 1970s recession when women entered the workforce to supplement or replace income lost by their husbands

Figure 10.3 Violet Newstead (Lily Tomlin), Doralee Rhodes (Dolly Parton), and Judy Bernly (Jane Fonda) at the office in *9 to 5* (1980).

– or lost their husbands altogether. The 9-to-5-ers are surrounded by a typing pool made up of women who also need their low-level jobs, and shock waves ripple through the ranks when a young Hispanic woman is fired for discussing salary in the restroom. The comic little-old-lady muse in *Desk Set* is replaced by Roz (Elizabeth Wilson), the executive toady, spy, and Human Resources manager over the female staff. The office setting is bleak, bathed in unhealthy gray-green fluorescent light, and the working women's near-uniforms are drab browns and grays. The three protagonists are visible exceptions: Violet wears slim skirt suit separates in black and red and red lipstick and earrings; Doralee wears form-fitting country-inflected outfits with sequins and fringe; and newcomer Judy wears florals and pastels in country-club styles. She arrives for the first day of work in a floral print skirt suit with a pussy-bow pastel blouse and a hat, an outfit more suited to the Junior League than the office.

The film begins with a cross-cut montage of morning commuters walking, by 1980, a fully established cinematic code for commerce in the big city. The theme song, "9 to 5," became a breakout hit for Parton, with a driving beat that echoes the pounding of feet on pavement and clocks ticking.[22] This eye-level montage captures shot after shot of women's legs in high-heeled shoes, framed from knee-length hemline to sidewalk as the action moves right to left, left to right, across the screen; there is not a pant suit in sight.[23] Vignettes within this montage include a young woman missing her bus and another dropping a sheaf of papers. Close-ups of women anxiously checking watches and building clocks give faces to the teeming movement workward. As noted, the pedestrian montage can be traced back to Hitchcock and before but, in this period, it becomes a staple of working-women films, almost an obligatory sequence to establish the tone and milieu of the narrative.

The revenge plot of *9 to 5* is broadly drawn: Franklin Hart is well established as a "sexist, egotistical, lying, hypocritical bigot" who treats the office staff as his personal harem. Because he can apparently fire at will, the women comply with his demands for coffee, personal shopping, gassing up the car. Rather than a new-fangled office machine as in *Desk Set*, the bad boss functions as the corporate enemy within. Hart's oligarchical reign makes the workplace unbearable. He implies to the whole company that he is sleeping with the buxom Doralee, threatens to fire Judy over a photocopier mishap, does fire a woman who discussed her salary in the restroom. When he takes credit for Violet's efficiency plan and then passes her over for promotion, the die is cast. Trapped in a "pink collar ghetto," the three women commiserate over the lousy jobs that they need.

The three women meet and bond in a bar and later, over a joint, share their fantasies of comeuppance. This sequence serves as the conventional home-life scene of Act II. While we do see Violet at home fixing her garage-door opener, and Doralee snuggling with her husband, this snacks-and-dope evening in Doralee's comfy living room fulfills the same function as the dinner scenes in *It Should Happen to You* and *Desk Set*: time away from the workplace to assess the options. The 9-to-5-ers envision their revenge on Hart in genre-film vignettes: Judy imagines a big-game hunting scenario; Doralee, a Western varmint-roping; and Violet, a Disney-inflected poisoning by Snow White rather than the evil stepmother. This domestic respite of Act II devolves into a screwball sequence of actual (accidental) attempted murder and kidnapping of Hart, holding him in his own house while his wife and minion Roz are away. In his absence (and in his name), the protagonists implement a series of worker-friendly changes in Hart's department: flex-time scheduling, warm-colored decor and seating areas on the work floor, a day-care center, equity raises.

The second highest-grossing film of 1980, *9 to 5* exhibits the broad caricatures of the 1970s workplace but attributes Franklin Hart's misogyny more to corporate culture than to the man himself. When the Chairman of Board (Sterling Hayden, dressed as Colonel Sanders) arrives to congratulate Hart on his congenial improvements and efficiencies, Violet steps in to explain what were her own directives while Hart silently takes credit. The chairman summarily rewards Hart with a promotion to the branch office in the Brazilian jungle, and the afterword title cards tell us that Violet was promoted to vice-president, Doralee left for a career in country-and-western music, and Judy married the photocopier salesman. As a workplace comedy, *9 to 5* both updates and downgrades the career-gal narrative: it brings the story into the second big influx of women in the workforce in the twentieth century, and – perhaps realistically – focuses on the confined and limited nature of women's work in recession-era corporate America. The second highest-grossing film of 1980, it clearly touched a nerve.

Sydney Pollack's 1982 *Tootsie*[24] reverses genders in the *It Should Happen to You* storyline. Rather than making a name in order to trade on fame, actor Michael Dorsey (Dustin Hoffman) must eschew his fame and become a woman of the crowd to get work. A notorious perfectionist, who once put a commercial a half day over schedule because he wouldn't sit down as a tomato, Michael is so difficult that nobody will work with him. Only by reinventing himself as Dorothy Michaels, a character actress of a certain age, can Michael get the career he seeks. His quest for anonymity within a gender role is the obverse of Gladys Glover's: she wants to be known, and her Average American Girl persona in her means to an end. Michael cannot find work as his very distinctive self, and becomes an average American woman and a working one at that, as a means to his end. Both protagonists have love interests that question and cajole their progress, and both films end with coupling over career. But thirty years made a difference: Dorothy enters the ERA-era work world of double standards, pantyhose, and demeaning nicknames. The ricocheting gender lines in *Tootsie* allow for a comic examination of women in the work world and women as working actresses.[25]

Throughout the opening credit montage, we see Michael Dorsey working at his craft: applying character makeup, auditioning, teaching. He recites the actor's mantra: "There's no reason not to work. There's no work, but you gotta find ways to work." Michael's problem is that no one will hire him because he is so difficult. His quest for perfection exhausts everyone, including his beleaguered agent George Field (Sydney Pollack) who recites Michael's résumé of unpaid jobs: Harlem Theatre for the Blind, Strindberg in the Park, the People's Workshop at Syracuse. Almost on a dare to prove that someone, anyone, will work with him, Michael reads for the very daytime drama role for which he had coached his insecure friend Sandy (Terri Garr). He arrives in (female) character and nails it.

In this scene Michael auditions not just for the role of *Southwest General* hospital administrator Emily Kimberly but for the role he will come to inhabit: Dorothy Michaels. He enters this sequence as a fully realized character, and never plays the role as drag.[26] Indeed, Hoffman told *Screen International*, "the real thrill lies in the work ... Playing a man who impersonates a woman in 'Tootsie' was an enormous challenge. We all worked on it for a year or so ... attempting to create Dorothy Michaels, not as a transvestite type but as a real woman in a man's world."[27] When the soap director Ron Carlisle (Dabney Coleman, fresh from *9 to 5*) pronounces her "not right for this role, honey," Dorothy – channeling Michael – points out that she is a character actress and can adapt to the role. Ron wants a "type" to make a "statement," and Dorothy is too "soft and genteel, not threatening enough" – until she offers to "knee

Figure 10.4 Michael Dorsey's (Dustin Hoffman) first appearance as Dorothy Michaels in *Tootsie* (1982).

your balls right through the roof of your mouth." Then she delivers a speech that is pure Michael Dorsey: "You want some gross caricature of a woman to prove some idiotic point, like power makes women masculine or masculine women are ugly. Well, shame on the woman that lets you do that . . . and that includes you, dear." This final clause is directed at *Southwest General*'s producer Rita (Doris Belack), a chain-smoking, self-assured petite woman wearing Chanel. Dorothy's call to conscience lands her an audition and the role, and so Michael becomes a career woman. (It is worth noting that Michael's friend Sandy, whom he had coached for the role of Emily Kimberly, lists her options after losing yet another audition: "I'm gonna be a waitress. I'll be anything – I'll be a *wife*." Clearly the 1982 prospects were as limited as ever.)

This narrative follows the fish-out-of-water plot of many earlier working-girl films but Dorothy's difference is not gender alone. She is not the lone woman in a man's world: the television studio seems to employ equal numbers of men and women and, in addition to the female producer, there are a female stage manager and production assistants. The director is the only man on crew who has a speaking role although male cameramen and tape editors appear on-screen. Dorothy's strength, and how that translates to her on-screen character Emily Kimberly, runs the fish-out-of-water narrative. Early on she points out that she has a name, just like the male actors, and she expects Ron to use it. In her first scene on camera she avoids the hoary has-been John Van Horn's (George Gaynes) initiatory kiss by going off script. Dorothy's ad libs and riffs become a regular occurrence, as Dorothy cannot mouth the writers' platitudes about domestic violence, sexual harassment, and other contemporary women's issues. In response to the running storyline of Dr. Brewster's handsy treatment of the hospital's nursing staff, Emily Kimberly tells the tear-stained Nurse

Charles, "I'm going to give every nurse on this floor an electric cattle prod and instruct them to just zap him in his budoobies" and then phones her assistant to consult the yellow pages for "Farm Equipment – Retail." Such on-screen character work makes Emily Kimberly a breakout character, and the fan mail for Dorothy Michaels begins pouring in. Indeed, her newfound celebrity leads to enhanced media coverage of the kind Gladys Glover sought. A montage of magazine photo shoots shows her posing for the covers of *Cosmopolitan*, *Ms.*, *Woman's Day*, *Life* (in harem pants and headscarf), *TV Guide* (with beaming critic Gene Shallitt), *People* (with Andy Warhol), and *New York*. The range of readership of these magazines indicates that her role on *Southwest General* speaks to women across class and educational lines; the last three cut across gender lines, as well. Meanwhile, off-screen, Dorothy cocks a skeptical eyebrow at the director's relationship with Julie Nichols (Jessica Lange), and his side flings with the young women of the cast and crew.

Indeed, Dorothy's success leads Michael to envision more work for her. He begs his agent to get him a television special because,

> I feel that I have something to say to women. I've been an unemployed actor for 20 years, George. I know what it's like to sit by the phone, waiting for it to ring, and then when I finally get a job I have no control. Everybody else has all the power. I've got zip! If I could impart that experience to other women like me –.

George Fields points out that there *are* no other women like him, to which Michael counters that he is an actress, "a potentially great actress," who could play Medea, Ophelia, Lady Macbeth, even the Eleanor Roosevelt Story. Dorothy's ambition for better roles and different audiences isn't hampered by talent, gender, a bad boss or an evil corporate machine, as is often the case in career-girl films. Paradoxically, Michael's ambition for better roles and different audiences *for* Dorothy is hampered by all of the above.

The Act 2 domestic complication we have seen in other working-girl films arises on three levels. Michael Dorsey falls into a sexual relationship with Sandy, his actress friend who lost his breakthrough role, after she walks in on him stripping down in her bedroom. (Little did she know that he wanted to try on one of her dresses for Dorothy.) Michael falls for Julie Nichols on his first day on set but she knows him as Dorothy and treats him like a girlfriend. Julie's father Les (Charles Durning) falls for Dorothy after their few meetings in New York and courts her during Julie and Dorothy's hiatus visit to his upstate farm. This love hexagon is as weak as its weakest side, which is Michael. He lies to Sandy to spend time with Julie, but as Dorothy. He pines for Julie but, when he meets her as Michael, she throws a drink in his face. When he breaks character as Dorothy and tries to kiss her, Julie recoils and then apologizes for not being well adjusted enough. He agonizes about hurting Les, "the sweetest guy in the world," but thinks he can walk away from it all when his contract ends. On one fateful night, Dorothy babysits Julie's daughter Amy, makes a failed pass at Julie, goes dancing with Les who proposes, and comes home to be the object of a pass from soap cast member John Van Horn that ends only at the entrance of roommate Jeff Slater (Bill Murray). The implication that Dorothy lives with a younger man adds yet another layer of complication to the romantic subplots. Rather than becoming a mistaken-identity farce, however, the film demands thoughtful action from Michael and Dorothy, spurred on by Jeff, the only person besides his agent who knows Michael's secret. Hoffman describes the challenge of playing straight with Dorothy:

> I had to fall in love with my co-star in the series, Jessica Lange, and try to reveal it to her, in my woman's guise without any hint of lesbianism. Again, when her father, played beautifully by Charles Durning, falls for me, thinking of course that I am Dorothy, I had to play those scenes with great care and sensitivity, in order not to make his character look foolish and to counter accusations of bad taste.[28]

Having told Michael on his first morning on the soap not to play hard to get, Jeff predicts sardonically that Michael is going to hell. The hell, it turns out, is the job.

Tootsie offers a comic, but nonetheless pointed, look into sexual politics in the workplace and the dating arena of the early 1980s. Feminists are tempted to overanalyze the gender dynamics, arguing that the drag role (which they accept wholesale) explores constructions of self and gender but only from a male point of view. For example, Jane O. Newman avers: "The 'Tootsie trope' thus makes it possible for both critical texts and literary representations to appear to unmask the constructedness of gender and identity, when they in fact rely for their own formulations on universalizing the very gender constructs and fictions of stable selfhood that they critique."[29] (Like Laura Mulvey's insistence that the cinematic gaze is male, this condemnation may reveal more about the scholar's positionality than the text's.)

Dorothy's popularity leads the show to pick up her option, continuing the contract for another year. Suddenly the promise of work becomes a punishment and Michael is desperate to get Dorothy out of her role and himself out of Dorothy. An unexpected live taping allows for Emily Kimberly to reveal herself as Edward Kimberly, "the reckless brother of my [dead] sister Anthea." He (now) pronounces himself "proud and lucky and strong enough to be the woman that was the best part of my manhood, the best part of myself." While this statement resolves some of the film's inquiry into gender constructs on the small screen – and by implication the large screen as well – the subtext remains the need for work. Edward, in Michael's rambling ad lib exposition designed to get him (literally) out of Dorothy, returned to Southwest General in order to avenge the abuse his sister suffered as a nurse in a sexist workplace. The diegetic and metadiegetic stories both come back to work, and the experience of women in the workplace.

By 1989, when the Berlin Wall came down, the class ceiling was largely still in place, a condition explored in Mike Nichols's *Working Girl* of the previous year.[30] Tess McGill might as well be Carrie Meeber, coming as she does from working-class parochial Staten Island. Her secretarial job in a Wall Street financial firm has fueled her ambition but, like Michael Dorsey in *Tootsie*, she can't keep a job. Tess will not defer to the adrenaline and sex-fueled boys club of Wall Street. When finally assigned to a woman boss in Mergers and Acquisitions, Tess is able to envision a future. Katherine Parker (Sigourney Weaver) represents all that Tess aspires to and Tess soon learns to speak, dress, and carry herself as Katherine does. The key difference is that Katherine, while preaching the doctrine of teamwork, attempts to steal Tess's idea for a deal. A fortuitous skiing accident diverts the bad-boss plot while Tess has a Cinderella interlude, staying in Katherine's apartment, wearing her clothes, and keeping some of her social engagements. Tess never masquerades as Katherine, she simply code-switches out of Staten Island. The impersonation is class rather than gender, and it is equally challenging. Her overly permed near-mullet hair needs to become "serious" and she needs to "rethink the jewelry." She does not totter on high heels like Dorothy Michaels but she does briefly rise to fetch the coffee when it's mentioned at a meeting. When she returns to Staten Island for her best friend's engagement party, Tess confronts her previous life with the incredibly sleazy Mick (Alec Baldwin). His response to her transformation is, "Who died and made you Grace Kelly?" *Working Girl* in many ways stands as a culmination of the career-girl film narrative. It combines the girl-in-the-city trope of *It Should Happen To You* with the triumph of brains in *Desk Set*. The gleeful exploitation of female staff and the bad boss of *9 to 5* appear magnified in the Wall Street of *Working Girl*, and in the professional cross-dressing from *Tootsie*, albeit adjusted for class rather than gender. By 1988, this career-girl film would garner six Oscar nominations and fourth highest box office for its year. The working-girl film genre had come into its own.

Notes

1. Margaret Willis, "Working Women," *The Journal of Educational Sociology*, Volume 17, No. 8 (April 1944), p. 475.
2. Lisa Parks, "Watching the 'Working Gals': Fifties Sitcoms and the Repositioning of Women in Postwar American Culture," *Critical Matrix* 11.2 (1999), p. 45.
3. For more on this interdependency, see William Boddy, "The Studios Move into Prime Time: Hollywood and the Television Industry in the 1950s," *Cinema Journal* 24.4 (1985), pp. 23–37.

4. Garson Kanin, *It Should Happen to You,* directed by George Cukor (1954, Columbia).
5. Walter Rimler reports that Columbia commissioned Harold Arlen and Ted Koehler in 1933 to write a musical entitled "Let's Fall in Love." Arlen had a burst of inspiration, and they wrote the song on the train from New York to Hollywood, using only the conductor's four-note dinner chime. *Man That Got Away,* University of Illinois Press, 2015, pp. 36–7, May 22, 2017 <http://www.myilibrary.com?ID=809063>
6. Anne Friedberg, *Window Shopping: Cinema and the Postmodern,* (Berkeley: University of California Press, 1993), p. 35.
7. The gendered distinction of the domestic and public arenas was observed by Alexis de Toqueville in 1840 and promoted by Catherine Beecher and the proliferating women's magazines of the Gilded Age. Utterly an upper-class phenomenon in the nineteenth century, this binary thinking returned to public discourse after World War II as a means of palliating women's return to the home after wartime work and independence.
8. "Legitimate: Judy Holliday nets 24G for 4 weeks of touring strawhats in 'dream girl.'" (1951, August 15). *Variety (Archive: 1905–2000),* 183, pp. 55–6, 60. "Straw hat" tours played in rural and tertiary U.S. cities, such as Corning, NY and Matanuck, RI, in facilities that may actually have been "barns," the *Variety* parlance for non-purpose-built theaters.
9. "Pictures: Holliday Nay Cued Col's 'Blondes' Out." 1951. *Variety (Archive: 1905–2000),* 182 (6), pp. 3–4, 20.
10. "Pictures: Miss Hepburn Finds but Half Her Work in Studio, Remainder is for Publicity." *Variety (Archive: 1905–2000)* 108, no. 8 (November 1, 1932): p. 55.
11. Phoebe and Henry Ephron, *Desk Set,* directed by Walter Lang (1957; Twentieth Century-Fox), adapted from *The Desk Set* by William Marchant (1955).
12. Indeed, *It Should Happen to You* draper Jean Louis was nominated for best black-and-white costuming.
13. See Karen Hummel Kinsley, *Working Women: Contemporary Cinematic Costumes in "Desk Set" and "Working Girl,"* M.A. thesis, Graduate Center, CUNY, 2014. Written from the perspective of a theater draper, this thesis contains useful insights into cinema costuming but contains some regrettable misstatements in character names and plot moments.
14. Pamela Robertson Wojcik, *The Apartment Plot: Urban Living in American Film and Popular Culture, 1945 to 1975* (Durham, NC: Duke University Press, 2010), pp. 66–7.
15. Richard Quine's 1964 adaptation of *Sex and the Single Girl* borrows only the title and author name from Helen Gurley Brown's how-to book on financial and sexual independence for career gals. Recast as a battle-of-the-sexes farce within the emerging genre of Hollywood sex comedies, the film played upon the "Sex" part of the title more than the "Single Girl." Co-written by Joseph Heller (of *Catch*-22 fame), the film was clearly made for male and date-night consumption, with a classic elders (Henry Fonda and Lauren Bacall) and youngsters (Tony Curtis and Natalie Wood) comic structure à la *Much Ado About Nothing.* Beyond casting Natalie Wood as a twenty-three-year-old Ph.D. with a full research lab, the film has little to say about career women or their work.
16. The U.S. Census Bureau's *Statistical Abstract* for 1965 tallied the 1964 female work force aged 18–34 as 27,143,000, while women 45–54, Friedan's contemporaries, 10,725,000. http://www2.census.gov/library/publications/1965/compendia/statab/86ed/1965-03.pdf, No. 298.
17. Barbara Ehrenreich and Deirdre English, *For Her Own Good: 150 Years of*

Experts' Advice to Women (Garden City, NY: Anchor/Doubleday, 1978), p. 258.
18. "A Secretary is Not a Toy," *How to Succeed in Business Without Really Trying*, music and lyrics by Frank Loesser. Original Broadway Production, 1961; film adaptation, directed by David Swift, United Artists, 1967.
19. "No Visible Means of Support," originally an expression for a state of indigence, became in the 1960s a winking description of kept women (and men). The phrase was trademarked by the International Playtex Corporation in June 1972 as applying to girdles and brassieres, joining the "Cross Your Heart" slogan of the 1960s. See United States Patent and Trade Office database, http://tmsearch.uspto.gov/ .
20. These statistics do not distinguish between full and part-time employment but anecdotal evidence and cultural memory suggest that women in the 1980s were more often full-time employees than in the postwar boom, although often in subsistence-level clerk jobs. United States Census Bureau, Statistical Abstract of the United States, 1999, No. 1431, Marital Status of Women in the Civilian Labor Force: 1900 to 1998, p. 879.
21. Patricia Resnick, *9 to 5*, directed by Colin Higgins (1980, Twentieth Century-Fox).
22. The song also became "an anthem of 'Office America,'" first used in commercial spots by Emery Worldwide air cargo when the film aired on CBS-TV in 1985."Ad Agency News & Views: Emery Goes 'Nine-to-Five.'" *Back Stage (Archive: 1960–2000)* 26, No. 4 (January 25, 1985): p. 74.
23. Clearly wrapped before the 1980 MTA subway strike, this film shows the final season of women commuters wearing dress pumps on the way to work. During the eleven days without train service in April 1980, working women adopted running shoes for their extended walks to work, carrying their office pumps or leaving them in their desks. This shift was irreversible and, throughout the millennium, the office-worker fashion profile included white socks and tennis or running shoes over stockings or tights, and a large tote bag with the day's necessities. "Transit Strike: On Second Day, Strain Begins to Show," *New York Times* Metropolitan Report, April 3, 1980, B:1.
24. Larry Gelbart and Murray Shisgal, with Barry Levinson and Elaine May (uncredited), *Tootsie,* Directed by Sidney Pollack (1982; Columbia).
25. The *Tootsie* script went through several iterations from Larry Gelbart ($M*A*S*H$) and Murray Shisgal, with uncredited intervention by Barry Levinson and, most significantly, Elaine May. See Michael Sragow, "Ghostwriters: Unraveling the Enigma of Movie Authorship," *Film Comment*, Volume 19, No. 2 (March–April 1983), pp. 9–18. Stable URL: http://www.jstor.org/stable/43452681 (accessed: March 6, 2017, 18:09, UTC).
26. While 1982 critics and subsequent scholars have insisted on treating *Tootsie* as a drag show, it carries none of the signature elements of drag culture and performance. Charles Eidsvik's reductive reading is symptomatic: "Tootsie plays on (and through laughter, releases) anxieties about sexual identity and the unfairness of a society in which looks virtually are fate. Dorothy Michaels suffers the fate of most of us who are less than beautiful or handsome. We can laugh at 'her' suffering because it is part of a drag act." Charles Eidsvik, "'Tootsie' versus 'Mephisto': Characterization in a Cross-Cultural Context," *Film Criticism*, Vol. 13, No. 3 (spring, 1989), p. 16.
27. "People: PEOPLE – Dustin Feels Content to Bide His Time," *Screen International (Archive: 1976–2000)* No. 392 (April 30, 1983), p. 22.
28. "People: PEOPLE – Dustin Feels Content to Bide His Time." *Screen International (Archive: 1976–2000)* No. 392 (April 30, 1983), p. 22.
29. Jane O. Newman, "'Academic Tootsie': Women's Voices, Gender, and Textual

Ventriloquism in the German Language Academies," *The Eighteenth Century*, Vol. 35, No. 3 (1994), 241.
30. Kevin Wade, *Working Girl*, directed by Mike Nichols (1988; Twentieth Century-Fox).

Filmography

Cukor, George, 1954: *It Should Happen to You*.
Higgins, Colin, 1980: *9 to 5*.
Lang, Walter, 1957: *Desk Set*.
Nichols, Mike, 1988: *Working Girl*.

Bibliography

"Ad Agency News & Views: Emery Goes 'Nine-to-Five.'" *Back Stage (Archive: 1960–2000)* 26, No. 4, January 25, 1985, p. 74.
Dreiser, Theodore (1900), *Sister Carrie*, New York: Doubleday, 1900, Gutenberg Project, iBooks.
Eidsvik, Charles (1989), "'Tootsie' versus 'Mephisto:' Characterization in a Cross-Cultural Context," *Film Criticism*, Vol. 13, No. 3, spring, pp. 13–24.
Friedberg, Anne (1993), *Window Shopping: Cinema and the Postmodern*, Berkeley: University of California Press.
Newman, Jane O. (1994), "'Academic Tootsie': Women's Voices, Gender, and Textual Ventriloquism in the German Language Academies," in *The Eighteenth Century*, Vol. 35, No. 3, pp. 241–60.
Parks, Lisa (1999), "Watching the 'Working Gals': Fifties Sitcoms and the Repositioning of Women in Postwar American Culture," *Critical Matrix* 11.2, pp. 42–65.
"Pictures: Miss Hepburn Finds but Half Her Work in Studio, Remainder is for Publicity," *Variety (Archive: 1905–2000)* 108, No. 8, November 1, 1932, pp. 2, 55.
Rimler, Walter (2015), *Man That Got Away*, Champagne-Urbana: University of Illinois Press, May 22, 2017 <http://www.myilibrary.com?ID=809063>
Sragow, Michael (1983) "Ghostwriters: Unraveling the Enigma of Movie Authorship," *Film Comment*, Vol. 19, No. 2, March–April 1983, pp. 9–18. Stable URL. http://www.jstor.org/stable/43452681 (accessed: March 6, 2017 18:09 UTC.
Stemm-Wade, Megan (2012), "Careless Girls and Repentant Wives: Gender in Postwar Classroom Films," *The Journal of Popular Culture* 45.3, pp.611–27.
Willis, Margaret (1944), "Working Women," *The Journal of Educational Sociology*, Vol. 17, No. 8, April, pp. 473–8.
Wojcik, Pamela Robertson (2010), *The Apartment Plot: Urban Living in American Film and Popular Culture, 1945 to 1975*, Durham, NC: Duke University Press.

11. PARIS LOVES LOVERS AND AMERICANS LOVED PARIS: GENDER, CLASS, AND MODERNITY IN THE POSTWAR HOLLYWOOD MUSICAL

Steven Cohan

The popular and critical success of *An American in Paris* (1951, MGM, directed by Vincente Minnelli) inspired a number of Hollywood musicals that took their American characters to the City of Light. This cycle of 1950s musicals includes *Lovely to Look At* (1952, MGM, directed by Mervyn LeRoy), *April in Paris* (1952, Warner Bros., directed by David Butler), *Gentlemen Prefer Blondes* (Twentieth Century-Fox, 1953, directed by Howard Hawks), *The French Line* (1953, RKO, directed by Lloyd Bacon), *So This Is Paris* (1955, Universal International, directed by Richard Quine), *Gentlemen Marry Brunettes* (1955, United Artists, directed by Richard Sale), *Funny Face* (1957, Paramount, directed by Stanley Donen), *Silk Stockings* (1957, MGM, directed by Rouben Mamoulian), and *Les Girls* 1957, MGM, directed by George Cukor). Several months before *An American in Paris* was released, MGM brought out *Rich, Young, and Pretty* (1951, directed by Norman Taurog), which justly belongs to this cycle as well.

To be sure, during this same period other genres, such as romantic comedy and melodrama, took Paris for their setting. Nonetheless, these Paris musicals are distinctive as a postwar cycle. Unlike those other genres, which range across Europe and Asia for their foreign settings, and in contrast with the previous decade when musicals journeyed to South America, the Hollywood musical of the 1950s travels mainly to Paris whenever it leaves North America. Vanessa R. Schwartz, in fact, calls these Paris musicals "Frenchness" films, a category for her that includes other musicals actually set in belle époque France with French characters, such as *Gigi* (1958, MGM, directed by Vincente Minnelli) and

Can-Can (1960, Twentieth Century-Fox, directed by Walter Lang), along with many non-musical films such as *Moulin Rouge* (1953, United Artists, directed by John Huston), *Sabrina* (1954, Paramount, directed by Billy Wilder), *Lust for Life* (1956, MGM, directed by Vincente Minnelli), and *Irma La Douce* (1963, United Artists, directed by Billy Wilder). Schwartz writes about these films:

> Frenchness as the Belle Epoque – whether in American or French film – and its association with spectacle, color, movement, song, dance, girls bashing through posters, and the Can-Can itself, highlights the power of film as much as its depictions of France. Certain clichés that stood in for "France" had a particularly long shelf life. The Belle Époque "stuck" in film for a number of reasons, including the history of the American collecting of French Impressionists as well as the prolific reproduction of these French visual entertainment clichés in poster art. Long before Hollywood, art and commercial art shared the same palette in France. This may help explain why, aside from his lurid biography, Toulouse-Lautrec and his world appear as a leitmotif of the 1950s Frenchness films.[1]

Schwartz sees the Frenchness-film cycle contributing to the globalization of popular culture because, she argues, the films use belle époque imagery to "link the history of entertainment to a transnational context of development from [fin-de-siècle] France to [mid-century] America."[2] Recycling clichés about Paris stretching back to the turn of the century, "the films combined the titillation of Paris, a place known for sex and frivolity, with its association with artistic quality and cultural innovation . . ."[3]

It is telling, however, that in Schwartz's selection of films for extended discussion of their "Frenchness," only *Funny Face*, shot in large part on location, is contemporary both in its setting and in what the characters see and where they go while in Paris. This musical is about fashion photography, not the belle époque. As Gerald Mast stated about director Stanley Donen's visual style in *Funny Face*, "This is the way that color photographs, whether of fashion magazines, travel brochures, or movie travelogues, gives life to Paris. Donen draws a parallel between fashion and travel photography when his movie camera becomes a tourist, like [the main characters] themselves."[4] Accordingly, Schwartz uses *Funny Face* as an example of the Frenchness films' concern with promoting a tourist's gaze of Paris, in contrast with their counterpart, the Americana musicals of the 1940s and early '50s, which appealed to nostalgia. Schwartz's other extended examples in her chapter on Frenchness films – *Gigi*, *Moulin Rouge*, *Lust for Life*, and *French Can-Can* (1955, Gaumont, directed by Jean Renoir) – are all set in the belle époque era, and her other major example, *An American in Paris*, while contemporary for its period in its setting, explicitly harks back to that earlier era through its famous ballet sequence with its evocations of French impressionist painters.

What I am calling the Paris cycle of musicals, however, is not only concerned with the globalization of popular culture or with the Americanization of Paris – the other way that critics have read Frenchness in cinema according to Schwartz.[5] Rather, this group of musicals also registered mid-century anxieties about how gender and class differences could potentially disrupt postwar hegemony at home and challenge the ongoing masculinization of United States authority around the world. The Paris cycle of musicals I listed are all set in the present day; the musicals use an imaginary Paris as their emblem of postwar modernity; for the most part they feature American characters interacting with one another; these characters generally travel to Paris to work; the films themselves address an American audience for these reasons; and, with the exception of *An American in Paris*, they do not directly refer to the belle époque.

The stereotypical signs of Paris typically featured in these musicals may have originated in the last decades of the nineteenth century, as Schwartz points out, but they did not necessarily carry that historical significance for American viewers over fifty years later. In *Gentlemen Prefer Blondes*, when Lorelei Lee (Marilyn Monroe) and Dorothy Shaw (Jane Russell) arrive in Paris, a montage takes them from famous monuments (the Eiffel Tower, the Arc de Triomphe), to sidewalk cafes and boulevard eateries (Le Madrigal and others), and finally to houses of fashion (Schiaparelli, Dior, Lucien Lelong, Balenciaga, and so forth) where they go shopping like rich postwar American tourists on a grand European tour. But, as telling, the women's song, "When Love Goes Wrong," occurring shortly after the montage, then identifies Paris through the turbulence of mid-century French colonialism in Algeria because the chorus surrounding Monroe and Russell includes two young boys wearing fezzes, two sailors, two soldiers, and a gendarme.

Alternatively, in other musicals of this cycle, Paris is more simply "gay Paree," the city of wine, woman, and song where anything goes in contrast with straight-laced puritanical America. Even though the belle époque originated the clichés in this sense of Paris, the passing of time and the interruption of World War II have occluded that historical referent. The "gayness" of Paris now just as readily alludes to the city's offerings of all sorts of pleasurable commodities on display in high-priced boutiques as evidence of postwar European recovery or in racy nightclubs and cabarets with their scantily clad showgirls. The trailer for *April in Paris* describes the city as "Paris, capital of the world, with its moods and music, the Eiffel Tower, and an eyeful of gorgeous 'mamselles'." In *Gentlemen Marry Brunettes*, the first Paris musical actually shot on location there, two American "mamselles," the Jones sisters (Jane Russell, Jeanne Crain), keep auditioning for one Parisian night spot after another only to learn they are expected to perform wearing no more than jewels or feathers and their courage. The flashback sequences to their mother and aunt, the earlier Jones sister team in Paris, take place in the Roaring Twenties, not the belle époque. For that matter, if the Gershwin score in *An American in Paris* means to evoke the composer's Parisian influences, the period in question would also have to be the 1920s, the short time when the composer wrote "An American in Paris" while in France.

In what follows I first discuss briefly how *An American in Paris* establishes the cycle's straightforward ideological work in presuming the male's authority over the female and in implicitly linking this dominance to the United States's global stature as evident in its economic role in restoring Europe after World War II. I then turn to three musicals with strong romance plots and a male and female starring couple. My purpose is to consider how these Paris musicals undermine the cycle's obvious ideological agenda through their female leads' performances of numbers in concert with their narrative status as working women. Cyd Charisse in *Silk Stockings*, Audrey Hepburn in *Funny Face*, and Doris Day in *April in Paris* play characters who, at least until their films' closures, challenge the male characters musically, if not always narratively, with resistant values allied to their differently gendered and classed identities. For all the while Paris seduces her for "proper" heterosexual coupling, the working woman's initial refusal to identify with bourgeois values, rendered in song and dance to complement the musical treatment of her male co-star – Fred Astaire in *Silk Stockings* and *Funny Face*, and Ray Bolger in *April in Paris* – establishes a strong counterpoint to his equally classed and gendered authority in the narrative.

An American in Paris

As the cultural prize won back by the American army in World War II, Paris in this cycle of musicals means to confirm the patriarchal male's global authority as the personification of the American century. *An American in Paris* registers this ideology through its representation of the two genders. The plot revolves around the secret romance of Jerry Mulligan (Gene Kelly), otherwise beholden to his rich American patron Milo Roberts (Nina Foch), and Lise Bouvier (Leslie Caron), otherwise betrothed to cabaret entertainer Henri Baurel (Georges Guetary), friend of Jerry's best buddy Adam Cook (Oscar Levant). Yet, although Jerry and Lise dance together twice, first in a book number along a studio mock-up of the Seine for "Our Love is Here to Stay" and then in the titular fantasy ballet, the musical's songs are all sung by the men. Aside from Jerry's solo in "I Got Rhythm," which he performs with children after Milo buys two of his paintings, he and Henri celebrate their joy at unknowingly being in love with the same woman in "'S Wonderful, 'S

Figure 11.1 Jerry Mulligan (Gene Kelly) dances with Lise Bouvier (Leslie Caron) to "Love is here to stay" along the banks of the Seine in *An American in Paris* (1951).

Marvelous"; after making a date with Lise, Jerry sings and taps to "Tra La La" as Adam plays the piano; Henri solos with French showgirls in "Stairway to Paradise," and the three men burlesque old-fashioned waltzes in "By Strauss." That Milo only performs a narrative function, and does not appear in any musical numbers, reflects her marginality in the film as a wealthy and assertive American woman with a voracious appetite for young painters. As for Lise, she dances but does not sing.

The famous ballet, which features Kelly and Caron dancing together for nearly twenty minutes, reiterates in its staging the narrative conflict of Jerry's meeting and losing Lise. To call attention to this motif in the staging, the ballet is framed first by Lise leaving Jerry at the Black-and-White Ball to go off with Henri and, after the ballet finishes, by Henri returning her to Jerry to close the film on a happier note. Lise, in short, is the Parisian prize that the older Frenchman, a survivor of the Resistance during the war, hands over to the victorious American ex-GI who has remained in Paris to paint because, as Jerry states in his voice-over at the film's start, "Brother, if you can't paint in Paris, you better give up and marry the boss's daughter." His painting, which he says is all he ever wanted to do, explicitly aligns *An American in Paris* with belle époque Frenchness since, as Jerry also states to Lise, "I came to Paris to paint, like Utrillo did, and Rouault did, and Lautrec did." These artists then inspire the sets and costumes of the ballet along with its choreography. From the perspective offered by the ballet, *An American in Paris* looks back to the historical sources of modernism in the late nineteenth and early twentieth centuries in order to reclaim the cultural continuity that two world wars had disrupted and threatened to efface, and which America had restored and now over which it claims cultural authority.

The strong buddy element in *An American in Paris*, however, links this musical just as forcefully to specific ideological expressions of American masculinity in the 1940s and '50s, especially as visualized in Hollywood films of this period, Gene Kelly's other buddy musicals in particular.[6] In narrative and musical terms, Lise is the object of homosocial exchange between Jerry and Henri. The numbers in *An American in Paris* record both this homosocial subtext and Lise's function as an object of exchange between men. For not only does Leslie Caron not sing in this musical but Adam and Henri also mediate her character's single solo dance number, "Embraceable You," before she meets Jerry. As Henri describes the many exciting facets of her personality to Adam, Caron's dancing illustrates each change in her character's mood; moreover, each segment of her number is shown as a reflection in a wall mirror as the two men exchange brief comments about her. Thus the setup for the dancing suggests how Caron's one solo number works as a fantasy that the two men share about Lise, anticipating Henri's duet with Jerry on "'S Wonderful, 'S Marvelous." As she does for Henri and Jerry, then, Lise is a means of uniting the Frenchman and Adam too – a function emphasized in the recent Broadway adaptation which has Adam also falling in love with Lise.

The conservative ideological framework of *An American in Paris* stands out all the more when placed next to *Gentlemen Prefer Blondes* which inverts the gendered logic of the MGM classic. While *Blondes* concludes with Lorelei and Dorothy each getting married in a double wedding ceremony, the final shots first show the two couples as they exchange vows but then home in on the two women smiling at each other. This last shot makes perfect sense because Lorelei and Dorothy's loyalty to, and bond with, each other, which has driven the narrative and motivated their numbers together, trump whatever feelings they have for their mates. To be sure, according to the film's comic plotting, the nebbishy males seem to carry the day. Both Gus (Tom Noonan) and his father have the money that Lorelei craves and can obtain only through marriage, and the detective Ernie Malone (Elliott Reid), who has caught Dorothy's eye while spying on Lorelei, realizes that Sir Francis Beekman (Charles Coburn) has the diamond tiara that Lorelei has been suspected of stealing. As the two women walk down the aisle together, Dorothy quips to Lorelei that, on her wedding day, it is okay to say "yes," and her remark, while ironically underscored by

Russell's delivery, superficially contains the women in postwar domestic ideology; marriage, in other words, secures these two voluptuous females as confirmations of the two weaker males' patriarchal masculinity. Even so, Monroe and Russell perform all of the film's musical numbers, and their performances set the stage for how, at almost every moment in its narrative as well as the numbers, *Gentlemen Prefer Blondes* undercuts the supposed naturalness of femininity and heterosexual desiring.[7] With the two female stars always in command of the narrative and the numbers, *Gentlemen Prefer Blondes* acknowledges the era's patriarchal ideology, well evident in *An American in Paris*, by parodying and debunking it.

Silk Stockings

Of the three musicals I now want to look at, *Silk Stockings* is the most reconciliatory. Narratively, the opposition of bourgeois capitalism and Soviet socialism has a predetermined knockout conclusion so there would not have been much of a contest for viewers in 1957. In an analysis of *Silk Stockings* from 1975 that still holds up, Robin Wood identifies what he calls this film's "four main ideological impulses" that crisscross throughout the film to create its interesting contradictions. These are: 1. the "surface project" that states outright "you are better off under Capitalism"; 2. the concern with "woman as object" as an expression of the female's role in capitalistic society, which is confirmed by Cyd Charisse's solo, "Without Love," yet is also parodied by Janis Paige's "overtly vulgar musical numbers"; 3. the validation of entertainment over art, a thematic mainstay of many postwar MGM musicals; and 4. the freedom of self-expression and spontaneity versus an inhibiting and impersonal sociopolitical system.[8] For the last "dance is crucial," Wood states.[9] Indeed, he goes on to argue that "the vitality of the musical numbers in *Silk Stockings* itself transcends their local ideological functions," a point I wish to pursue.[10] But, before I do so, we first need to recall how thoroughly *Silk Stockings* associates American-ness with capitalism, female objectification, entertainment, and freedom of expression, without apparently calling attention to the contradictions arising from this syllogism, and, as much to the point, how Paris functions for *Silk Stockings* to bind together those four ideological threads.

Early in their relationship, Steve Canfield (Fred Astaire) asks Ninotchka Yoschenko (Cyd Charisse), "Can't you ever accept something because it's amusing or appealing?" When she replies, "It's best that way," he answers in turn, "I've never known anyone like you. I've never known anyone to resist enjoyment the way you do." In Steve's mind, Paris is the agent of such pleasures. "I didn't do anything to the commissars," he says of the three men who preceded Ninotchka in the city and were seduced by its pleasures. "Paris did. It did it to me. It will do it to you." While resisting his – and Paris's – charms at first, eventually an inebriated Ninotchka does capitulate, singing in "Without Love" that "For a woman to a man is just a woman./ But a man to a woman,/ Yes, a man to a woman is her life."

In a plot turn not from the original source, however, the comedy *Ninotchka* (1939, MGM, directed by Ernst Lubitsch), the couple soon quarrel bitterly over Steve's turning "Ode to a Tractor" by Boroff, considered the greatest living composer, into a popular song, "Josephine," for a musicalized version of a small portion of *War and Peace* starring former swimming star, Peggy Dayton (Paige). Their argument lays out the groundwork of their differences quite plainly in Cold War terms that, in turn, resonate for Wood's ideological reading. First, the couple differs over the popular versus the national. "That music belongs to the Russian people," Ninotchka claims. "What right have you to distort it?" "I'm afraid you don't understand," Steve replies. "In America we do this all the time. We make popular songs, and millions of people enjoy them." Score one for American popular culture over elitist high art! Second, the couple clash over the private versus the state. Steve believes that this quarrel has nothing to do with them personally but Ninotchka disagrees. "I am guilty of neglecting my duty, and betraying my whole way of life because of an emotional attachment," she states. "I thought you were all through with this twisted political thinking," Steve shouts back. Score another win for the personal over the political! "But does every woman kissed by you change her politics?" she counters. His rebuttal – that he saw "a carefully trained robot turn into a woman" and that she "can love the masses but to love one man scares the daylights out of you" – then raises the third and most profound difference: his authority versus her submission. Ninotchka's reply to Steve's rebuttal is worth quoting in full: "That, of course, is your opinion. It's always your opinion. It's what you want and what you think. Everything I do is wrong, and everything you do is right. You leave me nothing of my own. If that's your idea of love, yes, it scares the daylights out of me." She, Boroff, and the three commissars leave for Moscow that evening. Eventually, though, Steve finds a way to get her back to Paris and into his arms as his prospective bride.

Ninotchka's response that Steve leaves her nothing of her own which, in the closure of *Silk Stockings* seems to be the price of her expatriation from the Soviet Union and their future marriage, may reverberate much more forcefully, certainly more chillingly, today than it probably did in 1957. Her musical transformation, however, from "a carefully trained robot . . . into a woman" exerts pressure on this neat ideological closure which endorses Steve's version of popular pleasures and their consumption at the expense of Ninotchka's ability to think for herself. In the dance number "Silk Stockings," Ninotchka places Lenin's photo face down and indulges in Parisian fashion: as she dances throughout the Royal suite, she forsakes her drab green dress, black stockings, and sensible shoes for silk stockings, backless high heels, a waist cinch, hat, chemise, sparkling bracelet, and earrings, all previously purchased (though we have not seen her buy them) and hidden throughout the suite beneath the cushions of a chair or behind books, or concealed in objects such as an urn or typewriter.

Ninotchka's dancing in this number is not directed at anyone's gaze – unlike Peggy Dayton's "Satin and Silk," the number right before this one, which is aimed at seducing Boroff into allowing his music to be popularized. (Nor is it a seemingly private moment mediated by men, as is Lise's dance solo in *An American in Paris*.) To be sure, after "Silk Stockings," when Ninotchka emerges in the hotel lobby fully dressed in haute couture, Steve has to reassure her that she does not look foolish, calling her the most beautiful woman in Paris. But *during* the number, Ninotchka dances for her own pleasure not his, indulging in her own desires as she enjoys the sensuous fabrics and textures and, most of all, the freedom of her body as she moves around the room.

One may surely conclude that this number stages Ninotchka's capitulation to capitalism and its pleasures, just as it places her (and Charisse) under the unmediated male gaze of the camera. But at the same time, we also may realize that this number establishes what Ninotchka can potentially keep for herself – and what Steve cannot take from her. The privacy that enables her self-indulgence is central to what her dancing in this number stages. Then, in "Fated to be Mated," the big dance number with Steve that immediately precedes their quarrel, the choreography balances the two with recurring parallel and side-by-side moves to suggest their new parity as equals through their dancing. As John Mueller points out, the choreography makes use of a (rare for Astaire) "cantilevered hip lift," in which "Charisse exultantly swings her legs out into space and plants her feet at a distance, pulling Astaire around after her," thereby making *her* the center of gravity in their dancing even when her partner lifts her.[11] Todd Decker notes that this number "was a quickly assembled partner routine with little plot meaning," because it was put together hurriedly after a more ambitious bicycle routine failed to gel.[12] The male–female equality of the choreography, however, stages a reply of sorts to the couple's first dance duet when, after she claims that "dancing is a waste of time," Steve seduces Ninotchka into dancing to "All of You." "Fated to be Mated" extends the liberation she has experienced in private during "Silk Stockings" to her relationship with Steve and, coming right before their argument, it motivates her anger at his condescension when he belittles her viewpoint.

Charisse and Astaire do not dance together again in *Silk Stockings* but have parallel solo numbers, each evoking the blues. Astaire's, which unexpectedly makes Steve a nightclub performer in a Russian-themed establishment now owned by the three commissars in Paris, is an ambivalent response to the sudden popularity of rock and roll and Elvis Presley.[13] Its merits aside, as a diegetic show number "The Ritz Rock and Roll" has (at least implicitly) been well rehearsed and is bound by the spatial limits of the nightclub stage; moreover, the choreography includes segments in which the elegantly dressed Astaire, for all his lighter-than-air mobility, is literally grounded, for he is shown rolling on the stage floor. By contrast, shortly before this number "The Red Blues," featuring Charisse, is, in Wood's phrase, "the film's supreme expression of vitality through physical movement."[14] The spontaneous and exuberant dancing in "The Red Blues" erupts within the regulated space of communal housing inside the repressive Soviet Union. Ninotchka's fellow tenants begin the dance by bursting into her living quarters as they hear Boroff and his friends play his new Americanized tune, and she soon takes over the dance, becoming the center around which half a dozen men, doing steps that evoke various Russian folk dances, orbit in their choreographed movement as Charisse twirls, leaps, is lifted, and leads them in a line around the room. In the finale she spins and kicks, moving toward the camera until only her whirling legs are shown; then the dancers lift her onto the upper level of her room, and one man holds her up as she kicks; the number then concludes with her back on the ground level, spinning with one leg in the air. At the number's end, the dancers collapse on to the floor, smiling and laughing heartily.

Whereas Steve's subsequent riff on rock and roll is a show number performed on a stage for paying customers, Ninotchka's is extemporaneous, seemingly unrehearsed and happening on the spot in a spacious multilevel room, and it unites the community through their festive dancing. On one hand, "The Red Blues" conceivably shows that Steve has well taught Ninotchka the pleasures of Western freedom, and that the dancing, which erupts around and because of her, is seditious just as the American music that has inspired Boroff is addictive and a vital weapon for the United States in Cold War politics. On the other hand, "The Red Blues" bears comparable significance to "Silk Stockings" because it occurs without Steve's knowledge or controlling viewpoint. The dancing gives full expression to Ninotchka's energy which challenges both Soviet governance and Steve's authority. Hence the surprisingly muted tone of her return to Paris and to Steve in the film's closure.

Funny Face

Funny Face recounts a Pygmalion story of sorts, too, in which Astaire's character likewise teaches Audrey Hepburn's about the pleasures of fashion in Paris as a means of getting her to realize her "true" femininity but Hepburn's stardom exerts greater weight against his in the narrative as well as in her numbers. Jo Stockton (Hepburn) agrees to go to Paris to be the face and body of *Quality*, a glossy fashion magazine, because it will give her the opportunity to meet Professor Emile Flostre, the founder of "empathicalism," the film's hippy-dippy stand-in for existentialism which she calls "the most sensible

Figure 11.2 Fashion Editor Maggie Prescott (Kay Thompson), fashion photographer Dick Avery (Fred Astaire), and bookshop girl Jo Stockton (Audrey Hepburn) sing "Bonjour, Paris!" in *Funny Face* (1957).

approach to true understanding and peace of mind." Photographer Dick Avery (Astaire) assures Jo that she will love Paris, equating the city with "*la belle romance*" albeit in a highly exaggerated mode: "You'll have a ball," he tells her, evoking belle époque clichés. "You'd go to a party every night, drink nothing but champagne, swim in perfume, and a new love affair every hour on the hour."

Yet Jo, Dick, *Quality* editor Maggie Prescott (Kay Thompson) and her crew, all go to Paris to work, not to swim in perfume or drink champagne. The work, in fact, splits Jo in two. On one hand, dressed in her shapeless gray tweed jumper, Jo believes fashion magazines are "chi-chi and an unrealistic approach to self-impressions as well as economics." She's "a thinker," Maggie notes on their first meeting in the Greenwich Village bookshop where Jo works, and "a talker," Dick adds. And Jo's intent in traveling to Paris to work, remember, is to engage her intellect (though tellingly, as a sign that the film addresses Americans in the 1950s, she does not bother to learn French). On the other hand, dressed in Duval's haute couture, what had been "a waif, a gamine, a caterpillar," the designer declares, emerges as "a Bird of Paradise." Moreover, inspired by Dick as she falls in love with him, Jo eventually outgrows him in taking over the scenarios for their photo shoot in the famous centerpiece of *Funny Face*.

Fashion ultimately seems to win over intellect. For when Jo finally does meet Flostre, the man inflames Dick's jealousy. "When you attack Flostre, you attack my principles and the things I believe in," Jo declares to Dick shortly before her introduction to the press as The *Quality* Woman. "We're fortunate to have found out these things now . . . Don't you see? We can never reconcile our differences. They're too basic and too elemental." Their quarrel turns the press show into a disaster. The plot of *Funny Face*, however, does just what Jo says the couple cannot do; by revealing that Dick was correct to be jealous of Flostre, Jo must take the blame, realizing how deeply she has hurt Dick, and she therefore realigns her "principles and the things [she] believe[s] in." Jo returns to Duval's just in time for the fashion show to start; she and the clothes are a big hit; and she and Dick are reunited for a final song, "'S Wonderful, 'S Marvelous," and dance duet.

In her commentary on Hepburn's films, Rachel Moseley notes that the star establishes "an alternative and in some sense oppositional femininity at this historical moment." For instance, as in *Funny Face*, Hepburn's "association with black clothing is perhaps a key way in which she has come to be understood as representing 'intellect,' despite the negotiations made in the narratives of her films."[15] The Hepburn look, in fact, "slim black trousers, black turtle or polo neck and flat black ballet shoes" has become known as "student" or "Bohemian chic," and it stood out for her younger fans as an alternative to the star's association with haute couture, which *Funny Face* also celebrates in its plot and Givenchy gowns.[16] Gaylyn Studlar likewise points out the countercultural significance of Hepburn's black clothing in *Funny Face*. Though "high fashion is glorified visually and musically for bringing Jo a new identity as a mature and marriageable woman," Studlar asserts, the poster art for *Funny Face* features the star not in the Givenchy haute couture that make Jo into the *Quality* woman, and in which she falls in love with Dick, but in "black sweater, pants, and loafers; she reaches for the sky as her face registers a blessed out expression of soulfulness."[17] Furthermore, Hepburn's body is in the foreground and twice the size of her backgrounded co-star, Astaire, who dances behind her; and some of the advertising adds a large view of her head, too, all to exclaim that this is an Audrey Hepburn film.

The costume and pose in the ads are from Hepburn's modern jazz number, "Basal Metabolism."[18] "Basal Metabolism" may be an ironic title for this number since the phrase means the amount of energy needed by a body in a complete state of rest, yet Jo asks Dick before beginning the dance, "Isn't it time you realize that dancing is nothing more than a form of expression and release? There is no reason to be formal or cute about it. As a matter of fact I feel like expressing myself now. And I can certainly use the release." This number certainly affords Jo that sense of release and self-expression!

As it begins, Hepburn dances alone to atonal music, doing bends and turns, stretching and folding her tall, slim body, holding it in momentary poses, as a cringing Astaire watches in disbelief, his hand covering his mouth or pressed against the side of his head. Here the number's title may be apt. When two fellows join her from the stage, the choreography becomes somewhat more fluid as the music changes to a languorous "How Long Has this Been Going On?" and the three dancers move in slow, rhythmic relation with one another, their figures triangulating the space. The trio moves around the club until Hepburn returns to the stage and, as she begins playing with the strings on a bass and kicking a drum, the music changes to a faster "Funny Face." Now, the number's title seems less of a fit than before. The three return to the floor of the club, as patrons scramble to give them room, and Hepburn moves backward as the two men move forward, and vice versa. Then the three dancers swivel their hips, kick, bend, and stretch their arms to the music. With Astaire's viewing position reestablished in the frame, the two men move to the side as Hepburn kicks her leg high, undulates like a snake, does a spin. Her two male partners then each does a brief solo of his own and the three reunite to finish the dance, with one man doing handstands, another dancing on the stage, and Hepburn climbing onto a stool and then kneeling and doing kicks. For the finish, she is lifted back onto the stage where she hits the piano keys to sound a discordant note along with the music while her partners do acrobat poses; then she jumps down, spins, and comes to rest by falling backward on to the laps of two uninterested café patrons.

What are we to make of this number which, choreographically, is not like any other number in *Funny Face*? No song introduces "Basal Metabolism" which begins with ersatz modern jazz music composed by producer Roger Edens and then segues into arrangements of first Hepburn's and then Astaire's earlier solos. The number may seem like a send-up of Jo's endorsement of intellectual Paris because of its free form which makes Hepburn's movement seem awkward and jerky in contrast with the structured story-telling of "Let's Kiss and Make Up," Astaire's number almost immediately following this one.[19] Formally, this number is balanced against Astaire's apologetic solo in the courtyard of the hotel: each has three parts and two cutaways to the other star watching the dancer, and his dance outside her hotel is in many respects his answer to hers in the club. In any event, John Mueller sees "Basal Metabolism" "generally misfir[ing] as parody" because in *Funny Face*, he writes, "even studied freakiness comes out looking innocent and glamorous," although he appreciates the "nice finish" of Hepburn's collapsing on to the laps of those two café patrons who continue talking to each other as if she were not there.[20]

Yet, aside from whether or not it parodies French intellectual life, this number supplies the film's advertising art, indicating its importance for the film. The ads suggest how Hepburn's star text, itself conflicted, as scholars like Studlar and Moseley have well explained, may supply a counterforce to the narrative's trajectory which concludes with a repentant Jo in a Givenchy wedding dress: both scholars report how female viewers remember Hepburn in black from the early portion of *Funny Face*. In many respects, then, "Basal Metabolism" is the correlative in dance terms to Jo's intellectual and philosophical ambitions in making the journey to Paris. For, as Jerome Delameter points out, "The dance even seems to reflect the pattern of Hepburn's emotions throughout the film."[21] It is about expression and release, and the black outfit stands out as highly memorable because it, not the haute couture, gives Hepburn's body the freedom to be frenetic and crazy, to be unruly and unregulated.

Jo Stockton is not the only major female character in *Funny Face*, moreover. The musical's memorable opening number, "Think Pink," shows off the sophisticated nightclub style of Kay Thompson as Maggie Prescott, the powerful editor of *Quality* magazine. In the opening she is surrounded by assistants who, chirping "Yes, Miss Prescott," sound like a flock of birds as they trail after her through the corridors of *Quality*'s office building. With her throaty voice and tallish stature, Maggie is a "mannish" professional woman who, in 1957, probably seemed more of out place as a candidate for domestic heterosexual normality than she would today: middle-aged, apparently with little interest in romance or sex and driven only by her work, she wears a black pillbox hat pinned to the back of her head and a black tailored suit with white gloves, blouse, and scarf; her outfit does not emphasize or exaggerate her figure but, on the contrary, gives it a harsh straight line. A fast talker and quick thinker, Maggie steamrolls her way into the bookshop and throws Jo abruptly into the world of haute couture and fashion photography.

Maggie/Thompson ends up being an odd third figure in the romance plot of *Funny Face* for, with her prominence in the narrative, she stands out as a highly disinterested observer of the June–December pairing of Jo/Hepburn and Dick/Astaire. Two of her numbers parody fashion as the proper expression of femininity about which her magazine instructs "women everywhere" and which Dick takes seriously. Maggie orders everyone to "Think Pink" after she rejects the current issue of *Quality* for being "dreary," "dismal," "dull," and "depressing." Throwing a bolt of pink cloth toward the camera, she wraps the material around her body as she sings that she wouldn't dare to tell a woman what to think but, if she has to think, to think pink. A montage in the middle section, with well-known models like Suzy Parker in pink gowns, establishes the significance of Richard Avedon's photographic style for *Funny Face* but, at the same time, the montage opens up the number to a camp reading of the excesses of fashion, what with its imagery of girls and women all in pink and engaged in all sorts of activities (from brushing their teeth to jumping off a diving board to disembarking from a limo), edited with split screens, jump cuts, and slow-motion effects.

The third section of "Think Pink" resembles the style of Thompson's nightclub act with the Williams Brothers, and it further encourages a camp reading. This section begins with a dissolve from a model flying across the screen on a swing, a long pink scarf trailing behind her, back to the suite of *Quality* offices.

Here the row of office doors, arranged in a crescent on a slightly higher level than the main floor to form a stage, have been painted pink by seven chorus boys in white uniforms; they hop, twirl, bend, and step to the music in union as they sing that pink is "the latest word, you know." The boys are soon joined by Maggie's gaggle of female assistants, now all in pink outfits that match the color of the doors. Then, with the boys raising their arms above their heads as they repeat the song's chorus, Maggie, dressed in a charcoal tailored suit, enters through the double doors in the center of the crescent, her arms raised to make a V as she joins in the singing. Maggie takes over the song as the ensemble forms a triangle with her at the center, first with the painters spread out against the pink doors in back with the assistants in front of them; the two lines then reverse and switch back; each realignment of the triangular configuration directs the viewer's eye toward Maggie who gestures broadly with her arms while singing.

At the number's end, Dovitch, one of Maggie's staff members, arrives to tell her that the whole country is going pink, including the Union Pacific Railroad, and that he awaits news from TWA about pink planes, adding that, for the past two weeks, he hasn't seen a woman in anything but pink – except for Maggie who declares "I wouldn't be caught dead." Her comment nails the number's satire of fashion as consumption just as it highlights her nonconformity. But it is worth noting that, in a subsequent scene, with the pink craze having apparently receded and her assistants again wearing gray or other muted colors, Maggie *does* wear a pink blouse with a dark cranberry suit and matching pillbox hat when she summons Jo to her office for Dick to photograph as the new *Quality* woman. The idiosyncratic Maggie may have chosen pink hues at this point to stand out from the crowd, a reason she would not have been caught dead in that color when it was all the craze, but this scene is also the point when *Funny Face* must begin to take high fashion seriously because it sets up the Paris trip and Jo's agreeing to model as the price of her ticket there. However, following the montage in which Dick photographs Jo all over Paris and its surrounding countryside, and before their argument about Flostre's intentions toward Jo, Maggie's duet with her, "On How to Be Lovely," again takes the air out of fashion's high seriousness and elitist posturing.

At a run-through of the big international press conference (which Dick and Jo's fighting will ruin), Maggie instructs Jo on how to answer the questions about beauty that the journalists will throw at her. "As one lady to another," Maggie begins, then pauses and adds, "But I think first we ought to look like one lady to another." Both women are dressed in a simple white shirt and black pants so they wrap a blue fringed tablecloth around their waists and tie a matching napkin around their heads for makeshift skirts and kerchiefs. "You will be an authority on how to be lovely," Maggie states, and, when Jo confesses she has no idea what to say in response to journalists' questions, the older woman tells her to listen and repeat what she says.

As Maggie sings and Jo repeats the lyrics, each woman exaggerates stereotypical feminine demeanor in the ways they hold their arms, move their legs, pose their bodies, purse their lips, even how they bow and acknowledge imaginary applause at the end of the number; throughout, these gestures underline the performativity and artifice of femininity. The effect of Thompson's and Hepburn's exaggerated performance thus resembles female drag. Their feminine masquerading counterpoints the lyrics of the song which stress the innateness of being lovely because the secret, so they sing, is to be happy, smile, and take nothing seriously. As performed, then, "On How to Be Lovely" does just the opposite of what it supposedly means to accomplish in the narrative which is to have Maggie teach Jo what to say to the press as the *Quality* Woman. Much like "Basal Metabolism" and, despite the obvious difference in tone and style, this number disrupts the Pygmalion narrative of *Funny Face* because the two women's mocking of proper femininity exposes its unnaturalness by making fun of the passivity expected of a "lovely" woman of the sort that Jo eventually becomes as Dick's compliant lover.[22]

April in Paris

This earlier Paris musical, released a year after *An American in Paris*, is in many respects the polar opposite of the later *Silk Stockings* insofar as its plot revolves around a career politician working for the State Department, S. Winthrop Putnam (Ray Bolger), and a Broadway chorine, Ethel "Dynamite" Jackson (Doris Day) whose strongest character note is her working-class background and manners. The film's politics are, for Cold War America, also shakier than the conservative framework of *Silk Stockings*. Ethel causes Winthrop to loosen up and choose love over his career; and the career itself puts him in Washington, D.C. where, as a repeated joke has it, government departments and committees keep investigating one another for impropriety or malfeasance (but not for harboring Reds, though, in 1952, the inference would have been conceivable).

As the quintessential girl next door of 1950s musicals and comedies, Doris Day, like Audrey Hepburn, stood apart from the bosomy blondes (Marilyn Monroe, Jayne Mansfield, Mamie Van Doren) and sexy brunettes (Elizabeth Taylor, Joan Collins, Dana Wynter) who came to prominence with her as new female stars of this decade. But, whereas Hepburn's sophistication had European associations, Day was stubbornly middle American. Her early musicals, moreover, differ from the persona of the perennial virgin for which she was (quite wrongly, in my view) known after *Pillow Talk* (1959, Universal International, directed by Michael Gordon) revised her image by associating her with both fashion via Jean Louis's costumes and the sex comedy genre.[23] In her early musicals Day typically plays either the girl next door or a slightly older working woman, occasionally widowed with a young child, and as often she is a tomboy more comfortable wearing men's clothes and engaging in male activities, such as fixing cars or playing baseball. Her characters tend to be scrappy and spunky; they speak their mind and are not afraid to defy male authority. *Calamity Jane* (Warner Bros., 1953, directed by David Butler) is probably the fullest, if most eccentric, expression of this persona. As much to my point, *April in Paris* is the fullest narrative as well as musical expression of my argument about the disruptive impact of female performances upon the otherwise conservative ideology of the Paris musicals.

Made during only her fourth year at Warners, *April in Paris* has Day's showgirl character mistakenly invited to Paris as part of the State Department's group of older male artists and intellectuals attending the United States-sponsored International Festival of the Arts in Paris. The invitation accidentally sent to Ethel by Winthrop was meant for Ethel Barrymore. As Assistant Secretary to the Assistant to the Undersecretary of State, Winthrop is an efficient and regulated drone, in contrast with the Parisian entertainer Philippe Fouquet (Claude Dauphin) who, at first, cannot leave the United States because the Treasury Department has impounded his income to see how much he owes the IRS. Refused any assistance by Winthrop, Fouquet turns to the camera and states: "Ladies and Gentlemen, I do not like to criticize your government. But everything is regulations, forms, red tape, efficiency, no room for mistakes. Now, what would happen to this giant machine if one little human error should sneak in? Things wouldn't be so apple pie, believe me. This whole delicately balanced mechanism would go poof!" Winthrop is the United States government as a giant machine and Ethel will be the "little human error" that causes its mechanism to go "poof!"

This happens on board the ocean liner taking the American group to Paris and on which Philippe has managed to get a job as a waiter to cover his passage home. At first we see Ethel with Winthrop, his boss, and the others in their party who have eschewed French cuisine for a New England boiled dinner with poached egg. Even Ethel's crunching celery too loudly disturbs the ordered tranquility of their dinner. Nor does she understand how to use the silverware in the proper sequence until Philippe covertly helps her out. Overstepping his position as their waiter, Philippe changes their food order into something more French and then wants Winthrop to take Ethel to the ship's dance but without success because she is ordered to return to her cabin and study her French. Philippe invites her as his date instead. Turned away from the main salon, they head for the ship's kitchen where, after explaining to the staff "that the honor of France is at stake" because Ethel has done nothing but conjugate verbs for the four days she has been on the boat ("and it's a French boat!"), Philippe declares that they will have a dance there in the kitchen. Seated on a steel cooking island, Ethel starts to conjugate the verb *aller* as the kitchen staff joins in. Philippe sings "*Au près de ma Blonde*" as the staff and Ethel, sporting a chef's hat, dance around the kitchen, using utensils, champagne bottles, and carrots as props. A waiter, delivering bicarbonate of sodas to the Americans, informs them that he has never seen such a night and that Ethel, in "the true spirit of democracy," is dancing with everyone in the kitchen. Sent to find Ethel and tell her she will be returned to New York once they reach France, Winthrop enters as she is kicking up her heels on one of those steel islands.

By this point, the party in the kitchen has expanded to include men and women from the main salon who watch Ethel dance. In the meantime, some waiters implore Winthrop to drink toasts to the United States, then France, and so on up and down the alphabet of the United Nations, getting him drunk on champagne. Finishing her dance by flipping up the wide skirt of her gown, Ethel now breaks into her own song, "I'm Gonna Ring the Bell Tonight." She sings:

> For three nights straight,
> I've been forced to act sedate.
> And may I say I didn't like the role.
> Thanks to you my friends
> My pretense now ends.

Then, knocking off the hats of two cooks, she declares, "And you'll forgive me if I kind of lose control!" Ethel joyously segues into the verses, singing that she will ring the bell, rock the boat, and pop her cork. She dances around the kitchen as she sings, playfully interacting with all the staff, as a group of musicians follows her and she uses kitchen props to mime playing instruments. At the song's conclusion everyone joins in and "rocks the boat" along with her.

This number occurs in the middle of *April in Paris* and it redirects the romance plot by forming the proper couple. Before this number, though his response to Ethel has repeatedly been "what a built!," Winthrop was engaged to his boss's daughter, Marcia (Eve Miller), who thinks of herself as the force behind his career with the White House as her endgame. As a result of this number, however, Winthrop and Ethel fall in love. Their relationship immediately following the number disturbs the regulated and staid American world of Washington politics through plot machinations that begin with the couple repeatedly getting into each other's cabins by mistake. They decide to get married by the ship's captain but it turns out that the ceremony is performed by a busboy posing as the captain to avoid being caught while stealing the captain's liquor. Philippe and the busboy then have to sabotage

Ethel and Winthrop's cabins to prevent the couple from consummating their union. Finally, when the boat lands in France, Marcia surprises Winthrop and her father by flying there to meet them and, suspecting something, she keeps belittling Ethel out of jealousy; her spite prompts Ethel – already furious at Winthrop for wanting to delay announcing their marriage until after the Arts Festival – to smack Marcia across the face during the opening ceremony, resulting in the two women going at each other. "Dynamite" is a fitting nickname for Ethel Jackson.

"I'm Gonna Rock the Boat Tonight," which announces Ethel's refusal to be staid and compliant, also transforms Winthrop, breaking down his stuffy and repressed deportment. His release is expressed through Ray Bolger's comic dancing. Bolger has two dance solos in *April in Paris*. The first occurs after his boss praises the (mistaken) invitation to a chorus girl to represent American theater for being a great public relations stunt and a big career move, and Marcia then hints that the White House is next. Once alone in the spacious undersecretary's office, Winthrop imagines what it would be like to be president, talk-singing a state of the union address in which he announces that "the state of the state is great" after his sixth term. Entering another room of this office suite, he sings and, chest swelled and chin lifted, he struts and taps to "Life is Such a Pleasure." During his dance, Bolger's long rubbery legs stretch out and go backward, and he uses furniture as props: he gets stuck in a trash can; he kicks and bounces off the back of a heavy desk; he slips and lands on a stuffed chair, on which he bounces and from which he leaps into the air. The final segment of the dance occurs when he discovers his likeness in life-size paintings of Washington and Lincoln. In the center of the screen, Winthrop initiates a challenge dance with his two imaginary alter egos who quickly begin dancing in perfect sync with him until he gallops out of the room to sing the final line of the song.

That number is a private fantasy of being released from his orderly and inhibited life as a government employee with a fiancée who will manage his future for him. His joining Ethel in the reprise of "I'm Gonna Ring the Bell Tonight" aboard the ship therefore makes real the release he has hitherto only been able to imagine in solitude. An inebriated Winthrop asks Ethel to dance, announcing, "Don't fight it. I'm masterful tonight." He sings a reprise of the song and the pair mimes playing the melody, with Ethel using a ladle on pots and pans and he using one on empty bottles. Then, after she accidentally bops him on the head, Winthrop leads her back on to the open floor where they dance an energetic polka – until she bumps him from behind and he lands on a steamer, leading him into a frenetic solo dance. Jumping on to a steel island, he removes his jacket while dancing; he initially taps expertly in the center but then gets more reckless, dancing precariously along the edges of the island, almost falling, until he regains his balance and ends the solo by flying into the arms of the watching waiters. Ethel comments that Winthrop has turned out to be "pretty human," and he shows her just how human he has become by kissing her. Another choral reprise of the song concludes this sequence as the ship's workers lift Ethel and Withdrop in the air. The couple kiss and, looking at the camera, Philippe mutters, "poof!"

Philippe Fouquet's French figure is therefore important in mediating the relationship of Ethel and Winthrop. Philippe is the clichéd sign of Paris, the "French lover" like Charles Boyer or, more accurately, Pepé LePeu. He has a reputation for (implicitly) bedding one woman after another, even while working on the boat. So he naturally promises Ethel, before she begins her song in the ship's kitchen, that every night in Paris will be like this. "I'll unfreeze my accounts," he tells her, "you'll unfreeze me." After this number, the fallout from the musical explosion in the kitchen, which brings together Ethel and a thawed Winthrop, continues. In the film's third act, Ethel, banished from the Arts Festival for fighting with Marcia, partners Philippe on stage. Their number, "That's What Makes Paris Paree," begins as a competition between Ethel's loyalty to New York and Phillipe's espousing the "charms" of Paris, as she sings about the lack of a tub in the hotel with its old leaky pipes dating back to 1883, the unique and chic clothes that undress her financially, the taxi cabs that nearly run her over, and the "oh so awful Eifel Tower." As the number reaches its finish, though, Ethel finally succumbs to Paris's charms.

This number is the one time *April in Paris* does allude to the belle époque; but the showgirls, each with a standard poodle dyed to match her outfit, the male dancers in bowler hats and moustaches, the street pillars with signs of Parisian events, the stage backdrops that look like cartoonish renderings of the impressionist sets of the ballet in *An American in Paris*, the illuminated Eifel Tower in the background, all place the allusions in bold quotation marks. Furthermore, with Winthrop in the audience, Ethel is determined to make him jealous and pretends that Philippe is her lover, embracing and kissing him at the curtain call. To continue inflaming Winthrop's jealousy, Ethel follows Philippe home with Winthrop in hot pursuit, and they learn that Philippe's persona as the wanton French lover is all a pose because the truth – that he is married with five children – would be bad for business. Thus, it turns out that he has been masquerading as a Frenchified lover in quotation marks, too. Upon discovering this truth about Philippe's private life, Ethel declares, "Gay Paree. I'll never believe another story about Paris as long as I live."

This revelation does not diminish Philippe's importance for *April in Paris*, however. He performs what postwar America presumes is "Frenchness," and this construction of France keeps mediating the romance plot that unites Ethel and Winthrop. Recall that Philippe speaks directly to the American audience about what would happen if the "little human error" (Ethel) should disrupt the regimented government machine (Winthrop); Philippe takes Ethel to the ship's kitchen where she rocks the boat; and he witnesses the shipboard marriage ceremony but, discovering it is not official, helps to sabotage their cabins. Finally, when Winthrop's s jealousy turns to anger at Ethel, once the truth about Philippe's marital status comes out, she addresses the final song, "I Ask You," to the Frenchman. Ethel sings about the joys of love in her effort to convince Winthrop that she really loves him, and Philippe is a third wheel in this number.

Ask any Frenchman and he will agree, Ethel sings, and Philippe concurs from his upstairs window. As Ethel follows Winthrop as he leaves, the camera remains focused on Philippe who sings a verse about the couple. Then he bids adieu to the audience as his wife calls him to bed. In the meantime, with the Eiffel Tower in the background as an echo of the previous show number, Ethel and Winthrop decide to kiss and say goodbye forever. As they start to walk away, Philippe's voice can be heard singing the chorus, "Isn't love wonderful? I ask you." His final mediation causes the couple to realize their love again, and the film ends with a joke that winks at the artificial basis of Paris. Ethel looks at the Eifel tower and remarks, "isn't it beautiful?" Winthrop looks at her and replies, "what a built!" A dissolve to a close-up of Philippe saying, "poof!" is followed by a dissolve back to the couple in a clinch as the film ends.

Conclusion

These Paris musicals cohere as a cycle because of shared thematic elements that, in becoming "musicalized," get complicated beyond their surface meanings. Generally speaking, the cycle uses the modernity represented by a very American notion of "Paris" to link postwar recovery with the Cold War ideology defining United States global superiority and sovereignty, and the films associate this ideology with the Yankee masculinity of the films' male leads. In this context *Silk Stockings*, *Funny Face*, and *April in Paris* each views Paris as a backdrop of bourgeois sophistication and postwar modernity, making it their locale for a Pygmalion-type narrative in which an older man seeks to domesticate a younger, energetic, and unruly woman (Cyd Charisse's Soviet commissar in *Silk Stockings*, Audrey Hepburn's bohemian intellectual in *Funny Face*, Doris Day's working-class chorine in *April in Paris*). Yet she, in turn, at least musically challenges the status and authenticity of his comfortable hegemonic masculinity. To be sure, Astaire's and Bolger's numbers help to bring this challenge out, too, because the energy and romantic or comic eloquence of their dancing further belie the conventionality and age of their male characters; but, at least in the narratives, the gendered logic of their characters' masculinity works hard in an effort to contain their musical numbers.

In each film the female star's screen persona highlights in some way the liberating effects of her numbers. Charisse's coldness as a dramatic performer, quite effective for the characterization of Ninotchka, calls attention to the freedom of her two solo numbers and duet with Astaire in "Fated to be Mated." Hepburn's Cinderella persona, already established in other "Frenchness" films opposite older male co-stars, such as Humphrey Bogart and Gary Cooper, as well as Astaire, likewise makes her dancing stand out as a form of youthful resistance to the patriarchal romance of *Funny Face*. In that musical and in *Silk Stockings*, Paris liberates the inhibited younger female so that she will presumably take her place back in the States alongside her older lover in a companionate marriage. By comparison, Day's scrappy persona, yet to be made more sophisticated and sexualized at this stage of her career, drives the narrative as well as numbers of *April in Paris*. Additionally, the medium for her disruption of the orderly machine of American politics is an Americanized view of Paris as personified by Philippe, the licentious French poseur; he gives license to Ethel to rock the boat, which she handily does. While a less integrated and stylish musical than the other two, *April in Paris* is, in the context of my argument, the most disruptive of the ideological current underlying this 1950s cycle of Paris musicals.

Notes

1. Vanessa R. Schwartz, *It's So French! Hollywood, Paris, and the Making of Cosmopolitan Film Culture* (Chicago: University of Chicago Press, 2007), p. 52.
2. Ibid., p. 21.
3. Ibid., p. 28.
4. Gerald Mast, *Can't Help Singin': The American Musical On Stage and Screen* (Woodstock, NY: Overlook Press, 1987), p. 284.
5. Schwartz, *It's So French*, p. 20.
6. I am thinking of Kelly's three musicals with Frank Sinatra, *Anchors Aweigh* (1945), *Take Me Out to the Ball Game* (1949), and *On the Town* (1949) but also of his other musicals that partner him with a buddy who competes with the girl for his attention, such as *Cover Girl* (1944), and later on, *Singin' in the Rain* (1952), *Brigadoon* (1954), and *It's Always Fair Weather* (1955). See my chapter on Kelly in Steven Cohan, *Incongruous Entertainment: Camp, Cultural Value, and the MGM Musical* (Durham, NC: Duke University Press, 2007), pp. 149–99. On cinematic representations of masculinity during the period 1945–60 see Steven Cohan, *Masked Men: Masculinity and the Movies During the Fifties* (Bloomington, IN: Indiana University Press, 1997).
7. See, for instance, Lucie Arbuthbot and Gail Seneca, "Pretext and Text in *Gentlemen Prefer Blondes*" (1982), reprinted in Steven Cohan (ed.), *Hollywood Musicals, The Film Reader* (London: Routledge, 2002), pp. 77–85; and Alexander Doty, *Flaming Classics: Queering the Film Canon* (New York: Routledge, 2000), pp. 131–53.
8. Robin Wood, "Art and Ideology: Notes on *Silk Stockings*," in Rick Altman (ed.), *Genre: The Musical* (London: Routledge and Kegan Paul, 1981), pp. 62–5.
9. Ibid., p. 64.
10. Ibid., p. 67. Though I am talking mostly about Astaire's character as he functions for the narrative as the patriarchal American, I do not want to minimize how his dancing complicates this characterization. In one of the first pieces I wrote on the musical, "Feminizing the Song-and-Dance Man: Fred Astaire and the Spectacle

of Masculinity in the Hollywood Musical," in Steven Cohan and Ina Rae Hark (eds), *Screening the Male: Exploring Masculinities in Hollywood Cinema* (London: Routledge, 1993), pp. 46–69, I discussed how his dancing in his 1950s musicals produce an alternative (for the era) figuration of masculinity, and my argument there still holds. On *Silk Stockings* see pp. 48–9, 56–9. Nonetheless, here I am focusing on the function of Charisse's dancing in relation to Astaire's character and what he represents about America.

11. John Mueller, *Astaire Dancing: The Musical Films* (New York: Knopf, 1985), p. 397. See also Cohan, "'Feminizing the Song-and-Dance Man," pp. 58–9.
12. Todd Decker, *Music Makes Me: Fred Astaire and Jazz* (Berkeley: University of California Press, 2011), p. 69.
13. See Decker, *Music Makes Me*, pp. 235–8, for an account of this number's context in 1957, the television presence of Elvis Presley, and Astaire's own ongoing effort to be modern.
14. Wood. "Art and Ideology," p. 65.
15. Rachel Moseley, *Growing Up with Audrey Hepburn* (Manchester: Manchester University Press, 2002), p. 56.
16. Rachel Moseley, "Dress, Class and Audrey Hepburn: The Significance of the Cinderella Story" in Rachel Moseley (ed.), *Fashioning Film Stars: Dress, Culture, Identity* (London: BFI, 2005), p. 118. It is worth noting that, when her character goes to the apartment of the French intellectual Flostre in *Funny Face*, both are wearing the unisex and bohemian wardrobe of black turtleneck and black skinny pants.
17. Gaylyn Studlar, *Precocious Charms: Stars Performing Girlhood in Classical Hollywood Cinema* (Berkeley: University of California Press, 2013), p. 227.
18. In fact, the association of Hepburn with this clothing persisted. In 2006 the Gap revived the skinny black pant, renamed "the Audrey Hepburn Pant," and used a CGI-doctored version of "Basal Metabolism" in its television advertising. See Claire Molloy, "Transformation, Fashion, and *Funny Face*," in Jacqui Miller (ed.), *Fan Phenomena: Audrey Hepburn* (Bristol: Intellect Books, 2014), pp. 40–1.
19. See Cohan, "Feminizing the Song-and-Dance Man," pp. 59–61 for my discussion of how this number typifies the spectacular value of Astaire's dancing, which momentarily disrupts his character's patriarchal role.
20. Mueller, *Astaire Dancing*, p. 381.
21. Jerome Delamater, *Dance in the Hollywood Musical* (Ann Arbor: UMI Research Press, 1981), p. 106.
22. It is worth noting that, as additions to the score by George and Ira Gershwin, and as well as supplying the original music for "Basal Metabolism," producer Roger Edens wrote "Think Pink" and "On How to Be Lovely." Edens's camp sensibility is obvious in the MGM musicals he did with stars like Judy Garland, as I discuss in *Incongruous Entertainment*.
23. Tamar Jeffers McDonald explains "the virgin myth" in relation to Day's star text in *Doris Day Confidential: Hollywood, Sex, and Stardom* (London: I. B. Tauris, 2013). See also Tamar Jeffers, "*Pillow Talk*'s Repackaging of Doris Day: 'Under All those Dirndls . . .'" in Rachel Moseley (ed.), *Fashioning Film Stars: Dress, Culture, Identity* (London: BFI, 2005), pp. 50–61.

Bibliography

Arbuthbot, Lucie and Gail Seneca (2002), "Pretext and Text in *Gentlemen Prefer Blondes*" (1982), reprinted in Steven Cohan (ed.), *Hollywood Musicals, The Film Reader*, London: Routledge, pp. 77–85.

Cohan, Steven (1993), "Feminizing the Song-and-Dance Man: Fred Astaire and the Spectacle of Masculinity in the Hollywood Musical," in Steven Cohan and Ina Rae Hark (eds), *Screening the Male: Exploring Masculinities in Hollywood Cinema*, London: Routledge, pp. 46–69.

Cohan, Steven (1997), *Masked Men: Masculinity and the Movies During the Fifties*, Bloomington, IN: Indiana University Press.

Cohan, Steven (2007), *Incongruous Entertainment: Camp, Cultural Value, and the MGM Musical*, Durham, NC: Duke University Press.

Decker, Todd (2011), *Music Makes Me: Fred Astaire and Jazz*, Berkeley: University of California Press.

Delamater, Jerome (1981), *Dance in the Hollywood Musical*, Ann Arbor: UMI Research Press.

Doty, Alexander (2000), *Flaming Classics: Queering the Film Canon*, New York: Routledge.

Jeffers, Tamar (2005), "*Pillow Talk*'s Repackaging of Doris Day: 'Under All those Dirndls ...,'" in Rachel Moseley (ed.), *Fashioning Film Stars: Dress, Culture, Identity*, London: BFI, pp. 50–61.

McDonald, Tamar Jeffers (2013), *Doris Day Confidential: Hollywood, Sex, and Stardom*, London: I. B. Tauris.

Mast, Gerald (1987), *Can't Help Singin': The American Musical On Stage and Screen*, Woodstock, NY: Overlook Press.

Molloy, Claire (2014), "Transformation, Fashion, and *Funny Face*," in Jacqui Miller (ed.), *Fan Phenomena: Audrey Hepburn*, Bristol: Intellect Books, pp. 38–47.

Moseley, Rachel, *Growing Up with Audrey Hepburn*, (Manchester: Manchester University Press, 2002).

Moseley, Rachel (2005), "Dress, Class and Audrey Hepburn: The Significance of the Cinderella Story," in Rachel Moseley (ed.), *Fashioning Film Stars: Dress, Culture, Identity*, London: BFI, pp. 109–20.

Mueller, John (1985), *Astaire Dancing: The Musical Films*, New York: Knopf.

Schwartz, Vanessa R. (2007), *It's So French! Hollywood, Paris, and the Making of Cosmopolitan Film Culture*, Chicago: University of Chicago Press.

Studlar, Gaylyn (2013), *Precocious Charms: Stars Performing Girlhood in Classical Hollywood Cinema*, Berkeley: University of California Press.

Wood, Robin (1975), "Art and Ideology: Notes on *Silk Stockings*", reprinted in Rick Altman, ed., (1981), *Genre: The Musical*, London: Routledge and Kegan Paul, pp. 57–69.

12. STRAIGHT TO BABY: SCORING FEMALE JAZZ AGENCY AND NEW MASCULINITY IN HENRY MANCINI'S *PETER GUNN*

Kristin McGee

> People want to be smart, and when they listen to jazz with a modern story, they start to get the feeling, even though they don't know what they are doing. Any emotion can be inspired by jazz. It has a lot of sexual drive, and this is one way TV can employ sex in its stories without being questioned by the censors.
>
> Henry Mancini[1]

> Mancini intuited that he could write for the five or six players who might be pictured in a club scene and bring that music forward sometimes to take on the responsibilities of narrative scoring, with extensions, digressions, builds, and climaxes that matched the action on screen. He would use jazz in a storytelling capacity.[2]

INTRODUCTION

Three cultural *dispositifs* gain currency in jazz-informed media of the 1950s. The first is the rising visibility of the West Coast jazz musician after the success of Henry Mancini's crime jazz series *Peter Gunn*. The second and third relate to alternative gender stagings occurring within American culture resulting from a variety of jazz-informed media. The late 1950s, in particular, witnessed an unorthodox representation of the white working woman through what I shall categorize as a *female jazz agency*. The last but perhaps more restricting *dispositif* supported the image of the so-called *new man*, and the attendant notions of *'new masculinity'* connected to both jazz connoisseurship and a liberal sex politics presented in jazz-informed entertainment media, especially Mancini's *Peter Gunn*.

While important scholarship within film music studies uncovers much of the unique aesthetic and musical strategies developed by Mancini and others in the postwar period,[3] few scholars have examined the ways in which Mancini's music incorporated creative techniques to both reinforce and transgress accepted gendered representations within the crime detective and noir genre. Many argue that his hybrid compositional practices, which incorporated non-traditional music genres and especially jazz and popular music, were so compelling that they had a profound impact on film scoring from the 1960s on.[4] Yet most fail to interrogate how this captivating and flexible style affected our understanding of gender and sexuality at the cusp of the 1960s, an era emblemized by its progressive transformations within sociopolitical fields. Connected to such larger transformations is *Peter Gunn*'s immense popularity which partly resulted from Mancini's transformed positioning of jazz's dominant race and gender associations within symbolic media such as film and television.

The extreme popularity of Mancini's television scores conditioned film and television music consumers in the postwar period to favor more modern musical genres over the "patch-work" or cue-based romantic soundtracks of the classic Hollywood era. Part of this appeal owed itself to the laid-back and minimalistic style of West Coast cool jazz which prominently appeared in both narrative and diegetic sequences within the *Peter Gunn* series. Further the narratives connected to *Peter Gunn*'s use of cool jazz can be understood as deeply invested in promoting the so-called "new masculinity" of an ideal, middle-class, male consumer, one who positioned himself within an expanding network of distinctive representations of masculinity partly defined by the rising status of jazz as art.

This form of jazz, associated largely with an exclusively white masculinity, was perhaps most publicly epitomized by Hugh Hefner, a jazz sponsor, wealthy bachelor, upper-class elite, and modern media curator, whose controversial ideas about sex and women were well circulated. While Hefner's debates about gender significantly influenced the American consciousness in the 1950s and '60s, the image that the public more likely associated with this new masculine ideal, however, was the detective Peter Gunn with his love of modern (white) jazz, his cosmopolitan, independent way of life, his cool sexuality, and his easy-going "man about town" demeanor.[5] Therefore, jazz's positioning in *Peter Gunn*, but also in surrounding and related media, was critical for promoting and poetically staging not only this new cosmopolitan masculinity but also the materialist comforts to be gained from disavowing the black roots of urban jazz culture. Finally, this new masculinity sought to distance itself from earlier Hollywood representations of heteronormative romantic relationships with all of the burdens attached to monogamy and marriage. The coalescing of images of various professional and established wealthy white men with distinctive musical tastes within American media would all assist the circulation and growing acceptance of this new jazz-loving figure.

By the late 1950s, the incorporation of diegetic jazz in dominant visual media less often referenced the black origins of its circulation such as the innovative performances and recordings of West Coast black jazz musicians Wardell Gray and Dexter Gordon, and instead promoted the evolving figure of the intellectual white jazz artist as the center of the emerging jazz idiom.[6] The Gunn series, a narrative which predominantly depicts white musicians performing jazz, functioned not only to affirm the gendered relations between Hart and Gunn but also to elevate the artistic and critical appeal of the show and its connection to the culturally revered cool jazz genre. By representing white musicians as the normative image of the performing jazz musician, the show simultaneously elided the continued presence of prominent black jazz musicians in LA's many local jazz scenes such as Central Ave, once the spatial locus of modern jazz during the 1940s.

In his book *West Coast Jazz*, Ted Gioia portrays the tension surrounding the rise of the cool jazz moniker and the resulting resentment felt by many black West Coast musicians as they struggled to gain visibility in the postwar era. Further, Gioia dispels the myth of cool jazz lyricism as the defining feature of West Coast jazz, instead highlighting those soloists evolving from Central Avenue who played a very advanced style of modern jazz influenced especially by Charlie Parker's bebop performances on the west coast during 1945 to 1947. One example is his review of altoist Sonny Criss, whose technique was diligently influenced by Parker, but whose emotional style drew heavily from gospel and blues. According to Gioia, by the early 1950s, the moment in which cool jazz's international reputation was gaining commercial appeal, Central Avenue was a ghost town. Most reviews of West Coast jazz depicted its overall decline in the 1960s, even for the newly anointed white cool jazz players. Gioia confirms this image:

> By the early 1960s, West Coast jazz was already in decline, with shrinking audience for both recorded and live jazz. The breakdown of the Central Avenue scene a decade earlier now proved to be a harbinger of the collapse of the whole Southern California jazz community. Even the recently anointed stars of white West Coast jazz were being forced underground into studio work and other non-jazz gigs . . . As it was the 1960s were years of retrenchment in which major stars struggled and new names found it all the harder to make a reputation."[7]

The studio work to which Gioia refers was no more prominently and successfully enacted than in Mancini's use of West Coast jazz within *Peter Gunn*. In the series, the image of the weekly jazz musician with a steady gig, who was white, middle class, and well respected by the community, was something of a misnomer or at least a cultural elision but the series did much to revive the careers of a small group of musicians who managed to transition from touring big bands into the film and television industry after the war. The series also cemented the connection between the genre of the crime detective series and the local West Coast jazz scene but, rather than depicting the racial and gendered diversity of LA's jazz community, the series upheld the cult of the white jazz musician as the quintessential cool jazz performer, an image that would come at the expense of those black musicians having established the innovative new sounds of modern jazz over a decade earlier. Further, contributing to the erasure of jazz's complex cultural, but black-based, community origins during the 1940s, *Peter Gunn*'s fictional jazz world is coolly consumed by a range of character types and classes from detectives to mobsters and from middle-class whites to beatniks and circus performers, yet each of these represents members of the predominantly white working and middle class. In real life, however, the late 1950s was a period in which jazz was performed by smaller groups in smaller clubs consumed by smaller audiences. The jazz that fared well in such a climate was mixed mediated, well marketed in new media, such as high-fidelity recordings, and driven by combinations of new youth-oriented genres such as rock and roll and popular music.

While the new masculinity image was clearly connected to particular associations with modern jazz in 1950s media, within this chapter, I argue that Mancini's innovative musical scoring also facilitated a potent counterpart to the new jazz male, in his enactment of a *female jazz agency*, which especially resulted from his approach towards scoring gender within *Peter Gunn*. While the enactment of a hip, gentrified new man was effectuated in part by one's connection to, and appreciation of, cool (white) jazz, the space for positioning women as modern agents of this new jazz/film economy was less rigidly portrayed. In fact, as I reveal, Mancini's flexible scoring of music in connection to his work with female jazz vocalists before and during *Peter Gunn*'s broadcast years, provide a more complex and sometimes confusing image of the postwar modern woman. Moreover, the series's image of the modern working (white) woman and, more importantly, of an independent jazz musician was also connected to the increasingly respected West Coast sound.

Yet, in this series, Mancini's music appears both to promote female jazz agency while also containing it. First, his programming of diegetic performances of female jazz artists confirms women's role in postwar American jazz culture. Second, however, by doubling and reworking such progressive diegetic jazz performances into lighter, domesticated musical forms within "ambi-diegetic"[8] or purely narrative sequences, such female jazz agency is often undermined so that more traditional gendered positions could be maintained. In this chapter, I uncover such strategies within the filmed narratives of various episodes of *Peter Gunn* from 1959 but also by connecting the extratelevisual texts of various media to this female jazz agency, including Mancini's tie-in albums recorded in relation to the series, which quickly elided and displaced images of black jazz from the West Coast to the television screen in the postwar period.

Sounding Women in Classic Hollywood and Noir/Crime Genres

During the 1940s and 1950s, film noir's narratives featured depictions of the urban *demi-monde* with characters whose relations to love and family veered from the conventions of mainstream Hollywood A-list dramas.[9] Yet, even as noir offered more complex characters displaying greater psychological depth, its broader stories typically inscribed traditional heteronormative relationships. In the quickly produced, but often more experimental B-rated crime genres, male detectives, typically portrayed as single white men, maintained only fleeting connections to romantic partners as temporary love interests. Occasionally, women acted as collaborators in sleuthing pursuits but often transitioned into romantic partners for domestic unions, usually secured at the end of the film. In short, women' roles in these films were often secondary, acting as foils to prominent men.[10]

As Kathryn Kalinak reveals, dominant and hierarchical enactments of gender are well examined by film scholars, yet few have understood how the sound world of classic film originally established the gendered sonic expectations of noir narratives. Following Claudia Gorbman's famous treatise on narrative music, Kalinak argues that such gendered principles were first established in the 1930s and continue to ground our perception of film music codes.[11] During this formative period, composers exploited music's power to construct cultural or affective associations between the narrative and the musical content.[12] In particular, narrative music devices afforded the mapping of cultural identities on to particular character types.

Despite claims of music's abstract or non-narrative structure, film-music composers relied upon particular conventions to situate the gendered sound worlds of its characters. These include stock cues to reference stereotypical character types, musical genres with cultural and gendered associations, and compositional structures, such as particular harmonies and melodic techniques, to allude clearly to a woman's sexual or cultural status. Women's secondary position in relation to prominent men as objects of desire or excess, for example, could be clarified not only through the cinematic filming aesthetic that prioritized the "male gaze"[13] but also through a set of sonic conventions that would become standard in classical Hollywood scoring. Such conventions created a sonic world whose compositional structures and main motives in relation to representing women prominently reinforced the dominance of the masculinized perspective or, as Kalinak argues: "the Hollywood film itself ... created an image of women as the projection of its own (male) fear and desire."[14] Feminized musical cues were therefore composed to reinforce this larger masculine sonic world.

Recently, film-music scholars have interrogated established perceptions of women's roles in noir and crime film narratives to extend the sonic analyses of largely classic Hollywood gendered soundscapes. Through her investigation of various B-level noir and crime films from the 1940s, Catherine Haworth posits that women sometimes inhabited more complex roles which afforded agency and mobility across classic Hollywood archetypes.[15] Such mobility was achieved and supported musically through the use of both existing library music (cues) and newly composed musical sequences, albeit often only temporarily in the initial stages of a film's narrative. Haworth reveals that, ultimately, musical conventions would also be used to contain such mobility by fetishisticly or reductively highlighting gendered or cultural difference.[16] The agency of female detectives in 1940s noir/crime genres is contained as they acquiesce their working status to take up the romantic or domestic needs of male protagonists who eventually reinhabit their dominant roles as detectives. Musically this is rendered by occasionally allowing women agency in the sleuthing scenes while the scoring takes on more chromatic and tension-creating moods and, then again, reasserting their secondary romantic interest role with more classical leitmotif themes where the female amateur detective is scored with romantic upper-register strings or other feminine-identified orchestrations. As women moved from investigative to romantic roles in these films, critics quickly connected such transformations as projections of anxieties about the changing roles of women during the postwar era.[17]

Henry Mancini's Ambi-diegetic Jazz for Peter Gunn

Accepting that such scoring conventions for women of the noir and crime genre existed, it is conceivable that Henry Mancini, an experienced film arranger and big band composer of the war and postwar era, consciously navigated both film and popular music codes to enact sonically such identity markers as race, sexuality, and gender in the late 1950s. But to understand better Mancini's unique scoring practices, it is first important to recognize how the changing role of film and of recording in the late 1950s had an impact on his compositional style. Mancini's role as a television composer of the crime genre coincides with two important events: first, the collapse of the big movie-studio system; and second, the high-fidelity revolution in recording which hastened the commercial market for high-fidelity systems and for long-play albums in the postwar era.[18] This technology further motivated new recording techniques, such as multi-miked stereo recording. According to Mancini scholar John Caps, these two events facilitated Mancini's rise as the most important and popular film and television composer of the 1950s and '60s.[19] The introduction of the high-fidelity album also enabled Mancini to promote a relatively new music commodity, the tie-in album, which assisted the vertical integration of the film, television, and music industry during the 1950s.

Prior to *Peter Gunn*, Mancini had gained critical experience performing and arranging with big bands during and after the war; before the war he arranged for the Benny Goodman Big Band and, during the war, he was conscripted into the Air Force Band where he arranged and performed a variety of genres. After the war, Mancini worked for the newly formed Glenn Miller Orchestra led by Tex Beneke. These positions gained him a reputation as an arranger of jazz and popular music and also had a profound impact on his musical scoring of film and television during the 1950s.

In the early 1950s, Mancini left the big bands and moved to Los Angeles with the encouragement of his musical colleague and later wife Ginny O'Connor whom he met while working with the Glenn Miller Big Band. O'Connor sang with the professional popular group the Mello-Larks for whom Mancini arranged for the Miller band.[20] O'Connor, recognizing the sea changes the music industry was undergoing, encouraged Mancini to leave the big bands and settle into Hollywood where her family maintained connections with the film studios. After a recommendation from his wife, he was invited to work for Universal films to arrange a Dorsey Brothers short subject film.[21] This led to other small arranging assignments. At first, he began modestly, arranging for B-level films in a variety of genres from dramas, fantasy, to musical comedy and noir. Some of his first important films were only partially scored by him under the model of the industrial film soundtrack which employed arrangers, cue sheet compilers, script markers, musical directors, and main theme composers. Some of these films were dramas, such as *Green Dolphin Street* (1947) and *Meet Danny Wilson* (1951) starring Frank Sinatra, or comedies such as the Abbott and Costello comedy, *Abbott and Costello Go to Mars (1953)*, the fantasy films *City Beneath the Sea* (1953), and *Creature from the Black Lagoon* (1954), the jazz-centered biopic films, *The Glenn Miller Story* (1953) and *The Benny Goodman Story* (1956), and his first teen musical, *Rock, Pretty Baby* (1956). Just before *Peter Gunn*, in 1958, Mancini scored a dramatic film entitled *Flood Tide* featuring singer Julie London. With each of these films, Mancini acquired critical experience in scoring a variety of music genres as well as filmic genres and character types; this experience would influence his writing for his most popular series *Peter Gunn*.

For the most part, the scores on which Mancini assisted during the 1950s were the traditional and heavily industrial patchwork films drawn from large studio cue music libraries. His most important film, however, which would establish both his unique hybrid musical scoring style as well as the increasingly important role of the tie-in album, was Orson Welles's *Touch of Evil* (1958). In this experimental film, Welles had wanted diegetic "street" music including Afro-Cuban drumming, rock and roll, and jazz emanating from the bars and cafés of a Mexican/American border town. In an interview, Mancini identified how this new innovative use of both diegetic and source music was a concept he had cultivated even before Welles's aesthetic request: "Dramatic sequences in that score were really just another aspect of the source music that was already coming from the streets. That's exactly what Welles had wanted all along, although I must admit I was committed of [sic] that approach before I ever knew what Welles was thinking."[22] This approach would become critical for innovating the television and film soundtrack with his series *Peter Gunn* in 1959.

During the late 1950s, in the environment of the collapse of the major film studios, Mancini was released from his contract with Universal. In need of money, he developed his *Touch of Evil* soundtrack into an independent album of fully composed songs and shopped it to various record companies; most declined but the local Challenge Records eventually signed it, making this his first soundtrack album of a dramatic score.[23] This was also his fourth credited soundtrack album including two teen rock and roll musicals *Rock Pretty Baby* (1956) and *The Long Hot Summer* (1958) and the dramatic film *Driftwood and Dreams* (1957).

By 1958, Mancini was no longer on contract with Universal but he retained his studio lot pass which allowed him to network with producers and directors. In that year, he ran into television producer Blake Edwards who had been developing a series idea based upon a new kind of detective, one who was sophisticated and loved West Coast cool jazz. According to Caps, it was with Edwards that Mancini envisioned extending his prior scoring practice from *Touch of Evil* in which the relation between the diegetic music from the film's setting and the dramatic score would become both intertwined and more complex. In *Peter Gunn*, the musical narrative concept led to one of the most successful crime genre series ever and also established the groundbreaking popularity of Mancini's crime jazz genre through the new medium of the tie-in album.

Peter Gunn ran for over two years (1959–61) and produced 114 episodes, each featuring several jazz moments or diegetic performances. Because Mancini was dedicated to the new high-fidelity sound, rather than recording the music for *Peter Gunn* at the film/television studio, he hired a special, newly equipped hi-fi music studio with which to record his three tie-in albums: *Music from Peter Gunn* (RCA Victor), *More Music from Peter Gunn* (RCA Victor) and

Dreamsville (Columbia). *Dreamsville* was the only tie-in album to feature vocal arrangements composed from many of the series's instrumental themes. The first two albums featured instrumentals exclusively and most were full arrangements reworked from the series's weekly material. Each album featured many of the same musicians who recorded the soundtrack but Mancini also invited special guests including prominent West Coast musicians such as drummer Shelly Manne. Many of the recording artists from *Peter Gunn* had also worked in the war-era big bands such as Woody Herman, Stan Kenton, and Glen Miller. Other musicians were known to Mancini from Universal's film music division.[24]

The show's weekly budget of $2,000 could accommodate only twelve players but later, as the music became increasingly popular, Mancini expanded his weekly sessions to include five saxes, four winds, four trombones, and two trumpets, with drums, piano, vibes, and guitar as sidemen. The players from the West Coast jazz scene included bassist Rolly Bundock, drummer Jack Sperling, trumpeter Pete Candoli and his brother Conte, trumpet soloist Shelly Manne and the Nash brothers with Ted on saxophone and Dick as the series's leading trombone soloist.[25] Hollywood studio players were later added to fill out the album recordings, including pianists John Williams (the same Williams who would become one of the most famous film composers of the late twentieth century) and Jimmy Rowles.

The weekly crime series was the first to evoke the contemporary West Coast sounds of LA's jazz scene. Nearly every episode featured diegetic jazz sequences filmed at the fictional club, Mothers, apparently so named to placate television censors anxious about the weekly incursion of an urban jazz club into family viewing hours.[26] Within these sequences, detective Peter Gunn often wandered into the club after work to hear jazz, to steal a few romantic moments with jazz vocalist Edie Hart, or to meet with potential clients to discuss crime assignments. The combination of Gunn's love of jazz and his romantic interest with the leading vocalist of Mothers provided avenues for showcasing both cool jazz and several local jazz musicians, including Lola Albright who was an established film actor and pop jazz singer prior to 1958. In fact, Mancini suggested Hart for the part after arranging her album *Lola Wants You* in 1957 for CBS's Columbia Records.

Scoring Women in *Peter Gunn*

In the *Peter Gunn* series, Lola Albright[27] portrayed the show's sultry nightclub singer and romantic partner Edie Hart. Albright remained in the show for all three seasons, winning an Emmy for Best Supporting Actress in 1959. Albright first gained acclaim in the 1949 Hollywood Kirk Douglas boxing drama *Champion*. Although she began her film career performing musical roles, she was just as often cast as the femme fatale or troubled woman in noir pictures or serious dramas. In her early career, she appeared in several films with musical themes, including her debut, the musical comedy *The Unfinished Dance* in 1947. She later starred in *Silver Whip* (1953) in which she played a saloon singer, in Frank Sinatra's *The Tender Trap* (1955) as one of the women who tries to tempt Sinatra into marriage, and in Elvis Presley's *Kid Galahad* (1962).[28]

Many would argue that Albright's understated and cool performance as Hart in *Peter Gunn* would remain the high point of her acting and musical career. In 1992, Mancini reflected on Albright's depiction of the smoky nightclub's singer claiming: "She was perfect casting for that role because she had an off-the-cuff kind of jazz delivery that was very hard to find, just enough to believe that she'd be singing in that club and that she shouldn't be on Broadway or doing movies."[29] Part of the show's believability owed to the seemingly realistic network of musicians drawn from the West Coast scene of which Hart was a participant and local recording artist.

In *Peter Gunn*, Hart continued her trade as a jazz singer; she appeared in nearly every episode as the lounge singer at the small jazz club Mothers. Her secondary role was as Gunn's steady romantic partner. The shows portrayal of Hart's character was somewhat unusual in mid-century America in both its representation of female jazz agency and in her romantic relationship to *Peter Gunn* (see Figure 12.1). Throughout the series, Hart earns her living as an independent jazz musician who eventually gets her own nightclub at the end of season three. Beyond the series's fictional narrative, her television role buttressed her real-life status as a modern jazz singer collaborating with established LA jazz musicians both of whose reputations preceded the series but were enhanced by it (in the diegetic portions staged at Mothers and in the release of three highly popular tie-in albums). Albright is one of the regular artists employed in this small-scale postwar jazz club and her cool, reserved style of performing and singing coalesced around the image of West Coast jazz, which contributed greatly to this series's popularity and cultural cachet.

Mancini's use of jazz in the series served to elevate Hart/Albright's agency and to inscribe her cool and collected individuality. Yet, despite its highly revered modern take on the crime/noir soundtrack, jazz would also be used as narrative scoring to position her character in relation to the overall gendered and racial hierarchies presented within postwar America. This complex positioning of agency in the frame of normative gender expectations was achieved especially through Mancini's complex mixture of diegetic and non-diegetic scoring practices. The composer's fuzzy "in-between" or "ambi-diegetic"[30] incorporation of jazz was a novel element of the show and one already partially cultivated as an aesthetic practice in his scoring of Orson Welles's *Touch of Evil*.[31]

Figure 12.1 Peter Gunn and Edie Hart share a private moment on Mother's backstage balcony in Episode 1, *The Kill*.

To achieve sonic and narrative continuity, Mancini adapted diegetic material performed by the instrumental combo at Mothers into non-diegetic narrative cues such as for Hart's romantic interludes with Gunn. These served first and foremost to provide affective continuity for the series by linking particular motives and melodies to particular characters and places. Two prominent spaces for such ambi-diegetic jazz were the backstage balcony at Mothers or Pete's bachelor pad. These were also important spaces in reconfiguring Hart's role as a jazz musician into a supporting romantic partner. Equally important was music's narrative role in mediating Hart's professional status as an independent jazz musician. One might argue that these cues also served to contain her agency as an independent working woman. In this sense, Mancini drew from the narrative strategies of 1940s noir film-music composers who inserted particular genres and scoring techniques, such as late-romantic (feminized) orchestrations, to contain women's agency. Yet Mancini further complicates such techniques by altering the affective and gendered expectations connected to particular genres. Critical in this departure was his use of jazz for a greater *variety* of affective ends and in the ambi-diegetic musical sequences adapted from diegetic scenes intrinsic to the main plot (Gunn being a lover of jazz who frequents Mothers for information gathering and intimate intermissions). I'll return to this point in the specific analyses of particular scenes later in the chapter.

While the new masculinity of Gunn's character is reinforced by Gunn's independent lifestyle and appreciation of modern jazz, the associations of the female lead in the series did not necessary carry the same connotations, although jazz's connection to Hart's character is significantly more varied and complex than in prior noir scorings. For example, by composing romantic themes derived from the diegetic instrumental combo performances as the narrative and dramatic soundscape for Hart's secondary role as Gunn's love interest, her status is both complex and changing throughout the series. In these sensual interludes, one might expect the more conventional noir scoring of sultry saxophones and slurred, brassy tones to suggest the overt sexuality of an independent female jazz performer. Rather, Mancini's orchestration generally rejects such sonic clichés of sexual excess to favor shorter improvised solos provided by instruments with more subdued timbres.

Further, by avoiding the now clichéd use of stripper jazz to intimate a sensual mood between Hart and Gunn, Mancini maintains Hart's sophisticated and respectable (white, middle-class) image. Instead of a solo saxophone, he composes sequences with lighter textures and arrangements more connected to the cool jazz aesthetic. These included improvised melodies performed by the more reserved jazz guitar, flute or vibraphone. These lighter and dreamy textures would be featured on many of the tracks from the tie-in LPs. For example, "Dreamsville," an airy tune featuring Mancini's characteristic vibraphones, guitar, and piano, often provided the sonic backdrop for domestic, romantic interludes between various characters. These romantic pieces prioritized catchy but simple melodic phrases over jazz-oriented chord changes.

The easy-listening appeal of such narrative music referenced the growing popularity of the West Coast bachelor pad or exotica genre produced and marketed by well-known studio composers including Martin Denny and Les Baxter. This lighter but sophisticated jazz was marketed less as the work of live jazz musicians from LA's local scene and more as music produced by specialist composers (such as Mancini) to be consumed in domestic spaces, as technologically enhanced cultural flights to exotic locales. In the series, however, this light jazz underscored a new type of femininity driven by Edie's status as a respectable, mature but independent woman with modern, consumer-driven tastes. These sophisticated tastes were reinforced in scenes where Hart relaxes in her living room fashionably equipped with a hi-fi stereo system (enjoying her West Coast jazz collection), a plush white matching sofa set, shaggy rug, and fireplace, all of the accoutrements of a white, sophisticated, working woman, itself a relatively new character type in American media.

Peter Gunn's Gendered Ambi-diegesis: from Female Jazz agency to Hi-fi Domesticity

While Caps, Smith, and others argue that Mancini abandoned the classic Hollywood patchwork or cue-sheet scoring format for this series, I suggest rather that he adapted it to create motives that elicited, variously, complex moods, scenes, and character associations. In this sense, he rejected the strict use of leitmotifs to inscribe particular gendered character types. For example, in season one, Mancini typically reincorporated four to five diegetic pieces from Mothers into narrative music sequences to elicit various gendered, sexualized, and affective associations for the episode's main characters. The most common musical cues were implemented into three scenarios: scenes of romantic domesticity; scenes of sexual tension between Gunn and others; or the sensual late-night or backstage interludes between Gunn and Hart. For these three scene types and corollary affective associations, Mancini typically composed and programmed five themes into the series within the genre of light or crossover jazz; these were composed into full songs for his three tie-in albums. From the first two tie-in albums from season one, *Music from Peter Gunn* and *More Music from Peter Gunn*, five pieces satisfy the growing pop-jazz formula designed for both masculine consumption and for eliciting the range of heteronormative intimacy within the series. These are "Slow and Easy," "Soft Sounds," "Blues for Mothers," "Dreamsville," and "A Quiet Gass."

"Slow and Easy"

One of Mancini's favorite pieces featured throughout season one is the theme/piece "Slow and Easy." It appears in the very first episode, *The Kill*, to intimate the jazz-drenched amorous relationship between Gunn and Hart. We first hear the song at Mothers. The scene establishes Gunn's dedicated relationship to the club. The viewer first sees the marque of Mothers in neon lights against a dark, damp city street. More importantly, we hear a small combo improvising modern jazz which seeps from the concrete walls out on to the street. Next, we see Pete casually enter the club, apparently dropping by after work to relax to the sounds of Mothers's intimate style of jazz.

The club's regular jazz singer Edie Hart is first introduced with a dramatic bongo solo as she enters the stage to perform an unusually polyrhythmic version of "Day In Day Out" (Figure 12.2). This performance appears inspired by the mixed-genre eclecticism of West Coast cool jazz. The lyrics of this first performance foreshadow the steadiness of Gunn and Hart's relationship ("Can't you see it's love, can there be any doubt, when there it is, day in day out"). From his approving looks and contented smile, Gunn appears to enjoy the jazz combo in the company of the well-healed but well-weathered

"Mother," the owner of the club. He seems especially turned on by Hart's mixed-genre version of "Day In Day Out," a nod to the classic American songbook and a novel reworking of this standard in a Latin jazz-inspired jacket. After a few numbers, between Edie's sets Pete wanders to the balcony presumably to meet her, as if this is his habit. As Edie enters through the back door, the music to "Slow and Easy" is heard faintly in the background; the viewer is aware that the jazz combo plays on without Edie for the remainder of the set.

During her performance break, Edie first expresses her love for Gunn as he listens attentively to her; the background jazz meanders in and out of their conversation like a third party. He coolly reciprocates. Yet as if to diminish the seriousness of her declaration, Hart's tone is rather understated:

> HART: I really love you very much.
> GUNN: I really love *you* very much.
> HART: But not that much. I'm just one of your favorite singers in the all the world.
> GUNN: [turns closer to face and embraces her] One of my *very* favorite.
> HART: Uh huh, I know the type. I lost my voice you'd hate my guts.
> GUNN: You don't just sing like your voice.
> HART: Is it true what they say about you?
> GUNN: What do they say?
> HART: Pete Gunn for hire.
> GUNN: True.
> HART: Well I've saved up a few dollars. I'll buy ya a steak later.
> GUNN: I'll take a rain check. I've got to run an errand for Mother.
> HART: Gonna take you all night?
> GUNN: Hard to say.
> HART: I'll hang around, if you don't show up by three o'clock, [laughs softly], I'll kill myself . . .

Then, as the camera pans away from close-ups of the couple, we hear the urban sound of train noises. The back door opens with the jazz pianist Emit (played by pianist Bill Chadney)[32] calling Edie back to the stage. She leaves through the back door to resume her role as professional singer. In other words, as detective work is Gunn's main preoccupation, jazz is Hart's, even as she coyly jokes about her romantic dependence upon Gunn.

This first interaction, leading to Hart's love declaration, sets the stage for the couple's weekly romantic trysts. Further, it established the use of diegetic cool jazz as the culturally appropriate backdrop for this relationship. As the next examples will uncover, this unique positioning led to the transformed ideological and cultural associations attributed to jazz on the American screen at the end of the decade. From season one, this may be the only scene where "Slow and Easy" dramatizes the overt sensuality of Gunn and Hart's relationship. The next time the theme is introduced, it is used to suggest the calm and reassuring palette of their steadfast, domestic relationship.

In Episode 4 of season one, *The Blind Pianist*, for example, the theme is scored as narrative music for Gunn's return to his apartment late at night where he discovers Edie sleeping peacefully on his couch. The theme is rendered by trombones in harmony with lots of sweet vibrato. Throughout the series, vibrato emerges as an important marker of both gender and romance. As Jeff Smith notes, Mancini was not only a virtuoso melodic composer, he was also adept at turning "unusual sonorities into brilliant song hooks" for his crossover albums.[33] Sectional vibrato by the trombones often referenced the couple's quiet domestic romance, while solo saxophone vibrato intimated a more overt sexuality between Gunn and a dangerous sexual woman. In the midst of this sweet jazz rendition, Hart wakes up to complain about Gunn's cheap perfume stink; presumably he has been out with a floozy in his crime-solving endeavors. They talk in quiet intimate tones while the song continues in the background. In this first episode, "Slow and Easy" sets up the predictable and "easy" nature of their romance but, true to his flexible adaptation of jazz material, Mancini would adapt it to suggest other associations in differing contexts throughout the series.

The next time we hear this melody, it occurs in Episode 19, *Murder on the Midway*, to reflect the dangerous sexual allure of the very attractive "Rowena" (played by the beautiful Nita Talbot), a carnival-employed, belly dancer who performs a sensual dance for a fictional but repugnant orientalist prince who forced her into a harem as a young woman. This time the theme, performed by solo saxophone, is slower and bluesier in a style enhancing the extreme sexual energy between Gunn and this tempting, experienced man-eater, the quintessential noir femme fatale. Her allure is reinforced by the orientalist associations of her performance art (typically rendered by oboe and hand drums). Later we hear the theme again after Rowena and Gunn visit Mothers together, much to the dislike of Hart. As Gunn accompanies Rowena back to her tent, the theme reappears in the original arrangement as a mid-tempo blues performed again by trombones in the upper register. This time Rowena coyly offers an invitation at kissing distance: "I hope I loused up your romance." To which Gunn replies "It's possible" to which she says "Good more for me" before landing a long kiss on his mouth. The altered orchestration (solo saxophone versus sectional trombones), new tempos (medium versus slow) and use of blue notes and vibrato provided varied connotations for the level of sensuality and tension between Gunn and these female characters. Mancini would develop such scoring strategies with relatively few resources and a small group of musicians to stage a range of gendered and sexual affects in later episodes.

In Episode 24, *The Ugly Frame*, the tune is performed diegetically at Mothers as Gunn and Hart chat at the bar while a despondent Lieutenant Jacoby sits alone at a table. He worries about his upcoming hearing (he has been framed). This time Mancini forgoes the usual brass players for a more economic piano and guitar doubling. This paired-down arrangement effectively marks this version as a melancholy, solitary background for drinking one's blues away rather than sounds that would suggest a sensual invitation for romance.

We hear the theme again in Episode 26, *Keep Smiling*, in an after-hours gentleman's club for betting and jazz. As the blackmailing, attractive femme fatale Emily (played by Mara Corday) enters the club, the music transitions from slowly rendered small-group blues to a more up-tempo version of the tune. This time the lead melody on trombone and trumpet is played in a more aggressive New Orleans hot-jazz style. Gunn and the blackmailing Emily flirt relentlessly even though both are playing a part to ensnare the other in their scheme. This more chaotic hot-jazz rendition of the theme suggests not only sexual danger but also a possible link to the unpredictable world of crime and gambling. In this scene, Mancini relies upon prior associations of underworld jazz from both noir and the classic Hollywood period.

"Slow and Easy" could also be used to suggest sexual tension between the secondary characters embroiled in the main crime plot. In Episode 9, *Image of Sally*, this theme provides the backdrop for the doomed relationship of Sally and Si, the man just released from jail who took the rap for the main gangster Joe Nord. After serving his time, Si enters the apartment of his former girlfriend Sally Hall, the damsel in distress. Sally is now the property of Joe Nord but she wants out. She offers him a drink and he declines. She walks over to her record collection and puts on "Slow and Easy." Here the music is rendered by the sensual trombone theme with lots of blue notes and vibrato; its audibility marks the melancholy backdrop for these doomed but romantically invested lovers. By filming Sally's character playing the record, the music functions on various levels: diegetically, as a replica of a typical modern apartment (with a record player and LP collection); dramatically, to cue the destitution of these tragic lovers; and finally, within the industrial and commercial context of television and the recorded division of RCA Victor (Figure 12.3). Here it functions outside of the diegesis to promote the recorded version of Mancini's tie-in LP (*Music from Peter Gunn*) providing viewers a snippet of what they can consume in their own living rooms.

Finally, in Episode 11, *Death House Testament*, Gunn takes the bait of a sexy, sophisticated "brunette" who appears to be sleeping in her expensive car while her cute diamond-studded poodle peers curiously out of the window, drawing Gunn's attention as he passes by. Gunn wakes the woman and offers to drive her somewhere. She accepts. As Gunn gets into the car, she drapes her long legs over the front seat. She slides to the middle to be closer to Gunn so she can demand that he kiss her. He pauses, claiming he doesn't even know her name. She replies: "Sandra Leads" to which he coolly retorts "I always insist on a formal introduction." As he kisses her, he fishes through her purse to discover a small, feminine gun at which he asks "Alright Sandra – why are we so fond of each other?"

For this scene, the album arrangement of "Slow and Easy" is heard as narrative music, again rendered by sectional trombones in a slower tempo to provide the sexually charged music undergirding the feminine trap set up by this attractive woman and her dog. The contrasting arrangement of the bridge, however, establishes this character's upper-class identity as a wealthy white woman. The high-class background is enacted sonically by the doubling in octaves on three instruments which would come to be synonymous with Mancini's light pop jazz style – the guitar, piano, and vibraphones. In this arrangement, the lush major tonalities of the bridge are orchestrated in melodious and languid octaves and performed by the characteristic trio. This trio often framed the upper-class standing of prominent but sensual white women in the Gunn series, with the Victorian associations of the piano as an important intertextual sonic cue. Thus, the alluring sensuality of this female temptress is framed by her white upper-class identification, a musical, cultural and visual depiction we would often witness later in the crime jazz series of the Bond films.

In each of these episodes, "Slow and Easy" continuously references the jazz club Mothers and Hart's performances there. Therefore the connections to this setting act as an important precursor to both her professional work and her romantic relationship. Mancini's unique rescoring of such themes depended upon the gendered and professional associations of jazz and blues sonically enacted, variously and over time, within different settings to suggest a diverse range of character types and affective worlds. Further, Mancini resisted using musical themes as one-dimensional leitmotifs to stage statically the gendered, affective, and psychological dimension of the show's main characters. Rather, diegetic music was flexibly scored to suggest something slightly different about the various male–female interactions of the series characters as demanded by each new crime-driven or romantic situation. Through Mancini's artful orchestrations and the combined uses of narrative and diegetic or rather ambi-diegetic scorings, these themes successfully communicated to the viewer much about the level of intimacy, the danger of the alluring woman, the overt sexuality of the encounter, or the contented domesticity shared between Hart and Gunn who predictably reunite after hours in the comfortable environment of bachelor pads or working-women apartments. Finally, in Mancini's scoring, jazz would be fully instrumental in inviting a respectable white woman into its associative world of sex, romance, and professional performance.

DREAMSVILLE

The two albums connected to the series, *The Music of Peter Gunn* and *More Music from Peter Gunn*, profoundly expanded the commercial success and critical acclaim of Mancini as a film music composer during the 1950s and 1960s. They also facilitated the rise of the economic popularity of the new genre of pop jazz and the medium of the tie-in album.[34] Further, the two tie-in albums carrying the series title were the first blockbuster LPs released by a film and television soundtrack composer in the 1950s.[35] In 1959, Mancini recorded his first tie-in album for the series *Music from Peter Gunn* (LPM/LSP 1956) with RCA Victor. This album became the first television soundtrack to reach number one on the *Billboard* Pop LP charts in 1959, selling more than a million copies and winning a Grammy for Album of the Year, a feat unheard of for film music composers. The second album recorded, also in 1959 for RCA Victor, was *More Music from Peter Gunn* (RCA LMP 2040) which was favorably reviewed but not as popular as the first release.

Most scholars of Mancini (and *Peter Gunn*) cite and examine these two albums.[36] Yet Mancini also released a third tie-in album to feature the series's main female character Edie Hart, portrayed by singer and actress Lola Albright. This vocal album, entitled *Dreamsville*, was released in 1959 by Columbia records (CL 1327) and featured many of the same musicians from the other two albums (Figure 12.4). The album showcased vocal versions of various instrumental themes heard both in the series and recorded on the other two albums. For example, Mancini arranged new vocal versions of the instrumentals "Dreamsville," "Brief and Breezy," "Soft Sounds," "Slow and Easy," "Sorta Blue," and "Session at Pete's Pad" (as "Straight to Baby"), four of the five themes most often scored to indicate Edie's relation to Gunn in the series. But only two of the newly arranged vocals appear as performances by Edie Hart at Mothers in season one; these are "Brief and Breezy" (Episode 37) and "Straight to Baby" (performed in Episodes 31 and 34). Contributing to the aesthetic continuity between the three tie-in albums, *Dreamsville* featured themes from the other two LPs, yet most of the arrangements were made sweeter with the addition of strings, harp, and a production aesthetic featuring a warm and heavily reverberating soundstage. What are missing from these new vocal arrangements are the sultry saxophones of the instrumentals and Pete Condoli's loud, aggressive trumpet solos of the *Music from Peter Gunn* soundtrack. Moreover, *Dreamsville* departed from the strategy of the other two albums by focusing more upon the light pop jazz genre for Albright as the featured soloist. Finally, Mancini wrote only half of the material for Albright's *Dreamsville* album. Of the twelve tunes, the other six were popular torch or jazz songs, which favorably exhibited Albright's talents and range. Two of the vocal tracks not connected to the show's original theme music which did

Figure 12.2 Lola Albright and Henry Mancini's *Peter Gunn* tie-in album *Dreamsville* from 1959 (Columbia CL 1327).

appear dietetically as solo jazz performances by Hart at Mothers were "You're Driving Me Crazy, What Did I Do?" (Episode 34) and "Just You Just Me" (Episode 38).[37]

Even though the album's timbre and style are sweet and romantic, it featured many unusual orchestrations such as "Slow and Easy," arranged for flute, strings, piano, and guitar. The album's tune which most represented the *Peter Gunn* crime jazz sound is "Straight to Baby," a vocal version of "Session at Pete's Pad" with new lyrics written by Mancini's frequent collaborator Sammy Cahn. "Straight to Baby" is also one of only two original songs from the album to appear diegetically in season one.[38] It appears twice, but only once in its entirety, in *Love Me to Death*. In this episode, Hart sings the tune at

Mothers during the very first scene as Pete listens with enjoyment and admiration. Its main function is to provide the backdrop during Gunn's introduction to two wealthy sisters who hire Gunn to investigate their third sister's new (blackmailing) husband. Yet the episode's serious filmic attention to Albright's performance also effectively positioned the song as one of the album's featured numbers. Further, by featuring Hart/Albright singing what would have been a familiar but dramatically altered tune, the song functioned to showcase Albright's unique vocal jazz talent in the context of the larger aesthetic vision of Mancini's scoring. His flexible adaptation of ambi-diegetic jazz-flavored themes elicited particular moods while also showcasing the unique talents and sonorities of his revered musicians who themselves could improvise and adapt to different settings and moods. The new slower vocal arrangement in the key of E minor, a whole step up from the original instrumental of "Session at Pete's Pad," was a perfect vehicle to display Albright's cool and smoky alto register. The contrast to the original was striking: the first, a faster and assertive arrangement scored as narrative music to elicit the dangerous fight scenes between Gunn and various criminals. This new, slower, laid-back, and economic scoring rejected its original role as narrative music and rather supported the full appreciation of Albright/Hart's unembellished cool jazz vocal style in the diegetic setting.

Mancini sets up Albright's first verse with a simple II-V-I turnaround in bass, accompanied by brushes on trap set. This minimal background texture is embellished with only intermittent short piano mordents. In other words, the texture in the first four measures is light and cool. The form is also straight ahead and uncomplicated; a 32-bar form is embellished with only two short solos on piano and then vibes, pointing both to Mancini's distinctive arrangements which relied upon economical pairings of vibes with piano or guitar and drew from the West Coast sound that often promoted non-traditional big band solo instruments such as alto flute or vibes.

The song's cool jazz style and the poetic lyrics also established Hart's agency as a competent jazz performer in the West Coast style. Her utterance of jazz lingo with words and references such as "straight," "baby," and "I blow" marks this performance's connection to current beatnik appropriations of black culture and its mediation in literature, film, and popular culture. But the ambiguity of these phrases also facilitated a musical and poetic voice for Hart's enduring female desire of an ambiguous object. In her diegetic performance of these lyrics, Hart enacts an active female gaze for Gunn and for her love of the jazz performance. But her performance is open for interpretation because, from these lyrics and their delivery, we are not sure if Hart longs only for Gunn or for a romantic alliance within her preferred jazz space, the jazz club. From the song's main line "take me straight to baby" the term "baby" is usually reserved to refer *to* women as objects of desire in an earlier musical historical moment such as in classic film noir. At other times, in blues lingo, "baby" might refer *to* black men as objects in black women's blues poetics (Davis, Harrison). But this diegetic jazz performance also suggests another reading: it points rather to the integral relationship between performing jazz (an active stance) and desiring a man (an active stance). Hart longs to stay at her cherished jazz spot where she can blow and express her art with her baby at her side. In short, this artful diegetic scoring of a commercially released cool jazz vocal tune allows for variable interpretations and levels of artistic and gendered jazz agency.

Gendered Jazz Myths in Gunn's Noir Jazz

While the diegetic performances of Edie Hart as well as the tie-in album of *Dreamsville* did much to promote the idea of the independent female jazz artist within the genre of crime jazz, Mancini also supported other performances for female jazz vocalists in this series. These performances expanded the images of professional jazz women but simultaneously reinscribed older myths surrounding the blues and jazz singer, especially those enacted within earlier Hollywood films with narratives treating black women musicians as victims of male culture.

Several episodes from season one featured a number of musical artists not connected to Mothers's jazz combo. The first was the prolific and respected LA trumpeter and soloist Shorty Rogers who collaborated with many West Coast jazz bands during the 1950s, including those of Stan Kenton and the Lighthouse Allstars. He also led his own group, Shorty Rogers and his Giants, and performed on other projects to release dozens of recordings during the 1950s and '60s. Rogers was also a frequent composer and arranger for film and television during the 1950s. Notably, Rogers's scores include *The Man with the Golden Arm* (1955) and *The Wild One* (1954), two contemporary films with crime and urban jazz and/or youth-oriented themes.

From Episode 5, *The Frog*, Gunn walks into Mothers to see the unknown Rogers taking a few choruses on "How High the Moon" before Hart/Albright takes over the head. After a neat and tight performance, Hart looks to Gunn and says "I don't think you know Shorty Rogers" to which Gunn casually responds "Hiya Shorty." Rogers is here filmed blowing his relatively unusual cool-toned flugelhorn.[39] During the pre-production of the series, Rogers had been invited to record the theme song for the show under his name, an invitation he turned down for Mancini, so his appearance as guest soloist here was not surprising.[40] As a respected composer and trumpet player with several West Coast groups, his performance served to buttress the show's connection to both the LA jazz scene and the increasingly trendy West Coast sound in the late 1950s.

A second featured musician, who performed a central role in a later episode *Lynn's Blues* (episode nine) and its larger jazz-driven narrative, was the jazz and pop vocalist Linda Lawson, an actor and musician who worked extensively in television and film. In addition to television and film appearances, she performed as a nightclub singer at various clubs including the Sands Hotel in Las Vegas. Her performances also contributed to the expansion of jazz labels such as Verve in the 1950s and '60s into the crossover jazz and pop market as well as the domestic market for hi-fi stereo systems.

This episode perpetuated older Hollywood noir narratives which linked jazz culture to organized crime. In films and in journalistic accounts, the jazz public was well familiarized with images of the speakeasies from the 1920s; many were jazz joints owned by notorious mobsters such as Al Capone. Chicago jazz clubs were well-known repositories for bootlegged alcohol during prohibition and these clubs' violent histories reveal the unwanted relationships between jazz musicians and mob bosses. In one notorious example, Chicago's famous Green Mill Cabaret singer Joe Lewis was attacked, his tongue cut out, and left for dead by mobster and club owner Machinegun Jack McGurn (Al Capone's leading hitman) after Lewis threatened to leave for another club.[41] Yet, like this story, most of our knowledge of the connections between jazz musicians and organized crime emerges from anecdotes later retold by agents and musicians (notably Louis Armstrong or Frank Sinatra). But such narratives rarely depicted stories of jazz women's intimidation by crime bosses in jazz sites. Women performers similarly suffered such economic and performance pressures, however, while also being subjected to unwanted sexual advances from unscrupulous nightclub bosses.[42]

While Hart's character rarely interacts with criminal characters, thus maintaining her respectability, in this episode Lynn Martel, performed by Linda Lawson, is the talented but compromised singer forced to perform under the unscrupulous terms of a crime boss. Therefore this episode attempted to promote an older jazz narrative. Yet, even though her middle-class, respectable position in society is suggested through her friendship with Hart, her blues-inflected performances provide the pretext to incorporate the jazz mob story.

The first scene opens in the hotel lobby with a patron entering the elevator. The elevator is stopped at mid-floor and the man is shot from above. The next scene opens in the hotel ballroom to feature a nearly catatonic jazz singer (Lynn Martel) exuding her grief through her torch song as she sings "blue is the color of the sea, till my lover left me." Martel exits the stage in mid-phrase, too despondent to continue. Her desperation is caused by her forced contract with the club's owner Babe Santana, a crime boss character who carries a knife and threatens Gunn after he attempted to console Lynn in her dressing room.

The plot appears to have been inspired by Peggy Lee's character in *Pete Kelly's Blues* from 1955 which takes place in a Kansas City speakeasy from the 1920s. Again, the familiar figure of the victimized, exploited blues woman provides the dominant narrative of jazz women,[43] who are almost always singers. In contrast to both this episode and to *Pete Kelly's Blues*, however, in reality most blues women were black, and this new version of the blues singer myth displaces the black progeny of blues and jazz singing. Earlier images of blues singers were first projected in the experimental sound films of the 1920s and 1930s with performances by both Bessie Smith and Billie Holiday.[44] Yet, in *Peter Gunn*, this tragic female jazz figure provides a brief counter to Edie's straight-arrow, respectable, middle-class demeanor; Edie is both a stable romantic figure and a jazz artist isolated from the excesses of crime and prostitution. While Martel's forced, and therefore less respectable, sexual relationship is indirectly referenced, Edie's chasteness is reinforced by her committed relationship with Gunn even as she appears nonchalant in her half-hearted complaints of his absence.

In this episode, in keeping with the jazz-mob narrative, the criminals are Italian but, to balance such blatant stereotypes, the most corrupt and powerful businessman in the narrative is an Anglo-Saxon man by the name of Nat Krueger (this might be a good corollary to Joe Glaser's and Al Capone's connections to jazz in the 1920s). Fortunately (sarcasm intended), we later discover that Lynn is not really from a criminal or "immigrant" background but that she has unwittingly found herself affiliating with such types because of her jazz singer profession. The episode reinforces her "wrong place at the wrong time" circumstance when Edie reassures Gunn that she has family in the Midwest and was a "sweet, normal girl" before she got wrapped up with Santana. With the help of Edie, Gunn's role is to save Martel from her crime boss. After she tries to kill herself with gas, Gunn literally slaps some sense into her (she apparently required once again aggressive cajoling from a strong man). He escorts her back to Edie's apartment to recover. The two are followed by Krueger and eventually a car chase ensues between Krueger, Jacoby, and the police. Krueger is caught and Lynn returns to the hotel for one last performance to sing her signature song "Meaning of the Blues."

This signature song, composed by Bobby Troupe (who hosted the ABC Stars of Jazz television program in the mid-1950s) would have been familiar to audiences because it was popularized by Julie London in 1957. Lawson had also recently recorded this song in a compilation album arranged by Mancini entitled *Songs for My Boyfriend* (1957 Verve 2097) with Linda Leigh, Marlene Willis, and Joan O'Brien. In other words, Mancini draws from his strategy of ambi-diegetic music not only to represent functional jazz myths of victimized blues singers working in crime-driven nightclubs but also by making connections to contemporaneous vocal jazz performances of popular singers promoted by the expanding crossover jazz record labels such as Verve. Mancini would increasingly rely upon this savvy cross-promotional marketing

Figure 12.3 Lynn Martel (Linda Lawson) sings her "Meaning of the Blues" in Peter Gunn's "Lynn's Blues."

technique in his other compilation soundtracks which could make connections between the cultural fictions of television and film and the cultural and affective connections of real-life performances of popular music. With such a strategy, the show's cultural and contemporary significance is reinforced by such real-world connections to pop culture.[45]

Linda Lawson released her solo album *Introducing Linda Lawson* in 1960, shortly after her appearance on *Peter Gunn*, with the independent Chancellor label in which she recorded a variety of torch songs and blues-oriented jazz ballads such as "Mood Indigo," "The Meaning of the Blues," and "But Beautiful." The album featured prominent modern jazz musicians from the West Coast including Bud Shank on alto sax, Jimmy Rowles on piano, Al Porcino on trumpet, Mel Lewis on drums, and Frank Rosolina on trombone.[46] It was conducted and arranged by Marty Paich, a composer and arranger often compared to Mancini in this period because of his blending of jazz and other genres within high-fidelity arrangements for home stereo systems. Jimmy Rowles had also recorded on Mancini's two LPs for the Gunn series. Both

Paich and Mancini had often worked with the same group of white studio/jazz musicians from the West Coast jazz scene.

In the postwar period, struggling jazz companies expanded into the vocal jazz and crossover market with compilation albums featuring sensual ballads by attractive and mostly white female jazz or torch song singers, such as Linda Lawson. Many crossover vocal jazz albums featured attractive performers who presented star Hollywood qualities and therefore these albums established connections to television or film. Of course, Mancini had also released such an album featuring Lola Albright in his *Dreamsville* LP. While the exotica or bachelor-pad light jazz of the 1950s and '60s were often instrumental music with exotic instrumentations and soundscapes, vocalists were not often historicized as part of the genre, with the exception of Yma Sumac who recorded a number of Hollywood-inspired exotica albums during the 1950s. Apart from Yma Sumac, women rarely contributed to this new crossover market as composers, lead performers, or producers, yet images of women were prominently positioned on record covers as sensual, exotic objects. In short, the genre performed almost exclusively for men and by men positioned a highly sensual, exotic, and feminized image to market such consumer products as masculine.

Conclusion

Mancini's postwar connection to the bachelor-pad sounds of Martin Denny or to *Playboy*-era cocktail jazz were clear, especially as these currents sought to market their music to a multigenerational, upwardly mobile, male, postwar audience. By combining jazz and pop into easy-listening melodies with mostly instrumental arrangements and the addition of the occasional torch song by a beautiful female vocalist, Mancini's work successfully appealed to a more mature audience, one that preferred listening to high-quality arrangements performed by the best (white) studio jazz musicians over visiting late-night (black) jazz clubs. The bachelor-pad or easy-listening genre was also perfect for the series's setting, in that it provided the soundstage for various living-room scenes to market Mancini's music but also to promote the new masculine consumer, whether engaged in romantic, escapist, exotic fantasies or simply seeking after-work relaxation. Such new objects of consumerism, from the hi-fi stereo system to the adult record collection of worldly sophisticated jazz sounds, provided the necessary accoutrements to cement Gunn and, by association, Mancini's musical status as the most adept composer to score this new consumer-driven masculinity for the upwardly mobile man.

Further, in the *Peter Gunn* series, the secondary appearances by guests, such as singer Linda Lawson and trumpeter Shorty Rogers, reveal Mancini's (and Edwards's) efforts in supporting the careers of musicians connected to the broader jazz scene of the West Coast. In such cameo appearances, Mancini's use of ambi-diegetic jazz further buttressed the cool image of West Coast jazz in connection with Peter Gunn's new masculinity. Sometimes, such appearances also made real connections to the performative spaces of West Coast jazz; at other times, as in the depiction of torch singer Lynn Martel, older gendered jazz myths were reconfigured into the gentrified spaces of a mediated white jazz world within this fictional space. Yet the gendered images, enacted musically and within the larger narrative of *Peter Gunn*, complicated the dominance and sexism of this new masculinity in providing one of the first serious narrative representations of an independent jazz woman. By combining many vocal performances and uses of ambi-diegetic jazz within the series, Mancini's scoring enabled a level of creative agency for Albright's character which elevated her artistic creditably and connected her to the broader professional world of West Coast jazz. His masterly ability flexibly to adapt diegetic jazz for the filmic goals of affective, spatial, and narrative cuing, however, also served to reinforce more established and normative gender positions in postwar America where women supposedly sought long-term monogamous relationships and desired a life of domestic comforts and economic dependability. Because this normative gendered desire is treated with a coy and ironic stance and because it fails to materialize in the Gunn series, this may be one of the first enactments of female jazz agency, in conjunction with representations of female desire, which is not limited, sonically or visually, to temporary forms of agency typically staged in the service of the dominant man prior to the late 1950s.[47]

Ultimately, the *Peter Gunn* series reinforced Hefner's elitist and gentrified concept of a consumerist-driven, urban, and independent new man, one resistant to the bonds of marriage and open for sexual adventures which were partly facilitated through an appreciation of high jazz. But to forget that this same series was one of only a few to promote professional hi-fi recordings of female jazz vocalists, while dramatizing an enduring image of an independent professional artist with considerable jazz agency when most of the new crossover hi-fi exotic or cool jazz recordings featured male artists exclusively, would be to oversimplify the gender politics of such jazz-centered media and their connections to the cool jazz rage of the West Coast which, increasingly, gained cultural capital as it displaced images of black jazz throughout the world. These progressive images of gender and jazz in no small part set the stage for mediating the radical transformations of race, gender, and sex politics that would explode during the 1960s within the counterculture.

NOTES

1. Mancini cited in David Butler, *Jazz Noir: Listening to Music from Phantom Lady to the Last Seduction* (London: Praeger, 2002) p. 150.
2. Caps, *Henry Mancini: Reinventing Film Music*, p. 46.

3. For analyses of Henry Mancini's crime jazz scores see Jeff Smith, "That Money Making Moon River Sound: Thematic Organization and Orchestration in the Film Music of Henry Mancini," in James Buhler, Caryl Flinn and David Neumeyer (eds) *Music and Cinema* (Middletown, CT: Wesleyan University Press, 2000), pp. 247–71; John Caps, *Henry Mancini: Reinventing Film Music* (Urbana, IL: University of Illinois Press, 2012); and Morris Holbrook, *Music, Movies, Meanings and Markets: Cinemajazzamatazz* (London: Routledge, 2011).
4. See especially Caps, "Big Screen, Little Screen," *Henry Mancini: Reinventing Film Music*, pp. 44–61; Holbrook "Introduction to Part I and II," in *Music, Movies, Meanings and Markets: Cinemajazzamatazz*, pp. 56–62, 144–8; and Smith "That Money Making Moon River Sound."
5. Yet other behind-the-scenes workers, such as producers and writers, including the show's writer and creator Blake Edwards also gained a reputation throughout Los Angeles as a jazz lover and attractive, charming bachelor. This type of educated, flexible and less rigid man assisted the growing acceptance of the new masculinity.
6. Butler and others point to the representation of West Coast jazz during the 1950s in both film and other related media as prioritizing the cult of the white jazz musician. For Butler, the band leader who provided the most visible image of this new sound was Stan Kenton with his Innovations in Modern Music Orchestra. Kenton's orchestras provided white audiences an image that facilitated the idealization of white jazz musicians. See David Butler, "Touch of Kenton: Jazz in 1950s Film Noir," in *Jazz Noir*, p. 111. For other discussions of the cult of the white jazz musician see Krin Gabbard "Jazz Becomes Art" *Jammin' at the Margins: Jazz and the American Cinema* (Chicago: University of Chicago Press, 1996), pp. 101–37; and John Gennari, *Blowin Hot and Cool: Jazz and Its Critics* (Chicago: University of Chicago Press, 2006) p. 182.
7. Ted Gioia, *West Coast Jazz: Modern Jazz in California 1945–1960* (New York: Quartet Books, 1992), p. 133. For an alternative discussion and representation by many of the important black musicians emerging from Central Avenue, see Clora Bryant, Buddy Collete, William Green et al., *Central Avenue Sounds: Jazz in Los Angeles* (Berkeley and Los Angeles: University of California Press, 1998).
8. Holbrook, *Music, Movies, Meanings and Markets*, p. 145.
9. Fred Pfeil, "Home Fires Burning: Family Noir in Blue Velvet and Terminator 2," in Joan Copjec (ed.), *Shades of Noir* (London: Verso, 1993).
10. Catherine Haworth, "Detective Agency?: Scoring the Amateur Female Investigator in 1940s Hollywood," *Music and Letters* 93/4 (2012), pp. 543–73.
11. Kalinak proposes Max Steiner as the twentieth-century composer who most rigorously established Hollywood film music-scoring conventions, both through the conviction of his aesthetic principles and with the dogma with which he promoted these convictions. Such conventions include the selective use of non-diegetic music for dramatic purposes, a correspondence between that music and the narrative, the synchronization between narrative action and music (as in the technique of mickey mousing), and the use of the leitmotif as a structural framework. See Katherine Kalinak, "Chapter Five: Every character should have a theme: *The Informer*, Max Steiner and the Classical Film Score," *Settling the Score: Music and the Classical Hollywood Score* (Madison: University of Wisconsin Press 1992), pp. 113–34.
12. Kalinak, *Settling the Score*, p. 113.
13. Laura Mulvey, *Visual and Other Pleasures* (New York: Palgrave 1989).
14. Kalinak, *Settling the Score*, p. 120.
15. Haworth, "Detective Agency?: Scoring the Amateur Female Investigator in 1940s Hollywood."

16. Haworth, "Detective Agency?: Scoring the Amateur Female Investigator in 1940s Hollywood," p. 545.
17. Yvonne Tasker reviews the critique of this anxiety in *Working Girls: Gender and Sexuality in Popular Cinema* (London and New York: Routledge 1998), p. 92. Of course, these were anxieties reflecting the positions of middle-class white women as non-white working-class women had frequently worked to sustain themselves and their families. For a comprehensive historical account of Black women's labor in the United States see, for example, Jacqueline Jones, *Labor of Love, Labor of Sorrow: Black Women, Work and the Family, from Slavery to the Present* (New York: Basic Books, 2010).
18. See Smith, "That Money Making Moon River Sound" and Caps, *Henry Mancini: Reinventing Film Music*.
19. Ibid., pp. 1–2.
20. Ibid., p. 14
21. Ibid., p. 21.
22. Ibid., p. 41.
23. Ibid., p. 42.
24. Mancini, "Did They Mention the Music?", p. 192.
25. Caps, *Henry Mancini: Reinventing Film Music*, p. 47.
26. Mancini, "Did They Mention the Music?", p. 191.
27. Albright was born in Akron, Ohio. Her parents were gospel musicians and she studied music throughout her childhood. See Mike Barnes, "Lola Albright, Sultry Actress in 'Peter Gunn' and Kirk Douglas's 'Champion', Dies at 92" in the *Hollywood Reporter*, March 24, 2017. Accessed May 8, 2017: http://www.hollywoodreporter.com/news/lola-albright-dead-peter-gunn-champion-actress-was-92-988635.
28. Barnes "Lola Albright, Sultry Actress in 'Peter Gunn' and Kirk Douglas's 'Champion', Dies at 92".
29. This was requoted from a 1992 interview which I could not locate but it is reinserted in this tribute to Albright in an obituary: Mat Schudel "Lola Albright, alluring actress in stylish 'Peter Gunn' TV series, dies at 92" in *The Washington Post*, March 25, 2017. Accessed: May 8, 2017: https://www.washingtonpost.com/entertainment/lola-albright-alluring-actress-in-stylish-peter-gunn-tv-series-dies-at-92/2017/03/25/e1e25bc0-116b-11e7-9d5a-a83e627dc120_story.html?utm_term=.c696b3c0e89c.
30. Anahid Kassabian *Hearing Film: Tracking Identifications in Contemporary Hollywood Film Music* (London: Routledge, 2001); and Holbrook, *Music, Movies, Meanings and Markets*, p. xix.
31. Morris Holbrook defines this category in relation to the narrative and affective prompting elicited by diegetic music's reappearance within the narrative film score, as is often the case with diegetic jazz within *Peter Gunn*. He situates this category outside of diegetic or non-diegetic occurrences stating: "ambi-diegetic music refers to on-screen music produced inside the film (like diegetic music) that plays a role in furthering the movie's dramatic development (as is typical of non-diegetic music). When on-screen performers play a jazz piece in a manner that advances the plot, comments on the nature of a character's persona, or reinforces a key theme, we have a case of ambi-diegesis." Morris's main example is the related jazz-inflected film *Pete Kelly's Blues* (1995), which similarly utilized jazz to comment upon the character's psychological and affective world, as well as to forward the narrative of the film, Holbrook, *Music, Movies, Meanings and Markets*, p. xix.
32. This was asserted by Peter Gunn journalist Quigley on his *Peter Gunn* website: Mike Quigley, "Seasons 1, 2 and 3," *Peter Gunn Episode Guide*. Accessed February 18, 2017, http://www.petergunn.tv/

33. Smith, "That Money Making Moon River Sound", p. 257.
34. Ibid.
35. Mancini et al, "Did They Mention the Music?", p. 193.
36. Smith, "That Money Making Moon River Sound"; Holbrook, *Music, Movies, Meanings and Markets*, pp. 226–34; and Caps, "Henry Mancini: Reinventing Film Music," pp. 47–59.
37. Other vocal jazz and classic American songbook arrangements not performed in *Peter Gunn* but recorded for the album were "It's Always You" famously sung by Frank Sinatra in the film *Road to Zanzibar*; "Two Sleepy People," composed by Hoagy Carmichael in 1938, "They Didn't Believe Me" composed by Jerome Kern and "We Kiss in a Shadow" from *The King and I*.
38. Hart sings "What Did I Do? You're Driving Me Crazy" in Episode 34 of season one, *Bullet for a Badge*.
39. Rogers was one of the first to incorporate the flugelhorn into modern jazz recordings in the 1950s.
40. Mancini et al., "Did They Mention the Music?" p. 193.
41. Patrick Sisson "An Oral History of the Green Mill" in *The Chicago Reader*, March 20, 2014. Accessed May 10, 2017: https://www.chicagoreader.com/chicago/uptown-greenmilljazz-bar-history-owner-bartender-musicians/Content?oid=12784766.
42. For examples of either sexual or social non-musical expectations of jazz women see Sherrie Tucker, *Swing Shift: All-Girl Bands of the 1940s* (Durham, NC: Duke University Press, 2000), pp. 246–7, 303–5. For a review of the misconceptions concerning performing women musicians in the USO see Kristin McGee, *Some Liked It Hot: Jazz women in Film and Television 1928–1959* (Middletown, CT: Wesleyan University Press 2009), p. 143.
43. See Daphne Duval Harrison, *Black Pearls: Blues Queens of the 1920s* (New Brunswick, NJ: Rutgers University Press, 1990) and Angela Davis, *Blues Legacies and Black Feminism: Gertrude "Ma" Smith, Bessie Smith, and Billie Holiday* (New York: Vintage, 1999).
44. Paramount's *St. Louis Blues* (1929) starred Bessie Smith as a love-worn, whiskey-drinking, blues singer who laments her no-good, two-timing man, and the Duke Ellington film *Symphony in Black* (Paramount 1935) featured a young Billie Holiday, rejected and jealous of her boyfriend's new romantic partner as she cathartically sings "That Man."
45. This practice would become more common and relevant for popular music compilation soundtracks in movies of the counterculture such as *The Graduate* (MGM, 1967) and *Easy Rider* (Warner Bros., 1969).
46. According to jazz journalist Marc Myers, Chancellor Records was a Philadelphia label with a Hollywood presence thanks to Am-Par, the music subsidiary of the American Broadcasting Company (ABC). Myers also lists the many fine West Coast musicians featured on Lawson's album: Al Porcino, Stu Williamson and Jack Sheldon (tp); Frank Rosolino (tb); Bud Shank (as); Bill Perkins (ts); Med Flory (bar); Jimmy Rowles (p); Bill Pittman (g); Joe Mondragon (b); Mel Lewis (d); and the Hollywood String Ensemble. See Myers's website "Introducing Linda Lawson" *JazzWax*. Accessed 5 May 5, 2017, http://www.jazzwax.com/2013/02/introducing-linda-lawson.html
47. This filmic device, allowing women only temporary agency, was, of course, typical of earlier aural and visual depictions of women within 1940s noir and crime detective genres. See Haworth, "Detective Agency?: Scoring the Amateur Female Investigator in 1940s Hollywood," and Ann Kaplan, *Women in Film Noir* (London: BFI, 1998).

Filmography

Edwards, Blake, 1958–1961: *Peter Gunn*.
Wells, Orson, 1958: *Touch of Evil*.

Discography

Lola Albright and Henry Mancini, *Dreamsville* (1959, Columbia CL 1327).
Linda Lawson, *Introducing Linda Lawson* (1960, Chancellor).
Henry Mancini, *Songs for my Boyfriend* (1957, Verve 2097).
Henry Mancini, *Music from Peter Gunn* (1959, RCA Victor LPM/LSP 1956).
Henry Mancini, *More Music from Peter Gunn* (1959, RCA Victor LMP 2040).

Bibliography

Brown, Royal (1994), *Overtones and Undertones: Reading Film Music*, Berkeley and Los Angeles: University of California Press.
Bryant, Clora, Buddy Collete, William Green, et al. (1998), *Central Avenue Sounds: Jazz in Los Angeles*, Berkeley and Los Angeles: University of California Press.
Butler, David (2002), *Jazz Noir: Listening to Music from Phantom Lady to the Last Seduction*, London: Praeger.
Caps, John (2012), *Henry Mancini: Reinventing Film Music*, Urbana, IL: University of Illinois Press.
Davis, Angela (1999), *Blues Legacies and Black Feminism: Gertrude "Ma" Smith, Bessie Smith, and Billie Holiday*, New York: Vintage.
Ehrenreich, Barbara (1987), *The Hearts of Men: American Dreams and the Flight from Commitment*, New York: Anchor Books.
Flinn, Caryl (1992), *Strains of Utopian: Gender, Nostalgia, and Hollywood Film Music*, Princeton, NJ: Princeton University Press.
Ford, Phil (2008), "Jazz Exotica and the Naked City," *Journal of Musicological Research* 27, 2008, pp. 113–33.
Gabbard, Krim (1996), *Jammin' at the Margins: Jazz and American Cinema*, Chicago: University of Chicago Press
Gennari, John (2006), *Blowin Hot and Cool: Jazz and Its Critics*, Chicago: University of Chicago Press.
Gioia, Ted (1992), *West Coast Jazz: Modern Jazz in California 1945–1960*, New York: Quartet Books.
Gorbman, Claudia (1987), *Unheard Melodies: Narrative Film Music*, London: BFI.
Harrison, Daphne Duval (1990), *Black Pearls: Blues Queens of the 1920s*, New Brunswick, NJ: Rutgers University Press.
Haworth, Catherine (2012), "Detective Agency?: Scoring the Amateur Female Investigator in 1940s Hollywood," *Music and Letters* 93/4, 2012, pp. 543–73.
Holbrook, Morris (2011), *Music, Movies, Meanings and Markets: Cinemajazzamatazz*, London: Routledge.
Kalinak, Katherine (1992), *Settling the Score: Music and the Classical Hollywood Score*, Madison, WI: University of Wisconsin Press.
Kaplan, Ann (1998), *Women in Film Noir*, London: BFI.
Kassabian, Anahid (2001), *Hearing Film: Tracking Identifications in Contemporary Hollywood Film Music*, London: Routledge.
Leeper, Jill (2001), "Crossing Musical Borders: The Soundtrack for *Touch of Evil*," in Wojcik, Pamela Robertson and Arthur Knight (eds), *Soundtrack Available:*

Essays on Film and Popular Music, Durham, NC: Duke University Press, pp. 226–43.

Manning, Joe (2014), "Mancini's Peter Gunn Score Launched Dozens of Careers," *Mornings on Maple Street* (accessed February 20, 2017), http://morningsonmaplestreet.com/2014/11/26/mancinis-peter-gunn-score-page-one/

Mancini, Henry and Gene Lees, (1989), "Did They Mention the Music?," in Mervyn Cooke, ed., *The Hollywood Film Music Reader*, Oxford: Oxford University Press.

Mulvey, Laura (1989), *Visual and Other Pleasures*, New York: Palgrave.

Naremore, James (2008), *More Than Night: Film Noir in its Contexts*, Berkeley and Los Angeles: University of Los Angeles Press.

Ness, Richard (2008), "A Lotta Night Music: The Sound of Film Noir," in *Cinema Journal*, 47/2, pp. 52–70.

Pfeil, Fred (1993), "Home Fires Burning: Family Noir in Blue Velvet and Terminator 2," in Joan Copjec, ed., *Shades of Noir*, London: Verso.

Quigley, Mike, "Seasons, 1, 2, and 3", *Peter Gunn Episode Guide*, (accessed February 18, 2017), http://www.petergunn.tv/

Russell, George (1959), "Review of the Soundtrack for Peter Gunn," *Jazz Review* 2/5, pp. 18–19.

Smith, Jeff (2000), "That Money Making Moon River Sound: Thematic Organization and Orchestration in the Film Music of Henry Mancini," in James Buhler, Caryl Flinn and David Neumeyer, eds, *Music and Cinema*, Hanover, CT: Wesleyan University Press, pp. 247–71.

Stanfield, Peter (2005), *Body and Soul: Jazz and Blues in American Film, 1927–63*, Urbana and Chicago: University of Illinois Press.

Tasker, Yvonne (1998), *Working Girls: Gender and Sexuality in Popular Cinema*, London and New York: Routledge.

Ursini, James (2004), "Angst at Sixty Fields per Second," in Alain Silver and James Ursini, eds, *Film Noir Reader*, New York: Limelight, pp. 275–87.

Whitey, Elizabeth (2001), "TV Gets Jazz: The Evolution of Action TV Music," in Bill Osgerby and Anna Gough Yates, eds, *Action TV: Tough Guys, Smooth Operators and Foxy Chicks*, London: Routledge, pp. 191–204.

INDEX

African American, 18, 39, 85, 92, 146, 157, 160, 165, 173–8, 183
Albright, Lola, 236, 245–6, 252
alien, 3, 21, 22–30, 36, 101, 126, 127, 128, 132, 136, 137, 145, 146
American in Paris, An, 206, 207–10
April in Paris, 219–55
Astaire, Fred, 7, 207, 210–13, 213–19, 224, 225
atomic, 1, 6, 26, 39, 52, 75, 93, 99, 159
atomic kitchen, 161
atomic ranch, 161
Aykroyd, Dan, 156

Bachelor in Paradise, A, 155
Bad Seed, The, 127, 136–7, 140
Belushi, John, 156
Berlin Wall, 1, 2, 43, 51, 145, 161, 182, 200
Berry, Chuck, 8
Big Heat, The, 99, 100, 101, 107, 109, 110, 111, 113, 116
Billboard, 245
Biskind, Peter, 21, 30, 31
Blackboard Jungle, 65, 66–7
Bradbury, Ray, 22–5
Brain Eaters, The, 28
Brown, Helen Gurley, 173, 190

Buchholz, Horst, 51–3
Burbs, The, 158

Cagney, James, 47–54, 58, 60–1
Caine, Michael, 37–9
Caron, Leslie, 207–9
Cavell, Stanley, 130, 142
Cavett, Dick, 18
Charisse, Cyd, 201–13
Claudine, 176–8
Coleman, Dabney, 193, 196
Come Blow Your Horn, 168
Communism, 2, 12, 32, 35, 56, 126
Crack in the Picture Window, The, 154
Crowther, Bosley, 71, 79, 82, 83, 90, 95, 97
Cukor, George, 183, 184, 185
Curtiz, Michael, 60, 83, 96

Darin, Bobby, 170
Day, Doris, 147, 152–3, 168, 172, 207, 219, 224
Dee, Sandra, 13, 169–70, 172
Desk Set, 11, 183, 187–92, 193–5, 200
Desperate Hours, The, 127, 132–3
Dr. Strangelove, 42, 43, 59, 92–3
Dont Look Back, 15–17

INDEX

Douglas, Kirk, 100, 236
Dylan, Bob, 15–17

Easy Rider, 14–15, 20, 256

Fonda, Jane, 173, 193, 194
Fonda, Peter, 14–15
Ford, Glenn, 66–7, 84, 107, 112, 153
Freud, Sigmund (Freudian), 34, 52, 68, 77, 124, 142
Funny Face, 213–19

Garner, James, 147–8
Garr, Teri, 156, 196
Gazebo, The, 153
Gentleman's Agreement, 70–3
Gentlemen Prefer Blondes, 187, 204, 206, 209–10
Gimme Shelter, 18
Girl Can't Help It, The, 12–13, 43
Grant, Cary, 80, 82, 83, 89, 144, 152
Guide for the Married Man, A, 155
Gunning, Tom, 100

Half Angel, 127, 130–2, 140
Hanks, Tom, 158
Hatful of Rain, A, 65, 73–4
Hefner, Hugh, 229, 233, 253
Heinlein, Robert, 28–9
Hendrix, Jimi, 14, 17, 18
Hepburn, Audrey, 172, 214–19, 224, 225
Hepburn, Katharine, 11, 188–90
Hitchcock, Alfred, 42, 74, 159, 163, 194
Hoffman, Dustin, 196, 197, 199
Holliday, Judy, 172, 183–7
Hopper, Dennis, 14–15
House + Home, 150, 151
HUAC (House Un-American Activities Committee), 1, 2, 3, 4, 86, 129, 137–8, 187
Hurt, Mary Beth, 159–60
Huston, John, 52, 118, 205

If a Man Answers, 167, 169–70
Interrupted Melody, 80, 82, 84, 85, 87, 88, 90, 92
Invasion of the Body Snatchers, 28, 30–3
Ipcress File, The, 37–9
It Came From Outer Space, 27–9

It Should Happen To You, 183–7, 189, 191, 193–6

Jailhouse Rock, 9–12

Kael, Pauline, 59, 61
Kazan, Elia, 63, 70, 72
Keaton, Michael, 155–6
Kelly, Gene, 155, 207–10
Kennan, George, 75, 76
Kerr, Jean, 153
Korean War, 21, 33, 34, 36, 73, 90, 130

Lancaster, Burt, 69, 141
Lange, Jessica, 198
Lemmon, Jack, 183
Levittown, 144, 146, 150
Lippmann, Walter, 75–6
Little Richard, 12–13
Lonely Crowd, The, 153–4
Los Angeles, 11, 18, 53, 72, 138, 160, 234

Man in the Gray Flannel Suit, The, 127, 128–30, 137, 140
Manchurian Candidate, The, 33–9
Mancini, Henry, 228–9, 231–2, 233–53
Marx, Karl (Marxism), 2, 4, 55
Matthau, Walter, 155
McCarthy, Joseph, 4, 35–6, 99, 123, 150
McCarthy, Kevin
McGivern, William, 100–20
Miller, Glenn, 234
Mr. Blandings Builds His Dream House, 144–5, 151–2, 165
Mr. Mom, 155–6
Mitchum, Robert, 99, 117
Money Pit, The, 151–2
Moriarty, Cathy, 156
Mulvey, Laura, 199, 254, 256
Murray, Bill, 199
My Son John, 126–8, 136

Neighbors, 156
Newman, Paul, 156–7
Niebuhr, Reinhold, 64
Night and Day, 82, 83, 85, 87–9, 90
9 to 5, 195–7, 200
North by Northwest, 3, 42

INDEX

O'Brien, Edmond, 12, 36, 101, 102, 110, 117–18
One, Two, Three, 43, 46–59
Organization Man, The, 67, 145

Palmer, R. Barton, 63, 64, 76
Parents, 158–60
Parton, Dolly, 193–5
PCA (Production Code Administration), 63, 65
Peck, Gregory, 70–3
Peter Gunn, 5, 228–53
Pillow Talk, 163, 167–8, 169–70, 172, 219
Playboy, 35, 59–60, 112, 167–70, 252
Please Don't Eat the Daisies, 152–3, 165
Poitier, Sidney, 67, 175–6
Polan, Dana, 64
Presley, Elvis, 6, 9–12, 13, 212, 237
Prowler, The, 100, 109, 113, 115, 116, 117

Quaid, Randy, 159–60

Raisin in the Sun, A, 174–7
Rally 'Round the Flag Boys!, 156–7
Reisman, David, 154, 156
Reynolds, Debbie, 153
Rock Around the Clock, 6–7, 8
Rogue Cop, 101–8, 118, 119
Rothman, William, 16
Russia (Russian), 18, 47, 49, 52, 54, 55, 75, 76, 141, 142, 163, 211, 212

Sex and the Single Girl, 172, 173, 190, 191
Shaw, Tony, 2
Shield for Murder, 100, 101, 102, 104, 108, 110–16, 118, 119
Shulman, Max, 155–6

Siegel, Don, 100, 30–3
Silk Stockings, 210–13
Silver, Alain, 121–2, 258
Smith, Jeff, 2, 242
Smothers Brothers Comedy Hour, 18
Sobchack, Vivian, 22, 31
Something Wild, 135–6
Soviet, 2, 6, 35, 42–3, 47, 51, 55, 75–6, 124–5, 126–7, 165, 210, 211, 213, 224
Spigel, Lynn, 164, 165
Stratton Story, The, 80, 83–4, 85
suburb (suburbs, suburbia), 3, 4, 5, 26, 70, 71, 101, 104, 112–16, 128, 137, 144–62, 170–8
Sunrise at Campobello, 86–8
Swimmer, The, 128, 139–41

Tender Trap, The, 167, 169, 237
That Funny Feeling, 141–2, 167, 172
This Is Spinal Tap, 18–19
Thrill of It All!, The, 147–9
Tomlin, Lily, 193–4
Tootsie, 196–200
Touch of Evil, 235
Tracy, Spencer, 11, 188–9
Twist Around the Clock, 8

Ursini, James, 258

Variety, 7, 11, 13, 14, 19–20, 187, 201

Welles, Orson, 235, 237
Whyte, William H., 67–8, 145
Wilder, Billy, 42–59, 205
With A Song In My Heart, 80, 82, 87, 90, 91–2, 94
Woodstock, 17–18
Woodward, Joanne, 157
Working Girl, 200

EU representative:
Easy Access System Europe
Mustamäe tee 50, 10621 Tallinn, Estonia
Gpsr.requests@easproject.com